While engaged in writing his *Studies of the Spanish Mystics* in 1927, Professor Peers first realized the need for an accurate and modern translation of the works of St. John of the Cross, "to whom," he writes, "I have long had great devotion—to whom, indeed, I owe more than to any other writer outside the Scriptures." He accordingly set about preparing a fresh, accurate, and critical translation, and was able to work in close co-operation with the editor of the definitive Spanish text published in 1929–31. The result has been a monument of scholarship and devoted research, hailed in its turn as a standard work.

"Professor Peers' translation has superseded all previous ones . . . the English reader can now approach the meaning of St. John of the Cross as nearly as possible without reading the original."   *Catholic Herald*

"So sublime is this poetry that it scarcely seems to belong to this world at all; it is hardly capable of being assessed by literary criteria. More ardent in its passion than any profane poetry, its form is as elegant and exquisite as plastic and as highly figured as any of the finest works of the Renaissance. The spirit of God has passed through these poems every one, beautifying and sanctifying them on its way."

Marcelino Menéndez Pelayo

"E. Allison Peers' translation is the most faithful that has appeared in any European language."

The Times (London)

SPIRITUAL CANTICLE

by

Saint John of the Cross
DOCTOR OF THE CHURCH

THIRD REVISED EDITION

Translated, edited, and with an introduction
by E. ALLISON PEERS
from the critical edition of
P. SILVERIO DE SANTA TERESA, C.D.

IMAGE BOOKS

A Division of Doubleday & Company, Inc.
Garden City, New York

IMAGE BOOKS EDITION 1961
by special arrangement with the Newman Press

ISBN: 0-385-08919-8
Printed in the United States of America

CONTENTS

SPIRITUAL CANTICLE, SECOND REDACTION

[1] The 'Annotations' which are prefaced to certain stanzas have for convenience been placed under the preceding stanzas.

PRINCIPAL ABBREVIATIONS

A.V. = Authorized Version of the Bible (1611).

D.V. = Douai Version of the Bible (1609).

C.W.S.T.J. = *The Complete Works of Saint Teresa of Jesus,* translated and edited by E. Allison Peers from the critical edition of P. Silverio de Santa Teresa, C.D. London, Sheed and Ward, 1946. 3 vols.

H. = E. Allison Peers: *Handbook to the Life and Times of St. Teresa and St. John of the Cross.* London, Burns, Oates and Washbourne, 1951. 2 vols.

LL. = *The Letters of Saint Teresa of Jesus,* translated and edited by E. Allison Peers from the critical edition of P. Silverio de Santa Teresa, C.D. London, Burns, Oates and Washbourne, 1951. 2 vols.

N.L.M. = National Library of Spain (Biblioteca Nacional), Madrid.

Obras (P. Silv.) = *Obras de San Juan de la Cruz,* Doctor de la Iglesia, editadas y anotadas por el P. Silverio da Santa Teresa, C.D. Burgos, 1929–31. 5 vols.

S.S.M. = E. Allison Peers: *Studies of the Spanish Mystics.* Vol. I, London, Sheldon Press, 1927; 2nd ed., London, S.P.C.K., 1951. Vol. II, London, Sheldon Press, 1930.

Sobrino. = José Antonio de Sobrino, S.J.: *Estudios sobre San Juan de la Cruz y nuevos textos de su obra.* Madrid, 1950.

REFERENCE TABLE

INTRODUCTION

The 'Spiritual Canticle': Composition and Argument

It was in his Toledo dungeon, where, in the course of the fierce struggles between the Calced and Discalced Carmelites, he was imprisoned as a recalcitrant friar, that St. John of the Cross composed the poem which we know as the *Spiritual Canticle*. In one of the darkest of dark nights which he had to endure, we can imagine him breaking into a song wrung from him by the sense of his Beloved's absence, a song as passionately inspired and as skilfully wrought as any that have ever come from human lips.

Although at most only the first thirty stanzas of the poem were written in the prison, and the pregnant exposition of it which forms the bulk of this volume is of a considerably later date, the entire composition is popularly connected with the experiences of Toledo, on account of the sense of desolation conveyed by the first stanza. It is a singularly ardent spirit that inspires the verses. Into them the Saint put his entire soul —and only from the commentary do we learn how much meaning is stored behind the vivid poetic imagery, of which much was taken from the *Song of Songs,* though some of it, as one likes to think, may have been suggested by the fragrance and verdure which surrounded his later life in fertile Andalusia.

The *Song of Songs* has always exercised a subtle charm upon those who have 'fallen in love with God.' Using the simple metaphor of Spouse and Bride, the sacred writer sketches a series of rapid dialogues between God and the soul, made brilliant with the most suggestive colours of nature. The fragrant vineyard, the fig-tree laden with fruit, the voice of the turtle-dove and the springing of the flowers, the spikenard and saffron, calamus and cinnamon, myrrh and aloes, the fruitful valleys and green hills, flocks of goats, young roes, streams of Lebanon, beds of spices and gardens of lilies—all these and more speak to the mystic of the object of his love. So they spoke to St. John of the Cross, and one may be tempted to assert that never in their long and crowded history have the Songs inspired a greater masterpiece.

So instinct with beauty were the images of the *Spiritual Canticle,* and so captivating was the music of its rhythm, that many of the religious who first heard it found that it frequently recurred to the memory. Before long the Saint was continually being importuned to expound the poem. After some time, one of the dearest spiritual daughters, both of St. John of the Cross and of St. Teresa—Ana de Jesús—prevailed upon him to write a formal commentary upon it. His verses, it seems, were by this time on the lips of all nuns of the Discalced, and, as each would interpret them after her own manner, it was felt that their author should make an interpretation of them which would be authoritative.

Besides the original stanzas of the *Canticle* which had been written at Toledo, a number were composed at Baeza, while the last five were penned, and the poem was completed, at Granada. The commentary was begun at El Calvario (1578–9) and finished in 1584, when the Saint was acting as Prior and Confessor to the Discalced Carmelite nuns of Granada. Unlike the expositions of the *Ascent of Mount Carmel* and the *Dark Night,* it adheres very closely to the text of the poem, and never allows the reader, as do the other commentaries at times, to forget it altogether. Partly for this reason the *Spiritual Canticle* will be found to have a lighter and a more poetic quality in its prose, more rapidity in the play of its symbols and metaphors, less proportion and harmony in its exposition and less erudition and density in its reasoning.

The Saint himself, in the commentary on the line 'The Bride has entered' of Stanza XXVII,[1] describes the argument of the whole book in a few words when he writes the following passage:

In order that we may expound the arrangement of these

[1] [Note that P. Silverio's numbering of the stanzas corresponds to that of the first version given in the text below.]

stanzas the more clearly, and describe the soul's habitual progress ere it come to this estate of the Spiritual Marriage, which is the highest of those that, with the help of God, we are now to describe, and to which the soul has now come, it is to be noted that first of all it exercised itself in the trials and bitternesses of mortification, and in meditation, as the soul said at the beginning, from the first stanza down to that which says: 'Scattering a thousand graces.' Afterward it passed through the pains and straits of love which have been described in the stanzas following, as far as that which says: 'Withdraw them, Beloved.' And in addition to this, the soul then relates how it has received great communications and many visits from its Beloved, wherein it has reached ever-increasing perfection and knowledge in His love, so much so that, passing beyond all things, and even beyond itself, it has surrendered itself to Him through union of love in the Spiritual Betrothal, wherein, as one that is now betrothed, it has received from the Spouse great gifts and jewels, even as it has described in its song, from the stanza wherein this Divine betrothal was made, and which says: 'Withdraw them, Beloved.'[2]

According to this passage, the soul, having exercised herself in the 'trials and bitternesses of mortification, and in meditation,' feels sudden and enkindling touches of love for God which impel her to go forth in search of the Beloved (Stanzas I–IV), to tell him how she languishes, suffers and dies.

For the soul that loves truly suffers ordinarily from feeling the absence of God in these three ways aforesaid, according to the three faculties of the soul, which are understanding, will and memory. She languishes in the understanding, because she sees not God, Who is the health of the understanding. She suffers as to the will, because she lacks the possession of God, Who is the rest, refreshment and delight of the will. She dies as to the memory, because, remembering that she lacks all the blessings of the understanding, which are the sight of God, and all the delights of the will, which are the possession

2 Cf. p. 173, below.

of Him, and that it is likewise very possible to be deprived of Him for ever, she suffers at this memory as it were death.[3]

Leaping with irresistible impulse across the 'frontiers' (as the Bride expresses it) of the repugnance of the flesh for the spirit, she enquires of the woods, the thickets, the meadows and the flowers, if He that wounded her soul has passed that way; and the creatures, in a sublime and solemn hymn, make reply:

> Rare gifts he scatterèd
> As through these woods and groves he pass'd apace,
> Turning, as on he sped,
> And clothing every place
> With loveliest reflection of his face.

This answer of the creatures, bearing witness to the greatness and excellence of God, enkindles her yet more with Divine love and increases the agony of her wound, so that she enters what the Saint calls the 'pains and straits of love.' The wound becomes, as it were, a festering sore, incurable, leading her into the afflictions and perils of death. She breaks out into the impassioned cry:

> O crystal spring so fair,
> Might now within thy silvery depths appear,
> E'en as I linger there,
> Those features ever dear
> Which on my soul I carry graven clear!

Then God our Lord, moved by these heartfelt cries, approaches the soul, who, unaccustomed to such greatness, is drawn out from herself and falls into ecstasy, so that her natural life seems to be endangered. Unable, as she feels, to suffer such an excess of Divine beauty, she cries to the Beloved:

> Withdraw thy gaze apart,
> For lo! I soar aloft.

[3] Commentary to Stanza II, line 5. In these lines is described the incipient love of the Bride, developed in conformity with the teaching of the *Ascent of Mount Carmel* and the *Dark Night*.

Her love is still very imperfect, and therefore somewhat pre-
cipitate, or, as the Saint himself calls it, 'impatient,' like the
love of Rachel when, because she had no children, she said to
Jacob, *Da mihi liberos, alioquin moriar.* These impetuosities
of love, which come after long exercise in the virtues and
severe mortifications, are wonderfully described and analysed
here by our great psychologist of mysticism. His entire description of this early period of Divine love, with its exuberances
and impetuosities, and also with its evident signs of imperfection and inexperience, is drawn with a master-hand. Gradually, and perfectly naturally, without the slightest brusqueness,
he leads us into the next and much more important stage in
the progress of the loving soul, called the Spiritual Betrothal.
We come, as it were, to a bridge that conducts us from the violent love which breaks forth in the heart to a love which is
tranquil and at peace. Frequently characterized as it is by
raptures, ecstasies and other extraordinary manifestations of
grace, the transition suggests to St. John of the Cross a digres-
sion treating of these phenomena, but he refrains from making it because the phenomena have been so 'admirably' described by St. Teresa. This modest commendation,[4] it may be
said in passing, is the only example of a eulogy of any except
the sacred authors which St. John of the Cross makes in all
his writings. For that very reason, in spite of the restraint of
its language, it is one of the most eloquent which St. Teresa
ever received.

It is the twelfth stanza that may most properly be described
as forming the bridge just mentioned, and as leading the soul
from her unquiet, restless, violent affection into an enviably
happy state of tranquillity and rest, surpassed only by the
great goal of Union. From the twelfth stanza to the twenty-
seventh, the Saint is writing of the Spiritual Betrothal between
the soul and God, and describing its effects upon the soul and
the soul's progress within it. The 'Annotation' of the beautiful
expositions to Stanzas XIII and XIV synthesizes the effects
which the Betrothal causes in the soul. The high mountains,
the solitary wooded valleys, the tumultuous rivers, the breezes

4 See p. 96, below.

that whisper in contrast with the tranquil night, the silent music, the rising of the dawn—these and all the other similitudes are borrowed from Nature by one that is immersed in an ocean of love, so that the supreme beauty of the Beloved palpitates in his spirit, and he sings with unsurpassed inspiration. The similitudes continue in the following stanzas, in which the Bride describes, now the 'flowery bed' which the Beloved is preparing for her (XV), now the cellars of spiced wine and the Divine balsam (XVI, XVII), now the secret and most delectable science of love that she learns in the Beloved's bosom (XVIII, XIX). She loses herself, only to find herself again in the Divine heart, where she delights to make garlands of flowers 'gathered in the cool mornings' (XX, XXI). She takes her God prisoner in the golden mesh of her fair hair (XXII) and His eyes look upon her, leaving an impress of His Divine grace (XXIII).

It would seem, from the language of these stanzas, as if, in this state, the soul already had fruition of full and perfect happiness. And yet it is not so. Across the apparently clear blue sky are already floating some ominous clouds, which threaten to hide from the soul the Sun of her love, the source of her indescribable joy. The Betrothal is not the indissoluble bond of Union. Covetous men may yet seek after the soul, to put an end to her bliss, or, at least, to sully the pure and delectable stream from which she is hiding. Mindful of these dangers, the Bride once more speaks in tones of gentle melancholy (XXIV):

> Ah, scorn me not, I pray,
> For if, in truth, uncomely once was I,
> Thy beauty came one day,
> And cloth'd my misery:
> Look then on me, thus shrouded, as I cry.

She knows that passions, appetites, imaginations, stirred up by her fierce enemy the devil, may well visit her and disturb this her peace. So she conjures the creatures to drive away these little foxes (XXV), lest they ruin her vineyard. She implores the 'dead north wind' to cease and the south wind, 'that wakenest love,' to breathe fragrance into her garden. She would have her spiritual life, not killed, but enriched and quickened.

Complete and unchangeable peace, a cloudless sky and spotless radiance can be enjoyed only in the highest state of all, that of perfection. For this the mystic has no name, so sublime is it; and, being as unable to describe it as to name it, he has recourse to the current symbol of daily life which corresponds to it most nearly. He calls it the Spiritual Marriage (XXVII).

The Bride enters here 'into the pleasant garden of her desire.' Her head 'reclining on the gentle arms of the Beloved,' she rests at her pleasure:

The soul having now done all in her power that the foxes may be driven away and the north wind may depart, since these have been hindrances and inconveniences impeding the perfect delight of the estate of the Spiritual Marriage; and having likewise invoked and obtained the breeze of the Holy Spirit (as has been described in the two preceding stanzas) which is the proper disposition and means for the perfection of this estate: it now remains to treat, in this stanza, of this estate, wherein the Spouse now speaks to the soul, calling her His Bride, and says two things. He says, first, that the soul, having issued forth victoriously, has now attained to this delectable estate of the Spiritual Marriage which both He and she had so greatly desired. The second thing that He does is to enumerate the properties of the said estate, of which properties the soul now has fruition in Him, and these are for her to rest at her pleasure and for her neck to recline upon the gentle arms of the Beloved.[5]

In the last thirteen stanzas of the poem the Saint develops his wonderful teaching upon the highest summit of perfection in the love of God which the soul can reach in this life, in which 'the Spouse reveals His wondrous secrets to the soul with great readiness and frequency, and describes His works to her, for true and perfect love can keep nothing hidden. And in particular He communicates to her sweet mysteries concerning His Incarnation and the mode and way of human

[5] Stanza XXVII, Exposition (p. 172, below).

redemption' (XXVIII). By means of the 'pleasant lyres,' which signify the sweetness now enjoyed by the soul, and of the 'sirens' song,' which 'signifies the delight that He has ever in the soul,' He brings to an end all the operations and passions which before this had been able to trouble her quiet and peaceful joy in the Beloved. God now wills that all these shall cease, so that without any hindrance the soul may have fruition 'of the delight, peace and sweetness of this union' (XXIX, XXX). The soul, for her part, finding herself in possession of these rich and precious gifts of the Beloved, and being eager to retain them, conjures the nymphs of Judæa (that is, the lower part of human nature) not so much as to 'touch the thresholds' of the mansions in which she and the Beloved dwell (XXXI). Once she has succeeded in dispelling them she turns to the Beloved and, with unspeakable tenderness, cries to Him once more (XXXII) and is lovingly greeted in response (XXXIII). So, in the form of a dialogue of love, continues the incomparably beautiful idyll of this spiritual epithalamium until the Bride is completely transformed in the Beloved.

This, briefly, is the argument of the *Spiritual Canticle,* one of the loveliest poems that the human heart has ever conceived, or the human mind expressed. No man has known more of love than this Carmelite friar; few have known as much; and nowhere, certainly, outside Holy Scripture, is such knowledge expressed with greater profundity and eloquence than in this poem and its exposition.

The book is a gift of God to man. Few, it is true, are capable of savouring to the full its exquisite fragrance; only here and there do elect souls, like St. Teresa of the Child Jesus, the Little Flower, taste the plenitude of its spiritual satisfaction. Yet it is none the less a book for every true Christian who would partake of the choicest fruit of the tree of faith. All can find much in it to instruct and inspire them; and many who have devoted their lives to the love of God count it among the dearest of their possessions.

Copies of the 'Spiritual Canticle'

Many copies were made of this book, both in the lifetime of its author and shortly after his death. It may be because it was published twelve years later than his other works that the copies of it are more numerous. Of the first redaction of the *Canticle* nine copies are known, all of early date. Those most like the Sanlúcar copy (to which reference will shortly be made) are the manuscript of Gayangos (MS. 17,558 of the National Library, Madrid), the two of Valladolid and the edition of Brussels (Cf. p. 32, below). To a second group of copies, which show considerable discrepancies from these, belonged no doubt the manuscript on which was based the edition of the *Canticle* published at Madrid in 1630 by P. Jerónimo de San José. As the copies of this second group are also of early date, it cannot be said that these variants are not the work of the Saint, who may well have retouched other copies than that of Sanlúcar, though we have no certain knowledge that he did.

Copy of Sanlúcar de Barrameda. Of all the copies which have come down to us, the most interesting is that highly valued Codex which is in the possession of the Discalced Carmelite nuns of Sanlúcar de Barrameda, in the province of Cadiz, and which contains many interlinear and marginal notes in the hand of St. John of the Cross himself, as well as a most important note on the title-page, to which we shall presently refer.

In 1928 was published a facsimile edition of this copy,[6] which contains the Saint's principal poems, as well as the *Spiritual Canticle*. The title-page reads: 'Exposition of the stanzas which treat of the exercise of love between the Soul and Christ the Spouse, wherein are touched upon and expounded some points and effects of prayer, at the request of Mother Ana de Jesús, Prioress of the Discalced nuns at San José of

[6] *Cántico Espiritual y Poesías de San Juan de la Cruz, según el Códice de Sanlúcar de Barrameda.* Edición del P. Silverio de Santa Teresa, C.D. Burgos, Tipografía de El Monte Carmelo, 1928.

Granada. The year 1584.' There follows a sketch of some artistic merit, and at the bottom of the page we read: 'This book is the rough copy of which a fair copy has already been made. Fray Juan de la Cruz.'

As the foundation of the convent of Carmelite nuns at Barrameda dates only from 1644, and it is not known how the Codex came into their possession, we can only make conjectures as to its earlier history. Its importance, which is so great as to give it primacy over all other known copies of St. John of the Cross's writings, consists in the numerous manuscript notes in his hand. Some of these correct errors of the amanuensis, others make additions to the text, while others again note down ideas which occurred to the Saint after the copy was made. All these are shown in the facsimile edition and are noted in the text below, as they occur.[7]

In the eighteenth century, P. Andrés de la Encarnación began work on a new edition of the works of St. John of the Cross[8] and in the course of it made a careful and reflective study of these manuscript notes. The conclusion to which he came (1757), and which independent investigators unanimously confirmed, was that the hand in which all these additions are written is unquestionably the Saint's. Further, he said, it is clear from the title-page of the Sanlúcar Codex that two expositions of the *Spiritual Canticle* were composed by its author, and it is reasonable to suppose that the notes in that Codex were written with a view to their amplification in the second version. Carmelite critics since the time of P. Andrés have concurred in approving his conclusions, and sufficient specimens of St. John of the Cross's handwriting are now readily available for others to be able to form a judgment.[9] Investigators will not forget that the notes in the Sanlúcar Codex are marginal or interlinear, and that their author was therefore considerably cramped for space: this will account

[7] [In the translation below, only such notes as are relevant to the English rendering are, of course, given.]

[8] Cf. *Ascent of Mount Carmel,* p. lxxix, Image Books; Garden City, New York; 1958.

[9] Cf. *Autógrafos del Místico Doctor S. Juan de la Cruz,* Toledo, 1913; Baruzi: *Aphorismes de St. Jean de la Croix,* Bordeaux, 1904; etc.

for certain differences of a general kind between the caligraphy of the notes and such writings as the Saint's letters in which his pen moved more freely. On the other hand, the nature of these very differences makes it extremely unlikely that the notes could have been the work of a forger.

Down to the present time nobody appears to have impugned the authenticity of the Sanlúcar notes, although M. Baruzi throws doubt upon the subscription on the title-page, both on internal and on partly external evidence.[10] Further reference will be made to this subject later.

We now add some notes on the other copies of the *Spiritual Canticle*, prefacing each with the abbreviation by which it is designated in the footnotes to the text below, and adding in brackets the usual description which is given of it, which, except where otherwise stated, indicates where it may be found.

V (Discalced Carmelite Nuns of Valladolid). Quite possibly a contemporary MS., well preserved, which differs only slightly from the Sanlúcar copy.

Vd (Discalced Carmelite Nuns of Valladolid). A second copy, very similar to the preceding but somewhat more carefully made. Neither V nor Vd has marginal notes of any kind.

G (Gayangos). This copy formerly belonged to the historian Gayangos and is now in the National Library, Madrid (MS. 17,558). End of sixteenth century. It follows the Sanlúcar Codex throughout.

Bj (Discalced Carmelite Nuns of Bujalance). End of sixteenth century or beginning of seventeenth. Somewhat carelessly transcribed. There are differences between the stanzas at the beginning of the commentary and the same stanzas in the body of the text. A corrector has emended a number of the errors, probably without reference to any other copy. There are many variants from the Sanlúcar copy, especially in Stanzas I–V, VIII, XIII, XX, XXIV, XXV, XXXVIII, XXXIX.

Lch (Discalced Carmelite Nuns of Loeches). End of sixteenth century. A carefully made copy having marginal cor-

---

[10] [P. Silverio summarizes M. Baruzi's contention in Vol. III, pp. xxi–xxiii, of his edition.]

rections by the copyist. The many variants from Sanlúcar are similar to those of Bj, but not identical with them.

Gr (Granada: Colegio del Sacro Monte). Of comparatively recent acquisition. History unknown; there is no foundation for the natural supposition that it originally belonged to the Convento de los Mártires, Granada, where the Saint once lived, or for the more probable one that it was made for one of his Granada penitents. Date very early, possibly contemporary with the life of the Saint. Variants from Sanlúcar very similar to those of Bj and Lch.

8,654 (MS. 8,654, N.L.M.). History unknown, but date possibly in the first third of the seventeenth century. Text similar to Bj, Lch, Gr. Title reads: 'Spiritual stanzas wherein is touched the substance of the sacred Book of the Songs of Solomon, with a copious explanation of all the verses therein contained, full of admirable spiritual and mystical instruction for devout spiritual souls desirous of perfection and favoured by Our Lord, composed and expounded by our father Fray John of the Cross, first Discalced Carmelite[11] and Definitor in Chief of this Order.'

Bz (MS. 8,795, N.L.M.). This has already been referred to in the introduction to the *Dark Night;*[12] it formerly belonged to the Discalced Carmelite nuns of Baeza. Text similar to Bj, Lch, Gr.

Second Redaction of the 'Spiritual Canticle'

In speaking of the Sanlúcar Codex we pointed out that the Saint, in his own writing, described it as the 'rough copy' from which a 'fair copy' had already been made. The Codex of the Discalced Carmelite nuns of Jaén, with which we shall presently deal, and many others which are based upon it, incorporate a considerable number of the author's notes, either literally or in a modified and amplified form.

---

[11] [The word 'Carmelite' here is masculine. St. John of the Cross was in fact the first man to be admitted into the Reform.]
[12] Cf. *Dark Night of the Soul,* Image Books; Garden City, New York; 1959.

The *Canticle,* in this revised form, has been called the 'New Spiritual Canticle,' or a 'new form' of the *Canticle* or a 'second redaction,' the Sanlúcar copy, in this last case, representing the first. The name which we give to this form of the treatise is in itself of small importance, save as indicating its user's opinion of the significance of the variations. These are of three chief kinds: (1) the stanzas are linked with one another by means of an 'Annotation,' which is nearly always completely new; (2) the notes made by the Saint in the Sanlúcar copy are included in some form; (3) the order of the stanzas is re-arranged, in conformity with the subject-matter. It is clear that, though this redaction of the *Canticle* is in no sense a new work, it is greatly changed in appearance throughout. All the stanzas have been revised, and most of them amplified—there being relatively few passages omitted which are in the Sanlúcar Codex. From the prologue (to which is added an 'Argument') onwards, there is hardly a stanza without some considerable change.

We may imagine the Saint writing the *Canticle* in its first form with almost feverish haste, for we can guess what the solitary of La Peñuela meant when he described the stanzas as having been written 'with a certain degree of fervour of love for God.'[13] And we imagine, too, his sternly disciplined mind at work, revising his own commentary, modifying its plan, providing it with a brief preliminary synopsis, connecting each stanza logically with the next[14]—all these modifications bespeak the careful teacher: they are improvements in method, not changes in substance.

Then, too, he adds long paragraphs to his expositions, so that the second redaction is a quarter as long again as the first. He incorporates about one hundred of the notes which he had made in the margins of the 'rough copy.' He adds to the poem and its exposition a new stanza, placed after the tenth,[15] probably because its introduction renders more natural and more progressive the increasing desire of the soul to

13 Prologue [p. 39, below].
14 Except Stanzas II, III, IV, V, VII, which alone have no annotations.
15 [See pp. 292–300, below.]

see God. There is no reason whatever, on internal grounds, to impugn the authenticity of this stanza: it is as like the Saint's in style as are any of its companions.

Finally, the Saint varies the order of the stanzas, in the way indicated by the following table, which also indicates in detail other differences between the two redactions [B = Codex of Sanlúcar de Barrameda; J = Codex of Jaén; St. = stanza; A = Annotation; § = Paragraph in this edition].

[Prologue] B, J.
[Argument] J only.

Stanzas

B	J	
1	1	A in J only. Text greatly changed and §§ 7–12 added to it.
2	2	Text considerably changed.
3	3	Exposition greatly changed, especially that of the first and second lines.
4	4	B = J.
5	5	B = J. Last paragraph of B is used in J as A to St. 6.
6	6	Few and unimportant changes.
7	7	Few and unimportant changes. Last paragraph of B is used in J as A to St. 8.
8	8	Text considerably changed.
9	9	A in J only. Text somewhat changed.
10	10	A in J only. Changes in the last two lines.
11	12	A in J only. Text somewhat changed. § 9 in J only.
12	13	A in J only. Otherwise B = J.
13	14	The A in J is composed of the first lines of the exposition of B and a few more added to them. Otherwise few and unimportant changes.
14	15	Few changes. §§ 29–30 in J only.
15	24	A in J only. Text considerably changed.[16]
16	25	A in J only. Commentary on the last two lines somewhat changed.
17	26	A in J only. Commentary, especially on line 4, considerably changed.

[16] [This entry is omitted from the table as given by P. Silverio.]

18 27 A and § 8 in J only.

19 28 A in J only. Commentaries on ll. 4, 5, greatly changed.

20 29 A in J only. At the beginning of the commentary on the last line J adds a few lines.

21 30 A and §§ 10, 11 in J only.

22 31 A in J only. J adds a paragraph to the commentary on l. 3. Many changes in the commentary on ll. 4, 5.

23 32 A and § 9 in J only. Changes in the last two lines.

24 33 A in J only. § 4 in J greatly enlarged. Many and important changes elsewhere and additions to the commentary on l. 5.

25 16 A in J only and considerable changes in the text.

26 17 A in J only and considerable changes in the text.

27 22 A in J only and considerable changes in the text, especially in the commentary on l. 1.

28 23 Exposition in B becomes (with some changes) A in J. New exposition written for J; changes in commentary; and new § (6) in J.

29 20 A in J only. Exposition greatly changed. Commentary has few changes. §§ 12, 13, 14 are new in J.

30 21 Text greatly changed.

31 18 A in J only. Text somewhat changed.

32 19 A in J only. Considerable changes in commentary on ll. 3–5.

33 34 A in J only. A few lines are added to the commentary on l. 1, and many changes are made in the rest of the text.

34 35 The A in J is taken from the text of B, § 2 in J is new and the commentary on l. 5 is greatly changed.

35 36 A in J only. Commentary greatly changed.

36 37 A in J only. Commentary considerably changed.

37 38 A in J only. Some of the paragraphs are greatly changed.

38 39 A and § 2 in J only. Commentaries, especially those on ll. 1, 2, considerably changed.

39 40 J changes first lines of A, which is also the Exposition, and introduces many changes elsewhere.

It will be seen that, with regard to the position of the stanzas, the first fourteen stanzas and the last seven maintain their original position, the different numbering being due to the introduction of Stanza XI in the second redaction. The remaining stanzas are all re-arranged, though the majority of these are still similarly grouped: thus Stanzas XV–XXIV of the first redaction become Stanzas XXIV–XXXIII in the second, and the following are re-arranged in groups of two.

B	J	B	J
25	16	29	20
26	17	30	21
27	22	31	18
28	23	32	19

Yet we repeat that, in spite of all these changes, the *Spiritual Canticle* remains fundamentally the same. The argument of the book as given in Stanza XXVII of the first redaction and quoted above[17] is repeated in the corresponding stanza (XXII) of the second redaction, with much amplification and many changes which can be studied in the text of our edition.[18] The comparison will show the essential identity of the two plans: there are two modifications, neither of which can fairly be said to affect it.

(i) In the first redaction, fifteen stanzas describe the betrothal of the soul with Jesus Christ. In the second, only five (XII, XIII, XIV, XXV, XXVI) treat of this subject, the other ten (XV–XXIV) being transferred to the description of the Spiritual Marriage. Apparently these last seemed to the Saint better suited to a description of the most perfect state than to that of one which has not the same permanence and is liable to be interrupted by the agencies described in the poem. For this reason, too, four stanzas (XXXI, XXXII, XXIX, XXX) which in the first redaction describe, in one form or another, the disquiet experienced by the soul when it fears to lose its Beloved, and which had been assigned to the Spiritual Marriage, are in the second redaction transferred to the Betrothal. As it seems to us, the change is a distinct improvement and

---

17 [See p. 19, above.]
18 [See pp. 371–7, below.]

leaves the two states referred to much more precisely differen-
tiated and clearly described.

(ii) 'And the last stanzas,' runs the second redaction, 'treat
of the beatific estate, to which only the soul in that perfect
estate aspires.'[19] In conformity with this, the latter part of
the commentary is modified in order to introduce these desires of the soul for everlasting glory, the one means of attaining eternal union with the Beloved.

Of these modifications, which St. John of the Cross made in
the *Spiritual Canticle* (recalling those of St. Teresa in the *Way
of Perfection*),[20] very little account was taken by his contemporaries. There are very early descriptions which speak of
the forty stanzas of the poem, but none of them gives any idea
of the number or the importance of the changes made in the
thirty-nine. Even so celebrated and learned a critic as P. Jerónimo de San José cannot have been aware of their significance
when in his edition, as we shall shortly see, he merely added
to the first redaction of the *Canticle* a stanza which he had
seen in other copies. No more enlightened was P. Andrés de
Jesús María, who, when publishing the second redaction, in
1703, complained bitterly of what he called the infidelities and
omissions of previous editors, who had, of course, been working from the first redaction. Later commentators followed the
steps of one or the other of these. Only P. Andrés de la Encarnación, as written testimony left by him proves, perceived
that there were two separate redactions of the *Canticle*, and
even he did not grasp the full significance of this discovery.

As neither the first biographers of St. John of the Cross nor
any of his contemporaries provide us with details as to how
he composed his treatises, we have no information as to the
manner or date of the composition of this second redaction of
the *Canticle*. Since the two have so much in common, and
the Saint was greatly occupied at the probable time to which
we are referring, he no doubt worked upon some copy of
the first redaction rather than wrote out the whole work anew,
rewriting merely those stanzas into which he was introducing
important modifications. When the revised work was com-

[19] [See p. 239, below.]
[20] [See *C.W.S.T.J.*, II, xix–xxi.]

pleted in this way he would entrust the making of a fair copy to a competent amanuensis. This copy may well be the beautifully written Codex which now belongs to the Discalced Carmelite nuns of Jaén and to which we shall presently return.

As to the date of the second redaction, it would probably be not much later than that of the completion of the first redaction—viz., 1584. The second was certainly finished in August 1586, since M. Ana de Jesús, with her own hands, gave a copy of it, which she had received from the Saint,[21] to M. Isabel de la Encarnación when the latter was still a novice at Granada, and this could not have been later than the departure of M. Ana for Madrid in August 1586, since the two never met again.

Further, in the commentary on Stanza XXXI, there is a reference to the 'exposition of the four stanzas which begin "O living flame of love"' as having been already composed.[22] This exposition we know to have been completed towards the end of 1585, soon after the Saint was elected Vicar-Provincial of Andalusia.

Once again, the reference to St. Teresa, already quoted from the commentary on Stanza XIII, speaks, both in the first (XII) and in the second redaction (XIII), of her works as about to be published. Since the decree, with which St. John of the Cross was concerned, authorizing the printing of her works, is dated September 1, 1586, he would undoubtedly have changed this phrase had the second redaction been made after that date. Although this is by no means a conclusive deduction, it seems, together with the other available evidence, to indicate the approximate date already postulated for the second redaction.

Copies of the Second Redaction of the 'Canticle'

Copies of the second redaction began to be made immediately it became known, and, of the nine which have come down to us, the greater number date from the sixteenth cen-

[21] [Cf. P. Silverio's edition, Vol. III, p. xli.]
[22] Cf. p. 434, below.

tury. The most important is the Codex of Jaén, from which
the variants are comparatively insignificant, and with which
we deal first in order.

Codex of Jaén. This copy, which was the one given by St.
John of the Cross to M. Ana de Jesús, belongs to the Discalced Carmelite nuns of Jaén. Though by no means free from
small inaccuracies, it was evidently made with great care. Its
writing is not unlike that of the Saint: for centuries, indeed, it
passed as his, and was so considered by its first editor, P.
Andrés de Jesús María (1703). The copy was given by M.
Isabel de la Encarnación, Prioress at Jaén (who had received
it from M. Ana de Jesús)[23] to M. Clara de la Cruz, a later
Prioress; both Prioresses made solemn and explicit declara-
tions as to its history, which thus goes back directly to St.
John of the Cross himself.

Av (Discalced Carmelite Nuns, Convent of San José, Avila).
A well-preserved copy, written with great care in two hands;
both these belong to the end of the sixteenth century. The
text has few and unimportant variants from Jaén.

Bg (Discalced Carmelite Friars, Burgos). Possibly contemporary in date with St. John of the Cross. The text hardly differs from Jaén except in copyist's errors. The prologue is
wanting and the forty stanzas come at the end of the commentary instead of following the argument.

A (Discalced Carmelite Friars, Alba de Tormes). Already
described (Cf. *Ascent of Mount Carmel*, p. 6, Image Books;
Garden City, New York; 1958). The only title which it gives
to the work is *Via illuminativa*. The text has fewer variants
from Jaén than any other copy but Av.

B (MS. 6,624, N.L.M.). Already described (Cf. *Ascent of
Mount Carmel*, p. 7, Image Books; Garden City, New York;
1958). Begins, without title, at the word 'Prologue.' Text has
a fair number of variants from Jaén, the most marked of
which occur in Stanza XIII.

Bz (MS. 8,492, N.L.M.). End of sixteenth century. Somewhat carelessly copied, but with few save unintentional or unimportant variants from Jaén.

[23] See p. 14, above.

Sg (Discalced Carmelite Friars, Segovia). Lacks two folios and has many omissions. Contains more variants from Jaén than does Av, Bg or A; many of them appear to be aiming at greater clearness. Omits commentary on Stanza XIII, line 3, and Stanza XV, line 3. The Codex is described on its title-page as an 'Ancient copy of the book of the Songs of our father St. John of the Cross, sanctified by the contact of his sacred hand and . . . appearing to contain some, though but a little, of his handwriting in corrections of the first twelve folios.' This last belief is no longer maintained.

G (MS. 18,160) and *Ej* (MS. 12,411), both in the National Library, Madrid, follow Sg in their general lines and are somewhat carelessly transcribed. Both end with Stanza XXXVIII.[24] G, which has already been mentioned (Cf. *Ascent of Mount Carmel*, p. 8; *Dark Night of the Soul*, p. 30, Image Books; Garden City, New York; 1958; 1959), formerly belonged to Gayangos: it has innumerable errors and occasionally abbreviates with some care. *Ej* (described in *Dark Night of the Soul*, p. 30, Image Books; Garden City, New York; 1959) omits lines and even paragraphs and is of no great importance.

Certain Editions of the 'Spiritual Canticle'

Neither in the first collected edition of the works of St. John of the Cross (1618) nor in the second edition (1619) does the *Spiritual Canticle* find a place. The times were not favourable for the publication of anything that might appear to be a commentary on the *Song of Songs,* on account of the use made of that book by the Illuminists,[25] who were especially strong in certain parts of the Peninsula. The first country to publish the *Spiritual Canticle* was France, the translation, by René Gaultier, published at Paris in 1622, antedating the first edition in Spanish by five years.

In 1627, at Brussels, was published the first Spanish edition.

---

24 Cf. p. 473, n. 32, below.
25 [See *S.S.M.,* I, 37: 2nd. ed. I, 30.]

Like Gaultier's translation, it is based on the first redaction and agrees very closely with the Sanlúcar Codex: it is referred to in our notes as *Br*. A number of errors in this edition are probably caused by the proof-correctors' ignorance of Spanish. In the same year (1627) an Italian translation of the works of St. John of the Cross, including the *Spiritual Canticle,* appeared in Rome. The next Spanish edition of St. John of the Cross, that of Madrid, 1630 (*Md*), has already been referred to (Cf. *Ascent of Mount Carmel,* pp. lxxii–lxxiii, Image Books; Garden City, New York; 1958). It gives to P. Jerónimo de San José the honour of being the first to publish the *Spiritual Canticle* in Spain. P. Jerónimo follows the Lch group of copies, which have a good many variants from the Sanlúcar Codex, as noted above.[26] There are few omissions in his text; occasionally he makes brief additions in the interests of precision, or in order to modify some phrase which might be unfortunately interpreted, much as did P. Salablanca in the *Ascent of Mount Carmel* and other treatises of his Alcalá edition.[27] He also adds a few Latin texts to those given in the Codices of the first redaction. He includes Stanza XI of the Jaén redaction, which, if he was not acquainted with the Jaén copy, he no doubt took from Av. His edition served as a model for all its successors in the seventeenth century.

A Latin edition of the Works, published at Cologne in 1639, did much to spread a knowledge of them in German-speaking countries. The next important edition is that of Seville (*S*), published in 1703 by P. Andrés de Jesús María, referred to above;[28] it reproduced the Jaén MS. with considerable fidelity, adding a few Latin texts to the Saint's Spanish versions of them.

Until the publication (1912–14) of the three-volume Toledo edition of the works of St. John of the Cross by P. Gerardo de San Juan de la Cruz, the Seville edition was fairly generally followed. P. Gerardo gave to the Jaén redaction of

26 See p. 23, above.

27 See *Ascent of Mount Carmel,* p. lxix, Image Books; Garden City, New York; 1958.

28 Cf. *Ascent of Mount Carmel,* p. lxxiv, Image Books; Garden City, New York; 1958.

the *Spiritual Canticle* the place of honour in his second volume, publishing the Sanlúcar redaction, with most of the Saint's manuscript notes, as an appendix.

The Present Edition

The importance of the Sanlúcar MS., as containing the Saint's notes, is so exceptional (especially as the extant autographs of St. John of the Cross are very few) that we publish it first in order (as is also demanded by its date); following it is the second redaction, on the basis of the Codex of Jaén.

The chief variants from the Sanlúcar Codex are given in footnotes, save that, where their number is very large, the passages in question are printed separately in the form of an appendix (pp. 488–520, below). These passages involve Stanzas I, II, III, IV, VIII, XIII (line 4), XX (Exposition only), XXIV, XXV, XXXVIII, XXXIX; the authorities which show these variants are Bz, Gr, Lch, Bj, 8,654 and Md.

When we began work upon this edition we studied as thoroughly as possible, and in (we believe) an entirely unprejudiced spirit, the arguments which have been alleged in recent years against the genuineness of the second redaction of the *Canticle,* as contained in the Codex of Jaén. It was our intention, should these arguments convince us, not to publish this redaction at all. In view of the nature of the first redaction, the genuineness of which none can impugn, it seemed to us that comparatively little would be lost were the second redaction proved to be apocryphal. We could not find such great differences between the two as to feel that, if genuine, the second would add enormously to the value of the treatise or the reputation of its author. We had had no hesitation in denying to St. Teresa certain writings which have been traditionally ascribed to her, and elsewhere in this edition it will be seen that we have had to deny others to St. John of the Cross. In the same way we were perfectly prepared to be persuaded that the Jaén redaction of the *Canticle* was apocryphal.

But the arguments alleged have wholly failed to convince us, and, as a result, we print the second redaction immediately after the first, and elsewhere in this edition deal with the arguments alleged against its genuineness.[29] This second redaction appears to us to be a genuine and original work of St. John of the Cross and the Jaén MS. the most authoritative of its various versions. In the notes to the second redaction will be found the principal discrepancies from it contained in the other codices described above. We have not given them all, since the majority are due to the carelessness of copyists and of no great significance. Only in the Seville edition of 1703 do the variants occasionally involve attempts to improve upon the original otherwise than by substituting one word for another when the copyist was unable to understand a word or considered it obscure.

Translator's Note

As explained in the Translator's Preface (*Ascent of Mount Carmel*, p. xviii, Image Books; Garden City, New York; 1958), the foregoing introduction, like the other introductions in this edition, is an abridgement of the long prologue placed by P. Silverio at the head of his edition of the *Spiritual Canticle* (*Obras*, Vol. III, pp. vii–lxiv). At the conclusion of the volume (pp. 453–516) comes a detailed discussion of the genuineness of the second redaction of the *Canticle,* which takes the form of a reply to the contentions of the French Benedictine, Dom Philippe Chevallier, who is the protagonist in the attack upon this redaction. We have not thought it either necessary or advisable to reproduce or excerpt from this discussion, which cannot be intelligently followed in any great detail without a knowledge of French and Spanish. We may, however, summarize P. Silverio's chief conclusions:

1. No conclusive proofs, either external or internal, have up to the present been alleged against the genuineness of the Jaén Codex and its group, which we therefore persist in regarding as the work of St. John of the Cross.

2. Stanza XI of this second redaction is undoubtedly gen-

[29] [See Translator's Note, below.]

uine, and takes a natural place in the development of the
Saint's theme, as revised by him.

3. The changes in the order of certain stanzas already referred to are due to the Saint's desire to give greater precision
to his descriptions of the Spiritual Betrothal and the Spiritual
Marriage.

4. The references to the soul's desires for the eternal possession of God in the beatific state which, in the second redaction, are attributed to the perfect, correspond to manuscript
notes made by the Saint in the commentary on the final stanzas, in the Sanlúcar Codex, with a view to future development, which he executed in the second redaction.

Translator's Note to the Second Edition

Thirty years have now passed since, in his article 'Le *Cantique spirituel* de Saint Jean de la Croix a-t-il été interpolé?'
(*Bulletin Hispanique*, 1922), Dom Philippe Chevallier
launched his first attack upon the Jaén redaction, of which
he rejected the authenticity, citing also *Amores de Dios y el
alma*, a commentary on the *Spiritual Canticle* written by an
Augustinian, P. Agustín Antolínez, as the source of the commentary on a stanza which he regarded as an interpolation.
Subsequently Dom Philippe Chevallier published further articles (notably in *Vie Spirituelle*, 1926) and a critical edition
of the *Spiritual Canticle* (1930), with notes and a French translation, in defence of his thesis, which received powerful support, notably from Jean Baruzi (1924), but also met with much
opposition.

The controversy, as it stood in 1930, was judicially summed
up in English by I. I. Macdonald (*Modern Language Review*,
1930, XXV, 165–84). Since then, however, it has continued
and developed considerably, and in 1948 was given new life
by the appearance of Jean Krynen's *Le 'Cantique Spirituel'
de Saint Jean de la Croix commenté et refondu au XVII°
siècle*. M. Krynen compares Antolínez's commentary, first with
the admittedly authentic commentary of St. John of the Cross,
and then with the redaction in the 1703 edition, concluding

that, while Antolínez undoubtedly used the former, the latter was composed at a later date than his (Antolínez's) commentary, and draws on it continually. Further, he holds that the 'absolutely fundamental' doctrinal differences between the two redactions correspond to the doctrinal developments which occurred within the Carmelite school of mystical theology during the first post-Teresan generation, and ascribes the 1703 redaction to either the most distinguished member of that generation, P. Tomás de Jesús, or one of his disciples. This book has provoked voluminous criticism from Carmelite scholars and others, and an agreed solution of the problem seems as far off as ever.

As it is impossible to summarize briefly arguments which involve textual criticism, the reader is referred to that section of the bibliography in this edition (Cf. *The Complete Works of St. John of the Cross,* E. Allison Peers; Vol. III, p. 419 ff.) which deals with the controversy, and in which all contributions of outstanding importance have been included.

SPIRITUAL CANTICLE

Exposition of the stanzas which treat of the exercise of love between the Soul and Christ the Spouse, wherein are touched upon and expounded some points and effects of prayer, at the request of Mother Ana de Jesús, Prioress of the Discalced at San José of Granada. The year 1584.[1]

PROLOGUE

Forasmuch as these stanzas, religious Mother,[2] appear to be written[3] with a certain degree of fervour of love for God, Whose wisdom and love are so vast that, as is said in the Book of Wisdom,[4] they reach from one end to another, and the soul which is informed and moved by Him has to some extent this same abundance and impetus in its words, I do not now think of expounding all the breadth and plenteousness imbued in them by the fertile spirit of love, for it would be ignorance to think that sayings of love understood mystically, such as those of the present stanzas, can be fairly ex-

---

[1] This is the title given in the Codex of Sanlúcar de Barrameda, from which some other manuscripts slightly differ. For the title of 8,654 see p. 24, above.

[2] The Venerable Ana de Jesús (Lobera), Prioress of the Discalced Carmelites of Granada. She was under the direction of the Saint, when he composed this treatise at her instances, and not at those of St. Teresa, as is said in the edition of Rome (1627). Of this venerable Mother much has already been said in the *Biblioteca Mística Carmelitana* [and in H, *ad loc.*]. Suffice it here to recall that she was a woman of great spirituality and a friend of St. Teresa, of Fray Luis de León and of St. John of the Cross. She introduced the Reform of St. Teresa into France and Belgium and died at Brussels on March 4, 1621. She was born on November 25, 1545, at Medina del Campo.

[3] The Codex of Bujalance begins: 'Forasmuch as these stanzas appear to be written after a religious manner.' Bz and Md omit: 'religious Mother.'

[4] Wisdom viii, 1.

plained by words of any kind. For the Spirit of the Lord, Who helps our infirmity, as Saint Paul says, dwells in us and makes intercession for us, with groanings unutterable, pleading for that which we cannot well understand or comprehend, so as to express it ourselves.[5] For who can write down that which He reveals to loving souls wherein He dwells? And who can set forth in words that which He makes them to feel? And lastly, who can express that which He makes them to desire? Of a surety, none; nay, indeed, not the very souls through whom He passes. It is for this reason that, by means of figures, comparisons and similitudes, they allow something of that which they feel to overflow and utter secret mysteries[6] from the abundance of the Spirit, rather than explain these things rationally. These similitudes, if they be not read with the simplicity of the spirit of love and understanding embodied in them, appear to be nonsense rather than the expression of reason, as may be seen in the divine Songs of Solomon and in other books of Divine Scripture, where, since the Holy Spirit cannot[7] express the abundance of His meaning in common and vulgar terms, He utters mysteries[8] in strange figures and similitudes. Whence it follows that no words of holy doctors, albeit they have said much and may yet say more, can ever expound these things fully, neither could they be expounded in words of any kind. That which is expounded of them, therefore, is ordinarily the least part of that which they contain.

2. Since these Stanzas, then, have been composed under the influence of a love which comes from abounding mystical understanding, they cannot be fairly expounded, nor shall I attempt so to expound them, but only to throw upon them some light of a general kind (since your Reverence has so desired). And this I think to be best, for the sayings of love are better left in their fullness, so that everyone may pluck advantage from them according to his manner and to the measure of his spirit, than abbreviated in a sense to which not every

[5] Romans viii, 26.
[6] G, V, Vd, Br: 'mystical secrets.'
[7] Lch, 8,654, Md: 'desires not to.'
[8] G, V, Vd, Br: 'speaks mystically.'

taste can accommodate itself. And thus, although they are expounded after a certain manner, there is no reason why anyone should be bound to this exposition. For mystical wisdom (which comes through love, whereof the present Stanzas treat) needs not to be understood distinctly in order to produce love and affection in the soul; it is like to faith, whereby we love God without understanding Him.

3. I shall therefore be very brief, although I shall be unable to refrain from extending myself in certain places where the matter requires it, and where occasion offers to expound and treat certain points and effects of prayer, for since there are many such in the Stanzas I cannot refrain from treating of some. But I shall leave aside the commonest of them and note briefly the most extraordinary, which come to pass in those[9] that, by the favour of God, have left behind the beginners' state. And this for two reasons: the one, that there are so many things written for beginners; the other, that I speak herein with your Reverence by your command, and to your Reverence Our Lord has granted the favour of drawing you forth from these beginnings and leading you farther onward into the bosom of His Divine love. Thus I trust that, although I write here of certain points of scholastic theology concerning the interior commerce of the soul with its God, it will not be in vain to have talked somewhat after the manner of pure spirit; for though your Reverence may lack the practice of scholastic theology, wherein are comprehended Divine verities, you lack not that of mystical theology, which is attained through love, and wherein these verities are not only known but also experienced.

4. And to the end that all I say (which I desire to submit to better judgment, and entirely so to that of Holy Mother Church) may be the better received, I think not to affirm aught that is mine, trusting to my own experience, or to that of other spiritual persons of which I have known, or to that which I have heard from them (although I purpose to make use of both) unless it be confirmed and expounded by authorities from Divine Scripture, at the least in those things

9 Md: 'those souls.'

which appear to be the most difficult of comprehension. Wherein I shall follow this manner—to wit, that first I shall set down the text in its Latin and then shall expound it with respect to the subject which it illustrates. And first I shall set down all the Stanzas together, and then in order shall set down each one separately with intent to expound it;[10] whereof I shall expound each line, setting it down at the beginning of its exposition.

END OF THE PROLOGUE

SONGS BETWEEN THE SOUL AND THE SPOUSE[1]

Bride

1. Whither hast thou hidden thyself, And hast left me, O Beloved, to my sighing?

   Thou didst flee like the hart,[2] having wounded me: I went out after thee, calling,[3] and thou wert gone.[4]

2. Shepherds, ye that go Yonder, through the sheepcotes, to the hill,

   If perchance ye see him that I most love, Tell ye him that I languish, suffer and die.

3. Seeking my loves, I will go o'er yonder mountains[5] and banks;

   I will neither pluck the flowers nor fear the wild beasts; I will pass by the mighty and cross the frontiers.

---

[10] Lch, 8,654, Md: 'I shall expound them, setting down each one separately, with the exposition thereof, in order.'

[1] The stanzas are not numbered in the original.

[2] Bj, Bz, G, V, Md: 'Like (a) hart.' 8,654: 'That didst flee like (a) hart.'

[3] 'I went out sadly calling' is a copyist's error in one version.

[4] Br: 'thou wert already gone.' Lch: 'and thou wert already gone.'

[5] G, V: 'fields.'

Question to the Creatures

4. O woods and thickets Planted by the hand of the Beloved![6]
   O meadow of verdure, enamelled with flowers, Say if he has passed by you.

Answer of the Creatures

5. Scattering a thousand graces, He passed through these groves in haste,
   And, looking upon them as he went, Left them, by his glance[7] alone, clothed with beauty.[8]

Bride

6. Ah, who will be able to heal me! Surrender thou thyself now completely.[9]
   From to-day do thou send me now[10] no other messenger,
   For they cannot tell me what I wish.

7. And all those that serve Relate[11] to me a thousand graces of thee,
   And all wound me the more And something that they are stammering leaves me dying.

8. But how, O life,[12] dost thou persevere, Since thou livest not where thou livest,

[6] Lch, 8,654, Md: 'of my Beloved.'

[7] [The word translated 'glance' is *figura*, elsewhere in the text rendered 'face,' 'image,' 'form.']

[8] G, Lch, V, 8,654, Md: 'with his beauty.'

[9] [*Lit.*, 'Complete the surrendering of thyself now truly.']

[10] Lch, V omit 'now.'

[11] [*Lit.*, 'are relating.']

[12] Gr, Lch, 8,654, Br, Md: 'O soul.'

And since the arrows make thee to die which thou receivest
　　From the conceptions of the Beloved which thou formest
　　within thee?

9. Since thou hast wounded this heart,   Wherefore didst
　　thou not heal it?
　　And wherefore, having robbed me of it, hast thou left it thus
　　　And takest not the prey that thou hast spoiled?

10. Quench thou my griefs,   Since none suffices to remove
　　them,
　　And let mine eyes behold thee,   Since thou art their light
　　　and for thee alone I wish to have them.

11. O crystalline fount,   If on that thy silvered surface
　　Thou wouldst of a sudden form[13] the eyes desired   Which
　　　I bear outlined in my inmost parts!

12. Withdraw them, Beloved, for I fly away.

The Spouse

　　　　　　　　　　　　　　　　Return thou, dove,
For the wounded hart appears on the hill   At the air of thy
　　flight, and takes refreshment.

The Bride

13. My Beloved, the mountains,   The solitary, wooded valleys,
　　The strange islands, the sonorous rivers,   The whisper of
　　　the amorous breezes,

14. The tranquil night,   At the time of the rising of the dawn,
　　The silent music, the sounding solitude,   The supper that
　　　recreates and enkindles love.

[13] G: 'show.'

15. Our flowery bed,   Encompassed with dens of lions,
Hung[14] with purple and builded in peace,   Crowned[15]
with a thousand shields of gold.

16. In the track of[16] thy footprint   The young girls[17] run
along by the way.
At the touch of a spark, at the spiced wine,   Flows forth[18]
the Divine balsam.

17. In the inner cellar, of my Beloved have I drunk,   And,
when I went forth over all this meadow,
Then knew I naught   And lost the flock which I followed
aforetime.

18. There he gave me his breast;   There he taught me a science
most delectable;
And I gave myself to him indeed, reserving nothing;   There
I promised him to be his bride.

19. My soul has employed[19] itself   And all my possessions
in his service:
Now I guard no flock nor have I now other office,   For
now my exercise is in loving alone.

20. If, then, on the common land,   From henceforth I am
neither seen nor found,
You will say that I am lost;   That, wandering love-stricken,
I lost my way[20] and was found.[21]

21. With flowers and emeralds   Gathered in the cool mornings[22]
We will make the garlands flowering in thy love   And
interwoven with one hair from my head.

---

[14] So (*tendido*) Bj, Gr, Lch. Bz, G, V, Vd, Br, Md have *teñido:*
'dyed.' 8,654 has *De. púrpura vestido:* 'clothed with purple.'
[15] V, Vd: 'Surrounded.'
[16] [Or simply 'behind,' 'after,' as in the current Spanish phrase.]
[17] Bz, V: 'the youths.'
[18] [*Lit.,* 'emissions of,' without a verb.]
[19] V: 'surrendered.'
[20] [Or 'I became lost.']
[21] [*ganada, lit.,* 'gained.']
[22] Lch: 'mountains.'

22. By that hair alone   Which thou regardedst fluttering on
    my neck,

    Beholding it upon my neck, thou wert captivated,   And
    wert wounded by one of mine eyes.

23. When thou didst look on[23] me,   Thine eyes imprinted upon
    me thy grace;[24]

    For this cause didst thou love me greatly,   Whereby mine
    eyes deserved to adore that which they saw in thee.

24. Despise me not,   For, if thou didst find me swarthy,
    Now canst thou indeed look upon me,   Since thou didst
    look upon me and leave in me grace and beauty.

25. Catch us the foxes,   For our vineyard is now in flower,
    While we make a bunch of roses,   And let none appear
    upon the hill.[25]

26. Stay thee, dead north wind.   Come, south wind, that awak-
    enest love;[26]

    Breathe through my garden and let its odours flow,   And
    the Beloved shall pasture[27] among the flowers.

Spouse

27. The Bride has entered   Into the pleasant garden of her
    desire,[28]

    And at her pleasure rests,   Her neck reclining on the gentle
    arms of the Beloved.

28. Beneath the apple-tree,   There wert thou betrothed to me;

[23] [The verb is *mirar,* more conveniently translated 'regard' in
Stanza XXII and its commentary.]

[24] Bj: 'their grace.'

[25] Bj: 'upon the countryside.'

[26] [*Lit.,* 'loves.']

[27] G reads *parezca* for *pacerá:* i.e., 'And let the Beloved appear . . .'

[28] [*Lit.,* 'pleasant desired garden.']

There did I give thee my hand   And thou wert redeemed
where thy[29] mother had been corrupted.

29. Birds of swift wing,[30]   Lions, harts, leaping does,
Mountains, valleys, banks, waters, breezes, heats,   And
terrors that keep watch by night,

30. By the pleasant lyres   And by the sirens' song, I conjure
you,
Cease your wrath[31] and touch not the wall,   That the Bride
may sleep more securely.

Bride

31. O nymphs of Judaea,   While mid the flowers and rose-
trees the ambar sends forth perfume,
Dwell in the outskirts   And desire not to touch our thresholds.

32. Hide thyself, dearest one,   And look with thy face upon
the mountains,
And desire not to speak,   But look upon her companions[32]
who travels mid strange islands.

Spouse

33. The little white dove   Has returned to the ark with the
bough,
And now the turtle-dove   Has found the mate of her desire[33] on the green banks.

---

[29] The original has *su* (his, her) for *tu* (thy): a clear error.
[30] [*Lit.*, 'the light birds.']
[31] [*Lit.*, 'Let your wraths cease.']
[32] Some MSS. have *campañas* ('countries') for *compañas*
('companions,' *fem.*).
[33] [*Lit.*, 'her desired mate.']

34. In solitude she lived   And in solitude now has built her nest,

    And in solitude her dear one alone guides her,   Who likewise in solitude was wounded by love.

Bride

35. Let us rejoice, Beloved,   And let us go to see ourselves in thy beauty,

    To the mountain or the hill where flows the pure water;

    Let us enter farther into the thicket.

36. And then we shall go forth   To the lofty caverns of the rock which are well hidden,

    And there shall we enter   And taste the new wine of the pomegranates.

37. There wouldst thou show me   That which my[34] soul desired,[35]

    And there at once, my life, wouldst thou give me   That which thou gavest me the other day.

38. The breathing of the air,   The song of the sweet philomel,

    The grove and its beauty in the serene night,   With a flame that consumes and gives no pain.[36]

39. For none saw it,   Neither did Aminadab[37] appear,

    And there was a rest from the siege,   And the cavalry came down[38] at the sight of the waters.

[34] Bz: 'thy.'

[35] [The verb is not *desear*, but *pretender*, to aim at, lay claim to, strive for.]

[36] Bz: 'and burns not at all.'

[37] The copyist of Vd, not understanding this word, wrote *a mi nada*, thus causing the line to read: 'neither did aught appear to me.'

[38] ['Dismounted' is a more appropriate rendering here, but the nature of the commentary favours a word of more general meaning.]

END

BEGINNETH THE EXPOSITION OF THE STANZAS BETWEEN THE BRIDE AND THE SPOUSE

STANZA THE FIRST[1]

Whither hast thou hidden thyself,   And hast left me, O Beloved, to my sighing?
Thou didst flee like the hart, having wounded me: I went out after thee, calling, and thou wert gone.

Exposition

In this first stanza, the soul that is enamoured of the Word, the Son of God, her Spouse, desiring to be united with Him through clear and essential vision, sets forth her love's anxieties, reproaching Him for His absence, the more so because, being wounded by her love, for the which she has abandoned all things, yea even herself, she has still to suffer the absence of her Beloved and is not yet loosed from her mortal flesh that she may be able to have fruition of Him in the glory of eternity. And thus she says:

Whither hast thou hidden thyself?

2. It is as though she said: O Word, my Spouse, show me the place where Thou art hidden. Wherein she begs Him to manifest His Divine Essence; for the place where the Son of God is hidden is, as Saint John[2] says, 'the bosom of the Father,' which is the Divine Essence, the which is removed and hidden from every mortal eye and from all understanding.

---

[1] [In the first Appendix to Vol. III of P. Silverio's edition, some important variant passages from the Granada group of MSS. are given. These are translated in the Appendix, pp. 488–520, below. The notes that are given here with respect to these passages refer only to G, V, Vd, Br.]

[2] St. John i, 18.

This Isaias signified when he said: 'Verily Thou art a hidden God.'[3] Here it is to be noted that, however lofty are the communications of a soul with God in this life, and the revelations of His presence, and however high and exalted is its knowledge of Him, they are not God in His Essence, nor have they aught to do with Him. For in truth He is still hidden from the soul, and it ever beseems the soul, amid[4] all these grandeurs, to consider Him as hidden, and to seek Him as One hidden, saying: 'Whither hast Thou hidden Thyself?' For neither is a sublime communication of Him nor a sensible revelation of His presence a clearer testimony of His presence, nor is aridity or the want of all these things in the soul the less clear testimony thereof. For which cause says the prophet Job: *Si venerit ad me, non videbo eum; et si abierit, non intelligam.*[5] Which signifies: If He (that is to say, God) comes to me, I shall not see Him; and if He departs, I shall not understand Him. Wherein is to be understood that, if the soul should experience any great communication or knowledge of God, or any other feeling, it must not for that reason persuade itself that it possesses God more completely or is more deeply in God; nor that that which it feels and understands is God in His Essence, however profound such experiences may be; and, if all these sensible and intelligible communications fail, it must not think that for that reason God is failing it.[6] For in reality the one estate can give no assurance to a soul that it is in His grace, neither can the other, that it is outside it. As the Wise Man says: *Nemo scit utrum amore an odio dignus sit.*[7] Which is to say: No mortal man can know if he be worthy of the grace or of the hatred of God. So that the intent of the soul in this present line is not merely to beg for sensible and affective devotion, wherein there is neither certainty nor clear evidence of the possession of the Spouse in this life by grace,

---

[3] Isaias xlv, 15. The Saint here corrects (a copyist's error) *escogido* to *escondido.*

[4] [*Lit.,* 'above.']

[5] Job ix, 11.

[6] [Or 'is wanting to it,' 'is absent from it,' but the original has the same verb where we have rendered 'fail . . . is failing.']

[7] Ecclesiastes ix, 1.

but also to beg for the presence and clear vision of His Essence, wherewith it desires to be given assurance and satisfaction in glory.

3. This same thing was signified by the Bride in the Divine Songs when, desiring union and fellowship with the Divinity of the Word her Spouse, she begged the Father for it, saying: *Indica mihi, ubi pascas, ubi cubes in meridie.*[8] Which is to say: Show me where Thou feedest, and where Thou liest in the midday. For to enquire of Him where He fed was to beg that she might be shown the Essence of the Divine Word, for the Father glories not, save in the Word, His only Son, neither feeds upon aught else. And to beg Him to show her where He lay in the midday was to beg that selfsame thing, since the Father lies not, neither is present in any place, save in His Son, in Whom He lies, communicating to Him all His Essence—'in the midday,' which is in Eternity, where He ever begets Him. It is this pasture, then, where the Father feeds, and this flowery bed of the Divine Word, whereon He lies hidden from every mortal creature, that the Bride-Soul entreats when she says: 'Whither hast Thou hidden Thyself?'

4. And it is to be observed, if one would learn how to find this Spouse (so far as may be in this life), that the Word, together with the Father and the Holy Spirit, is hidden essentially in the inmost centre of the soul. Wherefore the soul that would find Him through union of love must go forth and hide itself from all created things according to the will, and enter within itself in deepest recollection, communing there with God in loving and affectionate fellowship, esteeming all that is in the world as though it were not. Hence Saint Augustine, speaking with God in the *Soliloquies,* said: 'I found Thee not, O Lord, without, because I erred in seeking Thee without that wert within.'[9] He is, then, hidden within the soul, and there the good contemplative must seek Him, saying: 'Whither hast Thou hidden Thyself?'

And hast left me, O Beloved, to my sighing?

[8] Canticles i, 6.
[9] *Soliloquies,* Chap. xxxi [cf. p. 244, n. 22].

5. The Bride calls Him 'Beloved,' in order the more to move and incline Him to her prayer, for, when God is loved indeed, He hears the prayers of His lover with great readiness; and then in truth He can be called Beloved when the soul is wholly with Him and has not its heart set on aught that is outside Him. Some call the Spouse 'Beloved' when He is not in truth their Beloved, because they have not their heart wholly with Him; and thus, before the Spouse, their petition is of less effect.

6. And in the words which she then says: 'And hast left me to my sighing,' it is to be observed that the absence of the Beloved is a continual sighing in the heart of the lover, because apart from Him she loves naught, rests in naught and finds relief in naught; whence a man will know by this if he have indeed love toward God—namely, if he be content with aught that is less than God. To this sighing Saint Paul referred clearly when he said: *Nos intra nos gemimus, expectantes adoptionem filiorum Dei.*[10] That is: We groan within ourselves, waiting for the adoption and possession of sons of God. Which is as though he said: Within our heart, where we have the pledge, we feel that which afflicts us—to wit, the absence. This, then, is the sighing which the soul ever makes, for sorrow at the absence of her Beloved, above all when, having enjoyed some kind of sweet and delectable communion with Him, she is left dry and alone. For this cause she grieves greatly, and says next:

Thou didst flee like the hart,

7. Here it is to be observed that in the Songs the Bride compares the Spouse to the hart and the mountain goat, saying: *Similis est dilectus meus capræ hinnuloque cervorum.*[11] That is: My Beloved is like to the goat, and to the young of the harts. And this because of the swiftness wherewith He hides and reveals Himself, as the Beloved is wont to do in the visits which He makes to the soul, and in the withdrawals and absences which He makes them experience after such visits.

[10] Romans viii, 23.
[11] Canticles ii, 9.

In this way He makes them to grieve the more bitterly for His absence, as the soul now declares when she says:

Having wounded me:

8. Which is as though she had said: Not sufficient of themselves were the sorrow and grief which I suffer ordinarily in Thy absence: Thou didst wound me yet more, by love, with Thine arrow; and, having increased my passion and desire for the sight of Thee, didst flee with the swiftness of the hart and allowedst not Thyself to be in the smallest degree comprehended.

9. For the further exposition of this line we must know that, beside many other different ways wherein God visits the soul, wounding it and upraising it in love, He is wont to bestow on it certain enkindling touches of love, which like a fiery arrow strike and pierce the soul and leave it wholly cauterized with the fire of love. And these are properly called the wounds of love, whereof the soul here speaks. So greatly do these wounds enkindle the will in affection that the soul finds itself burning in the fire and flame of love, so much so that it appears to be consumed in that flame, which causes it to go forth from itself and be wholly renewed and enter upon another mode of being, like the phœnix, that is burned up and re-born anew. Of this David speaks and says: *Inflammatum est cor meum, et renes mei commutati sunt et ego ad nihilum redactus sum, et nescivi.*[12] Which is to say: My heart was kindled and my reins were changed and I was brought to nothing and I knew not. The desires and affections, which the Prophet here describes as reins, are all stirred, and in that loving enkindlement of the heart are changed into Divine affections, and the soul through love is reduced to naught, and knows naught, save love only. And at this season of love there takes place this stirring of these reins of the desires of the will, which is much like to a torture of yearning to see God—so much so that the rigour wherewith love treats the soul seems to it intolerable; not because it has been wounded thereby[13] (for aforetime it held such wounds of love to be

[12] Psalm lxxii, 21 [A.V., lxxiii, 21–2].
[13] G, V, Vd: 'wounded by love.'

health), but because it is left thus wounded and grieving, and has not been wounded further, even to the point of death, in the which case it would see itself united with Him in a clear and revealed vision of perfect love. Wherefore the soul magnifies or describes the pain of the wound of love caused her by this absence, and says: 'Having wounded me.'

10. And thus there comes to pass in the soul this grief[14] that is so great, inasmuch as when God inflicts upon the soul that wound of love its will rises with sudden celerity to the possession of the Beloved, Whom it has felt to be near by reason of that His touch of love which it has experienced. And with equal celerity it feels His absence and is conscious of sighing thereat, since in one and the same moment He disappears from the soul and hides Himself, and it remains in emptiness and with the greater sorrow and sighing according to the greatness of its desire to possess Him. For these visits of love that wound are not like[15] others wherein God is wont to refresh and satisfy the soul by filling it with gentle peace and repose. These visits He makes to wound the soul rather than to heal it, and to afflict rather than to satisfy, since they serve but to quicken the knowledge and increase the desire, and, consequently, the pain. These are called wounds of love, and are most delectable to the soul, for which cause it would fain be ever dying a thousand deaths from these lance-thrusts, for they cause it to issue forth from itself and enter into God. This the Bride expresses in the line following, saying:

I went out after thee, calling, and thou wert gone.

11. There can be no medicine for the wounds of love save that which comes from him that dealt the wounds. For this cause the soul says that she went out, calling—that is, after Him that had wounded her—begging for medicine and crying out at the violence of the burning[16] that was caused by the wound. And it must be known that this going out is under-

[14] Vd, Br: 'thought.' G, V omit several words here.
[15] The Sanlúcar amanuensis omitted 'like,' which the Saint himself inserts.
[16] [*Lit.*, 'strength of the fire.']

stood in two ways: the one, a going forth from all things, which she does by despising and abhorring them; the other, a going forth from herself, by forgetting and neglecting herself, which she does by holy abhorrence of herself[17] through love of God; and this raises her after such wise that it makes her to go out from herself and from her judgment[18] and the ways that are natural to her, and to call for God. And to these two ways of going forth the soul refers when she says: 'I went out'; for both these, and no less, are needful for one that would go after God and enter within Him. And thus it is as though she said: By this Thy touch and wound of love, my Spouse, Thou hast drawn me forth, not only from all things, from which Thou hast far withdrawn me, but likewise from myself (for truly it seems at such a time that God is drawing the soul away from her very flesh) and hast raised me up to Thyself, so that I cry for Thee and loose myself from all things that I may cling to Thee.[19] 'And Thou wert gone.'

12. As though she had said: At the time when I desired to possess Thy presence I found Thee not, and for Thy sake I remained empty and loosed from all things, and yet I bound not myself to Thee; I was buffeted woefully by[20] the gales of love and found support neither in myself nor in Thee. This going forth in order to go to God, as the soul here terms it, is called by the Bride in the Songs to 'rise,' where she says: *Surgam et circuibo civitatem, per vicos et plateas quæram quem diligit anima mea, quæsivi illum et non inveni.*[21] Which signifies: I will rise and go about the city; in the streets and the broad ways I will seek Him Whom my soul loveth. I sought Him and I found Him not. This rising is here understood, spiritually, as of an ascent from the low to the high, which is the same as to go out from oneself—that is, from one's own low way of life and love of self to the high

---

[17] G, V: 'by despising and abhorring herself.'

[18] [*Lit., quicios,* 'hinges.' Cf. the metaphorical English phrase 'to become unhinged.']

[19] The Saint corrects the amanuensis' error: 'may loose myself from Thee.'

[20] [*Lit., penando en,* 'suffering,' 'agonizing in.']

[21] [Canticles iii, 2.]

love of God. But she gives it to be understood that she was afflicted because she found Him not. Thus one that is enamoured of God goes through this life ever in affliction, for he is already surrendered to God, and has expectation of being paid in the same coin—to wit, by the surrender to him of the clear possession and vision of God, for which he 'calls' and which in this life is not granted him. He has lost himself already for love of God, yet has found no gain to compensate him for his loss, for he lacks the said[22] possession of the Beloved for which he lost himself. Wherefore, if a man goes about afflicted for God, it is a sign that he has given himself to God and that he loves Him.

13. This affliction and sorrow for the absence of God is wont to be so great in those that are approaching ever nearer to perfection, at the time of these Divine wounds, that, if the Lord provided not for them, they would die. For, as they have kept the palate of the will and the spirit clean, healthy and well prepared for God, and as in that experience whereof we have spoken He gives them to taste something of the sweetness of love, for which they yearn above all things, therefore do they likewise suffer above all things. For there is shown to them in glimpses an immense good and it is not granted to them; wherefore their affliction and torment are unspeakable.

STANZA II

Shepherds, ye that go   Yonder, through the sheepcotes, to the hill,
If perchance ye see him that I most love,   Tell ye him that I languish, suffer and die.

Exposition

In this Stanza the soul seeks to make use of intercessors and intermediaries with her Beloved, begging them to tell Him of her pain and affliction; for it is a characteristic of the lover,

[22] G, V: 'the Divine.'

when she cannot commune with her Beloved because of His
absence, to do so by the best means that she may. And so at
this point the soul would fain use her desires, affections and
sighs as messengers, who are also able to make known the
secrets of her heart. And thus she says:

Shepherds, ye that go

2. Calling the affections and desires shepherds, because they
feed the soul on spiritual good things. For shepherd[1] signifies
'one who feeds,' and by their means God communicates Himself to her (which without them He does not). And she says:
'Ye that go.' That is to say, Ye that go forth from pure love;
because they go not all to God, but those only that go forth
from faithful love.

Yonder, through the sheepcotes, to the hill,

3. By the 'sheepcotes' she means the choirs of the angels,
by whose ministry, from choir to choir, our sighs and prayers
travel to God; Whom she calls 'the hill,' because the hill is
high, and, even so, God is the greatest of all heights; and
because in God, as on the hill, are spied out[2] and seen all
things. To Him go our prayers, which the angels offer Him,
as we have said; for it is they who offer Him our prayers and
desires,[3] according as the angel said to holy Tobias, in these
words: *Quando orabas cum lachrymis et sepeliebas, etc., ego
obtuli orationem tuam Domino.*[4] Which is to say: When
thou didst pray with tears and didst bury the dead, I offered
thy prayer unto the Lord. We can likewise understand by
these shepherds of whom the soul here speaks the angels
themselves, for not only do they bear our messages to God
but they also bring God's messages to our souls, feeding our
souls, like good shepherds, with sweet inspirations and communications from God, which He also creates by means of

[1] [The Spanish word is *pastor,* which is more appropriate here
than 'shepherd.']
[2] ['. . . Como en el *otero,* se *otean* y ven todas las cosas.' The
play upon words cannot be rendered in English.]
[3] V, Vd, Br omit: 'and desires.'
[4] Tobias xii, 12.

them. And they protect us from the wolves, who are the evil
spirits, and defend us from them like good shepherds.

If perchance ye see . . .

4. This is as much as to say: If my good fortune and happiness are such that ye reach His presence so that He sees you
and hears you. Here it is to be observed that, although it is
true that God knows and understands all things, and sees and
observes even the least of the thoughts of the soul, yet He is
said to see our necessities, or to hear them, when He relieves
them or fulfils them; for not all necessities or all petitions
reach such a point that God hears them in order to fulfil
them, until in His eyes the number of them is sufficient and
there has arrived the proper time and season to grant them
or relieve them.[5] And then He is said to see them or to hear
them, as may be seen in the Book of Exodus, where, after the
four hundred years during which the children of Israel had
been afflicted in the bondage of Egypt, God said to Moses:
*Vidi afflictionem populi mei in Egipto et clamorem ejus audivi
et descendi liberare eum.*[6] That is: I have seen the affliction
of My people and have heard their cry; and I am come down
to deliver them. Yet He had ever seen it, but He said that He
had seen it only when He willed to fulfil their request by His
deed. Even so said Saint Gabriel to Zacharias: *Ne timeas,
Zacharia, quoniam exaudita est deprecatio tua.*[7] Which is to
say: Fear not, Zacharias, for thy prayer is heard. That is, He
now granted him the son for which he had been begging Him
many years; yet He had ever heard him. And thus it is to be
understood by every soul that, albeit God may not at once
hearken to its necessity and prayer, yet it follows not that, if
they merit it, He will not hearken to them when the time is
opportune and due. For, as David says, He is *Adjutor in
opportunitatibus in tribulatione.*[8] That is: a helper in due
time and in tribulation. This, then, is signified here by the

[5] Br has: 'grant them or hear them,' and omits: 'and . . . to hear
them.'
[6] Exodus iii, 7, 8.
[7] St. Luke i, 13.
[8] Psalm ix, 10 [A.V., ix, 9].

soul that says, 'If perchance ye see . . .': 'If by my good fortune the time and season has arrived wherein my desires and petitions have reached the point at which He[9] sees them to fulfil them for me.'

. . . him that I most love,[10]

5. That is to say: more than all things; and, speaking ideally, when the soul loves Him more than all things is when naught that presents itself to her impedes her from doing and suffering, whatsoever it be, for His sake. To Him, then, Whom she most loves, she sends her desires as messengers with the petition of her needs and afflictions, saying:

Tell ye him that I languish, suffer and die.

6. Three kinds of need the soul represents here, to wit: languor, suffering and death; for the soul that loves truly suffers ordinarily from feeling the absence of God in these three ways aforesaid, according to the three faculties of the soul, which are understanding, will and memory. She languishes in the understanding, because she sees not God, Who is the health of the understanding. She suffers as to the will, because she lacks the possession of God, Who is the rest, refreshment and delight of the will. She dies as to the memory, because, remembering that she lacks all the blessings of the understanding, which are the sight of God, and all the delights of the will, which are the possession of Him, and that it is likewise very possible to be deprived of Him for ever, she suffers at this memory as it were death.

7. These three needs Jeremias likewise represented to God, saying: *Recordare paupertatis meæ, absynti et fellis.*[11] Which is to say: Remember my poverty, the wormwood and the gall. The poverty refers to the understanding, because to it belong the riches of the wisdom of God, wherein, as Saint Paul says,

[9] The Sanlúcar amanuensis had 'God,' which the Saint altered to 'He.'

[10] Br reads, obviously in error [*hoy* for *yo*]: 'Him that to-day I most love.'

[11] Lamentations iii, 19.

are hid all the treasures of God.[12] The wormwood, which is
a herb most bitter, refers to the will, for to this faculty belongs
the sweetness of the possession of God: lacking which, the
soul is left with bitterness, even as the Angel said to Saint
John in the Apocalypse, in these words: *Accipe librum, et
devora illum, et faciet amaricari ventrem tuum.*[13] Which is
to say: Take the book and eat it up; and it shall make thy
belly bitter—the belly being taken to mean the will. The gall
refers to the memory, and signifies the death of the soul, even
as Moses writes in Deuteronomy, when he speaks of the
damned, saying: *Fe draconum vinum eorum, et venenum
aspidum insanabile.*[14] That is: Their wine will be the gall of
dragons and the venom of asps, which is incurable. This signifies there the lack of God, which is the death of the soul;
and these three needs and afflictions are founded upon the
three theological virtues—faith, charity and hope—which relate
to the three faculties aforementioned: understanding, will and
memory.

8. And it is to be observed that in the line aforementioned
the soul does no more than represent her need and affliction
to the Beloved. For one that loves discreetly has no care to
beg for that which he lacks and desires, but only shows forth
his need, so that the Beloved may do that which seems good
to Him.[15] As when the Blessed Virgin spake to the beloved
Son at the wedding in Cana of Galilee, not begging Him
directly for wine, but saying: 'They have no wine.'[16] Or as
when the sisters of Lazarus sent to Him, not to say that He
should heal their brother, but to tell Him to see how he whom
He loved was sick.[17] And the reason for which it is better for
the lover to show forth his need to the Beloved than to beg
Him to fulfil it is threefold. First, because the Lord knows

[12] Colossians ii, 3.

[13] Apocalypse x, 9.

[14] Deuteronomy xxxii, 33.

[15] V, Vd: 'For one that loves discreetly does no more than show
forth his need and suffering to the Beloved, without begging for
that which he lacks and desires, so that the Beloved may do that
which seems good to Him.' G omits a few sentences here.

[16] St. John ii, 3.

[17] St. John xi, 3.

our necessities better than we ourselves; second, because the Beloved has the greater compassion when He beholds the necessity of His lover and is moved when He sees his resignation; third, because the soul is on surer ground with respect to self-love and love of possession if she represents her need than if she begs Him for that whereof she believes herself to have need. It is precisely this that the soul does in this present line, where she represents her three necessities. For to say: 'Tell ye Him that I languish, suffer and die' is, as it were, to say: Since I languish, and He alone is my health, may He give me my health. Since I suffer, and He alone is my rest, may He give me my rest. Since I die, and He alone is my life, may He give me my life.[18]

STANZA III

**Seeking my loves,   I will go o'er yonder mountains and banks;
I will neither pluck the flowers nor fear the wild beasts;   I will
pass by the mighty and cross the frontiers.**

Exposition

Not content with prayers and desires, and with making use of intercessors in order that she may speak with the Beloved, as she did in the preceding stanzas, the soul, over and above all this, sets to work herself to seek Him. This she says in this stanza that she must do: in the search for her Beloved she must practise virtues and mortifications in the contemplative and the active life; and to this end she must accept no comforts or good things, nor must all the powers and snares[1]

---

[18] Br omits a few words here, through an error of the copyist or printer, reading: 'Since I suffer, and He alone is my life, may He give me life.'

[1] G, V omit: 'and snares.'

of the three enemies—world, devil and flesh—suffice to detain and hinder her. So she says:

Seeking my loves,

2. That is to say, my Beloved.

I will go o'er yonder mountains and banks;

3. The virtues she calls 'mountains': first, by reason of their loftiness; second, because of the difficulty and toil which are experienced in climbing them, through the practice of the contemplative life. And she describes as 'banks' the mortifications and subjections and self-despising which she practises in this respect in the active life; for in order to acquire the virtues there is need of both. This, then, is as much as to say: Seeking my Beloved, I will ever put into practice the lofty virtues and abase myself in mortifications and things lowly. This she says, because the way to seek God is ever to be doing good in God, and mortifying evil in oneself, after the manner following:

I will neither pluck the flowers . . .

4. Inasmuch as in order to seek God it is needful to have a heart that is detached and strong, free from all evil things and from good things that are not simply God, the soul speaks, in this present line and in those which follow, of the liberty and the courage which she must have in order to seek Him. And herein she says that she will not pluck the flowers that she may find on the way, whereby she means all the pleasures and satisfactions and delights which may be offered her in this life and which might obstruct her road if she should desire to pluck or accept them. These things are of three kinds: temporal, sensual and spiritual. And because they all occupy the heart, and, if the soul should pay heed to them or abide in them, are an impediment to its attainment of such detachment of spirit as is needful in order to follow the straight road to Christ, she says that in seeking Him she will not pluck all these flowers aforementioned. And thus it is as if she had said: I will not set my heart upon the riches and good things

which the world offers, nor will I accept the satisfactions and delights of my flesh, neither will I pay heed to the pleasures and consolations of my spirit, in such manner as to be kept from seeking my loves over the mountains and banks of virtues and trials. This she says because she has accepted the counsel which the prophet David has given to those that go by this road, saying: *Divitiæ si affluant nolite cor apponere.*[2] That is: If riches abound, apply not your heart to them. This, too, she understands of sensual pleasures, as also of the majority of[3] temporal blessings and spiritual consolations. Here it is to be observed that not only do temporal blessings and corporeal delights hinder us and turn us aside from the road to God, but likewise spiritual delights and consolations, if we attach ourselves to them or seek after them, obstruct the road to the Cross of our Spouse Christ. Wherefore it behoves him that will go forward not to turn aside and pluck these flowers. And not only so, but it behoves him also to have the courage and the fortitude to say:

> . . . nor fear the wild beasts;
> I will pass by the mighty and cross the frontiers.

5. In these lines the Bride speaks of the three enemies of the soul, which are world, devil and flesh, and these are they that war upon her and make her way difficult.[4] By the 'wild beasts' she understands the world; by the 'mighty,' the devil; and by the 'frontiers,' the flesh.

6. She calls the world 'wild beasts,' because to the imagination of the soul that sets out upon the road to God the world seems to be represented after the manner of wild beasts, which threaten her fiercely, and this principally in three ways. First, the favour of the world will leave her, and she will lose friends, credit,[5] reputation and even property. Secondly—a wild beast no less terrifying—she must be able to bear the renunciation for ever of the satisfactions and delights of the world, and of all worldly comforts. Thirdly—and this is worse

---

[2] Psalm lxi, 11 [A.V., lxii, 10].
[3] MSS. and editions: 'as of other,' etc.
[4] Br: 'full of difficulties.'
[5] G: 'friends, knowledge, credit.' V, Vd, Br add: 'favour.'

still—the tongues of men will rise up against her, and will mock her, and will proffer many sayings and gibes against her, and will set her at naught. These things are wont to prejudice certain souls in such a way that it becomes supremely difficult for them, not only to persevere against these wild beasts, but even to be able to set out upon the road at all.

7. But a few more generous souls[6] are wont to meet other wild beasts, which are more interior and spiritual—difficulties and temptations, tribulations and trials of many kinds through which they must needs pass. Such God sends to those whom He will raise to high perfection, by proving and refining them as gold in the fire, even as in one place David says: *Multæ tribulationes justorum.*[7] That is: Many are the afflictions of the just, but out of them all will the Lord deliver them. But the soul that loves indeed, that prizes her Beloved above all things and that trusts in His love and favour, finds it not hard to say: 'Nor will I fear the wild beasts.'

I will pass by the mighty and cross the frontiers.

8. Evil spirits, who are the second enemy, she calls 'the mighty,' because with a great display of strength they endeavour to seize the passes of this road, and likewise because their temptations and wiles are stronger and harder to overcome,[8] and more difficult to penetrate, than those of the world and the flesh, and furthermore because they reinforce themselves with these other two enemies, the world and the flesh, in order to make vigorous warfare upon the soul. Wherefore David, speaking of them, calls them mighty, saying: *Fortes quæsierunt animam meam.*[9] Which signifies: The mighty sought after my soul. Concerning their might, the prophet Job says also: 'There is no power upon earth that can be compared with that of the devil, who was made to fear no one.'[10] That is, no human power can be compared with his; and thus, only the Divine power suffices to be able

---

[6] G, V, Vd, Br: 'But a few securer souls.'
[7] Psalm xxxiii, 20 [A.V., xxxiv, 19].
[8] Br omits: 'to overcome.'
[9] Psalm liii, 5 [A.V., liv, 3].
[10] Job xli, 24 [A.V., xli, 33].

to conquer him and only the Divine light to penetrate his wiles. Wherefore the soul that is to overcome his might will be unable to do so without prayer, nor will it be able to penetrate his deceits without humility and mortification. Hence Saint Paul, in counselling the faithful, says these words: *Induite vos armaturam Dei, ut possitis stare adversus insidias diaboli, quoniam non est nobis colluctatio adversus carnem et sanguinem.*[11] Which signifies: Put on the armour of God, that you may be able to stand against the deceits of the devil, for our wrestling is not against flesh and blood. By blood he means the world; and by the armour of God, prayer and the Cross of Christ, wherein is the humility and mortification whereof we have spoken.

9. The soul also says that she will cross[12] the frontiers, whereby, as we have said, she indicates the repugnance which the flesh has of its nature to the spirit and the rebellions which it makes against it. As Saint Paul says:[13] *Caro enim concupiscit adversus spiritum.*[14] That is: For the flesh lusteth against the spirit. It sets itself, as it were, upon the frontier, and resists those that travel on the spiritual road. And these frontiers the soul must cross, by surmounting these difficulties and, by the force and resolution of the spirit, overthrowing all the desires of sense and the natural affections; for, so long as these remain in the soul, the spirit is impeded by their weight so that it cannot pass on to true life and spiritual delight. This Saint Paul sets clearly before us, saying: *Si spiritu facta carnis mortificaveritis, vivetis.*[15] That is: If by the spirit you mortify the inclinations and desires of the flesh, you shall live. This, then, is the procedure which the soul says in this stanza that she must needs follow in order to seek her Beloved along this road. Briefly, she must have constancy and resolution not to stoop to pluck the flowers; courage not to

[11] Ephesians vi, 11.
[12] Br: 'crosses.'
[13] G, V, Vd, Br read: 'whereby she indicates, as Saint Paul says,' and omit all that stands between these two phrases in the text.
[14] Galatians v, 17.
[15] Romans viii, 13.

fear the wild beasts;[16] and strength to pass by the mighty and cross the frontiers; and she must determine only to go over the mountains and banks, which are the virtues,[17] after the manner already expounded.

STANZA IV

**O woods and thickets　Planted by the hand of the Beloved![1]
O meadow of verdure, enamelled with flowers,　Say if he has
　　passed by you.**

Exposition

After the soul has described[2] the way wherein she will prepare herself for setting out upon this road, namely, by courage not to turn aside after delights and pleasures, and fortitude to conquer temptations and difficulties, wherein consists the practice of self-knowledge, which is the first thing that the soul must achieve in order to come to the knowledge of God, she now, in this stanza, sets out upon her road, through consideration and knowledge of the creatures, to the knowledge of her Beloved, their Creator. For, after the practice of self-knowledge, this consideration of the creatures is the first thing in order upon this spiritual road to the knowledge of God; by means of them the soul considers His greatness and excellence, according to that word of the Apostle where he says: *Invisibilia enim ipsius a creatura mundi per ea quæ facta sunt intellecta conspiciuntur.*[3] Which is as much as to say: The invisible things of God are known by the soul through the

---

[16] G, V, Vd, Br omit this phrase.

[17] The Sanlúcar copy had not the words 'which are the virtues,' which were added by the Saint and are not found in the other versions.

[1] The same variants occur here as in the stanza of the complete poem. See p. 43, n. 6, above.

[2] G, V, Vd: 'given' [i.e., shown].

[3] Romans i, 20.

invisible and created visible things. The soul, then, in this stanza, speaks with the creatures, asking them for news of her Beloved. And it is to be observed that, as Saint Augustine says,[4] the question that the soul puts to the creatures is the meditation that she makes by their means upon their Creator. And thus in this stanza is contained a meditation on the elements and on the other lower creatures,[5] and a meditation upon the heavens and upon the other creatures and material things that God has created therein, and likewise a meditation upon the celestial spirits. She says:

O woods and thickets

2. She describes as 'woods' the elements, which are earth, water, air and fire; for, like the most pleasant woods, they are peopled thickly with creatures, which here she calls 'thickets' by reason of their great number and the many differences which there are between those in each element. In the earth, innumerable varieties of animals and plants;[6] in the water, innumerable different species of fish; and in the air, a great diversity of birds; while the element of fire concurs with all in animating and preserving them; and thus each kind of animal lives in its element, and is set and planted therein as in its own wood and region where it is born and nurtured. And in truth, God so commanded when He created them:[7] He commanded the earth to produce plants and animals; and the sea and the waters, fish; while He made the air the dwelling-place of birds. Wherefore, when the soul sees that thus He commanded and thus it was done, she says as in the line that follows:

Planted by the hand of the Beloved!

[4] *Confessions*, Bk. X, Chap. vi.
[5] G, V, Vd: 'And thus this meditation treats of the elements and all the other creatures.'
[6] The words 'and plants' are an addition of the Saint's, not found in the MSS. or the old editions.
[7] Genesis i.

3. In this line is the following consideration—namely,[8] that these varieties and wonders could be made and nurtured only by the hand of the Beloved, God. Here it is to be observed that she says intentionally 'by the hand of the Beloved'; for albeit God performs many other things by the hands of others, as by angels or men, He never performed the act of creation, neither performs it, save by His own hand. And thus the soul is greatly moved to love her Beloved, God, by the consideration of the creatures, seeing that these are things that have been made by His own hand. And she says furthermore:[9]

O meadow of verdure,

4. This consideration is upon Heaven, which she calls 'meadow of verdure,' because the things that are created therein[10] have ever unfading greenness[11] and neither perish nor wither with time; and in them, as among fresh verdure, the just take their pleasure and delight; in the which consideration likewise is comprehended all the diversity of the beauteous stars and other celestial planets.

5. This name of verdure the Church gives likewise to heavenly things when, praying to God for the souls of the departed, and speaking to them, she says: *Constituat vos Dominus inter amœna virentia.* This signifies: May God set you among the delectable verdure.[12] And she says also that this meadow of verdure is likewise

Enamelled with flowers,

6. By these flowers she understands the angels and the holy souls, wherewith that place is adorned and beautified like a graceful and costly enamel upon an excellent vase of gold.

Say if he has passed by you.

[8] 'Namely' is added by the Saint and is not in the MSS.

[9] These four words are added by the Saint and are not in the MSS. or the old editions.

[10] G: 'because the things that are in Heaven.'

[11] V: 'because the things that are in Heaven endure, and are ever with unfading greenness.'

[12] C, V: 'celestial verdure.'

7. This question is the consideration spoken of above, and
it is as if she said: Say what excellences He has created in you.

STANZA V

**Scattering a thousand graces,   He passed through these groves
in haste,
And, looking upon them as he went,   Left them, by his glance
alone, clothed with beauty.[1]**

Exposition

In this stanza the creatures make answer to the soul, which
answer, as Saint Augustine says also in that same place,[2] is
the testimony which in themselves they bear to the soul concerning the greatness and excellence of God, and for which
the soul asks in its meditation. And thus that which is contained in this stanza is in its substance[3] that God created all
things with great facility and brevity[4] and in them left some
trace of Who He was; not only did He give them[5] being out
of nothing, but He even endowed them with innumerable
graces and virtues, making them beauteous with marvellous
orderliness and unfailing interdependence, and doing all this
through His wisdom whereby He created them, which is the
Word, His Only-begotten Son. She says, then, thus:

Scattering a thousand graces,

2. By these thousand graces which she says He scattered
as He went[6] is understood the innumerable multitude of the
creatures. She sets down here the greatest number, which is

---

[1] G, Lch, V, 8,654, Md: 'with his beauty.' See p. 43, n. 8, above.
[2] *Confessions*, Bk. X, Chap. vi.
[3] Sanlúcar, V, Vd, Br read: 'And thus that which is contained in
this stanza which in its substance is . . .'
[4] Br has only: 'with facility.'
[5] G, V, Vd, Br: 'leave them.'
[6] The Saint's correction of the copyist's 'would go' [*iba* for *iría*].

a thousand, in order to denote their multitude. She calls them
graces, by reason of the many graces wherewith He endowed
every creature; and, scattering them—that is to say, peopling
the whole world with them—,

He passed through these groves in haste,

3. To pass through the groves is to create the elements,
which here she calls groves. Through these she says He passed,
scattering a thousand graces, because He adorned them with
all the creatures, which are full of grace. And, moreover, He
scattered among them the thousand graces, giving them virtue
that they might be able to contribute to the generation and
conservation of them all. And she says that He passed, because the creatures are, as it were, a trace of the passing of
God, whereby are revealed His greatness,[7] power, wisdom
and other Divine virtues. And she says that this passing was
in haste, because the creatures are the lesser works of God,
Who made them as it were in passing. The greater works,
wherein He revealed Himself most clearly and which He
wrought most lovingly,[8] were those of the Incarnation of
the Word and the mysteries of the Christian faith, in comparison wherewith all the rest were wrought, as it were, in
passing, and in haste.

**And, looking upon them as he went,   Left them, by his glance[9]
alone, clothed with beauty.**

4. According to Saint Paul, the Son of God is the brightness of His glory and the figure of His substance.[10] It must
be known, then, that God looked at all things in this image
of His Son alone, which was to give them their natural being,
to communicate to them many natural gifts and graces and to
make them finished and perfect, even as He says in Genesis,
in these words: 'God saw all the things that He had made
and they were very good.'[11] To behold them and find them

---

[7] [*Lit.*, 'whereby traces are left of His greatness.']
[8] [*Lit.*, 'to which He paid most heed.']
[9] See p. 43, n. 7, above.
[10] Hebrews i, 3.
[11] Genesis i, 31.

very good was to make them very good in the Word, His
Son. And not only did He communicate to them their being
and their natural graces when He beheld them, as we have
said, but also in this image of His Son alone He left them
clothed with beauty, communicating to them supernatural
being. This was when He became man, and thus exalted man
in the beauty of God, and consequently exalted all the creatures in him, since in uniting Himself with man He united
Himself with the nature of them all. Wherefore said the
same Son of God: *Si ego exaltatus fuero a terra, omnia traham
ad me ipsum.*[12] That is: I, if I be lifted up from the earth,
will draw all things to Myself. And thus, in this lifting up of
the Incarnation of His Son, and in the glory of His resurrection according to the flesh, not only did the Father beautify
the creatures in part, but we can say[13] that He left them all
clothed with beauty and dignity.

5. But, besides all this, speaking now somewhat according
to the sense and the affection of contemplation, in the vivid
contemplation and knowledge of the creatures, the soul sees
with great clearness that there is in them such abundance of
graces and virtues and beauty wherewith God endowed them,
that, as it seems to her, they are all clothed with marvellous
natural beauty,[14] derived from and communicated by that
infinite supernatural beauty of the image of God, Whose beholding of them clothes the world and all the heavens with
beauty and joy; just as does also the opening of His hand
whereby, as David says: *Imples omne animal benedictione.*[15]
That is to say: Thou fillest every animal with blessing. And
therefore the soul, being wounded in love by this trace of the
beauty of her Beloved which she has known in the creatures,
yearns to behold that invisible beauty, and speaks as in the
stanza following.

[12] St. John xii, 32.
[13] Sanlúcar, 8,654, V, Vd, Br, Md: 'we shall be able to say.'
[14] G, V: 'abundance of graces and virtues and natural beauty.'
[15] Psalm cxliv, 16 [A.V., cxlv, 16]. Md completes the quotation
Aperis tu manum tuam . . . , but omits the Spanish translation
here given.

STANZA VI

Ah, who will be able to heal me!   Surrender thou thyself now
    completely.
From to-day do thou send me now[1] no other messenger,   For
    they cannot tell me what I wish.

Exposition

As the creatures have given the soul signs of her Beloved, by
revealing to her in themselves traces of His beauty and excellence, her love has increased, and in consequence the pain
which she feels at His absence has grown (for the more the
soul knows of God, the more grows her desire to see Him);
and when she sees that there is naught[2] that can cure her
pain save the sight and the presence of her Beloved, she mistrusts any other remedy, and in this stanza begs Him for the
surrender and possession of His presence, entreating Him from
that day forth to entertain her with no other knowledge and
communications from Himself, since these satisfy not her
desire and will, which is contented with naught less than the
sight and presence of Him. Wherefore, she says, let Him be
pleased to surrender Himself in truth, in complete and perfect
love, and thus she says:

Ah, who will be able to heal me!

2. As though she had said: Among all the delights of the
world and the satisfactions of the senses, and the consolations
and sweetness of the spirit, naught[3] of a truth will be able to
heal me, naught will be able to satisfy me. And since this is
so:

Surrender thou thyself now completely.[4]

[1] Lch, V omit 'now.'
[2] Br, Vd and the Sanlúcar amanuensis: 'and as there is naught.'
The correction, in the Saint's hand, agrees with all other versions.
[3] G, V: 'no one.'
[4] [See p. 43, n. 9, above.]

3. Here it is to be noted that any soul that truly loves cannot wish to gain satisfaction and contentment[5] until it truly possess God. For not only do all other things fail to satisfy it, but rather, as we have said, they increase its hunger and desire to see Him as He is. And thus, since each visit that the soul receives from the Beloved, whether it be of knowledge, or feeling, or any other communication soever (which are like messengers that communicate to the soul some knowledge of Who He is, increasing and awakening the desire the more, even as crumbs increase a great hunger), makes it grieve at being entertained with so little, the soul says: 'Surrender Thou Thyself now completely.'

4. Since all that can be known of God in this life, much though it be, is not complete knowledge,[6] for it is knowledge in part and very far off, while to know Him essentially is true knowledge, which the soul begs here, therefore she is not content with these other communications, and says next:

From to-day do thou send me now no other messenger,

5. As though she were to say: Permit me not henceforward to know Thee thus imperfectly through these messengers—to wit, by the knowledge and the feelings that I am given of Thee, so far distant and removed from that which my soul desires of Thee. For to one who grieves for Thy presence, well knowest Thou, my Spouse, that the messengers bring an increase of affliction: for the one reason, because with the knowledge of Thee that they give they re-open the wound; for the other, because they seem but to delay Thy coming. Wherefore from this day forth do Thou send me no more of such far distant knowledge, for if until now I could make shift with it, since I neither knew Thee nor loved Thee much, now the greatness of the love that I have to Thee cannot be satisfied with this earnest of knowledge: wherefore do Thou surrender Thyself completely. It is as if she said more clearly: This thing, O Lord my Spouse, that Thou art giving of Thyself in part to my soul, do Thou now give completely and

[5] G, V, Vd, Br omit: 'and contentment.'
[6] Md adds: 'that is, entire and perfect [knowledge] of God.'

wholly. And this thing that Thou art showing as in glimpses, do Thou now show completely and clearly. This that Thou art communicating through intermediaries, which is like to communicating Thyself in mockery, do Thou now communicate completely and truly, giving Thyself through Thyself. For at times in Thy visits it seems that Thou art about to give the jewel of the possession of Thyself, and, when my soul regards herself well, she finds herself without it; for Thou hidest it from her, which is as it were to give it in mockery. Surrender Thyself, then, completely, giving Thyself wholly to the whole of my soul, that it wholly may have Thee wholly, and be Thou pleased to send me no other messenger.

For they cannot tell me what I wish.

6. As though she were to say: I wish for Thee wholly, and they are unable and know not how to speak to me of Thee wholly; for naught on earth or in heaven can give the soul the knowledge which she desires to have of Thee, and thus they cannot tell me what I wish. In place of these messages,[7] therefore, be Thou Thyself messenger and messages both.

STANZA VII

And all those that serve   Relate to me a thousand graces of thee,
And all wound me the more   And something that they are stammering leaves me dying.

Exposition

In the last stanza the soul has described herself as being sick, or wounded with love for her Spouse, by reason of the knowledge of Him that the irrational creation has given her; and in this present stanza she describes herself as wounded with

[7] Only Sanlúcar, Lch and Md read thus. The other MSS. and Br: 'messengers.'

love by reason of a loftier knowledge of the Beloved that she receives through the rational creation—namely, angels and men, who are nobler than the former. And, furthermore, she says that not only is this so, but likewise that she is dying of love because of a wondrous immensity that is revealed to her through these creatures; yet she attains not to a complete revelation thereof, for she calls it here a 'something,'[1] since she cannot describe it, save that it is such that it makes the soul to be dying of love.

2. From this we may infer that in this business of loving[2] there are three kinds of pain which come to the soul from the Beloved, corresponding to three kinds of knowledge that can be had of Him. The first is called a wound; this is the slightest of the three and passes the most briefly,[3] as does a wound, because it is born of the knowledge that the soul receives from the creatures, which are the lowest works of God. And of this wound, which here we likewise call sickness, the Bride speaks in the Songs, saying: *Adjuro vos, filiæ Jerusalem, si inveneritis dilectum meum, ut nuntietis ei, quia amore langueo.*[4] Which signifies: I adjure you, O daughters of Jerusalem, if you find my Beloved, that you tell Him that I languish with love—meaning by the daughters of Jerusalem the creatures.

3. The second is called a sore, which takes firmer hold upon the soul than a wound, and for that reason lasts longer, for it is like a wound which has become a sore, wherewith the soul feels in truth that it goes about sorely wounded[5] by love. And this sore is made in the soul by means of the knowledge of the works of the Incarnation of the Word and mysteries of the faith; which, being greater works of God and

---

[1] [*Lit.,* 'an I know not what' (*un no sé qué*). The phrase is used, like the French *je ne sais quoi,* to denote something very indefinite.]

[2] Bz, G, Gr, V, Vd, Br: 'of love.'

[3] Lch: 'more vehemently.'

[4] Canticles v, 8.

[5] [This play upon words reflects the Spanish use of *llagar* (wound) in this paragraph, to correspond to *llaga* (sore), rather than *herir* (wound), as in the last paragraph, where it corresponds to *herida* (wound).]

comprehending within themselves a greater love than those of the creatures, produce a greater effect of love upon the soul: so that, if the first is as a wound, this second is as a continuous sore. Of this the Spouse in the Songs, addressing the soul, says: 'Thou hast ravished[6] My heart, My sister, thou hast ravished My heart with one of thine eyes, and with one hair of thy neck.'[7] Because the eye here signifies faith in the Incarnation[8] of the Spouse, and the hair signifies the love of the same Incarnation.

4. The third kind of pain in love is like to dying, which is as though the soul had the sore festered. The soul has become wholly festered, and lives while yet dying, until love slays it and so makes it to live the life of love, by transforming it into love. And this dying of love is effected in the soul by means of a touch of highest[9] knowledge of the Divinity, which thing is the 'something' whereof, as is said in this stanza, 'they are stammering.' This touch is neither continuous nor long,[10] for were it so the soul would loose itself from the body; but it passes quickly, and thus the soul remains dying of love, and dies the more seeing[11] that it cannot wholly die of love. This is called impatient love, which is described in Genesis, where the Scripture says that Rachel had such great desire to conceive that she said to her spouse Jacob: *Da mihi liberos, alioquin moriar.*[12] That is: Give me children or else I shall die. And the prophet Job said: *Quis mihi det, ut qui coepit ipse me conterat?*[13] Which is to say: Who will grant me that he that hath begun me, the same shall end me?

5. These twofold pains of love—namely, the sore and the dying—says the soul in this stanza, are caused in her by these rational creatures: the sore, in that place which says that they are relating to her a thousand graces of the Beloved in the

---

[6] [The original has the same word *llagar;* see last note.]
[7] Canticles iv, 9. Cf. pp. 153 ff., below.
[8] G, V, Vd, Br: 'signifies the Incarnation.'
[9] Md: 'loftiest.'
[10] Md: 'nor does it last long.'
[11] Bz, Gr, Lch, Bj: 'dies the more, while it loves, because . . .'
[12] Genesis xxx, 1.
[13] Job vi, 8–9.

mysteries and wisdom of God taught her by the faith; the dying, in that place which says that they are 'stammering,' which is the sense and knowledge of the Divinity revealed to the soul[14] in things that she hears said of God. She says, then, thus:

And all those that serve[15]

6. She means here, as we have said, by 'those that serve,' the rational creatures—angels and men—for these alone among all the creatures serve[16] God with understanding of Him. For that is the meaning of this word (*vagan*) which in Latin is *vacant*. Thus it is as much as to say: 'all those that serve[17] God.' Some do this by contemplating Him in Heaven and having fruition of Him, as do the angels; others, by loving and desiring Him upon earth, as do men. And because through these rational creatures the soul knows God more keenly (now by considering their excellence, which is greater than that of all things else created, now by that which they teach us of God: the ones inwardly by secret inspirations, like those of the angels, the others outwardly through the truths of the Scriptures) she says,

Relate[18] to me a thousand graces of thee,

7. That is, they reveal to me wondrous things of Thy grace and mercy in the works of Thy Incarnation and truths of faith which they expound to me concerning Thee, and relate to me more and more; for the more they desire to say, the more graces will they be able to reveal concerning Thee.[19]

And all wound me the more

[14] G, V, Br and the Sanlúcar Codex (which the Saint corrects) have 'concealed' (from) for 'revealed' (to)—an evident slip.
[15] [The Spanish has *vagan* (literally, 'wander'). The latter word is more appropriate in the poem, but the context of the commentary justifies our translation.]
[16] [*vacan.*]
[17] *Ibid.*
[18] [Cf. p. 43, n. 11, above.]
[19] Sanlúcar, G, Vd, Br read: 'of (*or* concerning) themselves' (*de sí*). Gr, Bz omit: 'concerning Thee.'

8. For the more the angels inspire me and the more men teach me concerning Thee, the more do they make me to be in love with Thee, and thus the more do all wound me with love.

And something that they are stammering leaves me dying.

9. As if she had said: But beyond the fact that these creatures wound me in the thousand graces which they reveal to me concerning Thee, there is something which, I feel, still remains to be said; a thing which I know has yet to be revealed; a clearly imprinted trace of God which is revealed to the soul, and which it has to follow; a most lofty understanding of God, which cannot be expressed, and for that reason is called a 'something'; and if the other thing that I understand inflicts upon me the wound and the sore of love, this that I cannot wholly understand, yet feel most deeply, slays me. This happens at times to souls that are already adept, to whom God grants the favour of giving, through that which they hear or see or understand, and sometimes without any of those means, a knowledge, clearly conveyed, wherein it is granted them to understand or to perceive the loftiness and greatness of God; and in this perception the soul experiences such sublime feelings of God that it understands clearly that all has yet to be understood; and that understanding and feeling that the Divinity is so vast that it cannot be perfectly understood is a most lofty understanding. And thus one of the great favours[20] that God grants fleetingly in this life is to give it to understand so clearly and to feel so deeply concerning God that it is able to understand clearly that it cannot understand or feel at all; for in some manner the soul is like those who see Him in Heaven, where those that know Him the best understand the most distinctly the infinitude that they still have to understand, while those that see Him least perceive less clearly than those that see most how much they have yet to see.

10. This, I think, one who has not experienced it will not succeed in understanding; but the soul that experiences it, seeing that it has yet to understand that which it feels so pro-

---

[20] Md: 'greatnesses and favours.'

foundly, calls it a 'something'; for, as it is not understood, so neither can it be expressed—although, as I have said, it can be felt. Wherefore the Bride says that the creatures are[21] stammering to her because they cannot perfectly explain themselves; for that is the meaning of 'stammer'—namely, to talk as do children, and not to convey and express perfectly that which they have to say.

11. Likewise, with respect to the other creatures, there come to the soul certain enlightenments in the manner that we have described (albeit they are not always so lofty) when God grants the soul the favour of unfolding to it the knowledge and perception of the spiritual power which is in them. They seem to be expressing grandeurs of God which they are unable to express perfectly, and it is as if they are going to express them, but fall short of making them understood, and thus it is a 'something that they are stammering.' And thus the soul proceeds with her complaint, and in the stanza following addresses her own life, saying:

STANZA VIII[1]

But how, O life,[2] dost thou persevere,   Since thou livest not where thou livest,
And since the arrows make thee to die which thou receivest
   From the conceptions of the Beloved which thou formest
   within thee?

Exposition

As the soul sees herself to be dying of love, even as she has just said, and sees also that she is not dying wholly, in such

---

[21] The Sanlúcar amanuensis wrote 'that they are,' which the Saint emends. He is copied by G, V, Vd and Br.

[1] [For the version of this chapter in the Granada group of MSS., see Appendix, pp. 505–6, below.]

[2] See p. 43, n. 12, above. Here Gr, 8,654, Br, Md have: 'O life.'

a way as to be able to have the fruition of love freely, she makes complaint of the duration of her bodily life, by reason of which her spiritual life is delayed. And thus in this stanza she addresses the very life of her soul, laying stress upon the pain which it causes her. The sense of this stanza is as follows: Life of my soul, how canst thou persevere in this bodily life, since it is death to thee and privation of that true life of thy God, wherein more truly than in the body thou livest in essence, love and desire? And albeit this were no cause for leaving the body of this death in order to live and enjoy the life of thy God, how canst thou still persevere in the body, since the wounds which thou receivest from the love of the grandeurs that are communicated to thee from thy Beloved are alone[3] sufficient to end thy life, together with the wounds of the vehement love caused in thee by that which thou feelest and understandest concerning Him—namely, the touches and wounds that slay with love? The lines continue:

But how, O life, dost thou persevere,   Since thou livest not where thou livest?

2. For the understanding hereof it is to be known that the soul lives in that which it loves rather than in the body which it animates, because it has not its life in the body, but rather gives it to the body, and lives in that which it loves. But beside this life of love, whereby the soul lives in whatsoever it loves, the soul has its natural and radical life in God, as have likewise all created things, according to the saying of Saint Paul: *In ipso vivimus, movemur et sumus.*[4] Which is as much as to say: In God we have our life and our movement and our being. And Saint John says: *Quod factum est, in ipso vita erat.*[5] That is: All that was made was life in God. And as the soul sees that she has her natural life in God, through the being that she has in Him, and likewise her spiritual life,

---

[3] 'Alone' is added by the Saint and found in G, V, Vd, Br.

[4] Acts xvii, 28.

[5] St. John i, 4. [The Vulgate, as quoted by the Saint, reads: 'Omnia per ipsum facta sunt, et sine ipso factum est nihil. Quod factum est, in ipso vita erat.' The modern punctuation ('. . . nihil quod factum est. In ipso vita erat') changes the meaning.]

through the love wherewith she loves Him, she complains because she is persevering so long in the life of the body, for this impedes her from truly living where she truly has her life, through essence and through love, as we have said. The insistence that the soul lays upon this is great, for she declares that she is suffering in two contrary ways—namely, in her natural life in the body and in her spiritual life in God, which in themselves are contrary; and since she lives in both she has perforce[6] to suffer great torment, for natural life is to her as death, since it deprives her of the spiritual life wherein she has employed all her being, life and operations through love and affection. And to explain more clearly the rigour of this life, she next says:[7]

Since the arrows make thee to die which thou receivest

3. As if she had said: And, apart from what I have said, how canst thou persevere in the body, since the touches of love (for this she means by 'arrows') which the Beloved inflicts upon thy heart suffice alone to deprive thee of thy life? These touches make the soul and the heart so fruitful in understanding and love of God that it may well be said that she has conception of God,[8] according as she says in the words which follow, namely:

From the conceptions of the Beloved which thou formest within thee?

4. That is to say, of the beauty, greatness and wisdom and virtues that thou understandest of Him.

[6] Br reads 'from without' [*por fuera*] for 'perforce' [*por fuerza*].
[7] This sentence is an addition by the Saint, not found in the MSS.
[8] G, V: 'that she receives it of God.'

STANZA IX

Since thou hast wounded this heart,   Wherefore didst thou not heal it?
And wherefore, having robbed me of it, hast thou left it thus
And takest not the prey that thou hast spoiled?

Exposition

In this stanza the Bride speaks once more with the Beloved, making complaint of her pain; for love that is impatient, such as the soul here reveals, allows itself no rest nor gives any respite to its grief, setting forth its yearnings in every wise until it finds a remedy. And as the soul sees herself wounded and alone, having no healer, nor any other medicine, save her Beloved, Who it was that wounded her, she asks Him why, since He wounded her heart with the love that comes from knowledge of Him, He has not healed her with the vision of His presence. And why (she asks further), since He has robbed her of her heart, through the love wherewith He has enamoured her, drawing her forth from her own power, has He left her thus, namely, drawn forth from her own power (for one that loves possesses his heart no longer, but has given it to the Beloved[1]) and has not placed her truly in His power, taking her to Himself in complete and perfect transformation of love in glory. She says, then:

Since thou hast wounded this heart,   Wherefore didst thou not heal it?

2. She makes not complaint because He has wounded her, for the more deeply the enamoured soul is wounded, the greater is her joy; but because, having wounded her heart, He did not heal it, by slaying it wholly; for so sweet and

[1] Bz, Gr, Lch, Bj, 8,654, Md omit: 'but has given it to the Beloved.'

so delectable are the wounds of love that if they succeed not
in slaying they cannot satisfy, but they are so delectable that
she would fain have them wound her even till they have
wholly slain her, wherefore she says this: 'Since Thou hast
wounded this heart, wherefore didst Thou not heal it?' As
though she had said: Wherefore, since Thou hast wounded
it even to the point of leaving a sore in it, dost Thou not
heal it by slaying it outright with love? Since Thou art the
cause of its wound in affliction[2] of love, be Thou the cause
of its health in death of love; for after this manner the heart
that is wounded with the pain of Thy[3] absence will be healed
with the delight and glory of Thy sweet presence. And she
adds:

And wherefore, having robbed me of it, hast thou left it thus

3. To rob is naught else than for a robber to dispossess
an owner of his possessions and to take possession thereof
himself. This plaint, then, the soul sets forth here to the Beloved,[4] enquiring of Him why, since He has robbed her of
her heart and taken it out of her power and possession, He
has abandoned it thus, without taking it truly into His own
possession and keeping it for Himself, as the robber does to
the spoils that he has robbed, by carrying them off with him.[5]

4. Wherefore he that has fallen in love is said to have his
heart robbed or raped from him[6] by the object of his love,
because it wanders far away from him and is set upon the
object of his love, and thus he has no heart of his own, for
it belongs to the person whom he loves. Wherefore the soul
may know well if it loves God or no; for, if it loves Him,

[2] The Sanlúcar copyist had 'sickness,' which the Saint emended.
Br, Md and the Codices copy 'sickness.'
[3] The Saint's correction for 'his.'
[4] 'To the Beloved' is an interlinear addition of the Saint's, found
neither in the Codices nor the editions.
[5] The last five words are added by the Saint and copied by G, V,
Vd, Br. Gr, Lch, 8,654, Bz, Md are more explicit, reading: '. . . he
has robbed, which would be to take her away from this life.'
[6] [The original has: *robado* ('robbed') *o arrobado* ('enraptured'):
the play upon the technical word *arrobado* cannot be reproduced in
English.]

it will have no heart for itself, but only for God, for, the more of it it has for itself, the less it has for God.

5. And whether or no the heart has indeed been stolen can be determined by whether it has yearnings for the Beloved, or cares for naught else save for Him, as the soul here declares. The reason is because the heart cannot be in peace and rest without possession,[7] and, when its affections are set, it has possession neither of itself nor of aught beside; and if, furthermore, it possesses not truly that which it loves, it cannot fail to be wearied until it possess it;[8] for until then the soul[9] is like to the empty vessel waiting to be filled, like to the hungry man that desires food, like to the sick man sighing for health, and like to one that is suspended in the air and has no place whereon to find a foothold. In that same case is the heart of one that has fallen in love, and it is this that the soul by experience feels here, saying: 'Wherefore hast Thou left it thus?' Which is to say, empty, hungry, lonely, wounded, sick of love, suspended in the air.

And takest not the prey that thou hast spoiled?

6. Which is to say: In order to fill it, and satisfy it, and accompany it, and heal it, giving it[10] perfect rest and a perfect abode in Thyself. The loving soul cannot fail to desire the recompense and wages of its love, for the sake of which recompense it serves the Beloved, for otherwise its love would not be true; the which wages and recompense are naught else, nor can the soul desire aught else, than greater love, until it attains to being[11] in perfection of love, which confers no payment save of itself, according as the prophet Job declared in these words, saying: *Sicut servus desiderat umbram, et*

[7] G, V, Vd, Br: 'without its possession.' Bz, Bj, Lch, Gr, 8,654, Md: 'without any possession.'

[8] Gr, Lch, Bj, 8,654, Md read for the last sentence ('and if . . . possess it'): 'whence it cannot fail to be fatigued until it possess that which it loves.'

[9] The Saint inserts 'the soul,' which is not found elsewhere; all other versions have 'it.'

[10] The Saint adds 'it,' remedying an evident error.

[11] The MSS. are divided between this reading and 'attains and is.' V has: 'until it attains to this perfection.'

sicut mercenarius præstolatur finem operis sui, sic et ego habui menses vacuos, et noctes laboriosas ennumeravi mihi. Si dormiero dicam: quando consurgam? et rursum spectabo vesperam et replebor doloribus usque ad tenebras.[12] Which signifies: As the servant earnestly desireth the shade, and as the hireling looketh for the end of his work, so I also had empty months and counted the nights wearisome and tedious for myself. If I lie down to sleep, I shall say: 'When will come the day when I shall arise?' And then I shall await the evening again, and shall be filled with sorrows till the darkness of night. After this manner the soul that is burning[13] and is enkindled in the love of God desires the fulfilment and perfection of love in order to find complete refreshment there; as the servant wearied with the summer desires the refreshment of the shade, and as the hireling awaits the end of his work, so does the soul await the end of hers. Here it is to be noted that the prophet Job said not that the hireling awaited the end of his labour, but the end of his work, in order to convey the idea that we are expressing—namely, that the soul that loves awaits not the end of its labour, but the end of its work. For its work is to love, and of this work, which is to love, the soul awaits the end and termination, which is the perfection and fulfilment of loving God. Until this comes, the soul is ever in the form described by Job in the passage aforementioned, holding the days and the months as empty and the nights as wearisome and tedious. In that which has been said it is signified how the soul that loves God must not claim nor hope for aught else from Him save the perfection of love.

[12] Job vii, 2–4. Bz, Bj, Gr, Lch, 8,654 omit the Latin text.

[13] For the archaic verb *estuando* Bj and Lch read *estribando* [resting, supporting, lying upon—it is translated 'find a foothold,' above] and G, V, Vd, Br *estando,* rendering the phrase: 'the soul that is being enkindled.' The Sanlúcar copyist had written *estaando* [an impossible form], which the Saint corrects.

STANZA X

**Quench thou my griefs,   Since none suffices to remove them,
And let mine eyes behold thee,   Since thou art their light and
    for thee alone I wish to have them.**

Exposition

The soul continues, then,[1] in the present stanza, entreating
the Beloved to be pleased now to set an end to her yearnings
and afflictions, since there is none other that suffices to do
this save only Himself; and she entreats Him to do it in such
a way that her eyes may behold Him, since He alone is the
light by which they see and she desires to use them for naught
else save for Him only. She says:

Quench thou my griefs,

2. The concupiscence of love has this one property, as has
been said,[2] that all that is not done and said in agreement
with that which the will loves wearies, fatigues and grieves
it, and makes it fretful, when it sees not the fulfilment of that
which it desires; and this, and the weariness which she has
to see God, the Bride here calls 'griefs,' to remove which
naught else suffices but the possession of the Beloved. Wherefore she entreats Him to quench them with His presence, and
to refresh them all, as cool water refreshes one that is wearied
with the heat. For this reason she here uses this word 'quench,'
to signify that she is suffering from the fire of love.

Since none suffices to remove them,

3. In order the better to move and persuade the Beloved
to fulfil her petition, the soul says that, since none other than
He suffices to satisfy her need, it must be He that shall quench

---

[1] 'Then,' like 'as has been said,' in § 2, below, is the Saint's addition, not found in any other version.
[2] See n. 1, above.

her griefs. Whence it is to be noted that God is very ready to comfort the soul and satisfy her in her needs and afflictions[3] when she neither has nor seeks to have any other satisfaction and comforts than Himself; and thus the soul that can find pleasure in naught apart from God cannot remain for long without a visitation from the Beloved.

And let mine eyes behold thee,

4. That is, let me see Thee face to face with the eyes of my soul.

Since thou art their light

5. Leaving aside the fact that God is supernatural light to the eyes of the soul, without which she is in darkness, the soul calls Him here, through her affection, 'light of her eyes,' in the way wherein the lover is wont to call the person whom he loves the 'light of his eyes,' to signify the love which he bears to her. And thus it is as if she had said in the two lines above mentioned: Since mine eyes have no other light, either of their nature or of love, let them behold Thee, for in every way Thou art their light. Of this light David felt the loss when with grief he said: *Lumen oculorum meorum et ipsum non est mecum.*[4] Which signifies: The light of mine eyes, even that is not with me.

And for thee alone I wish to have them.

6. In the last line the soul has shown how her eyes will be in darkness if they see not her Beloved, since He alone is their light, wherefore she constrains Him to give her this light of glory. And in the present line she desires to constrain Him yet more, saying that she wishes not to have them for aught else but Himself; for even as that soul is justly deprived of the Divine light who desires to set the eyes of her will on the light of possession of any other thing beside God, since she herself sets a hindrance to receiving it, even so also, in the same way, a soul merits that this be given her, if she

[3] Bz, 8,654, Gr, Lch, Bj, Md: 'to comfort and relieve the necessities of the soul. . . .'
[4] Psalm xxxvii, 11 [A.V., xxxviii, 10].

closes her eyes aforementioned[5] to all things, to open them
to her God only.

STANZA XI[1]

O crystalline fount,   If on that thy silvered surface[2]
Thou wouldst of a sudden form the eyes desired   Which I bear
   outlined in my inmost parts![3]

Exposition

As with so great a desire the soul desires union with the
Spouse, and sees that, in all the creatures, there is no relief,
neither any means to that end, she speaks again to faith as
to the one who shall give her the most vivid light from her
Beloved, considering faith as a means to that end; for indeed
there is no other way whereby a soul may come to true union
with God, according as the Spouse declares through Osee, saying: 'I will betroth thee to Me in faith.'[4] She says, then, to
faith, with great desire: O faith of Christ my Spouse! If thou
wouldst but show forth clearly the truths concerning my Beloved which obscurely and darkly thou hast infused into my
soul, so that that which thou containest in faith, which is unformed knowledge, thou mightest discover and reveal, withdrawing thyself from it, suddenly, formally and completely,
and turning it into a manifestation of glory! The line, then,
says:

O crystalline fount,

2. She calls faith 'crystalline' for two reasons: the first, because it is from Christ, her Spouse,[5] and the second, because

---

[5] Br has a curious version, 'the blessed eyes' [los dichosos ojos],
for 'her eyes aforementioned' [los dichos sus ojos]. [I feel sure
that, as P. Silverio hazards, this is a pure error.]
   [1] Before this stanza Md inserts that to be found on p. 291, below.
   [2] [semblantes, a plural, as we say 'features' in the sense of 'face.']
   [3] [Lit., 'entrails' (entrañas).]
   [4] Osee ii, 20.
   [5] [There is a play of words here, upon cristalina and Cristo.]

it has the properties of crystal in being pure in its truths, and
strong, and clear, free from errors and natural forms. And
she calls it 'fount,' because from it[6] there flow to the soul
the waters of all spiritual blessings. Hence Christ our Lord,
speaking with the Samaritan woman, called faith a fount, saying that in those that believed in Him He would make for
Himself a fount whose water should spring up into everlasting
life.[7] And this water was the spirit which they that believed
on Him should receive in their faith.[8]

If on that thy silvered surface[9]

3. The propositions and articles which faith sets before us
she calls a silvered surface. For the understanding of this and
of the other lines it must be noted that faith is compared to
silver with respect to the propositions which it teaches us, and
the truths and substance which they contain in themselves are
compared to gold; for that same substance which now we believe, clothed and covered with the silver of faith, we shall
behold and enjoy in the life to come, fully revealed and[10]
with the gold of the faith laid bare. Wherefore David, speaking thereof, says thus: 'If you sleep between the two lots, the
feathers of the dove shall be silvered, and the hinder parts
of her back shall be of the colour of gold.'[11] He means: If
we close the eyes of the understanding to things both above
and below (which he calls to 'sleep between') we shall remain
alone in faith, which he calls a dove, whose feathers, which
are the truths that it tells us, will be silvered, because in this
life faith sets them forth to us obscurely and veiled, for which
reason the Bride here calls them a silvered surface. But when
this faith shall have come to an end, which will be when it
is perfected through the clear vision of God, then the sub-

6 Md adds: 'being living.'
7 St. John iv, 14.
8 St. John vii, 39.
9 [See n. 2, p. 88. In sixteenth-century Spanish *semblante* was
often used in the plural, as it is here.]
10 The copyist had written 'or,' which the Saint emends to 'and.'
11 Psalm lxvii, 14 [A.V. lxviii, 13. A.V. interprets differently.
Cf. *Spanish Mysticism, a Preliminary Survey*, London, 1924, pp.
77–9, 193–5, for a mystical interpretation of this passage and com-
ments upon it].

stance of the faith[12] will remain, stripped of this veil of silver, and in colour as gold. So that faith gives and communicates to us God Himself, but covered with the silver of faith; but it fails not for that reason to give Him to us in truth, even as one that gives a vessel of silvered gold gives none the less a golden vessel because it is covered with silver. Wherefore, when the Bride in the Songs desired this possession of God, He promised it to her, so far as in this life may be, saying to her that He would make her earrings of gold, but enamelled with silver.[13] In these words He promised to give Himself to her, veiled by faith. The soul, then, now says to faith: 'Oh, if on that thy silvered surface . . . ,' by which she means the articles aforementioned, wherewith thou hast covered the gold of the Divine rays, which are the 'eyes desired,' whereof she next speaks, saying:

Thou wouldst of a sudden form the eyes desired

4. By the eyes are meant, as we said, the Divine truths and rays; which, as we have likewise said, are set forth to us by faith in its formless and hidden articles. And thus it is as if she were to say: Oh that Thou wouldst but give me these truths which Thou teachest me formlessly and darkly, and which are veiled in Thy articles of faith, clearly and formally revealed in them, according to the entreaty of my desire! And she calls these truths 'eyes' by reason of the greatness of the presence of the Beloved which she feels, so that it seems to her that she is ever gazing at it. Wherefore she says:

Which I bear outlined in my inmost parts!

5. She says that she bears these truths outlined in her inmost parts—that is to say, in her soul, according to the understanding and the will; for according to the understanding she has these truths infused into her soul by faith. And, because her knowledge of them is not perfect, she says that they are outlined: for, even as an outline is not a perfect painting,

[12] Md adds: 'that is, the truths that she teaches.'
[13] Canticles i, 10.

so the knowledge of faith is not perfect knowledge. Wherefore the truths that are infused into the soul through faith are as it were in outline, and when they are in clear vision they will be in the soul as a perfect and finished painting, according to the words of the Apostle, where he says: *Cum autem venerit quod perfectum est, evacuabitur quod ex parte est.*[14] Which signifies: When that which is perfect is come (namely, clear vision), then that which is in part (namely, the knowledge of faith) shall be done away.

6. But besides this outline of faith there is another outline in the soul of the lover, which is of love, and this is according to the will; wherein the image of the Beloved is outlined in such manner, and so completely and vividly pictured, when there is union of love, that it is true to say that the Beloved lives in the lover and the lover in the Beloved; and such manner of likeness does love make in the transformation of the two that are in love that it may be said that each is the other and that both are one. The reason for this is that in the union and transformation of love the one gives possession of itself to the other, and each one gives and abandons itself to the other and exchanges itself for the other. Thus each lives in the other, and the one is the other, and both are one through the transformation of love. It is this that Saint Paul meant when he said: *Vivo autem, jam non ego, vivit vero in me Christus.*[15] Which signifies: I live, yet not I, but Christ liveth in me. For in saying, 'I live, yet not I,' he meant that, although he lived, his life was not his own, because he was transformed in Christ and his life was divine rather than human. Wherefore he says that it was not he that lived but Christ that lived in him.

7. So that, according to this likeness of transformation, we can say that his life and the life of Christ were one life through union of love, which in Heaven will be perfectly accomplished in the Divine life in all those who shall merit being in God; for, being transformed in God, they will live the life of God, and not their own life, and yet it will be their own life, for the life of God will be their own life. And then they

---

[14] 1 Corinthians xiii, 10.
[15] Galatians ii, 20.

will say in truth: We live, yet not we, for God liveth in us. This may come to pass in this life, as in the case of Saint Paul—not, however, in a complete and perfect way, although the soul may reach such a transformation of love as the Spiritual Marriage, which is the highest estate that can be attained in this life; for everything may be called an outline of love by comparison with that perfect image of transformation in glory. But when this outline of transformation is attained in this life, it is a great and good happiness, because the Beloved is greatly pleased with it. For this reason, desiring that the Bride should grave Him upon her soul as an outline, He said to her in the Songs: 'Set Me as a seal upon thy heart, as a seal upon thine arm.'[16] The heart here signifies the soul, whereupon God is set in this life as the seal of an outline of faith, even as was said above; and the arm signifies the strong will, wherein it is as the seal of an outline of love, as we have just now said.

STANZA XII

Withdraw them, Beloved, for I fly away.

Return thou, dove,
For the wounded hart appears on the hill   At the air of thy flight, and takes refreshment.

Exposition

In the great desires and fervent affections of love which the soul has expressed in the preceding stanzas, the Beloved is wont to visit His Bride, in a way most lofty, most delicate and most loving, and with great strength of love. For ordinarily, the favours and visits of God to the soul are wont to be great in proportion to the fervours and yearnings of love which have preceded them. And, as the soul has just now desired these Divine eyes with such great yearning, even as she has just said in the foregoing stanza, the Beloved has revealed to her some rays of His greatness and divinity, as she

[16] Canticles viii, 6.

has desired. These rays were communicated with such loftiness and such power that the soul was made to issue forth
from herself in rapture and ecstasy, which at the first is accompanied by great suffering and natural fear. And thus the
soul, being unable to suffer excess in so frail a mortal form,
says in the present stanza: 'Withdraw them, Beloved.' That
is to say: Withdraw these Thy Divine eyes, for they make
me to soar aloft, issuing forth from myself in highest contemplation above that which my physical nature can bear.
This she says because it seemed to her that her soul was flying
out of her body, which is what she desired: for this reason
she begged Him to withdraw His eyes—that is, to communicate
them no longer to her in the flesh, since in this wise she could
neither bear them nor enjoy them as she would desire, but
to communicate them to her in the flight which she was about
to make from out of the flesh. But this desire and flight the
Spouse prevented, saying: Return, dove, for the communication which thou art now receiving from Me belongs not yet
to that estate of glory to which thou now aspirest. But return
thou to Me, for it is I Whom thou seekest, wounded as thou
art by love. And I also, Who am like to the hart wounded
by thy love, now begin to reveal Myself to thee in thy lofty
contemplation, and take recreation and refreshment in the
love of thy contemplation. Wherefore the soul says to the
Spouse:

Withdraw them, Beloved,

2. According as we have said, the soul, as befitted the great
desires which she had for these Divine eyes, which signify
Divinity,[1] received inwardly from the Beloved such communication and knowledge of God, that it compelled her to say:
'Withdraw them, Beloved.' For such is the wretchedness of
our physical nature in this life that that which is truest life
to the soul and which she desires with such great desire—
namely, the communication and knowledge of her Beloved,
when they come and are given to her—she cannot receive without its almost costing her[2] her life, so that when those eyes

---

[1] The copyist had written 'dignity,' which the Saint emends. All
other authorities read 'Divinity.'
[2] Vd, Br: 'taking away from her'; V, G: 'consuming.'

which she sought with so much solicitude and yearning, and by so many ways, are revealed to her, she may come to say: 'Withdraw them, Beloved.'

3. For at times the torture felt in such visits of rapture is so great that there is no torture which so wrenches asunder the bones and straitens the physical nature[3]—so much so that unless God provided for the soul its life would come to an end. And in truth, to the soul which experiences it, it seems indeed to be ended, because it feels as though the soul is detached from the flesh and the body is unprotected. The reason for this is that such favours cannot be received by one that is wholly in the flesh, because the spirit is raised up to commune with the Divine Spirit which comes to the soul, and thus it has perforce in some manner to abandon the flesh. And hence it is that the flesh has to suffer,[4] and, consequently, the soul that is in the flesh, through the unity which they have in one being.[5] Wherefore the great torture which the soul feels at the time of this kind of visit, and the great terror which comes to it as it sees itself treated in supernatural wise, cause it to say: 'Withdraw them, Beloved.'[6]

4. But it is not to be understood that, because the soul entreats Him to withdraw them, she desires their withdrawal; for that saying comes from natural fear, as we have said. Rather, though it should cost her far more, she would not willingly lose these visits and favours of the Beloved, because, although the physical nature suffers therein, the spirit soars to supernatural recollection, in order to have fruition of the Spirit of the Beloved,[7] since it is this that she has desired and entreated. Yet she would not desire to receive it in the

[3] G, V, Vd, Br: 'For at times the torture which she receives in such visits of rapture is so great that all the bones seem to be dislocated and the physical nature straitened.'

[4] G, V, Vd, Br: 'And thus by reason of being abandoned in some manner [by the soul], in its absence, the flesh has to suffer.'

[5] G, V, Vd, Br: 'through the unity which it has with its union.'

[6] G, V, Vd, Br: 'And this is the cause of the great grief (*sentimiento*), which is great torture for the flesh; whence it is that she says, and the grief makes her to say: "Withdraw them, Beloved."'

[7] G, V, Vd, Br: 'soars to recollection, which is its nature, the which is to have fruition of the Beloved.'

flesh, where it is impossible for it to be received perfectly, but only to a slight extent and with difficulty; she would rather receive it in the flight of the spirit[8] from out of the flesh, where she can have fruition of it freely. For this cause she said: 'Withdraw them, Beloved.' Which is to say: Cease to communicate them to me in the flesh.

For I fly away.

5. As though she had said: I fly away from the flesh that Thou mayest communicate them to me apart from it, since they are the cause making me fly from out of it. And that we may the better understand what flight is this, it is to be noted that, as we have said, in that visitation of the Divine Spirit the spirit of the soul is enraptured with great force, to commune with the Spirit, and abandons[9] the body, and ceases to experience feelings and to have its actions in the body, since it has them in God. For this cause said Saint Paul, with respect to that rapture of his, that he knew not if his soul was receiving it in the body, or out of the body.[10] It is not for this reason to be understood that the soul[11] abandons[12] and forsakes the body of natural life, but that it has not its actions in it. And it is for this reason that in these raptures and flights the body remains without its senses, and, although the greatest pains be inflicted upon it, it feels them not; for this is not like other swoons and trances, which are natural, so that their subjects return to themselves with the first touch of pain. And these feelings are experienced in such visitations by those who have not yet arrived at the estate of perfection, but who are travelling along the road in the estate of progressives; for those who have already attained receive all these communications in peace and gentle love, and these raptures cease, since they were communications preparing the soul for the communication which crowns all.[13]

8 Bj: 'but in the spirit, in the flight of the spirit.'

9 Vd, Bj, Br: 'destroys'; G: 'reveals'; V: 'forsakes.'

10 [2 Corinthians xii, 2.]

11 The Saint substitutes 'the soul' for 'it' and is followed by G, V, Vd and Br.

12 G, V, Vd, Br: 'destroys.'

13 [*Lit.*, 'preparing for the total communication.']

6. This would be a convenient place for treating of the different kinds of rapture and ecstasy and of other issuings forth and subtle flights of the spirit, which are accustomed to befall spiritual persons. But, since my intent is but to expound these stanzas briefly, as I promised in the prologue, these other things must remain for such as can treat them better than I. And I pass over the subject likewise because the Blessed Teresa of Jesus, our mother, left notes admirably written upon these things of the spirit, the which notes I hope in God will speedily be printed and brought to light. That, then, which the soul says here concerning flight is to be understood of rapture and ecstasy of the spirit in God. And next the Beloved says to her:

Return thou, dove,

7. Very willingly was the soul leaving the body upon that spiritual flight, thinking that its life was coming to an end, and that it would be able to have fruition of its Spouse for ever and remain with Him unhindered by a veil. But the Spouse prevented its flight, saying: 'Return thou, dove.' As though He had said: O dove, in the quick and lofty flight of thy contemplation, and in the love wherewith thou burnest, and the simplicity wherein thou goest (for the dove has these three properties), return thou from this lofty flight wherein thou aspirest to attain to possession of Me in truth, for not yet has the time arrived for such lofty knowledge. And adapt thyself to this lower knowledge that I now communicate to thee in this thy excess.

For the wounded hart . . .

8. The Spouse compares Himself to the hart, for by the hart He here means Himself. It must be known that the characteristic of the hart is to mount up to high places, and when wounded it goes with great haste to seek refreshment in the cool waters; and if it hears its mate complain and perceives that she is wounded it goes straightway to her and fondles and caresses her. Even so does the Spouse now, for, seeing that the Bride is wounded for love of Him, He comes when she sighs, wounded in like manner with love of her, for in

those that are in love with each other the wound of one is
the wound of both, and the two have one and the same feeling. And thus it is as if He had said: Return thou, My Bride,
for if thou goest wounded with love for Me, I also, like the
hart, come to thee wounded in this thy wound, Who am as
the hart; and I also appear on the heights. For which reason
He says:

. . . appears on the hill

9. That is, through the loftiness of thy contemplation which
thou hast in this flight. For contemplation is a lofty height,
from which in this life God begins to commune with the soul
and reveal Himself to it, but not completely. For this reason
He says not that He has appeared completely, but that He
'appears,' for, however sublime the degrees of knowledge of
God which are given to the soul in this life, they are all as
very devious appearances. There follows the third characteristic of the hart, whereof we spoke, which is that contained
in the line following:

At the air of thy flight, and takes refreshment.

10. By flight He means contemplation in that ecstasy
whereof we have spoken, and by the air He means that spirit
of love which this flight of contemplation produces in the soul.
And this love which is produced by the flight He here most
appropriately calls 'air'; for the Holy Spirit, Who is love, is
also compared to air in the Divine Scripture, since He is the
breath of the Father and the Son.[14] And, even as there He
is the air of the flight—that is, He proceeds from the contemplation and wisdom of the Father and the Son,[15] and is
breathed—so here the Spouse calls this love of the soul air,
because it proceeds from the contemplation and knowledge
which at this time the soul has of God. And it is to be noted
that the Spouse says not here that He is coming at the flight,
but at the air of the flight, for properly speaking God communicates not Himself to the soul through the flight of the
soul—which is, as we have said, the knowledge that it has of

[14] Br by a copyist's error omits 'the Father and.'
[15] Md adds: 'through the will.'

God—but through the love which comes from that knowledge; for, even as love is union of the Father and the Son, even so also is it union of the soul with God. Hence it comes that, although a soul have the loftiest[16] knowledge of God, and contemplation, and knowledge of all mysteries, yet if it have not love it profiteth it nothing, as Saint Paul says,[17] towards union with God. For as likewise that same Apostle said: *Charitatem habete, quod est vinculum perfectionis.*[18] That is to say: Have charity, which is the bond of perfection. This charity, then, and love of the soul, brings the Spouse running to drink of this fount of the love of His Bride, even as the fresh water-brooks bring the thirsting and wounded hart to taste their coolness. Wherefore the line continues: 'And takes refreshment.'

11. For even as the air brings coolness and refreshment to him that is fatigued with the heat, so does this air of love refresh and recreate him that burns with the fire of love. For this fire of love has such properties that the air which affords it coolness and refreshment is an increased fire of love; for, in the lover, love is a flame which burns with the desire of burning more, as does the flame of natural fire. Wherefore He here describes as refreshment the fulfilment of this desire of His to burn more in the ardour of love for His Bride, which is the air of her flight. And thus it is as though He said: It burns more at the ardour of thy flight, for one love enkindles another. Here it is to be noted that God sets not His grace and love in the soul save according to the will and love of the soul; for which cause he that is truly in love must see that this love fail not, for by this means, as we have said, it will (if we may so say) move God the more to have more love[19] for the soul and to find more refreshment in it. And, in order to follow after this charity, it must practise that which the Apostle says thereof, where he writes: 'Charity is patient, is kind; envieth not, doeth no evil, is not puffed up, is not ambitious, seeketh not her own, is not provoked,

16 Bj: 'greatest.'
17 1 Corinthians xiii, 2.
18 Colossians iii, 14.
19 [*a que Dios le tenga más amor.*]

thinketh no evil, rejoiceth not in iniquity but rejoiceth in the truth; beareth all things which have to be borne; believeth all things (that is, those which ought to be believed); hopeth all things; endureth all things'—namely, those which are in accord with charity.[20]

STANZAS XIII AND XIV

My Beloved, the mountains,   The solitary, wooded valleys, The strange islands, the sonorous rivers,   The whisper of the amorous breezes,

The tranquil night,   At the time of the rising of the dawn, The silent music, the sounding solitude,   The supper that recreates and enkindles love.

Annotation

Before we enter upon the exposition of these stanzas, it is necessary to explain, for the better intelligence thereof and of the stanzas which follow them, that by this spiritual flight which we have just described is denoted a lofty estate and union of love wherein after much spiritual exercise God is wont to place the soul, which is called spiritual betrothal with the Word, the Son of God. And at the beginning, when this is done for the first time, God communicates to the soul great things concerning Himself, beautifying it with greatness and majesty, decking it with gifts and virtues, and clothing it with knowledge and honour of God, just as if it were a bride on the day of her betrothal. And upon this happy day, not only is there an end of the soul's former vehement yearnings and plaints of love, but, being adorned with the good things which I am describing, she enters into an estate of peace and delight and sweetness of love, as is described in the present stanzas,

[20] 1 Corinthians xiii, 4–6.

wherein she does naught else but relate and sing the wonders of her Beloved, which she knows and enjoys in Him, by means of the aforementioned union of the betrothal. And thus, in the remainder of the stanzas following, she speaks not of pains or yearnings as she did aforetime, but of the communication and exercise of sweet and peaceful love with her Beloved, since in this estate all those other things are now ended. And it is to be noted that in these two stanzas is contained the most that God is wont to communicate to a soul at this time. But it is not to be understood that to all such as arrive at this estate He communicates all that is expounded in these two stanzas, nor that He does so according to one single way and degree of knowledge and feeling. For to some souls He gives more and to others less; to some after one manner and to others after another; though souls belonging to either category can be in this estate of the Spiritual Betrothal. But we set down here the highest that is possible because in this is comprehended all else. And the exposition follows.

Exposition of the Two Stanzas

2. Now as this little dove, which is the soul, was flying on the breezes of love above the waters of the flood (namely, those her fatigues and yearnings of love which she has described[1] up to this point) and found no rest for her foot,[2] upon this last flight which we have described, the compassionate father Noe put forth the hand of his mercy and caught her, and brought her into the ark of his charity and love, and this was at the time when, in the stanza that we have just expounded, the Spouse said: 'Return thou, dove.'

3. And it is to be noted that, even as in the ark of Noe, as the Divine Scripture tells us, there were many mansions for many different kinds[3] of animal, and every kind of food

---

[1] V, Vd, Br: 'which we have treated.'

[2] Gr, Lch, 8,654, Md add: 'even as the dove that flew out of the ark.'

[3] Gr, Lch, 8,654, Md: 'for every different kind.'

which they could eat, even so, in this flight which it makes to this Divine Ark of the bosom of God, the soul not only sees therein the many mansions which His Majesty described in Saint John,[4] saying that they were in His Father's house, but sees and knows that all kinds of food are there[5]—that is, all the grandeurs which can please the soul, which are all the things that are contained in the two stanzas above-mentioned, and are signified by those words used in common parlance, the substance of which is as follows.

4. In this Divine union the soul sees and tastes abundance and inestimable riches, finds all the rest and the recreation that it desires, and understands strange kinds of knowledge and secrets of God, which is another of those kinds of food that it likes best. It feels likewise in God an awful power and strength which transcends all other power and strength: it tastes a marvellous sweetness and spiritual delight, finds true rest and Divine light and has lofty experience of the knowledge of God, which shines forth in the harmony of the creatures and the acts of God. Likewise it feels itself to be full of good things, and empty of evil things and far withdrawn from them; and, above all, it experiences, and has fruition of, an inestimable feast of love, which confirms it in love, and this is the substance of that which is contained in the two stanzas aforementioned.

5. In these stanzas the Bride says that her Beloved is all these things, both in Himself and also for her;[6] for in that which God is wont to communicate in such excesses, the soul feels and knows the truth of that saying which the holy Francis uttered, namely: 'God mine, and all things.' Wherefore, since God is all things to the soul, and the good of them all, the communication of this excess is explained by the similitude of the goodness of the things[7] in the said stanzas, which we shall expound line by line. It must be understood that all

---

[4] St. John xiv, 2.
[5] Br omits: 'and knows that all kinds of food are there.'
[6] A corrupt reading has: 'and she awaits Him' [*y lo espera ella* for *y lo es para ella*]. Bj reads: 'and awaits her there' [*y la espera allá*]. Our reading is the Saint's correction.
[7] Bj, Bz: 'this excess of the abundance of things.'

that is expounded here is in God in an eminent and an infinite manner, or, to express it better, that each of these grandeurs which are spoken of is God, and they are all of them God; for, inasmuch as in this case the soul is united with God, it feels that all things are God in one simple being, even as Saint John felt when he said: *Quod factum est, in ipso vita erat.*[8] That is to say: That which was made in Him was life. It is not to be understood that, in that which the soul is here said to feel, it is, as it were, seeing things in the light, or creatures in God, but that in that possession the soul feels that all things are God to it. Neither is it to be understood that, because the soul has such lofty feelings concerning God in that which we are saying, it sees God essentially and clearly, for this is no more than a powerful and abundant communication, and a glimpse of that which He is in Himself, wherein the soul feels this goodness concerning the things which we shall expound in these lines, as follows:

My Beloved, the mountains,

6. The mountains have heights; they are abundant, extensive, beautiful, graceful, flowery and fragrant. These mountains my Beloved is to me.[9]

The solitary, wooded valleys,

7. The solitary valleys are quiet, pleasant, cool, shady, abounding in fresh water; and with the variety of their groves and the sweet song of the birds they greatly recreate and delight the senses, in their solitude and silence giving refreshment and rest. These valleys my Beloved is to me.

The strange islands,

8. The strange islands are girt around by the sea, and are far away over the sea, withdrawn and aloof from communication with men. Thus there are produced and bred in them things very different from those in our own experience, of very strange kinds and with virtues never seen by men, so

---

8 [See p. 80, n. 5, above.]
9 G omits this paragraph.

that they cause great surprise and wonder in those that see them. And thus, by reason of the great and marvellous wonders, and the strange knowledge, far removed from the knowledge of every day, that the soul sees in God, He is here called strange islands. There are two reasons for calling a man strange: either because he lives in retirement from men or because he is excellent and singular among other men in his deeds and works. For both these reasons the soul here speaks of God as strange; for not only has He all the strangeness of islands which have never been seen, but likewise His ways, counsels and works are very strange and new and marvellous to men.[10] And it is no marvel if God is strange to men who have never seen Him, since He is strange also to the holy angels and the souls[11] who see Him; for they cannot see Him perfectly, nor shall they so see Him, and until the last day of judgment they will continually be seeing in Him so many things that are new, according to His profound judgments, and concerning the works of His mercy and justice, that they will wonder continually and marvel ever more: so that not men alone, but likewise angels, can speak of Him as of strange islands.[12] Only to Himself is He not strange, neither to Himself is He new.

The sonorous rivers,[13]

9. Rivers have three properties: the first is that they assail and submerge all that they meet: the second, that they fill up all the low and hollow places that are in their path: the third, that their sound is such as to drown and take the place of all sounds else. And because in this communication of God

[10] Bz, 8,654, Gr, Lch, Bj, Md: 'And thus [the soul] speaks of God as strange, for both these reasons; because He has all the strangeness of islands which have never been seen, and because His ways and counsels are marvellous wonders.'

[11] Bz, Bj, Lch, Gr, 8,654, Md omit: 'and the souls.'

[12] Md: 'will ever know in Him so many things that are new according to the works of mercy and justice that they ever marvel; so that all, both angels and men, can speak of Him as of strange islands.'

[13] [For the version of §§ 9–11 in the Granada group of MSS. see Appendix I, pp. 506–8, below.]

which we are describing the soul feels most delectably in herself these three properties, she says that her Beloved is the sonorous rivers. With respect to the first property that the soul feels, it must be known that she feels herself to be assailed by the torrent[14] of the Spirit of God in this case, in such a manner, and taken possession of thereby with such force, that it seems to her that all the rivers of the world are coming upon her and assailing her, and she feels that all her actions[15] are whelmed thereby, and all the passions which she had aforetime. Yet, though this is an experience of such violence, it is not for that reason an experience of torment; for these rivers are rivers of peace, even as God declares through Isaias concerning this assault upon the soul,[16] saying: *Ecce ego declinabo super eam quasi fluvium pacis et quasi torrentem inundantem gloriam.*[17] Which is to say: Take note and be warned that I will come down upon her (that is to say, upon the soul) and assail her like a river of peace and like a torrent which overflows with glory as it advances. And thus this Divine assault which God makes upon the soul, resembling the assault of sonorous rivers, fills it wholly with peace and glory. The second property which the soul feels is that this Divine water at this time fills up the low places[18] of its humility and also fills the empty places of its desires, even as Saint Luke says: *Exaltavit humiles, exurientes implevit bonis.*[19] Which is to say: He hath exalted the humble and hath filled the hungry with good things. The third property that the soul feels in the sonorous rivers of its Beloved is a spiritual voice and sound which is above all sounds and above all voices, the which voice drowns every other voice and its sound exceeds all the sounds in the world. And in the exposition hereof we shall have to occupy ourselves for some little space.

10. This voice or sonorous sound of these rivers which the soul here describes is a fulfilment so abundant that it fills

[14] G, V, Vd, Br: 'by the current.'

[15] G, V, Br: 'all her occasions'—clearly an error.

[16] Both the Sanlúcar copyist and all the other MSS. read: 'saying concerning this assault upon the soul.' The correction is the Saint's.

[17] Isaias lxvi, 12.

[18] *bajos.* Br has *vasos* ('vessels').

[19] St. Luke i, 52-3.

the soul with good things, and a power so powerful that it
possesses the soul and appears to her not merely as the sound
of rivers, but as most powerful thunderings. But this voice
is a spiritual voice and is unaccompanied by those physical
sounds, and by the pain and trouble of them, but is accompanied rather by grandeur, strength, power, delight and glory;
and thus it is as an immense and inward sound and voice,
which clothes the soul with power and strength. This spiritual
voice and sound was heard in the spirits of the Apostles at
the time when the Holy Spirit, in a vehement torrent (as is
said in the Acts of the Apostles), descended upon them;[20]
when, in order that the spiritual voice that was speaking to
them from within might be made manifest, this sound was
heard from without as a vehement wind, in such wise that it
was heard by all who were in Jerusalem: whereby, as we
say, was denoted that which the Apostles received within
themselves, which was, as we have said, a fulfilment of power
and strength. And likewise, when the Lord Jesus was praying
to the Father in the peril and anguish which were caused Him
by His enemies, as is said in Saint John, there came to Him
an inward voice from Heaven, strengthening Him according
to His humanity, which sound the Jews heard from without,
and so solemn was it, and so mighty, that some said it had
thundered, and others, that an angel from Heaven had spoken
to Him;[21] and by that voice which was heard from without
was denoted and signified the strength and power given to
Christ, according to His humanity, within. By this it is not to
be understood that the soul fails to receive in the spirit the
sound of the spiritual voice. It must be noted that the spiritual voice is the effect which the voice makes upon the soul,
even as the physical voice impresses its sound upon the ear and
its intelligence upon the spirit. This was in the mind of
David when he said: *Ecce dabit voci suæ vocem virtutis.*[22]
Which signifies: Behold, God will give[23] to His voice a voice
of virtue, the which virtue is the voice within. When David

[20] Acts ii, 2.
[21] St. John xii, 28.
[22] Psalm lxvii, 34 [A.V., Psalm lxviii, 33].
[23] G, V, Vd, Br read: 'He' for 'Behold, God.'

said that He would give His voice a voice of virtue he meant
that to the outward voice, which is heard in outward wise,
He would give a voice of such virtue that it would be heard
within. By this it must be understood that God is an infinite
voice, and that, communicating Himself to the soul after the
said manner, He produces the effect of an immense voice.[24]

11. This voice Saint John heard in the Apocalypse, and he
says of the voice that he heard from Heaven: *Erat tanquam
vocem aquarum multarum, et tanquam vocem tonitrui
magni.*[25] Which is to say: That the voice which he heard was
as a voice of many waters and as the voice of a great thunder.
And that it may not be inferred that this voice, because it
was so great, was harsh and disagreeable, he adds at once
that this same voice was so soft that *erat sicut citharedorum
citharizantium in citharis suis.* Which signifies: It was as of
many harpers who harped upon their harps. And Ezechiel
says that this sound as of many waters was *quasi sonum
sublimis Dei,*[26] which is to say, as a sound of the Most High
God. That is, that He communicated Himself therein after
a manner most high and likewise most gentle. This voice is
infinite, for, as we said, it is God Himself Who communicates
Himself, speaking in the soul: but He limits Himself by the
capacity of each soul, uttering a voice of virtue such as befits
its limitations; and He produces in the soul great delight and
grandeur. For this cause the Bride said in the Songs: *Sonet
vox tua in auribus meis, vox enim tua dulcis.*[27] Which
signifies: Let Thy voice sound in my ears, for Thy voice is
sweet. The line continues:

The whisper of the amorous breezes,

12. Of two things the soul makes mention in this present
line, namely, of breezes and of a whisper. By the amorous
breezes are here understood the virtues and graces of the Be-

[24] G, V, Vd, Br read: [for 'He . . . voice'], 'the immense voice
produces an effect upon it.' So also reads the Sanlúcar copy; the
reading in the text above is the Saint's correction.
[25] Apocalypse xiv, 2.
[26] Ezechiel i, 24.
[27] Canticles ii, 14.

loved, which, by means of the said union of the Spouse, assail the soul, communicate themselves most lovingly and touch
it in its substance.[28] And by the whisper of these breezes is
meant a most lofty and most delectable knowledge of God,
and of His virtues, which overflows into the understanding
at the touch which these virtues of God effect in the substance
of the soul:[29] and this is the supreme delight which is contained in all things that the soul here experiences.[30]

13. And in order that what has been said may be the better understood, it must be noted that even as two things are
perceived in the air—namely, the touch thereof and the sound
or whisper—so in this communication of the Spouse two other
things are perceived—namely, feeling of delight, and knowledge. And even as the touch of the air is felt with the sense
of touch and the whisper of the same air is heard by the ear,
even so likewise the touch of the virtues of the Beloved is
felt and enjoyed in the sense of touch of this soul which is in
its substance;[31] and the knowledge of these virtues of God is
felt in the ear of the soul, which is in the understanding. And
it must be known likewise that the amorous breeze is said
to have come when it strikes delectably, satisfying the appetite of him that so greatly desired this refreshment, for then
the sense of touch is soothed and refreshed, and with this
soothing of the sense of touch the ear experiences great delight in the sound and whisper of the air, much more than
does the sense of touch in the touch of the air; for the sense
of hearing is more spiritual (or, to speak more exactly, comes
nearer to the spiritual) than the sense of touch; wherefore
the delight which it causes is more spiritual than that which is
caused by the sense of touch.

14. Precisely because this touch of God brings great satisfaction and comfort to the substance of the soul, and sweetly
fulfils its desire, which was to be in this union, the said union,

[28] Md adds: 'by means of loving knowledge.'

[29] The Saint corrects: 'in the ascent of the soul' (which is also
found in Bz) to 'in the substance of the soul.' Md adds: 'by means
of its faculties.'

[30] 'Here' is an addition of the Saint, copied only by G, V, Vd,
Br.

[31] Md adds: 'by means of the will.'

or touch, is spoken of as 'amorous breezes'; for, as we have said, in it are communicated to the soul, lovingly and sweetly, the virtues of the Beloved, whence is derived in the understanding the whisper of knowledge. And it is called a whisper, because even as the whisper which is caused by the air enters subtly into the organ of hearing, even so this most subtle and delicate knowledge enters with marvellous sweetness and delight into the inmost substance of the soul, which is a far greater delight than any other. The reason is that substance of understanding is given to it, stripped[32] of accidents[33] and imaginary forms, for it is given[34] to the understanding that is called by philosophers 'passive' or 'possible,' because it receives it passively, doing naught on its own behalf;[35] which is the principal delight of the soul, because it is in the understanding, wherein, as theologians say, consists fruition, which is to see God.[36] Since this whisper signifies the said substantial knowledge, some theologians think that our father Elias saw God in that gentle whisper of the breeze which he felt on the mount at the mouth of his cave. The Scripture calls it a gentle whisper of the breeze, because from the subtle and delicate communication of the Spirit knowledge was born to it in the understanding; and the soul here calls it a whisper of amorous breezes, because from the amorous communication of the virtues of her Beloved it overflows into her understanding, wherefore she calls it a 'whisper of the amorous breezes.'

15. This Divine whisper, which enters by the ear of the soul, is not only substance which I have called that of understanding, but likewise it is the manifestation of truths concerning the Divinity and the revelation of His hidden secrets; for ordinarily, whensoever some communication of God is

[32] G, V, Vd, Br omit part of this and the last sentence, reading: 'into the inmost substance of the soul, stripped of all accidents and imaginary forms.'

[33] Md: 'of other accidents.'

[34] The Saint thus corrects the 'which it gives' of the copy.

[35] Md: 'naught after its natural manner on its own behalf.'

[36] Md: 'which is the principal act of the soul; because it is in the understanding, wherein consists, as theologians say, the vision of God.'

found in the Divine Scriptures, and is said to enter by the ear, it is found to be a manifestation of these naked truths in the understanding, or a revelation of secrets of God, which are purely spiritual visions or revelations, given to the soul alone, without the help and aid of the senses, and so, when it is said that God communicates by the ear, that expression describes a very sublime and certain fact. Thus, when Saint Paul wished to describe the loftiness of his revelation, he said not, *Vidit arcana verba*, still less, *Gustavit arcana verba*, but *Audivit arcana verba, quæ non licet homini loqui*.[37] Which is as though he had said: I heard secret words which it is not lawful for a man to utter. As to this, it is thought that he saw God, as did our father Elias, in that whisper. For even as faith, as Saint Paul says likewise, comes by bodily hearing, even so that which faith teaches us, which is the substance of understanding, comes by spiritual hearing. This was clearly expressed by the prophet Job, when he spoke with God, Who had revealed Himself to him, saying: *Auditu auris audivi te*,[38] *nunc autem oculus meus videt te*.[39] That is to say: With the hearing of the ear I heard Thee, but now mine eye seeth Thee. Wherein it is clearly declared that to hear Him with the ear of the soul is to see Him with the eye of passive understanding whereof we spoke. Wherefore he says not: I heard Thee with the hearing 'of my ears,' but 'of my ear'; nor: I saw Thee 'with mine eyes,' but 'with mine eye,' which is the understanding. Wherefore this hearing of the soul is seeing with the understanding.[40]

16. And it is not to be understood that, because this which the soul understands is naked substance, as we have said, it is perfect and clear fruition[41] as in Heaven; for, although it is free from accidents, it is not for that reason clear, but rather it is dark, for it is contemplation, which, as Saint Dionysius says, is in this life a ray of darkness; wherefore we can say that it is a ray and image of fruition, inasmuch as it is in the

---

[37] 2 Corinthians xii, 4.

[38] The Saint's emendation for the copyist's *audivit*.

[39] Job xlii, 5.

[40] Lch paraphrases: 'This, therefore, that the soul understands is . . .'

[41] Md: 'vision.'

understanding, wherein consists fruition.[42] This substance of understanding, which the soul here calls a whisper, is the 'desired eyes,' whereof the soul said, when the Beloved revealed them to her, because she could not bear the perception of them: 'Withdraw them, Beloved.'

17. And, as I think that in this place a passage in Job is very much to the point, as confirming a great part of that which I have said of this rapture and betrothal, I will relate it here (although it may delay us a little longer) and I will expound the parts of it that are to our purpose. And first I will give it wholly in Latin, and then wholly in the vulgar tongue, and afterwards I will briefly expound that part of it which concerns our purpose; and having ended this I will continue the exposition of the lines of the next stanza. Eliphaz the Themanite, then, in the Book of Job, speaks after this manner: *Porro ad me dictum est verbum absconditum, et quasi furtive suscepit auris mea venas susurri eius, In horrore visionis nocturnæ, quando solet sopor occupare homines, pavor tenuit me, et tremor, et omnia ossa mea perterrita sunt: et cum spiritus me præsante, transiret, inhorruerunt pili carnis meæ: stetit quidam, cujus non agnosceban vultum, imago coram oculis meis, et vocem quasi auræ lenis audivi.*[43] Which in the vulgar tongue signifies: In truth a hidden word was spoken to me, and mine ear received as it were by stealth the veins of its whisper. In the horror of the vision[44] by night, when sleep is wont to occupy men, I was occupied by fear and trembling, and all my bones shook; and, as the spirit passed before my presence, the skin[45] of my flesh shrank; and there came before me One Whose countenance I knew not, an image before mine eyes, and I heard a voice of a gentle breeze. In this passage is contained almost all that we have here said concerning this rapture, from the twelfth stanza, which says: 'Withdraw them, Beloved,' down to this point. For in that which Eliphaz the Themanite says, namely, that a hidden word was spoken to him, is signified that hidden thing which was

[42] Md: 'wherein consists the said vision.'
[43] Job iv, 12–16.
[44] Vd, Br have 'visitation' erroneously.
[45] Md has: 'the hair' [cf. Job iv, 15, A.V.].

given to the soul, the greatness whereof it could not suffer, so that it said: 'Withdraw them, Beloved.'

18. In this saying that his ear received, as it were by stealth, the veins of its whisper, is signified the naked substance which, as we have said, is received by the understanding: for veins here denote inward substance, and the whisper signifies that communication and touch of the virtues from which the said substance of understanding is communicated to the understanding. And the soul here calls it a whisper, because such a communication is very gentle, even as in that other place she calls it 'amorous breezes,' because it communicates itself amorously. He says that he received it as it were by stealth, because even as that which is stolen belongs to another, even so that secret did not belong to man, speaking after the manner of nature: for he received that which was not according to his nature, wherefore it was not lawful for him to receive it, as it was not lawful for Saint Paul to repeat that which he had heard. Wherefore the other Prophet said twice: 'My secret to myself.'[46] And when Eliphaz speaks of the horror of the vision by night, when sleep is wont to occupy man, and says that he himself has been occupied by fear and trembling, he refers to the fear and trembling which is caused naturally in the soul by that communication of rapture which we said human nature could not suffer in the communication of the Spirit of God. For this Prophet declares here that, as at the time when men go to rest they are wont to be oppressed and terrified by a vision which they call a nightmare, which comes to them between sleep and waking—that is, at the point when sleep begins—even so at the time of this spiritual transit from the sleep of natural ignorance to the waking of supernatural knowledge, which is the beginning of rapture or ecstasy, the spiritual vision which is then communicated to them fills them with fear and trembling.

19. And he adds further that all his bones were terrified, or shaken. Which is as though he had said that they were moved and dislocated from out of their places; wherein is described the great dislocation of the bones which, as we have said, is

[46] Isaias xxiv, 16.

suffered at this time. This was clearly expressed by Daniel, when he saw the angel, and said: *Domine, in visione tua dissolutæ sunt compages meæ.*[47] That is: Lord, in Thy vision the joints of my bones have become loosed.[48] And in that which he then says, which is: 'And as the spirit passed before my presence'—that is to say, when He made my spirit pass beyond its limits and natural ways by means of the rapture whereof we have spoken—'the skin of my flesh shrank,' he describes that which we have said concerning the body, which in this transit is frozen so that the flesh shrinks like that of a dead man.

20. The passage continues: 'There was One Whose countenance I knew not, an image before mine eyes.' This One Who he says was present was God, Who communicated Himself after the manner aforementioned. And he says that he knew not His countenance, in order to indicate that in this communication and vision, most lofty though it be, the face and the Essence[49] of God are neither known nor seen. But he says that it was an image before his eyes: for, as we have said, that knowledge of the hidden word was most sublime, as it were the image and trace of God, but it is not to be understood that such knowledge is the essential vision of God.

21. The passage then concludes, saying: 'And I heard a voice of a gentle breeze.' By this is understood the whisper of the amorous breezes, to which the soul here likens her Beloved. It is not to be understood that these visits are always accompanied by these natural distresses and fears, which, as has been said, are the lot of those that are beginning to enter the estate of illumination and perfection, and to experience this kind of communication; for in others these things are accompanied rather by great sweetness. The exposition continues:

The tranquil night,

22. In this spiritual sleep which the soul has in the bosom of its Beloved, it possesses and enjoys all the calm and rest and

[47] Daniel x, 16.
[48] [*Lit.,* 'have opened.']
[49] Lch: 'presence.'

quiet of the peaceful night, and it receives in God, together with this, a profound and dark Divine intelligence. For this reason the Bride says that her Beloved is to her 'the tranquil night'

At the time of the rising[50] of the dawn,

23. But this tranquil night, she says, is not as the dark night, but as the night which is already near the rising of the morning:[51] for this calm and quiet in God is not complete darkness to the soul, as is the dark night, but it is tranquillity and quiet in the Divine light, in a new knowledge of God, wherein the spirit is most gently tranquil, being raised to the Divine light. And here she very fitly calls this Divine light the rising of the dawn, which means the morning; for, even as the rising of the morning dispels the darkness of the night and reveals the light of the day, even so this spirit that is tranquil and quiet in God is raised from the darkness of natural knowledge to the morning light of the supernatural knowledge of God—not brightly, but, as we say, darkly, like the night at the time of the rising of the dawn; for, even as the night at the time of such rising is neither wholly night nor wholly day, but, as men say, 'between two lights,'[52] so this Divine tranquillity and solitude is neither informed with the Divine light in all its clearness nor does it fail in some measure to participate thereof.

24. In this tranquillity the understanding sees itself raised up in a new and strange way, above all natural understanding, to the Divine light, much as one who, after a long sleep, opens his eyes to the light which he was not expecting. This knowledge, as I understand, was indicated by David when he said: *Vigilavi et factus sum sicut passer solitarius in tecto.*[53] Which signifies: I awakened and became like to the sparrow[54] all

[50] [The Spanish word (*levantes*) is plural here and throughout the paragraph following.]

[51] G, V, Vd, 8,654, Br: 'the rising of the dawn.'

[52] [This phrase (*entre dos luces*) is the current Spanish equivalent of 'twilight.']

[53] Psalm ci, 8 [A.V., cii, 7].

[54] The Spanish translation of *passer* throughout is 'bird' [*pâjaro*, the etymological descendant of *passer*].

alone on the house-top. As though he had said: I opened the
eyes of my understanding and found myself above all kinds
of natural knowledge, all alone, without them, upon the
house-top—that is, above all things here below. And he says
here that he became like to the sparrow that is all alone,
because in this manner of contemplation the spirit has the
properties of this sparrow, which are five. First, it ordinarily
perches upon the highest places, even as the spirit, in this
experience, engages in the highest contemplation. Second, it
ever keeps its beak turned towards the direction of the wind,
even as the spirit here turns the beak of its affection towards
the direction whence comes to it the spirit of love, which is
God. Third, it is ordinarily alone and will have no other bird
whatsoever near to it, so that, when any other perches beside
it, it flies away. Even so the spirit in this contemplation is withdrawn from all things, detached from them all and consenting
to naught save solitude in God. The fourth property is that it
sings very sweetly: even so does the spirit sing to God at this
time, for the praises which it makes to God are of sweetest
love, most delectable to itself and most precious to God.[55]
The fifth is that it is of no definite colour; even so is the perfect spirit, which in this excess not only has no colour of
sensual affection and love of self, but has not even any particular consideration of things above or below,[56] neither can
it speak thereof in any method or manner, for that which
possesses it is the fathomless knowledge of God, even as we
have said.

The silent music,

25. In that aforesaid tranquillity and silence of the night,
and in that knowledge of the Divine light, the soul is able to
see a marvellous fitness and disposition of Wisdom[57] in the
diversities of all its creatures and works, all and each of which

[55] Br: 'most delectable to itself, and most precious to itself, and
most precious to God.'
[56] Md: 'consideration of things below, or at times of things
above.'
[57] Bj, Bz, Gr, Lch, 8,654, Md: 'of the wisdom of God.'

are endowed with a certain response[58] to God, whereby each after its manner testifies to that which God is in it, so that it seems to hear a harmony of sublimest music surpassing all the concerts and melodies of the world. The Bride calls this music silent because, as we have said, it is a tranquil and quiet intelligence, without sound of voices; and in it are thus enjoyed both the sweetness of the music and the quiet of the silence. And so she says that her Beloved is this silent music, because this harmony of spiritual music is known and experienced in Him. Not only so, but likewise He is

The sounding solitude,

26. This is almost the same as silent music; for, although that music is silent to the senses and the natural faculties, it is a most sounding solitude to the spiritual faculties; for when these are alone and empty of all natural forms and apprehensions they can readily receive the spiritual sound most sonorously in the spirit of the excellence of God, in Himself and in His creatures, according to that which, as we said above, Saint John saw in spirit in the Apocalypse—namely, when he heard the voice of many harpers who harped upon their harps.[59] This was in the spirit: he speaks not of material harps,[60] but of a certain knowledge which he had of the praises of the blessed, which each one, according to his own degree of glory, makes to God continually. And this is like music, for, as each one possesses the gifts of God in a different degree, even so does each one sing the praises of God in a different degree, yet all make one harmony of love, just as in music.

27. After this same manner the soul is able to see, in that tranquil wisdom, how of all the creatures—not the higher creatures alone, but also the lower, according to that which each of them has received in itself from God—each one raises its voice in testimony to that which God is. She sees that each one after its manner exalts God, since it has God in itself according to its capacity; and thus all these voices make one

[58] G, V, Md: 'correspondence.'
[59] [See p. 106, § 11, above.]
[60] Lch: 'of natural harps.'

voice of music, extolling the greatness of God and His marvellous knowledge and wisdom. And it is this that the Holy Spirit signifies in the Book of Wisdom, where He says: *Spiritus Domini replevit orbem terrarum, et hoc quod continet omnia, scientiam habet vocis.*[61] Which is to say: The Spirit of the Lord hath filled the round world, and this world, which containeth all things that He hath made, hath knowledge[62] of the voice. This is that sounding solitude which, as we say, the soul knows here,[63] which is the testimony that all things give in themselves concerning God. And inasmuch as the soul receives this sounding music, not without solitude and withdrawal from all outward things, she calls them the silent music and the sounding solitude. This, she says, is her Beloved; and He is further

The supper that recreates and enkindles love.

28. To those that are loved suppers bring recreation, satisfaction and love. And because these three things are caused[64] by the Beloved in the soul in this sweet communication, the Bride here calls Him the supper that recreates and enkindles love. It is to be known that in Divine Scripture this word 'supper' is understood of the Divine vision; for, as supper is the end of the day's work and the beginning of the night's rest, so this knowledge which we have called tranquil gives to the soul a realization of the sure termination of things evil and the possession of things that are good, whereat it is more enkindled with love for God than it was before. Wherefore God is to the soul the supper which recreates it by being the termination of its evils, and enkindles it in love by being to it the possession of all things that are good.

[61] Wisdom i, 7.

[62] Lch: 'necessity.'

[63] The word 'here,' an addition of the Saint, is found also in G, V, Vd, Br.

[64] The copy had: 'And because this [supper] is caused.' The Saint emended it as shown in the text above. Bj, Bz, Lch, Md read: 'And because this [thing] is caused'; the remaining versions as in the text.

STANZA XV

**Our flowery bed,   Encompassed with dens of lions,
Hung with purple and builded in peace,   Crowned with a
thousand shields of gold.**

Exposition

In the last two stanzas the Bride has sung of the graces and
wonders of her Beloved, and in this stanza she sings of the
happy and high estate wherein she sees herself set, and of its
security, and of the riches of the gifts and virtues wherewith
she sees herself endowed and adorned, in the nuptial chamber
of union with her Spouse. She says that she is already one
with the Beloved, that she has the strong virtues, and charity
in perfection, and perfect peace, and that she is wholly enriched and beautified with gifts and beauty, such as it is possible to possess and enjoy in this life. Thus she says:

Our flowery bed,

2. This flowery bed is the bosom and love of the Beloved,
wherein the soul, that has become the Bride, is now united;
the which bed is flowery for her by reason of the union and
bond which has now been made between the two, by
means whereof are communicated to her the virtues, graces
and gifts of the Beloved. With these she is so greatly beautified, and is so rich and so full of delights, that she thinks herself to be upon a bed made of a variety of sweet flowers,
which delight her as she touches them and refresh her with
their fragrance; for the which cause she calls this union of
love a flowery bed. So the Bride calls it in the Songs, where
she says to the Beloved: *Lectulus noster floridus;*[1] that is: Our
flowery bed. She calls it 'ours,' because the same virtues and
the same love (namely, those of the Beloved) are common to

[1] Canticles i, 15.

both, and the same delight is common to both, even as the Holy Spirit says in the Proverbs, in these words: 'My delights are with the sons of men.'[2] She calls it flowery also, because in this estate the virtues are now perfect[3] in the soul and put into practice as works which are perfect and heroic, which thing could not be until the bed had become flowery in perfect union with God. Wherefore she says:

Encompassed with dens of lions,

3. By means of the strength and acrimony of the lion she here compares the virtues possessed by the soul in this estate to the dens of lions, which dens are most secure and protected from all other beasts, since these fear[4] the strength and boldness of the lion that is within, and hence not only dare not to enter, but dare not even to tarry near.[5] Thus each of the virtues, when the soul at last possesses them in perfection, is like a lion's den, wherein the Spouse dwells and is present, Who is strong as a lion, and is united with the soul in that virtue and in each of the other virtues; and the soul herself, united with Him in these same virtues, is like a strong lion, for there she is given the properties of the Beloved. And in this case the soul is so well protected and so strong in each virtue and with all of them together in this union of God, which is the flowery bed, that not only does the devil not presume to attack her, but he dares not even to appear before her, by reason of the great fear which he has of her,[6] when he sees her so greatly exalted and emboldened with the perfect virtues in the bed of the Beloved. For, when she is united with God in transformation of love, the devil fears her as he fears God Himself,[7] and dares not even look upon her; so greatly does the devil fear the soul that has perfection.

[2] Proverbs viii, 31.

[3] G, V, Vd, Br: 'preferred.'

[4] The copy reads 'have,' and the Saint made the obvious correction [*teniendo* to *temiendo*]. V, Br alone retain 'have.'

[5] Gr: 'but [dare] not even to pass.'

[6] V, Vd, G, Br omit the words: 'by . . . her.'

[7] Lch reads: 'totally as God Himself' [making bare sense in the original].

4. This bed of the soul is encompassed with these virtues because in this estate they are linked among themselves, strengthened mutually and united in the soul's complete perfection in such a way that there is no place in it where the devil can enter, and furthermore the soul is protected so that naught in the world, be it high or low, can cause her unrest, disturb her or move her; for, being now free from all disturbance of the natural passions, and withdrawn and detached from the torture and diversity of temporal things, the soul has sure[8] fruition of the participation of God. This is that which was desired by the Bride in the Songs, where she says: *Quis det te mihi fratrem meum sugentem ubera matris meæ, ut inveniam te solum foris, et deosculer te, et iam me nemo despiciat?*[9] Which is to say: Would that Thou mightest be given to me, my brother, to suck the breasts of my mother, so that I may find Thee alone without, and that I may kiss Thee and that no man may now despise me! This kiss is the union whereof we are speaking, wherein the soul is made equal with God through love.[10] Wherefore she has this desire, asking to be given the Beloved that He may be her brother, which phrase signifies and makes equality;[11] and that He may suck the breasts of her mother, which signifies the consuming of all the imperfections and desires of her nature which she has from her mother Eve; and that she may find Him alone without, that is, may be united with Him alone, far away from all things,[12] detached, according to the will and the desire, from them all: and thus none will despise her, that is to say, neither world nor flesh nor devil will attack her; for, when the soul is free and purged from all these things and united with God, none of them can annoy her. Hence it is that the soul in this estate enjoys an habitual sweetness and tranquillity which is never lost to her and never fails her.

5. But, over and above this habitual satisfaction and peace,

---

[8] Md modifies 'sure' by *como* ['as,' 'as it were'].

[9] Canticles viii, 1.

[10] [*en la cual se iguala con Dios por amor.*] Md modifies by adding: 'in a certain manner.'

[11] Md: 'and makes a certain manner of equality.'

[12] [*Lit.,* 'without (i.e. outside) all things.']

the flowers, or virtues, of this garden whereof we speak are
wont to open in the soul and diffuse their fragrance in it after
such manner that the soul seems to be, and in fact is, filled
with delights from God. And I said[13] that the flowers, or
virtues, which are in the soul are wont to open, because, although the soul is full of virtues in perfection, it is not always
actually enjoying them (although, as I have said, it does
habitually enjoy the peace and tranquillity which they cause
it); for we can say that in this life they are in the soul as
flowers in bud, tightly closed, in a garden—it is a marvellous
thing at times to see them all opening, by the work of the
Holy Spirit, and diffusing marvellous scent and fragrance in
great variety. For it will come to pass that the soul will see in
itself the flowers of the mountains whereof we spoke above,
which are the abundance and greatness and beauty of God;
with these will be intertwined the lilies of the wooded valleys,
which are rest, refreshment and protection; and then there
will be placed among them the fragrant roses of the strange
islands, which, as we said, are the strange kinds of knowledge
concerning God; and likewise it will be assailed by the fragrance of the water-lilies from the sounding rivers, which we
said were the greatness of God that fills the entire soul; and
intertwined and enlaced with these is the delicate scent of the
jasmine (which is the whisper of the amorous breezes),
whereof we said likewise that the soul has fruition in this estate; and furthermore all the other virtues and gifts which
come, as we said, from tranquil knowledge and silent music
and sonorous solitude and the delectable supper of love. And
the enjoyment and perception by the soul of these flowers is
at times of such a kind that the soul can say with complete
truth: 'Our flowery bed, encompassed with dens of lions.'
Happy the soul that in this life merits at times to taste the
fragrance of these Divine flowers. She says also that this bed
is

Hung[14] with purple

[13] G: 'I say.' Bj, Br, Md: 'She says.' The Saint corrects the
copy to 'I said.'

[14] G, V, Vd, Br, Md: 'dyed,' with corresponding changes in the
exposition.

6. By purple, in the Divine Scripture, is denoted charity; kings are clad in it and use it. The soul says that this flowery bed is hung with purple, because all virtues, riches and good things are sustained by it, flourish in it and have fruition only in the charity and love of the King of Heaven, without which love the soul could not enjoy this bed and its flowers. And thus all these virtues in the soul are, as it were, hung with the love of God, as with a substance which preserves them well; and they are, as it were, bathed in love, because all and each of them are ever enkindling the soul with love for God, and in all things and works they are moved by love to greater love. This is to be hung with purple. And she says that the bed is likewise

Builded in peace,

7. Each of the virtues is of itself peaceful, meek and strong; and consequently, in the soul that possesses them, are produced these three effects, namely: peace, meekness and strength. And because this bed is flowery, composed of the flowers of virtues, as we have said, which are all peaceful, meek and strong, hence it comes to pass that the bed is builded in peace, and the soul is peaceful, meek and strong; which are three properties that can be attacked in no war, whether of world, devil or flesh. And the virtues keep the soul so peaceful and secure that it seems to her that she is wholly builded in peace. And she says, furthermore, that this bed is likewise

Crowned with a thousand shields of gold.

8. She calls the virtues and gifts of the soul shields, saying thereof that the bed of the delight of the soul is crowned therewith; for not only do the virtues and gifts serve him that has gained them as a crown and prize, but they likewise serve him as a defence, and as strong shields against the vices which by their means he has conquered; wherefore the flowery bed is crowned with them as with a prize and defended by them as with the protection of a shield. And she says they are of gold, to denote the great worth of these virtues; the virtues are a crown and a defence. This very thing was said by the Bride in the Songs in other words, in this wise: *En lectulum*

Salomonis sexaginta fortes ambiunt ex fortissimis Israel, uniuscujusque ensis super femur suum propter timores noctur-nos.[15] Which signifies: Behold how threescore mighty men are about the bed of Solomon; the sword of each upon his thigh because of the fears of the nights.[16]

STANZA XVI

In the track of[1] thy footprint   The young girls run along by the way.

At the touch of a spark, at the spiced wine,   Flows forth the Divine balsam.

Exposition

In this stanza the Bride praises the Beloved for three favours which devout souls receive from Him, whereby they are the more incited and exalted to love God; of these, having experienced them in this estate, she here makes mention. The first, she says, is the sweetness which He gives them of Himself, and which is of such efficacy that it makes them to run very quickly upon the way of perfection. The second is a visit of love whereby they are suddenly enkindled in love. The third is abundance of charity infused into them, wherewith they are inebriated after such manner that their spirit is as greatly exalted with this inebriation as with the visit of love, so that they send forth praises to God, together with the delectable affections of love, saying as follows:

In the track of thy footprint

[15] Canticles iii, 7. *Mille clypei pendent ex ea, omnis armatura fortium.* This text the Saint puts in a marginal note. In the second redaction of the *Spiritual Canticle* he also glosses it, without, however, quoting it in Latin (cf. p. 387, below).

[16] Bz, Gr, Lch, 8,654, Bj, Md omit this translation.

[1] See p. 45, n. 16.

2. The footprint is the trace of Him Whose the footprint is, whereby the soul goes tracking and seeking out Him that made it. The sweetness and knowledge concerning Himself which God gives to the soul that seeks Him is the trace and footprint whereby it knows and seeks Him increasingly. Wherefore the soul says here to the Word its Spouse: 'In the track of Thy footprint'—that is, in the traces of sweetness which Thou imprintest upon them and wherewith Thou inspirest them, and in the fragrance of Thyself which Thou scatterest—

The young girls run along by the way.

3. This is to say that devout souls, with the youthful strength which they have received from the sweetness of Thy footprint, 'run along,'—that is, run in many places and after many manners (for this is the meaning of the phrase[2]) each one in the place and after the manner which God grants to it, according to its spirit and to the estate which it has reached, by means of a great variety of spiritual works and exercises, along the road of eternal life, which is evangelical perfection, on the which road they meet the Beloved in union of love after attaining detachment of the spirit from all things. This sweetness and this trace of Himself which God leaves in the soul lighten it greatly and make it to run after Him; for then the work done by the soul itself towards its journey along this road counts for very little or nothing; rather it is moved and attracted by this Divine footprint of God, not only to set forth, but to run along that road after many manners, as we have said. Wherefore the Bride in the Songs entreated the Spouse for this Divine attraction, saying: *Trahe me: post te curremus in odorem unguentorum tuorum.*[3] That is: Draw me after Thee and we will run to the fragrance of Thine ointments. And, after He has given her this Divine fragrance, she says: *In odorem unguentorum tuorum currimis: adolescent-*

---

[2] [i.e. of the Spanish word *discurrir*, translated 'run along.' A more literal rendering would be 'run about,' 'roam about,' which, however, scarcely fits the sense of the first half-line.]

[3] Canticles i, 2–3.

ulæ dilexerunt te nimis.[4] Which is to say: At the fragrance of Thine ointments we run; the young girls loved Thee greatly.[5] And David says: 'I ran the way of Thy commandments when Thou didst enlarge my heart.[6]

At the touch of a spark, at the spiced wine,   Flows forth the Divine balsam.

4. In the first two lines we have explained how souls in the track of the footprint of the Beloved run along by the way by means of exercises and outward works; now in these last lines the soul describes the exercise which these souls perform inwardly with the will, moved by two other favours and inward visits which the Beloved grants them, which she here calls the touch of a spark and spiced wine; and the inward exercise of the will which results from these two visits and is caused by them she calls the flowings forth of Divine balsam. With respect to the first point, it must be known that this touch of a spark which she mentions here is a most subtle touch which the Beloved inflicts upon the soul at times, even when she is least expecting it, so that her heart is enkindled in the fire of love, just as if a spark of fire had flown out and kindled it. Then, with great rapidity, as when one suddenly awakens, the will is enkindled in loving, desiring, praising, giving thanks, doing reverence, esteeming and praying to God with savour of love. These things she calls the flowings forth of Divine balsam, which, at the touch of the spark, issues forth from the Divine love which struck the spark, which is the Divine balsam, that comforts and heals the soul with its fragrance and substance.

5. Concerning this Divine touch the Bride speaks in the Songs after this manner: *Dilectus meus misit manum suam*

---

[4] *Ibid.*

[5] Md reads: 'And after He gave her this Divine fragrance, by the infusion or effusion thereof in her soul, she says shortly before: *Ideo adolescentulæ dilexerunt te, curremus in odorem unguentorum tuorum.* Therefore the young girls loved Thee, and with yearnings entreat Thee to bear them after Thee that they may run in Thy train.'

[6] Psalm cxviii, 32 [A.V., cxix, 32].

per foramen, et venter meus intremuit ad tactum ejus.[7] Which
is to say: My Beloved put His hand through the opening and
my bowels were moved at His touch. The touch of the Beloved is that touch of love which, as we here say, is inflicted
upon the soul; the hand is the favour which He grants it
therein; the opening whereby this hand has entered is the
manner[8] and mode and degree of perfection which the soul
possesses; for the touch is wont to be heavier or lighter according to this manner or that of the spiritual quality of the soul.
The moving of the bowels whereof she speaks is that of the
will whereupon the said touch is inflicted; and the moving
thereof is the rising within her of desires and affections towards God, the desiring, loving and praising of Him, and the
other things whereof we have spoken, which are the flowings
forth of balsam produced by that touch, even as we said.

The spiced wine.

6. This spiced wine is another and a far greater favour
which God grants at times to souls that have made progress,
inebriating them in the Holy Spirit with a wine of love that
is sweet, delectable and strong, for the which cause she calls
it spiced wine. For even as this spiced wine is prepared[9] with
many and divers spices that are fragrant and strong, so this
love, which is the love that God gives to those that are already
perfect, is prepared and made ready in their souls, and spiced
with the virtues which the soul has already gained. Seasoned
with these precious spices, this love infuses into the soul such
strength and abundance of sweet inebriation, in the visits that
God makes to her, that with its great efficacy and strength
it causes her to send forth to God these emissions or outflowings,[10] wherein she praises, loves and reverences Him, and
so forth, as we are saying here, and this with wondrous desires
to work and suffer for Him.

7. And it must be known that this favour of sweet inebria-

[7] Canticles v, 4.
[8] [Here again there is a play upon words, *manera* being used
where we translate both 'opening' and 'manner.']
[9] [*cocido:* 'prepared by means of fermentation.']
[10] Br: 'deceptions'; G: 'inebriations.'

tion passes not as quickly as the spark, for it is of greater duration. The spark touches and is gone, though its effect lasts for some time, and occasionally for a very long time, but the spiced wine and its effect are both accustomed to last long, and this, as I say, is love's sweetness in the soul. Sometimes it lasts for a day, or for two days; at other times, for many days, though not always at the same degree of intensity, since it weakens or increases, and the soul is unable to control it. Sometimes, when the soul has done nothing to produce it, it feels this sweet inebriation of its spirit and the enkindling of this Divine wine within its inmost substance, even as David says in these words: *Concaluit cor meum intra me, et in meditatione mea exardescet ignis.*[11] Which signifies: My heart grew hot within me and in my meditation fire will kindle. Sometimes the flowings forth of this inebriation of love last for as long as the inebriation; at other times, although the inebriation persists in the soul, it does so without the flowings forth aforementioned, and these, when they occur, are of greater or less intensity, according as the inebriation is of greater or less intensity. But the flowings forth or the effects of the spark habitually last longer than the spark itself; it leaves them in the soul, and they are more ardent than those which come from the inebriation, for at times this Divine spark leaves the soul consuming and burning away in love.

8. And, as we have spoken of wine that has been prepared by fermentation, it will be good at this point to note briefly the difference between fermented wine, which is called old, and new wine,[12] which will be the same as that between old and new lovers, and will provide a little instruction for spiritual persons. In new wine the lees have not yet been thrown off, and are not settled, wherefore the wine ferments, and its goodness and worth cannot be known until it has well settled on the lees and the fermentation has ceased.[13] Until that time there is great likelihood of its going bad; it has a rough and sharp taste, and to drink much of it is bad for the drinker; its strength is chiefly in the lees. In old wine the lees are di-

---

[11] Psalm xxxviii, 4 [A.V., xxxix, 3].
[12] Md differs verbally here [but the differences do not appear in translation].
[13] [*Lit.,* 'until it has well digested the lees and fury of them.']

gested and settled, so that there is no longer any fermentation going on in it as there is in new wine; it is quite evidently good, and quite safe from going bad, for that fermentation and bubbling of the lees which might cause it to do harm is all over; and thus well fermented wine very rarely goes bad or is spoiled. It has a pleasant flavour, and the strength is in the substance of the wine and no longer in the taste, wherefore a draught of it gives the drinker good health and makes him strong.

9. New lovers are compared to new wine: these are they that are beginning to serve God, for the fermentations of the wine of their love are taking place wholly without, in their senses, since they have not yet settled on the lees of weak and imperfect sense, and the strength of their love resides only in its sweetness. These lovers ordinarily derive the strength to work from sweetness of sense, and by this sweetness they are moved, so that such love as theirs cannot be trusted until its fermentations and coarse tastes of sense are over. For, even as these fermentations and heats of sense can incline the soul to good and perfect love and serve it as a good means thereto, when the lees of its imperfection have settled, even so it is very easy in these beginnings, when these tastes are still new, for the wine of love to fail and be spoiled as soon as fervour and sweetness of new things have failed. And these new lovers always have yearnings and fatigues caused by love, which come from the senses; it is meet for them to temper their draught, for, if they are very active while the wine is still fermenting, their natures will be ruined. These yearnings and fatigues of love are the taste of the new wine, which, as we said, is rough and sharp, and not sweetened as yet by perfect preparation, after which these yearnings of love will cease, as we shall shortly say.

10. This same comparison is made by the Wise Man in the Book of Ecclesiasticus, where he says: *Vinum novum amicus novus: veterascet, et cum suavitate bibes illud.*[14] Which signifies: The new friend is as new wine; it shall grow old and thou shalt drink it with pleasure. Wherefore old lovers, which are they that are practised and proved in the service

---

[14] Ecclesiasticus ix, 15 [A.V., ix, 10].

of the Spouse, are like old wine which has settled on the lees, so that it no longer has those fermentations[15] of the senses, or those fires and storms of fermentation[16] from without; the sweetness of the wine can be tasted in its substance, now that it is fermented and settled within the soul, and its taste is no longer in the senses, as with new lovers, but in the substance and savour of the spirit and truth in its works. And in these souls there shall be[17] no savours or fervours of sense, neither do they desire to experience them; for he that has his taste settled upon sense has often perforce[18] to suffer pains and displeasures of sense. And since these old lovers have no sweetness that has its roots in sense, they have no more yearnings and pains of love in sense and soul; and thus it is a marvel if these old friends fail God, for they are already far above that which might make them fail—namely, the lower senses—and in them the wine of love is not only fermented and purged of its lees, but is also seasoned with the spices, which, as we said, are virtues in perfection, and allow it not to go bad like new wine. For this reason says the author of Ecclesiasticus: *Amicum antiquum ne deseras, novus enim non erit similis illi.*[19] Which signifies: Forsake not the old friend, for the new will not be like to him. In this the soul's wine of love, then, well proved and spiced, the Beloved produces the Divine inebriation which we have mentioned and which causes sweet outflowings to go forth to God. So the sense of the last lines is as follows: At the touch of the spark wherewith Thou awakenest my soul, and at the spiced wine wherewith Thou lovingly inebriatest me, my soul sends to Thee its outflowings, which are the movements[20] and acts of love occasioned by Thee within it.

[15] Bj: 'those vapours.'

[16] ['Storms' is literally 'furies.'] Bj reads: 'furies and furious fires'; Bz reads: 'forces' for 'storms.'

[17] [*Lit.*, 'shall fall.'] Bz, Gr, Lch, 8,654, Md read: 'they see' for 'there shall be.'

[18] G, V, Vd, Br omit 'perforce.'

[19] Ecclesiasticus ix, 14 [A.V., ix, 10].

[20] G, V: 'deservings.'

STANZA XVII

In the inner cellar, of my Beloved have I drunk,   And, when I
   went forth over all this meadow,[1]
Then knew I naught[2]   And lost the flock which I followed
   aforetime.

Exposition

In this stanza the soul describes the sovereign favour which
God has granted her by gathering her into the depth of His
love, which is the union or transformation of love in God;
and she notes two effects which she has derived therefrom—
namely, forgetfulness and withdrawal[3] from all the things of
the world, and the mortification of all its tastes and desires.

In the inner cellar,

2. In order that I might say aught concerning this cellar,
and explain that which the soul intends to denote by it, it
would be needful that the Holy Spirit should take my hand
and move my pen. This cellar whereof the soul here speaks
is the last and most intimate degree of love to which the soul
may attain[4] in this life, wherefore she calls it the inner cellar—
that is to say, the innermost. From this it follows that there
are others less interior, which are the degrees of love whereby
the soul rises to this, the last of all. And we may say that
there are seven of these degrees or cellars of love, all of
which the soul comes to possess when she possesses in perfection the seven gifts of the Holy Spirit, in the manner wherein
she is able to receive them. And thus, when the soul attains
to perfect possession of the spirit of fear, she has likewise
in perfection the spirit of love, since that fear, which is the

[1] Bj, Gr, Vd, Br: 'over all that meadow.'
[2] V has 'nothing'; the other versions 'no thing.'
[3] G, V, Vd, Br: 'abnegation.'
[4] [*Lit.*, 'wherein the soul may be situated.']

last of the seven gifts, is filial,[5] and the perfect fear of a son proceeds from the perfect love of a father. Hence, when the Divine Scripture desires to call a man perfect in charity, it speaks of him as fearing God. Wherefore Isaias, prophesying the perfection of Christ, said: *Replebit eum spiritus timoris Domini.*[6] Which signifies: He shall be filled with the spirit of the fear of the Lord. And Saint Luke also describes the holy Simeon as full of fear, saying: *Erat vir justus, et timoratus,*[7] and this is also true of many others.

3. It must be known that many souls attain to the first cellars and enter therein, each according to the perfection of love which he possesses, but few in this life attain to this last and innermost perfection, for in this there comes to pass that perfect union with God which they call the Spiritual Marriage, whereof the soul speaks in this place. And that which God communicates to the soul in this most intimate union is completely ineffable, so that naught can be said thereof,[8] even as naught can be said concerning God Himself which may describe Him; for it is God Himself Who communicates this to the soul, and transforms her into Himself with marvellous glory, so that they are both in one, as we should say the window is one with the sun's ray, or coal with the fire, or the light of the stars with that of the sun—yet less essentially and completely so than will come to pass in the next life. And thus, in order to describe that which she receives from God in that cellar of union, the soul says naught else, nor do I believe that she could say aught more appropriate to express some part thereof, than the following line:

Of my Beloved have I drunk,[9]

4. For, even as a draught is diffused and shed through all the members and veins of the body, even so is this communication from God diffused substantially in the entire soul, or, to express it better, the soul is more nearly transformed into

[5] Bj: 'is spiritual.'

[6] Isaias xi, 3 [A.V., xi, 2].

[7] St. Luke ii, 25.

[8] Md: 'is almost ineffable and scarce anything can be said thereof.'

[9] Br omits 'have I drunk.'

God, according to which transformation the soul drinks of[10] its God according to its substance and its spiritual faculties. For according to the understanding it drinks[11] wisdom and knowledge; according to the will, it drinks[11] sweetest love; and, according to the memory, it drinks[12] recreation and delight in the remembrance and sense of glory. With respect to the first point, that the soul receives and drinks[12] delight substantially, the Bride herself says this, in the Canticles, after this manner: *Anima mea liquefacta est, ut sponsus locutus est*.[13] That is: My soul delighted[14] when the Spouse spake. The speaking of the Spouse signifies here His[15] communicating Himself to the soul. And that the understanding drinks wisdom is declared in the same book by the Bride, where, desiring to attain to this kiss of union and entreating the Spouse for it, she says: *Ibi me docebis, et dabo tibi poculum ex vino condito*.[16] That is: There Thou shalt teach me (namely, wisdom and knowledge in love); and I will give Thee a draught of spiced wine[17]—that is to say, of my love spiced with Thine, or, in other words, transformed into Thine.

5. With respect to the third point, which is that the will drinks there of love,[18] the Bride says this also in the said Book of the Songs, in these words: *Introduxit me Rex in cellam vinariam, ordinavit in me charitatem*.[19] Which is to say: He introduced me into the secret cellar and ordained charity in me; which is as much as to say: He gave me to drink love introduced into His love; or more clearly and properly speaking: He ordained in me His charity, accommodating

---

[10] G, Vd, Br: 'lives in.' [The change is only a slight one—*vive de* for *bebe de*—and *b*, *v* were (and are) in speech and in uneducated writing indistinguishable.]

[11] Vd, Br: 'lives.'

[12] Vd, Br: 'lives.'

[13] Canticles v, 6.

[14] [A poor translation. The Spanish (*se regaló*) does not correspond even approximately to *liquefacta est* ('melted').]

[15] Various versions omit 'His.'

[16] Canticles viii, 2.

[17] V, Vd, 8,654, Md [and P. Silverio's text]: read 'a spiced draught of wine.'

[18] Vd, Br: 'lives there on love.'

[19] Canticles ii, 4.

His own charity to me and making it mine: this is the drinking by the soul of the very love of its Beloved, which its Beloved infuses into it.[20]

6. Here it is to be known, with respect to the saying of
some that the will cannot love, save what the understanding
first understands, that this has to be understood after a natural
manner; for in the way of nature it is impossible to love if
one understands not first that which one is to love; but in
the supernatural way God can readily infuse love and increase
it without infusing or increasing distinct knowledge, as is given
to be understood in the passage quoted. And this is the experience of many spiritual persons, who oftentimes find themselves burning in the love of God without having a more
distinct knowledge of Him than aforetime; for[21] they can understand little amd love much, and they can understand much
and love little. But habitually those spiritual persons who have
not a very excellent understanding concerning God are wont
to excel in will; and infused faith suffices them in the stead
of intellectual knowledge; by means of which faith God infuses into them charity, and increases it within them, together
with the act thereof, which is to love more, even though their
knowledge be not increased, as we have said. And thus the
will can drink of love without the understanding drinking
anew of knowledge; although in the case of which we are
speaking, wherein the soul says that she drank[22] of her Beloved, inasmuch as there is union[23] in the inner cellar, which
is according to the three faculties of the soul, as we have said,
all of them drink together.

7. And with respect to the fourth point—namely, that the
soul drinks of its Beloved there according to the memory—
it is clear that the soul is enlightened with the light of the
understanding in remembering the good things which it is possessing and enjoying in the union of its Beloved.

[20] G, V, Vd, Br: 'the drinking by man of the very love of his
Beloved, which his Beloved infuses into him.'
[21] The Saint's addition, and the reading of G, V, Vd, Br.
[22] The Saint's correction of 'lived [on].'
[23] G, V, Vd, Br: 'inasmuch as He is loved.'

8. The Divine draught so greatly deifies and exalts the soul
and immerses it in God that

When I went forth

9. That is to say, this favour has completely passed away,
for although the soul is for ever in this high estate of marriage
after God has placed it therein, yet it is not for ever in actual
union according to the said faculties, although it is so according to the substance of the soul. But in this substantial union
of the soul the faculties[24] are also very frequently in union,
and drink in this cellar; the understanding by knowledge, the
will by love, etc. So, when the soul now says 'When I went
forth,' she understands not this of the essential or substantial
union which she now possesses, which is the estate aforementioned, but of the union[25] of the faculties, which is not continuous in this life, neither can be so. She says, then, that
when she went forth

Over all this meadow,

10. That is, over all this expanse of the world,

Then knew I naught

11. For that draught of the highest wisdom of God which
there she drank makes her forget[26] all the things of the world.
It seems to the soul that its former knowledge, and even the
knowledge of the whole world, is pure ignorance by comparison with that knowledge; and that deification which it possesses, and the exaltation of the mind in God wherein it is
as if enraptured, immersed in love, and become wholly absorbed in God, allows it not to take notice of any thing soever
in the world; so that it may well say: 'Then knew I naught.'
For it is withdrawn not only from all other things, but even

[24] Md modifies thus: '. . . although it is so according to the
substance of the soul, through a most excellent grace. But in this
gratuitous and substantial union of the soul the faculties . . . , etc.'
[25] Md: 'of the actual union.'
[26] Some versions read: 'Through that draught . . . drank, He
makes her forget.' The correction [a very slight one in the original]
is the Saint's.

from itself, and is annihilated, as though it were dissolved in love, which consists in passing from itself to the Beloved. This unknowing the Bride describes in the Songs, where, after having spoken of the union and the making of herself one with the Beloved, she says this word: *Nescivi;*[27] 'I knew not,' or 'I was ignorant.' The soul in such a condition will intervene little in things of others, since it remembers not even its own things; and the Spirit of God has this characteristic in the soul wherein He dwells, that He forthwith inclines it toward unknowing and makes it to be ignorant of all the things of others, especially things that are not to its profit. For the Spirit of God is recollected within the soul,[28] and goes not forth to things of others, and thus the soul remains in a complete unknowing.

12. It is not to be understood that the soul in this case loses its habits of knowledge, although these no longer dominate it, because in this union they are joined with a higher wisdom, and it is this which works; just as, when a small light unites with another that is great, it is the greater that overwhelms the lesser and gives light. It is in this sense that the soul 'knew naught' of those habits; and this, I suppose, will be the position in Heaven as concerning acquired knowledge: it will be of no[29] great importance to the righteous, for they will know more in the Divine wisdom than it can teach them. The soul, then, although it remains in that unknowing, suffers not the total loss of its knowledge, with respect to the things that it knew aforetime, but it loses the act and memory of things in that absorption of love, and this for two reasons: the one, because, as it is actually absorbed and immersed in that draught of love, it cannot actually be in aught else; the other, because that transformation in God

[27] Canticles vi, 11 [A.V., vi, 12]. Lch, Gr, 8,654, Md add: 'Which signifies.'

[28] The words 'within the soul' are the Saint's marginal addition and are not found in either Codices or editions.

[29] This word is conjectural. The whole passage ('although these no longer . . . teach them') is added by the Saint in the margin of the Codex of Sanlúcar de Barrameda, which is badly cut, so that many letters are missing. See the photograph on p. 225 of Vol. I of *Cántico Espiritual y Poesías,* ed. P. Silverio, Burgos, 1928.

makes it conform with His simplicity and purity, after such
manner as to leave it clean and pure and empty of all forms
and figures which it had aforetime, for the act has ever these
forms with it.[30] Just so, when the sun shines upon a window,
and infuses itself therein, it makes it bright, so that all the
stains and specks[31] which formerly appeared upon it are lost
from sight; but, when the sun departs again and completely
withdraws itself from the window, the mists[32] and stains appear upon it once more. In the soul, however, since the effect
of that act of love remains with it and endures, there likewise
endures[33] this, that it knows naught through its natural habits
but only through acts of knowledge; although from the nature
of the infused superior habit these habits persist with respect
to the exercises, the soul is dissolved in that transformation
wherein, inflamed and changed in love,[34] it was annihilated
and undone as to all that which was not love, and left so
that it knew naught else save love. This agrees with what we
said above concerning David, who writes: *Quia inflammatum
est cor meum, et renes mei commutati sunt et ego ad nihilum
redactus sum, et nescivi.*[35] Which is to say: For my heart
was inflamed, and together with it my reins also were changed,
and I was dissolved into nothing and I knew naught. For the
reins to be changed by reason of this inflaming of the heart
signifies for the soul to be changed in God, with all its desires,
after a new manner, and for all those old things, which it

[30] The phrase 'for . . . with it' is an interlinear addition of the
Saint's.

[31] [*Lit.*, 'short hairs.' The Spanish word (*pelillo*) is often used
in the sense of 'trifle.']

[32] [*nieblas*, a word often used by Spanish mystical writers in a
technical sense. Cf. p. 220, n. 17, below.]

[33] MSS. and editions have 'endures to some extent.' The Saint
suppressed the adverbial phrase.

[34] The whole of this sentence, down to this point, follows the
Saint's interlinear and marginal corrections, which, like those described in n. 29, p. 134, are mutilated. (*Cántico*, etc., ed. cit., I, p.
226.) The original version reads: '. . . remains with it and endures
to some extent, there likewise endures this, that it knows not, as
we have said, how great is the duration of the effect and relish of
that act, whereby, inflamed and changed . . . , etc.'

[35] Psalm lxxii, 21 [A.V., lxxiii, 21–2].

used aforetime, to be abandoned; for which reason the Psalm-
ist says that he was dissolved into nothing, and that he knew
naught, which, as we said, are the two effects caused by the
draught from this cellar of God. For not only is all that first
knowledge which the soul possessed annihilated, so that it
seems nothing at all to it by comparison with that highest
knowledge, but likewise all its former life and imperfections
are annihilated and the old man is renewed; wherefore there
follows this second effect that flows from this, which is contained in the line following:

And (I) lost the flock which I followed aforetime.

13. This signifies that, until the soul attains to this state
of perfection whereof we are speaking, however spiritual it
may be, there ever remains to it a little flock, as it were, consisting of some of its desires and petty tastes and other of
its imperfections—sometimes natural, sometimes spiritual—
after which it goes, endeavouring to pasture them while following them and satisfying them. For with respect to the understanding there are wont to remain to such souls certain
imperfections concerning the desire to know things. With respect to the will, they permit themselves to be carried away
by certain petty tastes and desires of their own. These may
be temporal, like the possession of certain small things, preference for one thing over another, and certain kinds of presumption, esteem and punctilio to which they pay heed, and
other little things which still reek and savour of the world.[36]
Or they may be natural, like food, drink and an inclination
for this rather than for that, and a choosing and desiring of
the best. Or, again, they may be spiritual, like the desire for
consolations from God and other irrelevances, which I might
never cease retailing, which things are wont to cling to spiritual men who are not yet perfect. And, with respect to the
memory, there are many varieties of things and cares and irrelevant reflections which draw the soul after them.

14. Sometimes, again, with respect to the four passions of

[36] G has: 'These may be either temporal or spiritual, as the
possession of a few little things which still reek and savour of the
world.'

the soul, there are many[37] useless hopes, joys, griefs and fears
after which the soul goes in pursuit. As to this flock aforesaid,
some are attracted by more of such things and others by less;
but they continually pursue them, until they enter this inner
cellar to drink and lose their flock entirely, becoming, as we
have said, wholly turned into love, wherein these flocks—that
is, these imperfections of the soul—are consumed more easily
than rust and mould upon metals are consumed in the fire.
So the soul feels itself to be free from all these childish likes
and dislikes and follies which it pursued, and it can indeed
say: 'I lost the flock which I followed aforetime.'

STANZA XVIII

**There he gave me his breast;   There he taught me a science
most delectable;[1]**
**And I gave myself to him indeed, reserving nothing;   There I
promised him to be his bride.**

Exposition

In this stanza the Bride describes the surrender which was
made upon either side in this spiritual betrothal, namely, that
betwixt herself and God; saying that, in that inner cellar of
love, they were united through the communication of Himself to her, when He gave her freely the breast of His love,
showing her therein wisdom and secrets; and likewise through
the communication of herself to Him, when she surrendered
herself to Him indeed[2] and wholly, without reserving aught
either for herself or for another, and declaring herself to be
His for ever. The line follows:

There he gave me his breast;

[37] G, V: 'a few.'
[1] Br: 'learned'; *sabiosa* for *sabrosa*.
[2] Lch reads: 'completely undone' (*toda deshêcha*) for 'indeed
and wholly' (*toda de hecho*).

2. For one to give the breast to another signifies to give
that one his love and friendship and to reveal to him his
secrets as to a friend. Thus, when the soul says that He gave
her His breast there, she means that He communicated to her
there His love and His secrets, which God grants to the soul
in this estate. Further, there is that which she says also in
this line following:[3]

There he taught me a science most delectable;

3. The delectable science which she says here that He
taught her is mystical theology—the secret[4] science of God,
which spiritual men call contemplation; this is most delectable,
since it is science through love, the which love is its master
and that which makes it to be wholly delectable. And inasmuch as God communicates to the soul this science and
knowledge in the love wherewith He communicates Himself
to her, it is delectable to her understanding, since it is a science which pertains thereto; and likewise it is delectable to
her will, since it consists in love, which pertains to the will.
She says next:

And I gave myself to him indeed, reserving nothing;

4. In that sweet draught of God, wherein, as we have said,
the soul is immersed in God, it surrenders itself, most willingly and with great sweetness,[5] to Him wholly, desiring to
be wholly His and never again to have aught in itself that
is alien from Him. God grants it, in the said union, the purity
and the perfection[6] which are necessary for this; for, inasmuch as He transforms the soul into Himself, He makes it
to be wholly His and empties it of all that it possessed and
that was alien from God. Wherefore the soul is indeed completely given up to God, reserving naught, not only according
to its will, but also according to its works, even as God has
given Himself freely to the soul. So these two wills are sur-

[3] The Saint interpolates 'following,' which is also found in G, V,
Vd, Br.
[4] Lch: 'the written.'
[5] Bj: 'humility.'
[6] Lch has a [clearly corrupt] variant reading here.

rendered, satisfied and given up the one to the other, so that neither shall fail the other, as in the faithfulness and stability of a betrothal. Wherefore the Bride adds these words:

There I promised him to be his bride.

5. For even as a maiden that is betrothed sets not her love upon another than her spouse, nor directs her thoughts[7] or her actions to any other, even so the soul in this estate has no longer any affections of the will or acts of knowledge of the understanding, nor any care or action which is not wholly turned to God, together with its desires. It is, as it were, Divine and deified, so that in even its first movements it has[8] naught whereto the will of God is opposed, in so far as it can understand. For even as in an imperfect soul its first movements at least, according to the understanding and according to the will and memory and desires, are as a general rule inclined[9] to evil and imperfection, even so, the soul in this estate, according to the understanding and will and memory and desires, in its first movements, is as a general rule moved and inclined to God, through the great help and stability which it already has in God and through its perfect conversion to that which is good. All this David clearly explained when he said, speaking of his soul in this estate: 'Shall not my soul perchance be subject to God? Yea, for from Him cometh my salvation, and He is my God and my Saviour; my Receiver, I shall not be any more moved.'[10] By saying 'my Receiver,' he means that, because his soul is received in God and united in Him, as we say here, he could not be moved against God any more.

[7] [Lit., 'her care.']

[8] Md adds: 'ordinarily.'

[9] V, Vd, Br have an erroneous reading here (indignados for inclinados).

[10] Psalm lxi, 2 [A.V., lxii, 1–2].

STANZA XIX

My soul has employed[1] itself   And all my possessions in his
service:
Now I guard no flock nor have I now other office,   For now
my exercise is in loving alone.[2]

Exposition

Inasmuch as in the last stanza the soul has said (or, rather,
the Bride has said) that she has given herself wholly to the
Spouse, and has reserved naught for herself, she now, in this
stanza, sets forth the manner and mode wherein she accomplishes this. She says that her soul and her body and her faculties and all her abilities are occupied, no longer in the things
which concern herself, but in those which pertain to the service of her Spouse. And that for this reason she no longer
goes about seeking her own gain, nor pursues her own tastes,
nor busies herself in other things, and in intercourse that has
naught to do with God, and is alien to Him. And that even
with God Himself she has no other style or manner of intercourse save the exercise of love, inasmuch as she has changed
and bartered that earlier mode of intercourse which she had
with Him into love, as she will now say:

My soul has employed itself

2. In saying that her soul has employed itself, the Bride
refers to the surrender of herself which she made to the Beloved in that union of love wherein her soul, with all its
faculties, understanding, will and memory, was dedicated and
subjected to His service. Her understanding she employs in
the understanding of those things that pertain most nearly to

[1] G, V, Gr: 'surrendered.' [Cf. the first words of § 2, below.]
[2] [On the imagery of this and the next stanza, see Dámaso
Alonso, *La Poesía de San Juan de la Cruz,* Madrid, 1942, pp.
137-8.]

His service in order to do them; her will, in loving all that
pleases God and in having affection of the will for God in
all things; and her memory, in caring for that which pertains
to His service and will be most pleasing to Him. And she
says further:

And all my possessions in his service:

3. By all her possessions she here understands all that pertains to the sensual part of the soul, which things, she says,
are employed in His service, even as is the rational or the
spiritual part whereof we have just spoken in the last line.
In this sensual part is included the body with all its senses
and faculties, both interior and exterior. In this line is understood also all ability of the nature and the reason, as we have
said—namely, the four passions, the natural and spiritual desires, and the other possessions of the soul, all of which
things, she says, are now employed in His service. For she
now orders the body according to God, rules and governs the
inward and outward senses according to God and directs their
actions towards Him; and all the four passions likewise she
keeps bound[3] to God; because she neither has enjoyment save
from God, neither has hope save in God, nor fears any save
God, neither does she grieve save according to God; and likewise her desires are directed alone to God, with all her cares.

4. All these possessions are now employed in God, in such
manner that all the parts thereof which we have described
tend,[4] in their first movements, without the soul's being conscious of it, to work in God and for God. For the understanding, the will and the memory go straightway to God; and the
affections, the senses, the desires and appetites, hope, joy and
all the rest of the soul's possessions are inclined to God from
the first moment, even though, as I say, the soul may not
realize that it is working for God. Wherefore the soul in such
case very frequently works for God, and is intent upon Him
and the things that pertain to Him, without thinking or remembering that it is doing aught for Him; for the use and

[3] Lch: 'ordered.'
[4] Md adds: 'ordinarily.'

habit which it has acquired in this manner of procedure deprives it of such realization and effort, and even of the fervent
acts[5] which it was wont to have at the beginning. And since
all these possessions are employed in God after the manner
aforesaid, the soul must needs likewise have that which it describes in the line following, namely:

Now I guard no flock

5. Which is as much as to say: Now I go no longer after
my tastes and desires; for, having set them upon God and
given them to Him, the soul no longer pastures them nor
guards them for herself. And not only does she say that she
no longer guards a flock, but she says further:

Nor have I now other office,

6. Many offices, and unprofitable ones, has the soul before
she goes so far as to make this gift and surrender to the Beloved of herself and of her possessions; for all the habits of
imperfections that she had may be described as so many occupations, which may have respect to speaking and thinking and
acting, and she was accustomed not to behave in these things
as is meet and fitting for perfection. With respect to this a
soul is ever inclined to some vicious employment which it
never completely conquers until it truly employs its possessions in the service of God; and, as we have said, all its words
and thoughts and actions are then of God, and it no longer
occupies itself in murmuring, nor in any other imperfection,
whether of speech or of the other faculties; and thus it is
as though she were to say: I am no longer occupied or busied
in other commerce or pastimes or things of the world.

For now my exercise is in loving alone.

7. This is as though she had said: All these faculties and
all the ability wherewith my soul and my body are provided,
which aforetime I employed to some extent upon other useless
things, I have set upon the exercise of love. This is that which

[5] Md adds: 'of sensible devotion.'

David says: *Fortitudinem meam ad te custodiam.*[6] Which signifies that all the ability of my soul and body is moved through love, that all that I do I do through love, and all that I suffer I suffer for love's sake.

8. Here it is to be noted that, when the soul attains to this estate, all its exercise, both of its spiritual part and of its sensual part,[7] be it in doing or in suffering, after whatsoever manner it be, causes it ever greater love and greater delight in God;[8] and even the very exercise of prayer and converse with God which it was frequently wont to have in considerations of a different kind and in other ways, is now wholly the exercise of love. So that, whether its commerce be with temporal things, or whether its exercise be concerning spiritual things,[9] a soul in this case can ever say: 'For now my exercise is in loving alone.'

9. Happy life and happy estate and happy the soul that arrives thereat, where all is now substance of love to it, and joy and delight of betrothal; wherein the Bride may indeed say to the Divine Spouse those words which she addresses to Him out of pure love in the Songs;[10] *Omnia poma nova, et vetera, servavi tibi.*[11] Which is as if she should say: My Beloved, I desire for Thy sake to have all that is hard and wearisome, and all that is sweet and delectable I desire for Thee. But the sense of this line, as we have interpreted it, is that the soul in this estate of the Spiritual Betrothal walks habitually in union of the love of God, which is the common and habitual presence of the loving will in God.[12]

[6] [Psalm lviii, 10: A.V., lix, 9.] This sentence is a marginal addition of the Saint's [cf. *Cántico,* etc., *ed. cit.,* II, p. 7], not found in Br, Md, or the Codices, which read: '. . . in the exercise of love; which signifies that all . . . , etc.'

[7] Bz, 8,654, Gr, Lch, Bj, Md: 'both that of its spiritual part, which is the soul, and that of its sensual part, which is the body.'

[8] Bz, 8,654, Gr, Lch, Bj, Md: 'in the Beloved.'

[9] Bz, 8,654, Gr, Lch, Bj, Md add: 'and commerce with God.'

[10] Bz, 8,654, Gr, Lch, Md: 'in the Divine Songs.'

[11] Canticles vii, 13.

[12] Gr, 8,654, Bj, Md: 'in the union of love, which is the common presence of the will in God.' Lch, Bj: 'in the union of love, which is as the presence of the loving will in God.'

STANZA XX

**If, then, on the common land,   From henceforth I am neither
seen nor found,
You will say that I am lost;   That, wandering love-stricken, I
lost my way and was found.[1]**

Exposition[2]

The soul, in this stanza, makes answer to a tacit reproach
uttered by those of the world,[3] which they are wont to direct
to such as give themselves truly to God; for they consider
them extravagant in their queerness and aloofness, and in their
general behaviour, and also say that they are useless in important matters and are lost with respect to all things that
the world prizes and esteems. This reproach the soul meets
in an excellent way, facing it very boldly and daringly, as
it faces all else that the world can impute to it, for, having
attained to a living love of God, it takes little heed thereof.
And not only so, but the Bride herself confesses it in this
stanza, and glories and boasts of having done such things and
become lost to the world and to herself for the sake of her
Beloved. And thus her meaning in this stanza, where she
speaks to those of the world, is that, if they no longer see
her in the places which she frequented formerly, following
the pastimes which she was wont to follow in the world, they
are to say and to believe that she has become lost to them
and is withdrawn from them, and that she considers this so
great a gain that she has herself desired thus to be lost in
going after her Beloved and seeking Him, enkindled as she
is with love for Him. And, that they may see how great a
gain to her is this loss, and may not consider it to be folly

---

[1] [*Lit.*, 'gained.']
[2] For the version of the Exposition in the Granada group of
MSS. see Appendix, p. 488, below.
[3] The last six words are the Saint's addition, which is found also
in G, V, Vd, Br.

or delusion, she says that this loss was her gain and that she became lost of set purpose.

If, then, on the common land,   From henceforth I am neither seen nor found,

2. By 'common land' is ordinarily meant a place common to all, where people are wont to come together to have solace and recreation, and where likewise shepherds pasture their flocks; and thus the soul here understands by this common land the world, where worldly folk pursue their pastimes and converse, and pasture the flocks of their desires. Herein the souls says to those of the world that if she is not seen or found as she was before she became wholly God's, they are to consider her, by reason of this very fact, as lost; and that they may say this, since she rejoices in it and desires them to say it. She adds:

You will say that I am lost;

3. He that loves is not abashed before the world concerning the works which he does for God, neither does he hide them with shame, even though the whole world condemn them. For he that is ashamed to confess the Son of God before men, and ceases to do His works, the same Son of God, as He says through Saint Luke, will be ashamed to confess him before His Father.[4] Wherefore the soul, with the courage of her love, takes pride in having been seen doing such work to the glory of her Beloved and having become lost therein to all things of the world. Wherefore she says: 'You will say that I am lost.'

4. Few spiritual persons attain to this perfect boldness and determination in their works; for although some behave thus, or attempt to do so, and some consider themselves to be very far advanced therein, they never completely lose themselves with respect to certain points, whether connected with the world or with their own natures, nor do they do work for Christ which is perfect and completely detached, looking not at what will be said of them or at what will appear. Such as these will be unable to say, 'You will say that I am lost,'

---

4 St. Luke ix, 26.

for they are not lost to themselves in their works; they are still ashamed to confess Christ in their works before men; they have respect for things of the world; they live not truly in Christ.

That, wandering love-stricken,

5. This is to say that, wandering stricken with love for God, and practising the virtues,

I lost my way[5] and was found.[6]

6. He that is indeed in love allows himself to be lost to all things else,[7] that he may have the greater gain as to that which he loves; wherefore the soul says here that she became lost—that is, that she allowed herself to be lost of set purpose. And this is after two manners, as follows. First, she is lost to herself: she takes no thought for herself in any way, but only for the Beloved; surrenders herself to Him freely and disinterestedly;[8] and in this wise becomes lost to herself, and desires no gain for herself in any way soever. Secondly, she is lost to all things, and takes no heed of aught[9] pertaining to herself, but only of those things that concern the Beloved; and this is to become lost, namely, to desire that others may gain her.[10]

7. Such is he that walks love-stricken for God, and that aspires to no gain or prize, but only to lose all things and to be lost to himself in his will for God's sake, which he holds as gain. And gain it is, even as Saint Paul declares when he says: *Mori lucrum.*[11] That is: My dying for Christ is my

[5] [Or 'I became lost,' as sometimes below.]

[6] [*Lit.*, 'gained,' and so throughout the paragraph. The play of words in n. 10 below, has greater point on this account.]

[7] In the margin the Saint here wrote 'two masters,' evidently struck with an idea which, as will be seen, he develops in the second redaction (see p. 420, below).

[8] [*Lit.*, 'without any interest'—evidently, in its context, a semi-metaphorical expression.]

[9] [*Lit.*, 'of all things.']

[10] [*que es tener gana que la ganen.* The play upon words is untranslatable. For 'gain,' understand 'find'; cf. n. 6, above.]

[11] [Philippians i, 21.]

spiritual gain as to all things and to Himself.[12] Wherefore
the soul says: 'I was found'; for he that cannot be lost after
this manner is not found, but is indeed lost, even as Our Lord
says in the Gospel, in these words: 'He who will gain his
life for himself, the same shall lose it; and he who loses his
life for My sake, the same shall gain it.'[13] And if we desire
to understand this said line more spiritually and more to the
purpose for the which it is here used, it must be known that,
when a soul on the spiritual road has reached such a point
that it has become lost to all natural modes and ways of progress in converse with God, so that it seeks Him no longer
by meditations or forms or feelings or any other means which
belong to creatures and to sense, but has passed beyond all
this and beyond all modes and manners of its own, having
converse with God and fruition of Him in faith and love:
then it says that it has indeed gained God, for indeed it has
become lost to all that is not God and to that which it is
in itself.[14]

STANZA XXI

**With flowers and emeralds   Gathered in the cool mornings[1]
We will make the garlands flowering in thy love   And interwoven with one hair from my head.**

Exposition

In this stanza the Bride speaks again with the Spouse in the
communion and refreshment of love, and that which she does
therein is to treat of the solace and delight that the Bride-
Soul and the Son of God have in the possession of the riches

[12] Md: 'My dying for Christ spiritually as to all things, and to
itself, is my gain, and as to Himself.'

[13] St. Matthew xvi, 25.

[14] The last eight words are the Saint's addition, and are copied
by G, V, Vd, Br.

[1] Lch: 'mountains.'

of each other's virtues and gifts and in the mutual exercise of these, having fruition thereof between themselves in the communion of the union of love. Therefore, in speaking with Him, she says that they will make rich garlands of gifts and virtues, acquired and gained in a pleasant and convenient season, beautified and made graceful in the[2] love which He has for her and sustained and preserved in the love which she has for Him. Wherefore she calls this fruition of the virtues making garlands of them; because in all of them, as in flowers that are in a garland, they both have joy in the mutual love which each bears to the other.

With flowers and emeralds

2. The flowers are the virtues of the soul and the emeralds are the gifts which it has of God. These flowers and emeralds are

Gathered in the cool mornings

3. This signifies that they are gained and acquired in youth, which is life's cool morning.[3] She says they are 'gathered,' because the virtues that are acquired in this time of youth are choice[4] and most acceptable to God, since in the season of youth there is more resistance on the part of the vices to their acquisition, and a greater inclination and readiness to lose them on the part of nature;[5] and also because, since the soul begins to pluck them from this season of her youth onward, the virtues which she acquires are much more perfect and more choice. She calls these times of youth the cool mornings, because even as the cool of the morning is more pleasant in spring than are other parts of the day, even so is the virtue

[2] The Saint altered 'His' to 'the.' The correction is not in the MSS. nor in Br or Md.

[3] [Lit., 'in the times of youth (juventudes) which are the cool mornings of the ages.']

[4] [The word translated 'choice' is escogidas, which has the double meaning of 'gathered,' and is thus used in the stanza, and of 'picked,' 'select,' 'choice,' in which sense it is used here.]

[5] G, V, Vd, Br: 'and on the part of nature, which is more inclined and ready to lose them.'

of youth before God. And these cool mornings may also be
interpreted as the acts of love wherein the virtues are
acquired, which are more pleasing to God than are cool mornings to the sons of men.

4. Likewise are understood here by the cool mornings
works which are performed at times of spiritual aridity and
hardship, which are denoted by the coolness of winter mornings; and these works, performed for God's sake at times of
spiritual aridity and hardship, are greatly prized by God, because the virtues and gifts are richly acquired therein. And
those which are acquired after this manner and with labour
are for the most part choicer, rarer and more lasting than
if they were acquired only at times of spiritual sweetness and
delight; and in aridity and hardship and labour and temptation virtue takes root, even as God said to Saint Paul, in these
words: *Virtus in infirmitate perficitur.*[6] That is: Virtue is
made perfect in weakness. Wherefore, in order to extol[7] the
excellence and the virtues whereof garlands are to be made
for the Beloved, it is well said: 'Gathered in the cool mornings,' because the Beloved has great joy only in those flowers
and emeralds—which are virtues and gifts—that are choice and
perfect, and not in those which are imperfect. Wherefore the
Bride-Soul says here that for Him, and of these flowers and
emeralds,

We will make the garlands

5. For the understanding hereof it must be known that all
the virtues and gifts which the soul, and God in the soul,
acquire, are in the soul as a garden of various flowers wherewith it is marvellously beautified, even as with a vesture of
rare variety. For the better comprehension hereof it must be
known that, even as the material flowers are gathered one by
one and made into the garland which is gradually formed
from them, so, after the same manner, as the spiritual flowers
of virtues and gifts are acquired one by one, they are gradually set in order in the soul. And, when they have all been

[6] 2 Corinthians xii, 9.
[7] Gr: 'contain.'

acquired, the garland of perfection is then completed in the soul, so that both the soul and the Spouse rejoice when they are beautified and adorned with this garland, even as in the estate of perfection. These are the garlands which the Bride says have to be made, and this is to gird and surround oneself with a variety of flowers and emeralds, which are perfect gifts and virtues, in order to appear worthily with this beauteous and precious adornment before the face of the King, and to merit being placed on an equality with Him, even as a queen by His side, which the soul merits through the beauty of its variety.[8] Thus David, speaking with Christ in such a case, said: *Astitit Regina a dextris tuis in vestitu deaurato, circumdata varietate*.[9] Which signifies: Upon Thy right hand did stand the queen in vesture of gold, surrounded with variety. Which is as much as to say: Upon Thy right hand did she stand vested in perfect love and surrounded with a variety of perfect virtues and gifts.[10] She says not: 'I alone will make the garlands,' nor yet 'Thou alone wilt make them,' but 'we will make them, both of us together'; for the virtues cannot be wrought by the soul alone, nor can she attain to them alone, without the help of God, neither does God work them alone in the soul without her co-operation; for, although it is true that every good gift and every perfect gift cometh from above, descending from the Father of lights, as Saint James says,[11] yet no such thing as this is received apart from the capacity and without the co-operation of the soul that receives it. The Bride, in the Songs, speaks of this with the Spouse, saying: *Trahe me: post te curremus in odorem*, etc.[12] Which signifies: Draw me after Thee, we will run. So the movement towards goodness must come from God, and from God alone, as is here declared; but the writer says not that he alone will

---

[8] G, V, Vd, Br: 'through the beauty of its virtue.' Bj: 'through the beauty of its sweetness.'

[9] Psalm xliv, 10 [A.V., xlv, 9].

[10] The Saint here wrote in the margin *Fulcite*, perhaps with the intention of adding something which he did not in fact carry out. [Cf. pp. 205, n. 15, 429, n. 47, below.]

[11] St. James i, 17.

[12] Canticles i, 3 [A.V., i, 4].

run, or she alone, but that they will run both of them together —that is, that God and the soul will work together.

6. This short line is understood with great propriety of the Church and of Christ, wherein His Bride, who is the Church, speaks with Him, saying: 'We will make the garlands.' By garlands are here understood all the holy souls begotten by Christ in the Church, each one of whom is as a garland adorned with flowers of virtues and gifts, and all of whom together are a garland for the head of Christ the Spouse. And likewise by the beauteous garlands can be understood the halos (which is another name for them), made likewise by Christ and the Church. These are of three kinds. The first is of the beauteous white flowers of all the Virgins, each with its halo of virginity, and all of them together will be a halo to be placed upon the head of Christ the Spouse. The second halo is that of the resplendent flowers of the holy Doctors, each with his halo as a doctor, and all of them together will be a halo to place upon the head of Christ above that of the Virgins.[13] The third is composed of the crimson carnations of the Martyrs, each one likewise with his martyr's halo,[14] all of which together will be one halo, forming as it were a crown to the halo of Christ the Spouse. So greatly beautified and so gracious to the sight with these three garlands will be Christ the Spouse that there will be said in Heaven that which the Bride says of Him in the Songs, namely: 'Go forth, daughters of Sion, and see King Solomon with the crown wherewith his mother crowned him on the day of his betrothal and on the day of the joy of his heart.'[15] We will make these garlands, then, she says,

Flowering in thy love

7. The flower which belongs to good works and virtues is the grace and virtue which they derive from the love of God, without which not only would they not be flowering but they would all be dry and worthless before God, even though hu-

---

[13] This sentence is omitted, through an oversight, from G, V, Vd, Br.

[14] G, V, Vd, Br: 'martyr's laurel.'

[15] [Canticles iii, 11.]

manly they were perfect. But because He gives His grace and love these works flower in His love.

And interwoven with one hair from my head.

8. This hair of hers is her will and the love which she has for the Beloved, the which love possesses and performs the same office as the thread in the garland; for, even as the thread binds and ties the flowers in the garland, so the love of the soul binds and ties the virtues in the soul and sustains them within her. For, as Saint Paul says, charity is the bond and link of perfection.[16] So that in this love of the soul the supernatural gifts and virtues are so essentially bound together that, if it were to break by failing God,[17] then all the virtues of the soul would become loosed and would fail, even as the flowers would fall apart if the thread of the garland were to be broken. So that it suffices not for God to have love towards us that He may give us virtues; we too must have love towards Him that we may receive and keep them. She says 'one hair' of her head, and not 'many hairs,' in order to convey the fact that her will is now set upon Him alone, and detached from all other hairs, which are strange affections for others. Herein she markedly insists upon the worth and price of these garlands of virtues; for, when love is single and firmly fixed upon God, in the way that is here described, the virtues are likewise perfect and complete, and flower freely in the love of God; for then the love which He has toward the soul is inestimable, even as the soul declares in the stanza following.

[16] Colossians iii, 14.
[17] [So the Spanish. The meaning is: 'if the *bond of love* were to break by the soul's failing God.']

STANZA XXII

By that hair alone   Which thou regardedst fluttering on my neck,
Beholding it upon my neck, thou wert captivated,   And wert wounded[1] by one of mine eyes.[2]

Exposition

Three things are signified by the soul in this stanza. First, she declares that that love wherewith the virtues are bound together is nothing less than a strong love, for in truth it must be such in order that the virtues may be preserved. Secondly, she says that God was greatly captivated by this her hair of love, seeing that it was one only and was so strong. Thirdly, she says that God was intimately enamoured of her, seeing the purity and integrity of her faith. And she says thus:

By that hair alone   Which thou regardedst fluttering on my neck,

2. The neck signifies that fortitude whereon, it is said, was fluttering the hair of love, wherewith are interwoven the virtues, and this is love in fortitude. For it suffices not, in order to keep the virtues together, that there be one hair only; it must also be strong, so that no contrary vice may break it in any part of the garland of perfection. For the virtues are bound together by this hair of the love of the soul in such a way that, if it were to break in any place, then, as we have

---

[1] [The verb is *llagar*, and so throughout this chapter. See p. 75, n. 5, above.]

[2] [The Saint is here following Canticles iv, 9. P. Crisógono (*San Juan de la Cruz*, etc., Madrid, 1929, Vol. II, p. 27) sees also (I am not sure with how much justification) the influence of a sonnet by Garcilaso de la Vega. Dámaso Alonso (*La Poesía de San Juan de la Cruz*, Madrid, 1942, pp. 140–2: cf. also pp. 35–6) also cites a possible MS. source, which, however, I should think it unlikely that the Saint used.]

said, they would all be lost; for, where one of the virtues is, there are they all, and likewise, where there is one lacking, they are lacking all. And she says that this hair fluttered upon her neck, because, in the fortitude of the soul—that is, upon the neck of the soul—this love flies toward God with great fortitude and lightness, without being hindered by aught soever. And, even as the breeze stirs the hair and causes it to flutter upon the neck, even so does the breeze of the Holy Spirit move and excite strong love that it may make flights to God; for, without this Divine wind, which moves the faculties to the practice of Divine love, the virtues work not, neither have any effect,[3] although they be in the soul. And, by saying that the Beloved regarded this hair fluttering upon her neck, she signifies how great is the love of God for strong love; for to regard is to behold with particular attention and esteem for that which one beholds, and strong love causes God to turn His eyes often to behold it.[4] She continues thus:[5]

Beholding it upon my neck,

3. This the soul says, in order to convey the fact that not alone did God prize and esteem this her love,[6] but likewise that He loved it, when He saw that it was strong; because for God to look[7] is for God to love, even as for God to regard is, as we have said, for Him to esteem that which He regards.[8] And in this line she speaks again of the neck, saying of the hair, 'Thou didst behold it upon my neck,' because, as has been said, that is the cause of His loving her so greatly, namely that He saw her in her fortitude, so that it is as if she

[3] [*Lit.*, 'make their effects.'] Bz, 8,654, Gr, Lch, Bj, Md omit 'neither have any effect.'

[4] Bz, 8,654, Gr, Lch, Bj, Md read: '. . . how great is the love of God for love [that is] strong and light in working, for to regard is to behold with particular attention and esteem. Strong love makes God observe greatly.'

[5] In the margin the Saint wrote: 'when love is weak, He beholds not the neck.'

[6] Bz, 8,654, Gr, Md: 'her strong love.'

[7] Bz, 8,654, Bj, Gr, Lch, Md: 'because the look of God.'

[8] Bz, 8,654, Gr, Lch, Bj, Md: 'even as the regarding of God is [His] estimating of the worth that there is in things and observing of it.'

had said: Thou didst love it when Thou didst see that it was strong, without weakness and fear, and alone, without any other love, fluttering with lightness and fervour. Whence it follows that

Thou wert captivated,

4. Oh, thing that art worthy of all acceptation[9] and joy, that God should be captivated by a hair! The cause of this so precious capture is that He stopped to behold (which is, as we have said, to love) this our lowly being. For if He, in His great mercy, had not first beheld us and loved us, as Saint John[10] says, and humbled Himself, He would never have been captivated by the fluttering of the hair[11] of our lowly love, since this love could not soar so high as to attain to the capture of this Divine Bird of the heights. But since He humbled Himself to look upon us and to incite us to fly upward ever higher, and thus gave worth to our love, He Himself was taken captive by this hair in its flight—that is, He Himself was glad and pleased and for that reason was captivated. This is the meaning of the phrase 'Beholding it upon my neck, Thou wert captivated'—and thus it is a credible thing that a bird of lowly flight may capture a royal eagle flying high, if the eagle descends to its lowliness, desiring to be caught.

And wert wounded by one of mine eyes.

5. By the eye is here understood faith. She says by 'one' of them alone, and that He was 'wounded' by it, because if the faith and fidelity of the soul toward God were not alone, but were mingled with respect or courtesy to some other, she would not succeed in wounding God by love. Wherefore it must be by but one eye alone that the Beloved is wounded, even as it is by one hair alone that He is taken captive. And the love wherewith the Spouse is taken captive by the Bride

[9] Br: 'action.'
[10] The MSS. and Br have 'Saint Paul.' [The reference seems to be to the preceding clause, i.e., to 1 St. John iv, 19. But if it were to the following clause, Saint Paul's Epistle to the Philippians ii, 7 would be intended. This is no doubt the cause of the confusion.]
[11] V, Vd, Br: 'neck.'

in this singleness and fidelity that He sees in her is so intimate that, if He was taken captive by the hair of her love, by the eye of her faith His captivity is made closer with so fast a knot that there is inflicted upon Him a wound of love, through the great tenderness of the affection wherewith He loves her, and she enters[12] into His love the more deeply.

6. This same figure of the hair and of the eye is used by the Spouse in the Songs, where He speaks with the Bride, saying: 'Thou hast wounded My heart, My sister; thou hast wounded My heart with one of thine eyes and with one hair of thy neck.'[13] Herein He twice declares that she has wounded His heart—namely, with the eye and with the hair. Wherefore the soul in this stanza describes these two things, as thanking the Beloved and acknowledging so great a favour, and likewise that she may rejoice and delight in having been so happy as to have found grace with her Beloved, all of which she attributes to Him in the following stanza, saying:

STANZA XXIII

When thou didst look on[1] me,   Thine eyes imprinted upon me thy grace;[2]
For this cause didst thou love me greatly,   Whereby mine eyes deserved to adore that which they saw in thee.

Exposition

It is the property of perfect love to be unwilling to accept or take aught for itself, and to attribute naught to itself, but all things to the Beloved. This is so even with our lower love—

---

[12] The Saint substitutes, in a marginal note, 'and He brings her' —a reading not found in the MSS.

[13] Canticles iv, 9. [The Spanish, in both phrases, has *en* ('in') for 'with.']

[1] [Cf. p. 46, n. 23, above.]

[2] See p. 46, n. 24, above. In this place the usual reading is 'their grace,' except in Lch, G, V, Md.

how much more, then, with love for God, which reason so
urgently requires of us! Wherefore, since in the last two stanzas the Bride appears to have been attributing something to
herself, as where she has said that she will make garlands
together with the Spouse, and that they will be interwoven
with a hair of her head, which is work of no small moment
and esteem; and since afterwards she declares, exultingly, that
the Spouse has been taken captive by this hair and wounded
by[3] her eye, wherein likewise she appears to be attributing
to herself great deserving; now in the present stanza she desires to explain her meaning and to correct an erroneous conclusion which might be drawn from this, for she is apprehensive and fearful that some worth and merit will be attributed
to her, and that for that reason[4] there will be attributed to
God less than that which is His due and than that which she
desires. So she attributes it all to Him, and at the same time
gives Him thanks for it, saying to Him that the reason for
His being taken captive by the hair of her love and wounded
by the eye of her faith is that He has granted her the favour
of looking upon her with love, and of thus making her graceful and pleasing in His sight; and that through this grace[5]
and worth which she has received of Him she has merited
His love,[6] and has now in herself become worthy to adore
her Beloved pleasingly and to do works worthy of His grace[7]
and love. The stanza continues:

When thou didst look on me,

2. That is to say, with affection of love, for we have already
said that for God to look signifies here for God to love.

Thine eyes imprinted upon me thy grace;[8]

[3] [*Lit.*, 'in'; and so in the following paragraphs.]
[4] Br omits the words 'some worth . . . for that reason.'
[5] Br: 'greatness.'
[6] Br has [a small change (*creció* for *mereció*) which makes the
phrase read:] 'her love has grown.'
[7] Br: 'greatness.'
[8] See p. 156, n. 2. Here Md also reads: 'their grace,' and only
G, Lch, V, Vd read 'thy grace.'

3. By the eyes of the Spouse is here understood His merciful Divinity, which, turning in mercy to the soul, imprints upon her and infuses in her His love and grace, beautifying her thereby and raising her up so as to make her the consort of His own Divinity. And, seeing the dignity and height wherein God has set her, the soul says:

For this cause didst thou love me greatly,

4. To love greatly[9] is more than to love simply: it is, as it were, to love doubly—that is, for two motives or causes. And thus in this line the soul describes the two motives and causes for love which He has towards her; for the which not only did He love her when He was taken captive by her hair, but He loved her greatly when He was wounded by her eye. And she says in this line that the reason for which He loved her so greatly and so intimately was that, when He looked upon her, He desired to grant her grace that He might be pleased with her, that she might give Him her love—that is, the hair—and that, by means of His charity, He might form faith in her, which is her eye. And thus she says: 'For this cause didst Thou love me greatly.' Because for God to set His grace in the soul is for Him to make her worthy and capable of His love; and thus it is as if she had said: Since Thou hadst set Thy grave in me, giving me pledges worthy of Thy love, therefore didst Thou love me greatly—that is, for that reason didst Thou give me more grace. This is that which is said by Saint John: *Dat gratiam pro gratia.*[10] Which signifies: He gives grace for the grace that He has given, which is to give more grace; or without His grace it is impossible to merit His grace.

5. For the understanding of this it is to be noted that, even as God loves naught apart from Himself,[11] even so He loves naught in a lower way than He loves Himself;[12] for He loves all things with respect to Himself and love has the final rea-

[9] [In the original 'love greatly' is represented by a compound verb, *adamar,* and the sentence begins by defining it: *adamar es amar mucho.*]

[10] St. John i, 16.

[11] Md adds: 'but with respect to Himself.'

[12] Bj, Bz add: 'that is, with less love than for Himself.'

son; thus He loves not things for that which they are in themselves. Wherefore for God to love the soul is for Him to set it, after a certain manner, in Himself, making it equal to Himself, and thus He loves the soul in Himself with the same love wherewith He loves Himself. Wherefore, in each of its acts, the soul merits the love of God, because, set as it is in this grace and in this lofty place, it merits God Himself in its every act. Wherefore the next line continues:

Whereby mine eyes deserved[13] . . .

6. In that favour and grace which the eyes of Thy mercy wrought in me so as to raise me to love of Thee, mine eyes found worth and became deserving

. . . to adore that which they saw in thee.

7. This is as much as to say: The faculties of my soul, O my Spouse, have deserved to rise and look upon Thee, though aforetime, with the wretchedness of their base works and possessions, they had fallen and were very low. For that the soul should be able to look upon God is that it should do works in the grace of God; and the eyes of the soul have had merit in adoration because they have adored in the grace of their God.[14] Enlightened and raised up as they are by His grace and favour, they have adored that which they have already seen in Him, and which they saw not aforetime by reason of their blindness and wretchedness. What, then, was it that they had already seen? They had seen greatness of virtues, abundance of sweetness, immense goodness, love and mercy in Him, numberless benefits which the soul has received of Him, both when it was in grace and when it was not so. All this the eyes of the soul have now deserved to adore meritoriously, because they are now full of grace. Before this they deserved neither to adore Him, nor to see Him, nor even to consider Him, for great is the[15] grossness and blindness of the soul that is without grace.

[13] [The original omits 'mine eyes' and adds it to the next line, where it occurs in the original of the stanza.]
[14] Br: 'in the greatness of God.'
[15] Br: 'for it is greatness of.'

STANZA XXIV[1]

**Despise me not,   For, if thou didst find me swarthy,
Now canst thou indeed look upon me,   Since thou didst look
upon me and leave in me grace and beauty.**

Exposition

The Bride now takes courage; and, esteeming herself with respect to the pledges and the reward which she has of her Beloved (seeing that, since these things come from Him, though
she of herself is of little worth and merits no esteem, she
merits to be esteemed because of them), makes bold to speak
to her Beloved, begging Him not to despise her or hold her
of no worth, since, if she once merited this by reason of the
baseness[2] of her fault and the wretchedness of her nature,
now, since first He looked upon her and adorned her with
His grace and clothed her with His beauty, He may well look
upon her for the second time, and many times more, and
increase her grace and beauty, since there is reason and cause
sufficient for this in His having looked upon her when she
merited it not neither had the means of doing so.

Despise me not,

2. As though she had said: Since this is so, do Thou not
hold me as of little worth.

For, if thou didst find me swarthy,

3. For if, ere Thou lookedst upon me, Thou didst find in
me baseness of faults and imperfections and wretchedness as
to my condition by nature,

Now canst thou indeed look upon me,   Since thou didst look
upon me

---

[1] [For the version of this chapter in the Granada group of MSS.
see Appendix, pp. 509–11.]
[2] G, V, Vd, Br: 'blindness.'

4. Since Thou didst look upon me, and take from me that miserable swarthy colour wherewith I was not fit to be seen, now canst Thou look upon me indeed, again and again; since not alone didst Thou take from me my swarthiness when first Thou lookedst upon me, but likewise Thou didst make me worthier to be seen, since with Thy look of love Thou didst

Leave in me grace and beauty.

5. Greatly is God pleased with the soul to whom He has given His grace, since He abides, well pleased, within her (which He was not wont to do before He gave it to her), and she is exalted and honoured by Him. For this cause He loves her with an ineffable love, and communicates to her ever more love in all her affections[3] and works; for the soul that has reached a high estate of love and is honoured in God's sight attains ever to more love and more honour from God, even as in the words of Saint John which we have quoted: *Dat gratiam pro gratia.*[4] And this God declares in speaking with Jacob His friend in the Book of Isaias,[5] saying: *Ex quo honorabilis factus es in oculis meis, et gloriosus, ego dilexi te.*[6] Which signifies: Since thou hast become honourable and glorious in Mine eyes, I have loved thee. Which is as much as to say: Since Mine eyes gave thee grace when first they looked upon thee, for which cause thou didst become honourable and glorious in My presence, thou hast merited more grace from My favours. The Bride speaks similarly to the daughters of Jerusalem in the Divine Songs, saying: *Nigra sum sed formosa filiæ Jerusalem, ideo dilexit me rex et introduxit me in cubiculum suum.*[7] Which is to say: I am swarthy, daughters of Jerusalem, but I am beautiful; wherefore the King has loved me and brought me into the interior of his bed. Which is as though she were to say: Daughters of Jeru-

---

[3] The Saint corrects 'effects' (*efectos*) to 'affections' (*afectos*). The former reading is found in G, V, Vd, Br. The words 'more love' are also added by the Saint and do not occur in G, V, Vd, Br.

[4] St. John i, 16.

[5] [*Lit.*, 'through Isaias.']

[6] Isaias xliii, 4.

[7] Canticles i, 4.

salem, marvel not because the King of Heaven has wrought
in me such great favours, bringing me into the interior of
His bed, for, though of myself I am swarthy, for which cause
I merited them not, I am made beautiful through Him, since
He has looked upon me and as a result has loved me.[8]

6. Well, my God, canst Thou now look upon that soul on
whom Thou lookedst once, and greatly canst Thou prize her,
since with Thy first look Thou didst leave pledges with her,
so that, not once alone, but many times, she merits the gaze
of Thy Divine eyes; for, as is said in the Book of Esther:
*Hoc honore condignus est quemcumque rex voluerit hon-
orare.*[9]

STANZA XXV[1]

**Catch us the foxes,   For our vineyard is now in flower,
While we make a bunch[2] of roses,   And let none appear upon
the hill.**

Exposition

The Bride, seeing that the virtues of her soul have now
reached the point of perfection, so that she is now enjoying
their delight and sweetness and fragrance, even as one enjoys
the sight and fragrance of plants when they are in full flower,
longs to continue this sweetness and desires that there may be
naught to hinder her from so doing. In this stanza, therefore,
she begs the angels and ministers of God to agree to keep
from her all such things as may tear down and crumple[3] the

---

[8] The Saint here adds a marginal note: *Omni habenti dabitur.*
See p. 446, below.

[9] Esther vi, 11.

[1] [For the version of this chapter in the Granada group of MSS.,
see Appendix, pp. 511–15, below.]

[2] [The word translated 'bunch' and 'nosegay' in this chapter is
piña, which means literally a pine-cone, or a cone-shaped cluster;
the significance of this will be seen in § 5, below.]

[3] [*ajar.*] Br has: [*aojar*] 'bewitch.'

said flower and fragrance of her virtues—as, for example, all the disturbances, temptations, causes of unrest, desires (if any remain[4]), imaginations and other motions, whether natural or spiritual, to which she here gives the name of foxes, which are wont to keep from the soul the flower of inward sweetness and quiet and peace, at the time when the soul in her virtues is most contentedly enjoying it, together with her Beloved. For the soul is wont at times to see in her spirit all the virtues which God has given to her (when He gives her that light), and then with wondrous delight and fragrance of love she gathers them all together and offers them to the Beloved as it were a bunch of flowers[5] (and the greater is her love, the larger is the bunch).[6] In accepting them—and accept them indeed He does—the Beloved at the same time accepts a great service; for together with the virtues the soul offers herself, which is the greatest service that she can render Him; and this delight that the soul receives from this kind of gift which she makes to the Beloved is one of the greatest delights that she is wont to receive in her intercourse with God. Thus the Bride desires that naught may keep her from this inward delight, which is the flowering vineyard, and desires that not only may these things aforementioned be taken from her, but that likewise she may be withdrawn far from all things, so that in all her exterior and interior desires and faculties there may be no form or image or other such thing to appear and present itself before the soul and the Beloved, who, withdrawn from all else and united with each other, are making this nosegay and having joy therein.

Catch us the foxes,   For our vineyard is now in flower,

2. The vineyard is the nursery of all the virtues, which is in the soul and which gives to the soul a wine of sweet savour. This vineyard of the soul is flowering when the soul is united with the Spouse according to the will and in the same Spouse is rejoicing and delighting itself in all these virtues together.

---

[4] This parenthesis is inserted by the Saint as an interlinear note, and is not copied by G, V, Vd, Br.

[5] G, V, Vd, Br: 'roses.'

[6] The parenthesis is added by the Saint.

At this season there are wont to resort to the memory and fancy, at certain times, many and various forms and imaginations, and to the sensual part of the soul many and various motions and desires which, as we have said, by their great subtlety and agility, trouble the soul and cause it to lose that inward tranquillity and sweetness wherein it was rejoicing. And besides this the evil spirits, who are very envious of the inward recollection and peace of the soul, are wont to introduce into the spirit horrors and disturbances and fears. All these things the Bride here calls foxes, for even as the shrewd and agile little foxes, with their subtle bounds, are in the habit of tearing down and ruining the blossom of the vineyards at the season when they are in flower, even so do the shrewd and malicious evil spirits, with like speed, by means of these disturbances and motions aforementioned, assail the devotion of holy souls.

3. This same request is made by the Bride in the Songs, where she says: *Capite nobis vulpes parvulas, quæ demoliuntur vineas: nam vinea nostra floruit.*[7] Which is to say: Drive us away the little foxes that spoil the vineyards, for our vineyard is flowering. And not for that reason alone does the soul desire them to be driven away, but likewise so that there may be room for that whereof she speaks in the line following.[8] Namely:

While we make a bunch of roses,

4. For at this season, when the soul is enjoying the flower of this vineyard and taking her delight upon the breast of her Beloved, it comes to pass that the virtues of the soul stand out clearly to view, as we have said, and are at their best, revealing themselves to her and bestowing upon her great sweetness and delight. These virtues the soul feels to be in herself and in God, so that they seem to her to be a pleasant vineyard, full of flower, belonging to them both, wherein both of them pasture and have delight. Then the soul gathers together all these virtues, and in each one of them and in all

[7] Canticles ii, 15.
[8] 'Why does it say the flower of the vineyard and not the fruit?' queries the Saint in a marginal note.

of them together makes most delectable acts of love. All these
she offers to the Beloved with great tenderness of love and
sweetness; and the Beloved Himself aids her herein, for without His favour and aid she could not thus gather together
the virtues and offer them to her Beloved. Wherefore she says:
'We make a nosegay,'—that is to say, the Beloved and I.

5. She calls this gathering together of virtues a cone or nosegay,[9] because even as a pine-cone[10] is strong,[11] and contains
within itself many pieces, strong and strongly bound together,
which are the pine-kernels, even so this cone or nosegay of
virtues which the soul makes for her Beloved is one single
piece of the soul's perfection, which firmly and in an ordered
manner embraces and contains within itself many perfections
and virtues which are very strong, and gifts which are very
precious, for all the perfections and virtues and gifts are ordered and combined into one firm perfection of the soul. Inasmuch as this perfection is being formed through the practice
of the virtues, and, when formed, is being offered to the Beloved by the soul in the spirit of love after the manner which
we are describing, it is fitting that the foxes aforementioned
be driven away so that they hinder not the said interior communication between the two. And not only does the soul in
this stanza make this request that she may be able to fashion
the nosegay well, but likewise she desires that which ensues
in the line following. Namely:

And let none appear upon the hill.

6. This Divine interior exercise also requires withdrawal
and detachment from all things that might present themselves
to the soul, whether from the lower part of a man, which
is that of the senses, or from the higher part, which is that
of the reason, in the which two parts are comprised the entire
harmony of the faculties and senses of the whole man, which
harmony the Bride here calls a hill, and begs that none may
appear thereon, that is to say, naught that pertains to any

[9] [By 'cone or nosegay' understand *piña*, and see p. 162, n. 2,
above.]
[10] [*piña*.]
[11] [*Lit.*, 'a strong piece.' Cf. the following clause.]

of these faculties or senses whereof we have spoken. It is thus as though she were to say: In all the spiritual faculties—namely, the understanding, the memory and the will—let there be no other considerations or affections or digressions; and in all the senses and faculties of the body, such as the imagination and the fancy, and the five exterior senses, let there be no other forms, images or figures of any natural objects or operations.

7. This the soul says here, since at this season of communication with God it is fitting that all the senses, whether interior or exterior, be empty and idle, for, at such a time, the more they set themselves to work, the more they disturb the soul. For, when the soul attains to interior union with God, the spiritual faculties no longer work in it, still less do the bodily faculties, inasmuch as the work of the union of love is already done, and thus the faculties have ceased to work, for when they reach their goal all medial operations come to an end. Thus that which the soul does at this time in the Beloved is to remain in the delectable[12] exercise of that which has already been wrought in it—namely, loving in continuation of the union of love. Let none, then, appear upon the hill; let the will alone be present in the surrender of itself and of all the virtues to the Beloved after the manner aforementioned.

STANZA XXVI

Stay thee, dead north wind.   Come, south wind, that awakenest love;
Breathe through my garden and let its odours flow,   And the Beloved shall pasture[1] among the flowers.

Exposition

Over and above the causes already mentioned, spiritual dryness might be a cause whereby in the Bride-Soul the inward

[12] This word is added by the Saint and is not copied by G, V, Vd, Br.
[1] See p. 46, n. 27. Here both G and V have: 'And let the Beloved appear . . .' while Vd has: 'And the Beloved shall appear . . .' (*parecerá*).

sweetness and substance[2] whereof we have spoken above might be quenched. Fearing[3] this, she does two things in this stanza. First, she shuts the door upon spiritual dryness, taking care not to become neglectful in devotion and so allow it to enter. The second thing that she does is to invoke the Holy Spirit, sustaining herself by means of prayer, so that by this means not only may dryness be kept without, but likewise[4] her devotion may be increased and she may put the virtues into practice[5] interiorly—all this to the end that her Beloved may have greater rejoicing and delight in them.

Stay thee, dead north wind.

2. The north wind is a cold and dry wind, and withers[6] the flowers; and because spiritual dryness[7] causes this same effect in the soul wherein it dwells, she calls it 'north wind'; and 'dead,' because it quenches and kills spiritual sweetness and substance;[8] because of the effect which it produces, she calls it 'dead north wind.' Desiring to maintain herself in the sweetness of her love, the Bride commands this dryness to stay itself: by this is to be understood that she takes care to do such things as may stay it, preserving and keeping the soul from aught that may arouse it.

Come, south wind, that awakenest love;

3. The south wind[9] is another wind, which is commonly[10] called *ábrego;* this is a peaceful breeze, which brings rain and

---

[2] [*jugo,* the sap or pith of a plant.]

[3] Gr, V, Vd, Br and Sanlúcar read, for *temiendo* ('fearing'), *teniendo* ('having').

[4] Bj omits 'not only . . . likewise.'

[5] Bz, Bj, G, V, Vd, Br: 'execution.'

[6] G, V, Vd, Md: 'a cold wind, and dries up and withers.'; Lch: 'which dries up and withers.'

[7] In the margin the Saint has added: 'The cause of this dryness is that the soul can do naught with its facilities until the Beloved moves them, putting them into actual practice.' [This sentence is reconstructed with some difficulty, the MS. not being clear.]

[8] [*jugo.*]

[9] [He uses the learned word *Austro; ábrego* is a popular word, meaning a south-west wind.]

[10] Bz, 8,654, Md: 'which in the vulgar tongue is . . .'

makes grass and plants[11] to grow and flowers to open and
scatter their fragrance; its effects are contrary to those of the
north wind. And thus by this breeze the soul here denotes the
Holy Spirit, Who, as she says, awakens love; for, when this
Divine breeze assails the soul, it enkindles it wholly and refreshes it and revives it and awakens the will and upraises the
desires which aforetime had fallen and were asleep, to the love
of God, in such manner that it may well be said thereof that
it awakens the love both of the Spouse and of the Bride.[12]

Breathe through my garden

4. We have said that the soul of the Bride is the vineyard
flowering in virtues; she[13] now likewise calls it here a garden,
wherein are planted the flowers of perfections and virtues
whereof we have spoken. And here it is to be noted that the
Bride says not: 'Breathe in my garden,' but 'Breathe through
my garden'; for there is a great difference between the breathing of God into the soul and the breathing of God through
the soul. To breathe[14] into the soul is to infuse into it grace,
gifts and virtues; and to breathe through the soul is for God
to touch the virtues and perfections which have already
been given to it, refreshing them and moving them so that
they may diffuse wondrous fragrance and sweetness. This is
just as when aromatic[15] spices are shaken; for, as soon as
they are set in motion, they shed the abundance of their
odour, which formerly was not present, or was not perceived
to so high a degree. For the virtues that the soul has acquired in itself it is not always actually feeling and enjoying;
because, as we have said, they are present in the soul during
this life like flowers enclosed in the bud, or like aromatic
spices covered over, the fragrance whereof is not perceived
until they are uncovered and shaken, as we have said.

[11] Gr, Lch, Bj, Bz, 8,654, Md omit 'and plants.'
[12] [*Lit.*, 'of Him and of her.'] These words are added by the
Saint and are not copied by the MSS.
[13] Gr, Lch, Bj, Bz, 8,654, Md: 'the Bride.'
[14] G, V, Vd, Br: 'For God to breathe.'
[15] The Saint's correction for 'Sarmatic,' an evident slip of the
copyist.

5. But at times God grants to the Bride-Soul such favours that, breathing with His Divine Spirit through this her flowering garden, He opens all these buds, or virtues, and uncovers these aromatic spices which are the gifts and perfections and riches of the soul, and, by opening this inward wealth and treasure, reveals all her beauty. And then it is a wondrous thing to see, and sweet to feel, the riches of the gifts which are revealed to the soul and the beauty of these flowers of the virtues[16] which are now all opened, each one diffusing the fragrance and sweetness which belongs to it. And this the Bride calls the flowing of the odours, as she says in the line following:

And let its odours flow,

6. These odours are at times so abundant that the soul thinks herself to be clothed with delights and bathed in inestimable glory—so much so that not only is she conscious of them within, but they are also wont to overflow without, to such an extent that all who are able to discern such things recognize it, and the soul in this case seems to them to be like a delectable garden, full of the delights and riches of God. And not only when these flowers are opened[17] can this be observed in these holy souls, but they bear within them habitually something[18] of greatness and dignity which causes others to stop and respect them by reason of the supernatural effect produced in them through their close and familiar intercourse with God, even as it is written of Moses, in the Book of Exodus, that they could not look upon his countenance by reason of the glory and honour which remained upon his person because he had spoken with God face to face.[19]

7. In this breathing of the Holy Spirit through the soul, which is His visitation of her in love, the Spouse, Who is the Son of God, communicates Himself to her after a lofty man-

---

[16] Md omits 'of the virtues.'

[17] From this point Lch omits a long passage, including the rest of this paragraph and the first half of the next, down to the words: 'He communicates Himself to her after a loftier manner.'

[18] [*un no sé qué.* Cf. p. 75, n. 1, above.]

[19] Exodus xxxiv, 30.

ner. To this end He first sends His Spirit, Who is His forerunner, as He did to the Apostles, to prepare for Him a dwelling for the soul His Bride, raising her up in delight, setting her garden in order, causing its flowers to open, revealing its gifts, and adorning her with the tapestry of His graces and riches. And thus with great desire the Bride-Soul desires all this—namely, that the north wind may depart, that the south wind may come and that it may breathe through the garden, for herein the soul gains many things together. She gains the fruition of the virtues which have been brought to the highest point of delectable exercise, as we have said. She gains the fruition of the Beloved in them, since by their means, as we have just said, He communicates Himself to her after a loftier manner and grants her more special favours than before. She also gains this, that the Beloved delights in her far more through this exercise of the virtues, and it is this that pleases her most, namely that her Beloved is pleased with her. She also gains the continuance and duration of this fragrance and sweetness of the virtues, which continues in the soul for as long as the Beloved is present after this manner, and the Bride is giving Him sweetness in her virtues, even as she says in the Songs, after this wise: *Cum esset Rex in accubitu suo, nardus mea dedit odorem suavitatis.*[20] This is as though she were to say: While the King was reclining in his reclining-chamber, which is my soul, my fragrant little tree gave forth fragrance of sweetness. By the fragrant little tree, which consists of many flowers, she here understands the nursery of many virtues which was said above to be in the soul, and which there she calls a flowering vineyard, or the nosegay of flowers which was spoken of later; and thus this tree gives forth the sweetness of its fragrance to God and to the soul, for as long as He dwells in her through communication of substance.

8. Wherefore it is greatly to be desired that every soul should pray for this breath of the Holy Spirit to breathe through its garden and for the flowing of its Divine odours. And because this is so necessary, and of such great good and

[20] Canticles i, 11 [A.V., i, 12].

glory for the soul, the Bride desired it in the Songs, and prayed for it, saying: *Surge Aquilo, et veni Auster, perfla hortum meum, et fluent aromata illius.*[21] This includes all that we have said in this stanza down to this point, and signifies: Rise up, north wind, and depart, and thou, south-west wind,[22] sweet and profitable wind, come and flow and breathe through my garden; and its fragrant and precious spices shall flow. And all this the soul desires, not for the delight and glory which come to her thereby, but because she knows that her Spouse delights therein. This is her preparation and prediction, that her Beloved Spouse, the Son of God, may come and take His delight in her; wherefore she says next:

And the Beloved shall pasture[23] among the flowers.

9. The soul here refers to this delight that the Son of God has in her at this time, and she gives it the name of pasture, which describes it with the greatest fitness, since pasturing or feeding is a thing that gives not only pleasure, but likewise sustenance; and even so the Son of God delights in the soul, and in these the soul's delights, and takes sustenance from her—that is, He continues in her, as in a place wherein He has great delight, since the place itself truly delights in Him. And it is this, as I understand, that He Himself meant, when He said, through the mouth of Solomon, in the Proverbs: 'My delights are with the sons of men'[24]—that is to say, when their delights are to be with Me, Who am the Son of God. And it is to be noted that she says not that He will pasture 'upon' the flowers, but 'among' the flowers; for the communication of the Spouse, and His delight, is in the soul, by means of the adornment of the virtues aforementioned. And it is upon the soul itself that He pastures, transforming it into Himself, when it is seasoned and prepared and made fragrant[25] with

---

[21] Canticles iv, 16.
[22] [*ábrego.*]
[23] See p. 46, n. 27, above.
[24] Proverbs viii, 31.
[25] [*Lit.,* 'seasoned and dressed and salted'—the metaphor of feeding is carried into the kitchen and developed in more detail than is possible in English.]

the flowers of virtues and gifts and perfections, which are the things[26] whereby and among which He pastures upon the soul. These things, by the power of His forerunner aforementioned, are rendering the soul pleasing and sweet to God; and this is the habit of the Spouse, to pasture upon the soul amid the fragrance of these flowers. And thus the Bride in the Songs, as one who well knows this habit of the Spouse, speaks in these words: *Dilectus meus descendit in hortum suum ad areolam aromatum, ut pascatur in hortis, et lilia colligat.*[27] Which signifies: My Beloved is gone down into His garden, to the beds and breezes[28] of the fragrant aromatic spices, to pasture in the gardens and to gather lilies for Himself.[29] And then she says: 'I for my Beloved, and my Beloved for me: He feedeth among the lilies.'[30] That is to say: He delights in my soul, which is the garden, among the lilies of my virtues and perfections and graces.

STANZA XXVII

The Bride has entered   Into the pleasant garden of her desire,[1] And at her pleasure rests,   Her neck reclining on the gentle arms of the Beloved.

Exposition

The soul having now done all in her power that the foxes may be driven away and the north wind may depart, since these have been hindrances and inconveniences impeding the perfect delight of the estate of the Spiritual Marriage; and

26 [*Lit.*, 'the sauce.']
27 Canticles vi, 1 [A.V., vi, 2–3].
28 [The Spanish has the singular form with plural meaning.]
29 Md omits 'aromatic,' and ends: 'to pasture on the lilies and to gather them for Himself.' Bz, 8,654, Bj, Lch, Gr are practically identical with Md.
30 Canticles vi, 2 [A.V., vi, 3].
1 [*Lit.*, 'pleasant desired garden.']

having likewise invoked and obtained the breeze of the Holy
Spirit (as has been described in the two preceding stanzas),
which is the proper disposition and means for the perfection
of this estate: it now remains to treat, in this stanza, of this
estate, wherein the Spouse now speaks to the soul, calling her
His Bride, and says two things. He says, first, that the soul,
having issued forth victoriously, has now attained to this delectable estate of the Spiritual Marriage which both He and she
had so greatly desired.[2] The second thing that He does is to
enumerate the properties of the said estate, of which properties the soul now has fruition in Him, and these are for her
to rest at her pleasure and for her neck to recline upon the
gentle arms of the Beloved, even as we shall now go on to
show in our exposition.

The Bride has entered

2. In order that we may expound the arrangement of these
stanzas the more clearly, and describe the soul's habitual
progress ere it come to this estate of the Spiritual Marriage,
which is the highest estate that, with the help of God, we have
now to describe, and to which the soul has now come, it is to
be noted that first of all it exercised itself in the trials and bitternesses of mortification, and in meditation,[3] as the soul said
at the beginning, from the first stanza down to that which
says: 'Scattering a thousand graces.'[4] Afterwards it passed
through the pains and straits of love which have been described in the stanzas following, as far as that which says:
'Withdraw them, Beloved.'[5] And in addition to this, the soul
then relates how it has received great communications and
many visits from its Beloved, wherein it has reached ever-
increasing perfection and knowledge in His love, so much so
that, passing beyond all things, and even beyond itself, it has
surrendered itself to Him through union of love in the Spiri-

---

[2] The MSS., Br and Md have: 'which she had so greatly desired.'
The addition of 'both He and' was made by the Saint.
[3] These three words are an addition by the Saint.
[4] [Stanza V.]
[5] [Stanza XII.]

tual Betrothal, wherein, as one that is now betrothed, it has received from the Spouse great gifts and jewels, even as it has described in its song, from the stanza wherein this Divine betrothal was made, and which says, 'Withdraw them, Beloved,[6] a spiritual [estate] the properties whereof it has been describing, down to this place, wherein the Spouse makes mention of it; wherefore its properties are being described down to this present place, which begins 'The Bride has entered. . . .' It now remains for the Spouse to make mention of the said Spiritual Marriage[7] between the soul aforementioned and the Son of God, her Spouse, which is far greater than the Betrothal because it is a total transformation in the Beloved (and thus I think that this estate is never without confirmation in grace, because the faithfulness of both is confirmed, that of the soul being confirmed in God),[8] wherein on either side there is made surrender, by total possession, of the one to the other in consummate union of love, as far as may be in this life, wherein the soul is made Divine and becomes God by participation, in so far as may be in this life, and thus this is the highest estate which in this life is attainable. For, even as in the consummation of marriage according to the flesh the two become one flesh, as says the Divine Scripture,[9] even so, when this Spiritual Marriage between God and the soul is consummated, there are two natures in one spirit and love of God. It is as when[10] the light of the star or of the candle is joined and united with the sun, so that that which shines is not the star or the candle but the sun, which

[6] Here there is a marginal addition by the Saint, the first line of which has been completely cut off. The remainder is represented by the words ('a spiritual . . . down to this present place') which immediately follow.

[7] The Saint's emendation for 'It has remained now for the Spiritual Marriage to come to pass. . . .' The MSS. do not copy this emendation.

[8] The bracketed parenthesis is a marginal addition made by the Saint. The words 'that of the soul,' 'in' [God] are conjectural; [were they omitted we should read: 'that of God being confirmed'— i.e. in the soul].

[9] Genesis ii, 24.

[10] 'When' is the Saint's addition, found also in Bj.

has absorbed the other lights in itself.[11] And of this estate the Spouse treats in the present line, saying: 'The Bride has entered'—that is to say, has gone out from all that is temporal and from all that is natural, and from all spiritual manners and modes and affections, and, having left behind and forgotten all temptations, disturbances, griefs, anxiety[12] and cares, is transformed in this sublime embrace.[13] Of this the following line goes on to treat, namely:

Into the pleasant garden of her desire,

3. This is as though she were to say: She has been transformed in God, Who it is that is here called a pleasant garden, by reason of the delectable and sweet repose which the soul finds in Him. The soul does not come to this garden of complete transformation (which is the joy and delight and glory of the Spiritual Marriage) without first passing through the Spiritual Betrothal and through the mutual and loyal love of those that are betrothed. For, after the soul has been for some time the Bride of the Son of God, in love which is sweet and perfect, God calls her and sets her in this His flowering garden for the consummation of this most happy estate of marriage with Him, wherein is effected such union of the two natures and such communication of the Divine nature to the human, that, while neither of them changes its being, each of them appears to be God. Although in this life this thing cannot come to pass perfectly, yet it surpasses everything that can be described or conceived.

4. This is very clearly expressed by the Spouse Himself in

[11] Md reads: '. . . or of the candle in the presence of the sun is joined and united with that of the sun, so that that which shines and absorbs the other lights in itself is the sun.' Bz, Lch, 8,654, Gr, Bj read similarly, but have 'united with it' for 'united with the sun.'

[12] [This noun, alone of the five, is singular.]

[13] Md (as also, with minute variations not affecting the sense, Bz, Lch, 8,654, Gr, Bj) reads: 'that is to say, from all that is temporal and natural, leaving outside all the temptations, disturbances, cares, anxieties and griefs, and forms and figures [both] corporal and imaginary, taking not advantage of them now as means for this sublime embrace. From all this she has entered.'

the Songs, where He invites the soul, now made His Bride, to this estate, saying: *Veni in hortum meum soror mea Sponsa, messui myrrham meam cum aromatibus meis.*[14] Which signifies: Come and enter into My garden, My sister, My spouse, for I have now gathered My myrrh with My fragrant spices. He calls her sister and spouse because this she was in the love and surrender of herself which she had made to Him before He called her to this estate of the Spiritual Marriage, where He says that He has now gathered His fragrant myrrh and aromatic spices, which are the fruits of the flowers,[15] now ripe and made ready for the soul, the which fruits are the delights and grandeurs that He Himself communicates to her in this estate—that is, He communicates them to her in Himself; for the which cause He is to her the pleasant garden of her desire. For the whole desire and aim of the soul, and that of God in all the works of the soul, is the consummation and perfection[16] of this estate, wherefore the soul never rests until she reaches Him; for in this estate she finds much greater abundance and fullness of God, and a peace more sure and stable, and a sweetness more perfect without compare than in the Spiritual Betrothal, since she is now placed in the arms of such a Spouse.[17] Of the soul in this estate is to be understood that which Saint Paul says to the Galatians, in these words: *Vivo autem, jam non ego, vivit vero in me Christus.*[18] That is: I live, yet not I, but Christ liveth in me. Wherefore, since the soul lives a life so happy and blessed as this life of God, let each one consider, if he can, what a life of the soul this will be, wherein neither can God perceive aught that is displeasing to Him, nor does the soul perceive it,[19] but the soul enjoys and perceives the delight

[14] Canticles v, 1.

[15] 'Of the flowers' is the Saint's addition, copied only by Bj, of the MSS., and not found in Br or Md.

[16] Bz, Lch, 8,654, Gr, Bj, Md omit 'and perfection.'

[17] 'Habitual embrace in (God?)': marginal note by the Saint.

[18] Galatians ii, 20.

[19] Bz, Lch, 8,654, Gr, Bj, Md read: 'And therefore, since the soul lives a life so happy, which is the life of God, let it consider, if it can, what a life will be this wherein the soul can now perceive naught that is unpleasing, neither does God perceive it.'

and glory of God in its very substance, which is now transformed in Him. Wherefore the stanza continues:

And at her pleasure rests, Her neck reclining . . .

5. The neck, as has been said above, denotes strength, for, by means of this strength, which the soul in this estate now possesses, is wrought this union; for the soul is incapable of receiving so close an embrace if it be not strong,[20] which strength is that wherewith the soul works, and practises the virtues, and conquers the vices; wherefore it is just that the soul should take its repose and rest after it has laboured, with its neck reclining

. . . on the gentle arms of the Beloved.

6. For the neck to recline on the arms of God is for it to have its strength now united—or rather, its weakness—in the strength of God; for the arms of God signify the strength of God,[21] wherein our weakness, reclining upon Him and transformed in Him, has now strength from God Himself. Wherefore it is very convenient to denote this estate of the Spiritual Marriage by this reclining of the neck on the gentle arms of the Beloved, since God is now both the strength and the gentleness of the soul, in Whom it is defended and protected from all evils and given the savour of good things. Hence the Bride in the Songs, being desirous of this estate, said to the Spouse: *Quis det te mihi fratrem meum, sugentem ubera matris meæ, ut inveniam te solum foris, et deosculer te, et iam me nemo despiciat?*[22] As though she were to say: Who would give Thee to me, my brother, that Thou mightest suck the breasts of my mother, so that I might find Thee alone without and might kiss Thee, and none would then despise me? By calling Him her brother, she denotes the equality which there is in the betrothal of love between the two before

[20] The words 'for, by means . . . be not strong' are a marginal note of the Saint's, included almost literally in the second redaction. [See p. 375, below.]

[21] G, V, Vd, 8,654, Br omit this phrase: 'for the arms . . . strength of God.'

[22] Canticles viii, 1.

they attain to this estate. By saying 'that Thou mightest suck the breasts of my mother,' she means, that Thou mightest quench and dry up in me the desires and passions, which are the breasts and the milk of Mother Eve in our flesh, and are a hindrance to this estate. And thus, she continues, when this is done, 'I might find Thee alone without'—that is: I might go out from all things, even from myself, in solitude and detachment of spirit, when once the aforementioned desires are dried up; and there I, being alone, 'might kiss Thee,' Who art alone—that is to say: My nature, now that it is alone and detached from all impurity, temporal, natural and spiritual, might be united[23] with Thee alone, with Thy nature alone, and without any other intermediaries,[24] which alone comes to pass in the Spiritual Marriage, which is the kiss of God by the soul, where none despises it or assaults it; for in this estate neither devil nor flesh nor world nor desires molest it. For herein is fulfilled that which is also said in the Canticles: *Iam enim hiems transiit, imber abiit et recessit, flores apparuerunt,* etc.[25] Which signifies: The winter is now past and the rain has gone and the flowers have appeared in our land.

STANZA XXVIII

**Beneath the apple-tree,   There wert thou betrothed to me;
There did I give thee my hand   And thou wert redeemed
where thy mother had been corrupted.**

Exposition

In this high estate of the Spiritual Marriage, the Spouse reveals His wondrous secrets to the soul with great readiness and frequency, and describes His works to her, for true and

[23] G, V, Vd, Br have: *si viniese* ('if it were to come') for *se uniese* ('might be united') [an inferior reading which involves some slight alterations in the English context].
[24] Md adds: 'save love.'
[25] Canticles ii, 11–12.

perfect love can keep nothing hidden. And in particular He communicates to her sweet mysteries[1] concerning His Incarnation, and the mode and way of human redemption, which is one of the highest works of God, and is thus most delectable to the soul. And so the Spouse does this in the present stanza, wherein is denoted how with great sweetness of love He reveals inwardly to the soul the mysteries aforementioned. And thus He speaks with her and tells her how by means of the Tree of the Cross she was betrothed to Him; how He gave her herein the favour of His mercy, being pleased to die for her and making her beauteous[2] after this manner. For He restored and redeemed her by the same means whereby human nature had been ruined, namely, by means of the Tree of Paradise, in our first mother, who was Eve. Thus the Spouse says:

Beneath the apple-tree,

2. Meaning by the apple-tree the Tree of the Cross whereon the Son of God redeemed human nature, and in consequence was betrothed to it, and consequently to every soul, giving to each soul in token thereof grace and pledges through the merits of His Passion. And thus He says to her:

There wert thou betrothed to me;
There did I give thee my hand

3. This is to say, the hand of My favour and help, raising thee up from thy miserable and low estate to be My companion and My betrothed.

And thou wert redeemed where thy mother had been corrupted.

4. For thy mother, human nature, was corrupted, in thy first parents, beneath the tree, and there likewise wert thou redeemed—namely, beneath the Tree of the Cross.[3] So that, if thy mother caused thy death beneath the tree, I gave thee

---

[1] The Saint corrects the 'matters' of the copy (also found in G, V, Vd, Br) to 'mysteries.'
[2] Many versions read: 'making her beauteously.'
[3] Canticles viii, 5.

life beneath the Tree of the Cross. After this manner God continues to reveal to the soul the ordinances and dispositions of His Wisdom; since He is able so wisely and beauteously to bring good from evil, and to ordain to our greater good that which was the cause of evil. That which is literally contained in this stanza is said by the same Spouse to the Bride in the Songs, where He says: *Sub arbore malo suscitavi te, ibi corrupta est mater tua, ibi violata est genitrix tua.*[4] Which signifies: Under the apple-tree I raised thee up; there thy mother was corrupted,[5] and there was she violated that bore thee.

STANZAS XXIX AND XXX

**Birds of swift wing,   Lions, harts, leaping does,
Mountains, valleys, banks, waters, breezes, heats,   And terrors
  that keep watch by night,**

**By the pleasant lyres   And by the sirens' song, I conjure you,
Cease your wrath and touch not the wall,   That the Bride may
  sleep more securely.**

Exposition

The Spouse continues, and, in these two stanzas, describes how, as by means of the pleasant lyres, which here signify the sweetness that is habitually enjoyed in this estate, and likewise by the sirens' song, which signifies the delight that He has ever in the soul, He has just brought to an end and conclusion all the operations and passions of the soul which aforetime were a certain impediment and hindrance[1] to peaceful

---

[4] *Ibid.*

[5] This is the reading (*estragada*) of Md, and all other authorities than Sanlúcar, Vd. 8,654, Br (*extraída,* 'drawn forth,' 'removed'), G, V, Lch (*destruída,* 'destroyed').

[1] [*sinsabor, lit.,* 'displeasure.']

pleasure and sweetness. These things, He says here, are the digressions of the imaginative fancy, and He conjures them to cease. Furthermore, He brings into control the two natural faculties, which formerly to some extent afflicted[2] the soul and which are the irascible and the concupiscible. And likewise, by means of these lyres and this song, He declares how in this estate, in so far as may be in this life, the three faculties of the soul—understanding, will and memory—are brought to perfection and set in working order. And likewise it is described herein how the four passions of the soul—namely: grief, hope, joy and fear—are mitigated and controlled by means of the satisfaction which the soul possesses, and which is denoted by the pleasant lyres and the sirens' song, as we shall now explain. All these hindrances God desires to cease, so that the soul, at her will and without any interruption, may have fruition of the delight, peace and sweetness of this union.

Birds of swift wing,

2. He calls the digressions of the imagination birds of swift wing, since they are light and subtle in their flight first in one direction and then in another. When the will, in quietness, is enjoying the delectable communication of the Beloved, they are apt to cause it displeasure,[3] and, by their subtle flights, to quench its joy. These the Beloved says that He conjures by the pleasant lyres, etc. That is to say that, since the sweetness and delight of the soul are now so abundant and frequent and strong that they could not hinder it as they were wont to do aforetime, when it had not reached so high an estate, they are to cease their restless flights, their impetuosities and their excesses. This is to be understood after the same manner in the other parts of this stanza which we have here to expound, as for example:

Lions, harts, leaping does,

3. By the lions are meant the acrimonies and impetuosities of the irascible faculty, which faculty is as bold and daring in

[2] Lch: 'fatigued.'
[3] [sinsabor.]

its acts as are lions. By the harts and the leaping does is understood the other faculty of the soul, which is the concupiscible—that is, the power of desire,[4] which has two effects:
the one is of cowardice and the other of boldness. It produces
the effects of cowardice when it finds that things[5] are inconvenient to itself, for at such times it withdraws and retires
within itself and behaves timidly,[6] and in these effects it is
compared to the hart; for even as harts possess this concupiscible faculty to a higher degree than many other animals, so,
too, they are very timid[7] and retiring. The effects of boldness
it produces when it finds that things are convenient to itself,
for then it retires not any more, neither behaves timidly, but
comes forth boldly to desire[8] them and accept them[9] with its
desires and affections. And as concerns these effects of boldness this faculty is compared to the does, which have such
concupiscence toward that which they desire, that not only do
they run towards it, but they even leap after it, for which
reason they are here called 'leaping.'

4. So that, in conjuring the lions, the Spouse restrains the
impetuosities and excesses of wrath; and in conjuring the
harts, He strengthens the concupiscible faculty with respect
to the cowardice and feebleness of mind which aforetime
caused it to shrink; and in conjuring the leaping does, He satisfies it and subdues the desires and appetites which aforetime
roamed restlessly about, leaping like does from one thing to
another, in order to satisfy that concupiscence which is now
satisfied by the pleasant lyres, whose sweetness it enjoys, and
by the sirens' song, upon the delight whereof it pastures. And
it is to be noted that it is not wrath and concupiscence which
the Spouse conjures here, for these faculties are never wanting in the soul, but their troublesome and disorderly acts,

---

[4] [*apetecer.*]

[5] Lch abbreviates: 'which has two effects: the one is of cowardice, which it excites when it finds things . . .' etc.

[6] [*Lit.,* 'behaves with cowardice.']

[7] [*Lit.,* 'very cowardly.']

[8] [*apetecer.*]

[9] Bz, Bj: 'and to ask for them.' Lch: 'and imitate them.'

which are denoted by the lions, harts and leaping does; it is necessary in this estate that these should cease.

Mountains, valleys and[10] banks,

5. By these three names are denoted the vicious and disorderly acts of the three faculties of the soul, which are memory, understanding and will, which acts are disorderly and vicious when they are carried to a high extreme, and likewise when they are at a low and defective extreme, or even when they are not at either extreme, but tend thereto in either direction. And thus by the mountains, which are very high, are signified acts which are extreme in being over-disorderly. By the valleys, which are very low, are signified the acts of these three faculties which are less extreme than is fitting. And by the banks, which are neither very high nor very low, yet, since they are not level, participate somewhat of the one extreme and of the other, are signified the acts of the faculties when these in some respect exceed or fail to reach that mean and level height of what is just. These acts, though not disorderly in the extreme, as they would be if they amounted to mortal sin, are nevertheless partially so, since they are either venial sins or imperfections, however slight, in the understanding, the memory and the will. All these acts which exceed what is just He conjures likewise, by the pleasant lyres and the aforementioned song, that they cease; the which lyres and song have brought the three faculties of the soul to such perfection of efficiency that they are completely occupied in the just operation which pertains to them, and this to such an extent that they avoid not only every extreme but also any tendency thereto. There follow the remaining lines:

Waters, breezes, heats, And terrors that keep watch by night.

6. By these four things, again, are understood the affections of the four passions, which, as we said, are grief, hope, joy and fear. By the waters are understood the affections of grief which afflict the soul; for they enter the soul like water, wherefore David said to God in speaking of them: *Salvum me fac*

---

10 ['And' appears here, though not in the stanza as written elsewhere.]

Deus, quoniam intraverunt aquæ usque ad animam meam.[11]
That is: Save me, my God, for the waters are come in even
unto my soul. By the breezes are understood the affections of
hope, for like the breezes they fly to desire that which is absent and is hoped for. Wherefore David says likewise: *Os
meum aperui, et attraxi spiritum, quia mandata tua desidera-
bam.*[12] As though he were to say: I opened the mouth of my
hope and drew in the breath of my desire, for I desired and
hoped for Thy commandments. By the heats are understood
the affections of the passion of joy, which enkindle the heart
like fire; wherefore the same David says: *Concaluit cor meum
intra me, et in meditatione mea exardescet ignis.*[13] Which
signifies: My heart grew hot within me and in my meditation
fire shall be enkindled; which is as much as to say: In my
meditation shall joy be enkindled. By the terrors that keep
watch by night are understood the affections of the other passion, which is fear; which affections, in spiritual persons that
have not yet reached this estate of the Spiritual Marriage
whereof we are speaking, are wont to be very great. At times
they come from God, when He desires to grant such persons
certain favours, as we have said above, and is wont to bring
fear and affright to their spirits, and likewise a shrinking to
their flesh and senses, since they have not fortified and perfected their nature and habituated it to these favours of God.
At times, again, they come from the devil, who, when God
grants the soul recollection and sweetness in Himself, becomes
very envious and greatly afflicted because of that blessing and
peace which have come to the soul, and contrives to set horror
and fear in its spirit, to hinder it from obtaining that blessing;
sometimes, he even threatens it within its very spirit. And
when he sees that he cannot reach the inmost part of the soul,
since it is deeply recollected and closely united with God, he
then attacks it from without, in its sensual part, and sets there
distraction[14] or inconstancy, and sensible afflictions[15] and

---

[11] Psalm lxviii, 1 [A.V., lxix, 1].
[12] Psalm cxviii, 131 [A.V., cxix, 131].
[13] Psalm xxxviii, 4 [A.V., xxxix, 3].
[14] [*Lit.*, 'he sets without, at least, in its sensual part, distraction.']
[15] [*aprietos.*] Lch has [*apetitos*], 'appetites.'

pains and horror, if haply by this means he may harry the
Bride in her marriage-chamber. These things the Spouse calls
terrors of the night, because they all come from evil spirits,
and because by their means the devil tries to diffuse darkness
in the soul by obscuring the Divine light wherein it is rejoicing.
He says of these fears that they keep watch, because their
effect is to cause the soul to watch and to awaken it from its
sweet inward sleep, and likewise because the evil spirits that
cause[16] them are ever watching to produce them. These
fears, coming from God, or from the devil, as I have said, are
infused, almost[17] passively, into the spirits of those who are
already spiritual; and I treat not here of other fears which are
temporal or natural, because it is not for spiritual people to
have such fears, whereas to have the spiritual fears aforementioned is proper to spiritual people.

7. So the Beloved likewise conjures all these four manners
of affection of the four passions of the soul, making them
to cease and be at rest, since He now gives to the Bride in this
estate riches and strength and satisfaction in the pleasant lyres
of His sweetness and the sirens' song of His delight, so that not
only can these things not reign within her but they cannot
even cause her the least degree of displeasure. For the grandeur and stability[18] of the soul in this estate are so complete
that, if formerly there reached the soul the waters of any
grief soever, even those of its own sins or of the sins of some
other person, which is what spiritual persons habitually feel
the most, now, although it still realizes their importance, they
cause it neither pain nor sorrow;[19] and it no longer feels
compassion,[20] though it performs the works of compassion
and has the perfection thereof; for in this estate the soul has
no longer that part of its virtues which was weak, but there
remains to it that which was strong, constant and perfect in
them; for in this transformation of love the soul acts as do the
angels, who apprehend perfectly things that are grievous with-

16 Bj: 'accuse.'
17 Md alone has 'almost.'
18 Br has *esta utilidad* ('this utility') for *estabilidad* ('stability').
19 Md: 'nor agonizing sorrow.'
20 Md adds: 'with anguish.'

out feeling grief, and perform works of mercy and compassion without feeling compassion; although occasionally and in occasional matters God bestows a favour upon the soul, granting it to feel sorrow and allowing it to suffer, that it may grow in merit, even as He did with the Virgin Mother and with Saint Paul;[21] but the estate does not imply this condition necessarily.

8. Neither does the soul grieve because of the desires of hope, for, being now satisfied, in so far as is possible in this life, by its union with God, it has naught to hope for with respect to the world, and naught to desire with respect to that which is spiritual, since it sees and feels itself to be full of the riches of God,[22] and thus, in life and in death, is conformed and reconciled to God's will. And thus the desire to see God which it experiences is without affliction.[23] The affections of joy, too, which were wont to be felt by the soul, to a greater or a lesser degree, seem to be in no way diminished, nor does their abundance cause it surprise. For its rejoicing is habitually so great that, like the sea, it is not diminished by the rivers that flow from it, neither is it increased by those that enter it; for it is within this soul that there is made that spring, the water whereof, as Christ says through Saint John, springs up to eternal life.[24] Finally, the terrors that keep watch by night fail to reach it, since it is so pure and so strong and so firmly fixed upon God in its repose that they can neither obscure it with their darkness, nor affright it with their terrors,[25] nor awaken it with their impetuosities; and thus naught can either reach it or molest it, since it has entered, as we have said, from all of these, into the pleasant garden of its desire, where it enjoys all peace, tastes all sweetness and delights itself in all delight, according as the condition and estate of this life allow. For of the soul in such an

[21] 'And with Saint Paul' is the Saint's addition [made in the original, not here, but, rather clumsily, at the end of the next clause]. It is not found in the MSS., in Br or in Md.

[22] Md adds: 'although it may grow in charity.'

[23] This sentence is an addition by the Saint, found neither in the other MSS. nor in Br or Md.

[24] St. John iv, 14.

[25] Bj: 'with their impetuosities.' Lch: 'with their fears.'

estate is understood that which the Wise Man says in the Proverbs, in these words: *Secura mens quasi juge convivium*.[26] That is: The soul that is secure and peaceful is like a continual feast; for, even as in a feast there are meats of all kinds delectable to the palate and music of all kinds sweet to the ear, even so the soul, in this continual feast which it experiences upon the bosom of its Beloved, enjoys all delight and tastes all sweetness.

9. Let it not appear to the reader of this that in what we have said we are indulging ourselves in mere words, for in truth, if it were necessary to explain that which passes through the soul that arrives at this happy estate, all words, and time itself, would fail us, and still the greater part would remain to be expounded; for, if the soul is enabled to reach the peace of God, which surpasses all that is of sense, then all that is of sense will remain bereft and mute at having to expound it. The lines continue:

By the pleasant lyres   And by the sirens' song, I conjure you.

10. We have already said that the pleasant lyres signify the sweetness of the soul in this estate, for, even as the music of the lyres fills the spirit with sweetness and refreshment, and it is so much absorbed and enraptured thereby that it is withdrawn from afflictions and distresses, even so does this sweetness keep the soul so completely within itself, that no affliction reaches it. Wherefore the Spouse conjures all the things that trouble[27] the faculties and passions to cease because of this sweetness. Furthermore, the song of the sirens, as has also been said, signifies the habitual delight which the soul possesses,[28] by the which likewise it is freed from all the hindrances and troublesome operations[29] aforementioned.[30] These are meant in the next line, which says:

[26] Proverbs xv, 15.
[27] [*a todas las molestias de.*] Bj has: [*a todas las bestias de*] 'all the beasts of.'
[28] The Saint has a marginal note here: 'The property of the sirens' song.'
[29] V, Vd, G, Gr, Lch, Br: 'operations [and] troubles.'
[30] The Saint's addition, not found in the editions or manuscripts.

Cease your wrath[31]

11. Indicating by wrath all the disorderly affections and operations whereof we have spoken. For, even as wrath is a certain impetuosity that goes beyond the limit of reason when it works viciously, so all the affections and operations aforementioned exceed the limits of tranquillity of the soul if they reign therein. Wherefore He says:

And touch not the wall,

12. By the wall is meant the rampart of peace and virtues and perfections which the soul now has, and by which it is now protected, which is the wall and defence of the garden of its Beloved. Wherefore He speaks of it thus in the Songs: *Hortus conclusus soror mea.*[32] Which signifies: My sister is a garden enclosed. Wherefore, He says, 'touch not this wall.'

That the Bride may sleep more securely.

13. That is to say, that she may delight the more according to her pleasure in the quiet and sweetness whereof she has fruition in the garden which she has entered, her neck reclining upon the gentle arms of the Beloved, so that there is now no door closed to the soul.[33]

[31] [*Lit.,* 'let your wraths cease.']
[32] Canticles iv, 12.
[33] The last clause is the Saint's marginal addition, found neither in the MSS. nor in Br or Md.

STANZA XXXI

O nymphs of Judaea,   While mid the flowers and rose-trees
the ambar sends forth perfume,
Dwell in the outskirts   And desire not to touch our thresholds.

Exposition

In the stanza it is the Bride that speaks, who, seeing herself
adorned, according to her higher and spiritual part, with such
rich and excellent gifts and delights, which come from her
Beloved, desires to preserve herself in the security and continual possession thereof, which, in the two preceding stanzas,
the Spouse has granted her. She sees that in her lower part—
namely, sensuality—there may be impediments, as in fact there
are,[1] which disturb so great a blessing. She therefore bids the
operations and motions of that her lower part to be stilled
in her faculties and senses, and not to pass beyond the limits
of their own region, that of the senses, nor to trouble or harass
the higher and spiritual part of the soul, lest it should be kept,
by any motion, howsoever small, from the blessing and sweetness which it enjoys. For if motions of the sensual part and
its faculties take place when the spirit is in fruition, they trouble and harass it all the more when they are busier and more
active.

O nymphs of Judaea,

2. By Judæa she means the lower part of the soul, which is
that of the senses. And she calls it Judæa, because it is weak
and carnal and of itself blind, even as are the Jewish people.
And by nymphs she means all the imaginations, fancies and
motions and affections of this lower part. All these she calls
nymphs, because, even as the nymphs attract lovers to them-

[1] This clause is an interlinear addition made by the Saint and
not found in the other authorities cited in these footnotes.

selves by their affectionate nature and their grace, so these operations and motions of sensuality contrive to attract the will pleasantly to themselves from the rational part of the soul, taking it away from that which is inward and making it to love that which is outward, which they themselves love and desire, and likewise moving the understanding and attracting it to be married and united with them after their base, sensual manner, contriving to bring into conformity and to unite the rational part with the sensual. You sensual motions and operations, then, she says:

While mid the flowers and rose-trees the ambar sends forth perfume,

3. The flowers are the virtues of the soul, as we said above. The rose-trees are the three faculties of the soul: understanding, memory and will; these bear roses and flowers of Divine conceptions and acts of love and of virtues. The ambar is the Divine Spirit Who dwells in the soul; and for this Divine ambar to send forth perfume amid the flowers and rose-trees is for it to communicate and scatter itself most sweetly in the faculties and virtues of the soul, thereby giving the soul a perfume of Divine sweetness. For so long, then, as this Divine Spirit is giving spiritual sweetness to my soul,

Dwell in the outskirts

4. In the outskirts of Judæa, which, we said, are the sensual part of the soul. Its outskirts are the inward sensual senses, such as the fancy, the imagination, the memory, wherein meet and gather the fancies and imaginations and forms of things. It is these which are here called nymphs, and which enter these outskirts of the inward senses through the gates of the outward senses, which are hearing, sight, smell, taste, touch; so that we may term all these faculties and senses of this sensual part outskirts, which are the suburbs that are without the city. For that which is called city in the soul is that most inward part, which is the rational part, and it is this that has capacity for communion with God, and the operations of which are contrary to those of sensuality. But since

there is natural communication between the dwellers in these
outskirts (which are the sensual part of the soul, these
dwellers being the nymphs of whom we speak) so that that
which is done in this part is habitually felt in the other more
inward part, which is the rational, and in consequence causes
itself to be noticed and disturbs that spiritual work which it
has in God, she tells them to dwell in her outskirts—that is,
to be stilled in the outward and inward senses of her sensual
part.

And desire not to touch our thresholds.

5. That is, touch not the higher part even in your first motions, for the first motions of the soul are the entrances and
the thresholds to an entrance therein, and, when they pass
from being first motions into the reason, they are crossing[2]
the thresholds; but, when they are naught but first motions,
they are said only to touch the thresholds or to knock at the
door, which happens when attacks upon the reason are made
by sensuality with regard to some disorderly act. The Bride
here not only bids these not to touch the soul; she even for-
bids considerations to do so which make not for the tranquillity and blessing whereof the soul has fruition. And thus this
sensual part, with all its faculties, its strength and its weak-
nesses, is already surrendered in this estate to the spirit. This
life is therefore a blessed one, like to that of the estate of
innocence wherein all the harmony and ability of man's sensual part served him for greater recreation and as a help to
a knowledge and love of God in peace and concord with his
higher part. Happy the soul that reaches this estate. But who
is he, and we will praise him? For he hath done wonderful
things in his life.[3]

6. This stanza has been placed here to describe the quiet
and secure peace of the soul that reaches this high estate; not
so that it may be thought that the soul here expresses this
desire—namely, that these nymphs shall be stilled—because

[2] A number of versions differ [almost imperceptibly in English].
G, V, Vd, Br read: 'when they pass from being first motions they
unite (*enlazan*) and are crossing . . .'
[3] [Ecclesiasticus xxxi, 9.]

they disturb the Bride in this estate, for they are already
stilled, as has been explained above; this desire belongs rather
to those who are progressing, and to those who have pro-
gressed, than to those who are now perfect, for over these
last the passions and motions have little or no empire.

STANZA XXXII

**Hide thyself, dearest one,   And look with thy face upon the
mountains,**
**And desire not to speak,   But look upon her companions[1] who
travels mid strange islands.**

Exposition

After the Spouse and the Bride have in the last stanzas re-
strained and enjoined silence upon the passions and faculties
of the soul, both sensual and spiritual, which might perturb
it, the Bride returns in this stanza to rejoice in her Beloved
with inward recollection of her soul, where He is united with
her in love, where secretly, in a glorious[2] manner,[3] He rejoices in her, and where the things that she experiences in
this recollection of her marriage with her Beloved are so lofty
and so delectable that she cannot describe them nor yet would
desire to do so; for they are such things as those whereof
Isaias says: *Secretum meum mihi, secretum meum mihi.*[4] And
thus to herself alone she possesses Him, and alone understands
Him, and alone rejoices in Him, and is glad to be alone with
Him;[5] wherefore her desire is that He may be deeply hidden
and greatly exalted and far removed[6] from all outward communication. In this respect she is like the merchant with the

---

[1] G, V: 'countries.' See p. 47, n. 32.
[2] [*Lit.*, 'great.']
[3] [*Lit.*, 'in great manner.'] Bj: 'in great love.'
[4] Isaias xxiv, 16.
[5] [*Lit.*, 'is glad that it is alone' (*sc.*, that she does these things).]
[6] Gr: 'and exalted and withdrawn.'

pearl, or, to express it better, like the man who, finding the
treasure hidden in the field, went and hid it with joy[7] and possessed it. It is this that the same soul now entreats of the
Spouse in this stanza, wherein with this desire she begs of
Him four things. First, that He will be pleased to have communion with her most inwardly in the hidden part of her soul.
Secondly, that He will illumine[8] her faculties with the glory
and greatness of His Divinity. Thirdly, that He will deal with
her so sublimely that none may wish or be able to describe
it, and that the outward and sensual part of her soul may
be unable to apprehend it. And fourthly, she begs Him to
fall in love with the many virtues that He has placed in her,
now that she is going to Him and soaring aloft through high
and noble knowledge of the Divinity, and through excesses
of love most strange and singular, surpassing such as she habitually experiences.

Hide thyself, dearest one,[9]

2. As though she were to say: Dear Spouse of mine, withdraw Thee into the inmost part of my soul, communicating
Thyself to it after a secret fashion, and manifesting[10] to it
Thy hidden wonders, which are far removed from all mortal eyes.

And look with thy face upon the mountains,

3. The face of God is His Divinity and the mountains are
the faculties of the soul—memory, understanding and will.
Thus it is as though she were to say: Assail my understanding
with Thy Divinity, giving it Divine intelligence; and my will,
giving and communicating to it Divine love; and my memory, with Divine possession of glory. Herein the soul prays
Him for all that for which she may pray, since[11] she is not

---

[7] Lch: 'went and bought it secretly.'

[8] [*Lit.*, 'assail.']

[9] [*Carillo*. On this word, see Dámaso Alonso, *La Poesía de San
Juan de la Cruz,* Madrid, 1942, p. 136.]

[10] Bj: 'communicating.'

[11] Bj has the emendation: 'This is the greatest communication
that she can pray for, since . . .' etc.

now being content with knowledge and communication of God from behind, such as God granted to Moses—that is, with a knowledge of Him by His effects and works;[12] but she desires to see the face of God, which is essential communication of His Divinity, without any kind of intermediary in the soul, through certain contact thereof with the Divinity. This is a thing far removed from all sense and accidents, inasmuch as it is the touch of pure substances—that is, of the soul[13] and the Divinity. Wherefore she says next:

And desire not to speak,

4. That is to say: And desire not to speak as Thou didst aforetime, when the communications that Thou workedst in me were such that Thou didst utter them to the outward senses, since they concerned things whereof these were capable, and were not so sublime and profound that the senses could not attain to them. But now let them be so sublime and so substantial, and so intimate, that Thou mayest not utter them to the outward senses, and that these may not be capable thereof. For substance cannot be communicated in the senses, and thus a thing that can be apprehended by sense is not essentially God. The soul, then, desiring here this essential communication of God, which is not apprehended by sense, prays Him that it may be of such a kind that He may not utter it to the senses. She says, then: Desire not to communicate Thyself in this way, which is so unworthy and so exterior that it can be communicated by sense and by speech.

But look upon her companions[14]

5. We have already said that for God to look is for Him to love; those whom the Bride here calls companions are the multitude of virtues and gifts and perfections and spiritual riches of the soul. It is thus as though she were to say: But rather do Thou turn inward, Dearest One, and fall in love with the companions—namely, the virtues and perfections which Thou hast set in my soul: so that, having come to love

---

[12] [Exodus xxxiii, 22–3.]

[13] Md adds: 'by means of the faculties aforementioned.'

[14] G, Lch, V, Md: 'countries.' See p. 47, n. 32, above.

my soul through them, Thou mayest hide Thyself in her and remain in her; for in truth, although they be Thine, yet, since Thou hast given them to her, they are hers[15] likewise.

Who travels mid strange islands.

6. That is, my soul, which travels to Thee through strange knowledge of Thee, and by ways and in manners that are strange, and far removed from all the senses, and from common natural knowledge. This is as though she were to say: Since my soul travels to Thee through strange knowledge that is far removed from the senses, do Thou communicate Thyself to her likewise after so inward and sublime a manner that Thy communication may be far removed from them all.

STANZA XXXIII

Spouse[1]

**The little white dove   Has returned to the ark with the bough,
And now the turtle-dove   Has found the mate of her desire on
the green banks.**

Exposition

In this stanza it is the Spouse Who speaks, singing of the purity which the Bride now has in this estate, and of the riches and the prize which she has won, through having prepared herself and laboured to come to Him. Likewise He sings of the great happiness which she has experienced in finding her Spouse in this union, and He describes the fulfilment of her desires and the delight and refreshment which she possesses

---

[15] The Saint adds 'hers,' which word is found also in G, V, Vd, Gr, Br.
[1] This word, inserted by the Saint, is only found in the Sanlúcar Codex.

in Him now that the labours and trials of her life and of the time past are over. He says, then:

The little white dove

2. He calls the soul a little white dove by reason of the whiteness and cleanness which it has received of the grace that it has found in God. This little dove, He says,

Has returned to the ark with the bough,

3. Here He makes a comparison between the soul and the dove from the ark of Noe, taking that coming and going of the dove to and from the ark as a figure of that which has come to pass in the soul in this case.[2] For, even as the dove that left the ark of Noe returned to it with an olive branch in its beak,[3] as a sign of the mercy of God in commanding the waters to withdraw from the earth, which was overwhelmed by the flood,[4] even so the soul in such case, which left the ark of God's Omnipotence when He created it, has flown over the waters of the flood of the sins, imperfections and afflictions and trials of this life, and returns to the ark, which is the bosom of its Creator, with the olive branch, which is the clemency and mercy that God has shown it in having brought it to so high an estate of perfection and having made the waters of sin to withdraw from the earth of the soul and given it victory,[5] notwithstanding all the war and assault of its enemies, which had ever striven to prevent this; wherefore the branch signifies victory over its enemies and also the reward of its merits. And thus not only does the little dove now return to the ark of its God, white and clean, even as it left that ark at its creation, but it also brings something with it—namely, the branch, which is the reward and the peace that it has obtained through its victory.

[2] Lch: 'in this estate.'
[3] Bz, Bj: 'in its mouth.'
[4] Genesis viii, 11.
[5] Bj: 'and gained victory.' Bz abbreviates: 'and having gained the victory in the whole war . . .' etc.

And now the turtle-dove   Has found the mate of her desire on the green banks.

4. He also calls the soul here a turtle-dove, because in this matter it has been like the little turtle-dove when it found the mate that it desired. And that this may be the better understood, it is to be known that it is written of the turtle-dove that when it finds not its mate[6] it neither sits upon the green bough, nor drinks of clear or cold water, nor settles beneath the shade, nor joins with other birds;[7] but when it is united with its Spouse it then has fruition of all this. All these properties are applicable to the soul; for, ere it reaches this spiritual union with its Beloved it must needs desire to be devoid of all delight (that is, not to sit upon the green bough), and all honour and glory of the world, and pleasure (which is not to drink the clear and cold water), and all refreshment and favour of the world (which is not to seek protection in the shade), desiring to rest in naught and sighing ever for solitude from all things until it find its Spouse.

5. And since the soul in such case, ere it reached this estate, went about in this way seeking its Beloved, like the turtle-dove, and neither finding nor desiring to find consolation or refreshment save only in Him, the same Spouse sings here of the end of the fatigues of the Bride and the fulfilment of her desires, saying that at last the turtle-dove has found the mate of her desire upon the green banks. This is to say that she now sits upon the green bough, delighting in her Beloved; and that she now drinks the clear water of sublime contemplation and wisdom of God, water which is cold, signifying the refreshment that she has in Him; and likewise settles beneath the shadow of His protection and favour, which she had so greatly desired, wherein she is comforted and refreshed after

---

[6] So Lch. The other versions (including the Sanlúcar Codex) read: 'consort.'

[7] This last phrase is the Saint's addition, found only in the Sanlúcar Codex. [The sentence as a whole, a paraphrase of a well-known Spanish ballad, 'Fontefrida,' is evidence that he was acquainted with this traditional form of art. See J. M. de Cossío, in *Boletín de la Biblioteca Menéndez Pelayo*, XI, 267, and Dámaso Alonso, *La Poesía de San Juan de la Cruz*, Madrid, 1942, p. 106.]

a delectable and Divine manner, even as she declares joyously in the Songs, saying: *Sub umbra illius, quem desideraveram sedi, et fructus ejus dulcis gutturi meo.*[8] Which is to say: I sat down under the shadow of Him that I had desired, and His fruit is sweet to my palate.

STANZA XXXIV

In solitude she lived   And in solitude now has built her nest, And in solitude her dear one alone guides her,   Who likewise in solitude was wounded by love.[1]

Exposition

Continuing, the Spouse describes the contentment which He derives from the solitude experienced by the soul before she reached this union, and that which He has from the solitude with respect to all fatigues and trials and hindrances which now is hers, since she has made a tranquil and delectable abode in her Beloved, and is free and far withdrawn from all things and the trouble which they bring. Likewise He manifests His pleasure that this solitude which the soul now possesses should have been a means whereby she could indeed be guided and moved by the Spouse, which could not be aforetime, since she had not then made her nest in solitude—that is, had not attained a habit of perfection and tranquillity[2] of solitude whereby she is now moved and guided to the Divine things of the Spirit of God. He says not only that He now guides her in this solitude, but that[3] He does it alone,

[8] Canticles ii, 3.
[1] [On this stanza, see K. Vossler, *La Poesía de la sóledad en España,* Buenos Aires, 1946, pp. 250–2.]
[2] 'Tranquillity' (*quietud*) is the Saint's emendation for 'virtue' (*virtud*), which was the word originally used in the Sanlúcar Codex and is in all the others, except Gr. Br and Md also have 'virtue.'
[3] Lch omits all that stands between 'tranquillity of solitude' and 'but that.'

communicating Himself to her without intermediaries—either angels, or men, or images, or forms;[4] and that, even as she has fallen in love with Him, so is He wounded with love for her in this solitude and liberty of spirit which comes to her through the solitude aforementioned. For this solitude He greatly loves, and thus says:

In solitude she lived

2. The little turtle-dove aforementioned, which is the soul, lived in solitude before it found the Beloved in this estate of union. For the soul that desires God is in no wise comforted or satisfied by any company soever; all things make and cause within it ever greater solitude until it find Him.

And in solitude now has built her nest,

3. The solitude wherein the soul lived aforetime was its desire to be without all the blessings of the world, for the sake of its Spouse, even as we have said of the turtle-dove. It strove to become perfect, and to acquire perfect solitude, wherein the soul attains to union with the Word, and consequently to all refreshment and rest. It is this that is signified by the nest which is here spoken of—namely, rest and repose. And it is thus as though He were to say: In that solitude wherein aforetime she lived, working therein with labour and anguish, because she was not perfect, she has now set her rest and refreshment, since she has now acquired this solitude perfectly in God. Of this says David, speaking spiritually: *Etenim passer invenit sibi domum, et turtur nidum ubi reponat pullos suos.*[5] Which signifies: The bird[6] has indeed found herself a house, and the turtle-dove a nest wherein to rear her young. That is, an abode in God where she may satisfy her desires and faculties.

---

4 Md adds: 'apart from the kinds of knowledge (*las inteligencias*) mentioned in the second line of stanza thirty-three' (in this edition stanza thirty-two).

5 Psalm lxxxiii, 4 [A.V., lxxxiv, 3]. G, Br, Vd, Lch also give this text.

6 See p. 113, n. 54, above.

And in solitude . . . guides her,

4. This signifies: In that solitude which the soul has with respect to all things and wherein she is alone with God, He guides and moves her and raises her to Divine things—that is to say, He raises her understanding to Divine intelligence, since it is now alone and stripped of all other strange and contradictory intelligence; and He moves her will freely to the love of God, for it is now alone and free from other affections; and He fills her memory with Divine knowledge, since it, too, is now alone and emptied of other imaginings and fancies. For, as soon as the soul disencumbers these faculties and voids them of all lower things and of all attachment[7] to higher things, leaving them in solitude, with naught else, God at once uses them for the invisible and Divine, and it is God Who guides the soul in this solitude, even as Saint Paul says concerning the perfect: *Qui spiritu Dei aguntur*, etc.[8] That is: They are moved by the Spirit of God. Which is the same as saying: In solitude there guides her . . .

. . . her dear one alone

5. This signifies that not only does He guide her in her solitude, but that it is He Himself alone Who works in her, using no other intermediary. For it is the characteristic of this union of the soul with God in the Spiritual Marriage that God works in her and communicates Himself to her alone, not now by means of angels, as aforetime, neither by means of her natural ability. For the outward and inward senses, and all creatures, and even the soul herself, have very little to do with the receiving of these great and supernatural favours which God grants in this estate: they belong not to the ability and natural working and diligence of the soul—He alone works them in her.[9] And the reason for this is that He finds

---

[7] [*propiedad*, 'love of possession,' 'sense of ownership'; cf. Vol. III; *The Complete Works of St. John of the Cross*, translated and edited by E. Allison Peers; The Newman Press; Westminster, Maryland, p. 202, n. 7.]

[8] Romans viii, 14.

[9] Md adds: 'and with her.'

her alone, as has been said, and thus He will give her no other company, nor will He have her profit by any other, or trust any other, save Himself only. And it is also fitting that, since the soul has now left all things and passed beyond all intermediaries, soaring above them all to God, God Himself should be her guide and the intermediary to Himself. Now that the soul has soared above everything, and is withdrawn from everything, none of these things is now of any profit or service to her that she may soar higher, save the Word Himself, which is the Spouse. And He is so greatly enamoured of Her that it is He alone Who desires to work these things. And so He next says:

Who likewise in solitude was wounded by love.

6. For, now that the soul has remained alone and is withdrawn from all things through love of Him,[10] He becomes greatly enamoured of her in that solitude, even as she also became enamoured of Him in solitude, being wounded within herself by love for Him; and thus He will not leave her alone, but, being in His turn wounded with love for her, through the solitude which she is experiencing because of Him, He alone guides her alone, causing her to surrender to Him, and fulfilling her desires, which He would not do in her had He not found her in solitude. Wherefore the same Spouse says of the soul through the Prophet Osee: *Ducam illam in solitudinem, et loquar ad cor eius.*[11] Which signifies: I will guide her into solitude and will there speak to her heart. He says that He will speak to her heart, meaning that He will give Himself to her, for to speak to the heart is to satisfy the heart, which is not satisfied with less than God.

[10] In the margin the Saint has written here: 'How, although the soul rejoices in company, it desires (*apetece*) solitude.'
[11] Osee ii, 14.

STANZA XXXV

Bride[1]

Let us rejoice, Beloved,   And let us go to see ourselves in thy beauty,
To the mountain or the hill where flows the pure water;   Let us enter farther into the thicket.

Exposition

Now that the perfect union of love is made between the soul and God, the soul desires to employ and exercise herself in the properties which pertain to love, and thus it is she who speaks in this stanza with the Spouse, praying Him for three things which are proper to love. First, she desires to receive the joy and sweetness of love, and for this she prays Him when she says: 'Let us rejoice, Beloved.' The second desire is that she may become like to the Beloved, and for this she prays Him when she says: 'Let us go to see ourselves in Thy beauty.' And the third desire is to delve into the things and secrets of the same Beloved, and to know them, and for this she prays Him when she says: 'Let us enter farther into the thicket.' There follows the line:

Let us rejoice, Beloved,

2. That is to say, in the communication of the sweetness of love, not only in that which we already have in the habitual joining together and union of us both, but in that which overflows in the exercise of affective and actual love, whether interiorly with the will in acts of affection, or exteriorly, in the performance of works belonging to the service of the Beloved. For, as we have said, love, where it has been firmly set, has this quality, that it desires ever to continue tasting its joys

---

[1] The Saint himself inserts this word, which is not copied by Br, Md or the MSS.

and sweetnesses, which are the exercise of loving interiorly and exteriorly, as we have said. All this the soul does that she may become more like to the Beloved, and thus she says next:

And let us go to see ourselves in thy beauty,

3. Which signifies: Let us so act that, by means of this exercise of love aforementioned, we may come to see ourselves in Thy beauty: that is, that we may be alike in beauty, and that Thy beauty may be such that, when one of us looks at the other, each may be like to Thee in Thy beauty, and may see himself in Thy beauty,[2] which will be the transforming of me in Thy beauty; and thus I shall see Thee in Thy beauty and Thou wilt see me in Thy beauty; and Thou wilt see Thyself in me in Thy beauty, and I shall see myself in Thee in Thy beauty; so that thus[3] I may be like to Thee in Thy beauty and Thou mayest be like to me in Thy beauty, and my beauty may be Thy beauty, and Thy beauty my beauty; and I shall be Thou in Thy beauty and Thou wilt be I in Thy beauty, because Thy beauty itself will be my beauty.[4] This is the adoption of the sons of God, who will truly say to God that which the Son Himself said through Saint John to the Eternal Father, in these words: *Omnia mea tua sunt, et tua mea sunt.*[5] Which signifies: Father, all My things are Thine and Thy things are Mine. He by essence, being the Son by nature; we by participation, being sons by adoption. And thus He spake, not only for Himself, Who is the Head, but for His whole mystical body, which is the Church.

To the mountain or the hill

4. This means to the knowledge of the morning,[6] as theo-

---

[2] This clause is omitted in G, Gr, V, Vd, Br.

[3] 'Thus' is added by the Saint, and not copied in Br, Md or the MSS.

[4] Bz, Bj, confused by this playing upon words, omit several phrases in the passage. 8,654 omits only 'and Thou mayest be like to me in Thy beauty.'

[5] St. John xvii, 10.

[6] Md adds: 'that is, to the knowledge like to that of the morning.' Bj reads: 'of matrimony' for 'of the morning.'

logians say, which is knowledge in the Divine Word, Who is here understood by the mountain; because the Word[7] is the loftiest essential Wisdom of God. Or let us go to the knowledge of the evening, which is the wisdom of God in His creatures and works and wondrous ordinances; this is here signified by the hill, which is lower than the mountain. When the soul, then, says: 'Let us go to the mountain to see ourselves in Thy beauty,' she means: Make me like to the beauty of Divine Wisdom, and inform me therewith; which Wisdom, as we say, is the Son of God. And when she says: 'Or let us go to the hill,' she is praying to be informed likewise by His Wisdom and His mysteries in His creatures and works, which also is beauty wherein the soul desires to see herself enlightened. The soul cannot see herself in the beauty of God and he made like to Him therein, save by being transformed in the Wisdom of God, wherein that which is above is seen and possessed;[8] wherefore she desires to go to the mountain or to the hill. *Vadam ad montem myrrhæ et ad collem thuris.*[9]

Where flows the pure water;

5. This signifies: Where the knowledge and wisdom of God, which here she calls pure water, are given to the understanding, clean and free from accidents and fancies, and clear from the darkness of ignorance. The soul has ever this desire to understand the Divine truths in a clear and pure way; and the more she loves, the more deeply she desires to penetrate them; wherefore she makes her third request, saying:

Let us enter farther into the thicket.

6. Into the thicket of Thy marvellous works and profound judgments, the multitude whereof[10] is so great, and of such great variety, that it may be called a thicket. For therein is abundant wisdom, so full of mysteries that it can be called

---

[7] Md: 'the Divine Word.'

[8] Md adds: 'as far as is possible in this life.'

[9] The quotation [Canticles iv, 6] is added by the Saint, and developed in the second redaction. [See p. 458, below.]

[10] 'That the multitude' is thus emended by the Saint; the emendation is followed by Lch, 8,654, G, V, Vd, Br, Md.

not only thick, but even curdled, according as David says in these words: *Mons Dei, mons pinguis, mons coagulatus, mons pinguis.*[11] Which is to say: The mountain of God is a mountain thick and a mountain curdled. And this thicket of wisdom and knowledge of God is so profound and vast that, for all that the soul may know thereof, she can ever enter farther still, so vast is it, and so incomprehensible are its riches, according as Saint Paul exclaims, saying: 'O the height of the riches of wisdom and knowledge of God! How incomprehensible are His judgments and incomprehensible His ways!'[12]

7. But the soul desires to enter this thicket and incomprehensibility of judgments and ways, because she is dying with desire to enter very far into the knowledge of them; for to have that knowledge is a priceless delight, exceeding all that can be felt. Wherefore David, speaking of their sweetness, said thus: *Judicia Domini vera, justificata in semetipsa, desiderabilia super aurum, et lapidem pretiosum multum, dulciora super mel et favum; nam et servus tuus dilexit ea.*[13] Which signifies: The judgments of God are true and have justice in themselves; they are more to be desired and are more coveted[14] than gold and than the precious stone of great worth; and they are sweet above honey and the honeycomb, so much so, that Thy servant loved and kept them. Wherefore the soul greatly desires to be immersed in these judgments and to have a deeper knowledge of them;[15] and to that end it would be a great consolation and joy to her to pass through all the afflictions and trials of the world, and through all else that might be a means thereto, howsoever difficult and grievous it might be.

8. And thus the thicket may be understood in this line as signifying trials and tribulations, wherein the soul also desires to enter when she says: 'Let us enter farther into the thicket.' That is to say, into trials and afflictions, insomuch as they

11 Psalm lxvii, 16 [A.V., lxviii, 16].
12 Romans xi, 33.
13 Psalm xviii, 11 [A.V., xix, 9–11].
14 Lch: 'they are more wondrous and to be coveted.'
15 *Fulcite me floribus*, adds the Saint in the margin of the Sanlúcar Codex.

are a means of entrance into the thicket of the delectable wisdom of God; for the purest suffering causes and entails the purest knowledge, and, in consequence, the purest and loftiest joy which comes from deepest penetration. So, not content with any manner of suffering, the soul says: 'Let us enter farther into the thicket.' Wherefore Job, desiring this suffering, said: *Quis det ut veniat petitio mea, et quod expecto, tribuat mihi Deus? Et qui coepit, ipse me conterat, solvat manum suam, et succidat me? Et hæc mihi sit consolatio, ut affligens me dolore, non parcat mihi?*[16] Which signifies: Who will grant that my petition may be fulfilled and that God may give me that for which I hope, and that He that began me may destroy[17] me and let loose His hand and cut me off, and that I may have this consolation, that He will afflict me with grief and will not pardon or relieve me?

9. Oh, that it might be perfectly understood how the soul cannot attain to the thicket of the wisdom and riches of God, save by entering into the thicket of many kinds of suffering and by setting thereupon its consolation and desire! And how the soul that of a truth desires wisdom first desires truly to enter farther into the thicket of the Cross, which is the road of life, which few enter![18] For the desire to enter into the thicket of wisdom and riches and favours of God comes to all; but the desire to enter into the thicket of trials and pains, for the sake of the Son of God, comes to few. Thus many would fain see themselves at the end, without passing along the road and way thereto.

[16] Job vi, 8–10.
[17] [*Desmenuzar*, 'break into small pieces.']
[18] In the margin the Saint adds: *Ut possitis compreheneder cum omnibus Sanctis, quæ sit longitudo et latitudo, altum et profundum.* In the second redaction he develops this text, without, however, reproducing it in Latin. [See p. 459, below.]

STANZA XXXVI

And then we shall go forth   To the lofty caverns of the rock
    which are well hidden,
And there shall we enter   And taste the new wine of the
    pomegranates.

Exposition

One of the causes which move the soul most to desire to enter
into this thicket of the wisdom of God and to have a knowledge of suffering[1] very deeply in His judgments, as we have
said, is that it may be able to pass on thence to a union of
its understanding and to a knowledge of the high mysteries
of the Incarnation of the Word, as of the soul's highest and
most delectable wisdom; to which clear knowledge it comes
not without having first entered into the thicket of knowledge
and experience of trials whereof we have spoken. And thus
the Bride in this stanza says that, after having entered farther
into this wisdom and these trials, they will proceed farther
still to a knowledge of the sublime mysteries of God and man,
which are sublimest in wisdom, and are hidden in God; and
that there they will enter, and the soul will be engulfed and
absorbed in them, and that she and the Spouse will rejoice
and have pleasure in the sweetness which is caused by the
knowledge of them, and of the virtues and attributes of God
which are revealed through them in God, such as justice,
mercy, wisdom, etc.

And then we shall go forth   To the lofty caverns of the
    rock . . .

2. The rock of which she here speaks is Christ, according
as Saint Paul says to the Corinthians: *Petra autem erat*

---

[1] All other versions read: 'and to suffer.' In the Sanlúcar Codex
the Saint makes the marginal addition to read as in the text.

Christus.[2] The lofty caverns are the lofty and high and deep mysteries in the wisdom of God which are in Christ, concerning the hypostatical union of human nature with the Divine Word, and the correspondence to this which is in the union of men in God, and in the agreement which there is between the justice and mercy of God as to the salvation of the human race in the manifestation of His judgments. These judgments are so high and so deep that they are very properly called lofty caverns: lofty, because of the height of their mysteries; caverns, because of the depth and profundity of their wisdom. For, even as caverns are profound and have many recesses, even so each of the mysteries that are in Christ is most profound in wisdom, and has many recesses, which are His secret judgments of predestination and foreknowledge with respect to the sons of men.[3] Wherefore she says next:

. . . which are well hidden,

3. So much so that, despite all the mysteries and wonders which have been discovered by holy doctors and understood by holy souls in this estate of life, there has remained much more to be said, and even to be understood, and thus there are great depths to be fathomed in Christ. For He is like an abundant mine with many recesses containing treasures, of which, for all that men try to fathom them, the end and bottom is never reached; rather in each recess men continue to find new veins of new riches on all sides, as Saint Paul said of Christ Himself in these words: *In quo sunt omnes thesauri sapientiæ et scientiæ Dei, absconditi*.[4] Which signifies: In Christ dwell hidden all the treasures and wisdom of God, whereinto the soul cannot enter and whereto it cannot attain, unless first, as we have said, it enter and pass into the thicket of exterior and interior suffering; and until God has granted it many other favours, both to the intellect and to the senses, and until many spiritual exercises have been first performed

---

[2] 1 Corinthians x, 4.

[3] Lch: 'of predestination and by essence in the eyes (*sic*) of men.'

[4] Colossians ii, 3.

by it. For all these things are inferior,[5] and are preparations
for coming to the lofty caverns of the knowledge of the mysteries of Christ, which is the loftiest wisdom attainable in this
life. Wherefore, when Moses prayed God to show him His
glory, He answered him that he would be unable to see it
in this life, but that He would show him 'all good'[6]—all, that
is, that in this life is possible. And it came to pass that, after
seeing him in the cleft of the rock, which is Christ, as we
have said, He showed him His back—that is, He gave him
a knowledge of the mysteries of His works, especially those
of the Incarnation of His Son.

4. Into these clefts, then, the soul desires earnestly to enter,
that it may be wholly absorbed[7] and inebriated and transformed in the love of the knowledge thereof, hiding itself in
the bosom of its Beloved. And to these clefts He invites it
in the Songs, saying: *Surge, propera, amica mea, speciosa
mea, et veni: columba mea in foraminibus petræ, in caverna
maceriæ.*[8] Which is to say: Arise and make haste, My friend,
My fair one, and come into the clefts of the rock and into
the cavern of the enclosure. These clefts are the caverns which
we are describing, whereof the Bride here says:

And there shall we enter

5. There shall we enter—that is, into that knowledge of Divine mysteries. She says not: 'I shall enter alone,' but 'We
shall enter'—that is, she and the Beloved—in order to explain
that it is not she who does this, but the Spouse with her; and
besides this, inasmuch as God and the soul are already united
in one in this estate of the Spiritual Marriage whereof we
are speaking, the soul does no work by itself without God.
And this which she says 'There shall we enter' is as much
as to say: There shall we be transformed in the transformation
of new knowledge and new acts and communications of love.
For, although it is true that the soul, when she says this,

[5] Lch: 'are very old.'
[6] Exodus xxxiii, 19.
[7] Bz, Bj: 'hidden.'
[8] Canticles ii, 13–14.

is already transformed by reason of the estate aforementioned, though, as we have said, in this wisdom there is naught added to her,[9] it does not therefore follow that she cannot in this estate have new enlightenments and transformations of new kinds of knowledge and Divine light. Indeed she has very frequent illuminations of new mysteries, communicated to her by God in the communication which is ever made between Him and the soul. And this communication He makes to her in Himself, and she enters into Him as it were afresh, according to the knowledge of those mysteries which she knows in Him; and in that knowledge she loves Him afresh most intimately and sublimely, being transformed into Him according to those new kinds of knowledge; and the sweetness and delight, which at that time she receives afresh, are altogether ineffable. Of these she speaks in the line following:

And taste the new wine of the pomegranates.

6. The pomegranates signify the Divine mysteries of Christ, and the lofty judgments of God, and the virtues and attributes which are known in God through the knowledge of these.[10] For, as the pomegranate has many small seeds, all of which have been born and are nourished in that one round orb,[11] so each virtue and attribute and mystery and judgment of God contains within itself a great multitude of seeds, which are the wondrous ordinances and effects of God, and are contained and nourished in the round or spherical orb[12] which is the virtue and mystery that belongs to those effects. And we refer here to the spherical or circular shape of the pomegranate, because by each pomegranate we here understand one virtue and attribute of God, which attribute or virtue of God is God Himself, which is denoted by the spherical or circular figure, because it has no beginning or end.[13]

[9] The parenthesis 'though . . . to her' is an addition of the Saint's and is found neither in Br, Md nor in the MSS.

[10] Md: 'of these mysteries.'

[11] [seno. The same word is rendered 'recess,' above.]

[12] [seno.]

[13] *Venter ejus eburneus, distinctus saphiris*—a marginal note by the Saint.

7. The new wine of these pomegranates, which the Bride says that they will taste, is the fruition which, in so far as may be in this estate, the soul receives in the knowledge and understanding of them, and the delight of the love of God which she tastes in them. And even as from many pomegranate seeds there comes but one new wine, even so, from all these wonders and grandeurs of God which are known by the soul, there comes forth and overflows for her one fruition and one delight of love alone, which she offers at once to God with great tenderness of the will. This in the Divine Songs she promised to the Spouse, if He granted her these kinds of sublime knowledge, saying: *Ibi me docebis, et dabo tibi poculum ex vino condito, et mustum malorum granatorum meorum.*[14] Which signifies: There Thou shalt teach me, and I will give Thee to drink of spiced wine and the new wine of my pomegranates. She calls them hers, although they are God's, since He has given them to her,[15] and she returns them to God Himself as though they were her own, and this she denotes when she says: 'We will taste the new wine of the pomegranates.' For as He tastes it, He gives it to her to taste, and, as she tastes it, she gives it to Him to taste, so that they both taste of it together.

[14] Canticles viii, 2.
[15] Vd, Br have: 'Since He has found them.'

STANZA XXXVII

**There wouldst thou show me   That which my soul desired,[1]
And there at once, my life, wouldst thou give me   That which
thou gavest me the other day.**

Exposition

The end for which the soul desired to enter those caverns
aforementioned was that she might reach (at least in so far as
this estate of life permits) the consummation of that which
she had ever desired, which is the complete and perfect love
communicated in this communication, for love is the end of
all;[2] and likewise that she might perfectly attain, after a spiritual manner, the uprightness[3] and cleanness of the estate of
original justness. And thus in this stanza she says two things.
The first is that there He would show her (namely, in that
transformation of knowledge) that which her soul desired in
all its acts and intentions,[4] which is to show her how to love
her Spouse perfectly as He loves Himself, together with the
other things which she expounds in the stanza following. The
second is that there, too, He would give her the cleanness and
purity which He gave her[5] in the original estate, or on the
day of her baptism, cleansing her completely from all her imperfections and darkness as she was cleansed then.[6]

[1] [The Spanish verb used here, *pretender*, means 'to desire' in
the sense of 'to aspire to, aim at' rather than in that of 'to wish
for, yearn for,' as elsewhere in the poem.]
[2] This last phrase is an addition made by the Saint and copied
nowhere.
[3] [*Lit.*, 'the right.'] Md: 'the rectitude.'
[4] Lch: 'in all its interior acts.'
[5] Md adds: 'in her first fathers.'
[6] The Saint adds in the margin the word *calculum*, introducing
an idea which he develops in the second redaction (see p. 472,
below).

There wouldst thou show me   That which my soul desired,[7]

2. This desire[8] is the equality of love which the soul ever desires,[9] both naturally and supernaturally, because the lover[10] cannot be satisfied if he feels not that he loves as much as he is loved. And, as the soul sees the truth of the vastness of the love wherewith God loves her, she desires not to love Him less[11] sublimely and perfectly, to which end she desires present transformation, because the soul cannot reach this equality and completeness of love save by the total transformation of her will in that of God, wherein the two wills are united after such manner that they become one. And thus there is equality of love,[12] for the will of the soul that is converted into the will of God is then wholly the will of God,[13] and the will of the soul is not lost but becomes the will of God. And thus the soul loves God with the will of God, which is also her own will; and thus she will love Him even as much as she is loved by God, since she loves Him with the will of God Himself, in the same love wherewith He loves her, which is the Holy Spirit,[14] Who is given to the soul, even as the Apostle says in these words: *Gratia Dei diffusa est in cordibus nostris per Spiritum Sanctum qui datus est nobis.*[15] Which sig-

[7] The Saint adds in the margin this note, which he expounds with some fullness in the second redaction (see p. 470, below): 'Although it is true that glory consists in the understanding, the end of the soul is to love.'

[8] [*pretensión.*]

[9] [*desea.*]

[10] Md: 'This desire is the equality or union of love, because the lover . . .', etc.

[11] Md: '. . . the truth and vastness of the love wherewith God loves her, she would not, if she could, love Him less . . .', etc. 'Truth and vastness' is altered by the Saint, in the Sanlúcar Codex, to 'truth of the vastness,' and this alteration is followed by G, V, Vd, Br.

[12] Md adds: 'in the sense in which the Apostle said: *Vivo ego, jam non ego, vivit vero in me Christus;* and thus in this sense there is equality of love.'

[13] G, V, Vd, Br omit 'is then wholly the will of God.'

[14] Md: 'which is also her will, in the sense mentioned, wherefore she will love Him with the loftiest love inspired by the Holy Spirit.'

[15] Romans v, 5.

nifies: The grace of God is shed abroad in our hearts by the Holy Spirit Who is given unto us. And thus the soul loves God in the Holy Spirit together with the Holy Spirit, not by means of Him, as by an instrument, but together with Him, by reason of the transformation, as we shall forthwith explain, and He supplies that which she lacks by her having been transformed in love with Him. Wherefore she says not that He will give her, but that He . . .[16]

3. And it is to be noted that the soul says not here: 'There wouldst Thou give me,' but 'There wouldst Thou show me.' For, although it is true that He gives her His love, yet she says very properly that He shows her love, that is, He shows her how to love Him as He loves Himself; for God, loving us first, shows us how to love Him purely and completely, as He loves us. And since, in this transformation, God, in communicating Himself to the soul, shows her love which is total, generous and pure, wherewith most lovingly He communicates Himself to her wholly, transforming her in Himself, and thus giving her His own love, as we said, wherewith she may love Him, therefore He is really showing her how to love—that is, He is placing an instrument in her hands, telling her how to use it, continually using it with her,[17] and thus the soul now loves God as much as she is loved by Him.[18] I do not mean that she will love God as much as He loves Himself, for this cannot be, but as much as she is loved by Him; for since she will know God even as she is known of Him, as she says . . . ,[19] since the love[20] of them both is one love. Wherefore the soul is not only instructed in loving, but is even made mistress of

[16] The whole of this passage ('And thus the soul loves God . . . but that He') is a marginal and interlinear addition, made by the Saint, and found only in the Sanlúcar Codex. The binder's knife has cut off approximately the last line of it.

[17] This phrase ('and . . . her') is an addition made by the Saint and found in none of the editions or copies.

[18] Md: 'and thus the soul here loves God with sublimest love, like unto that wherewith she is loved by Him.'

[19] At the bottom of the page the Saint wrote the sentence 'I do not . . . as she says' which is here incorporated in the text. Again the binder's knife has cut off the last line of this interpolation.

[20] Over this word, but without erasing it, the Saint has written 'wisdom.'

loving, united with the Master Himself, and consequently satisfied. For she is not satisfied until she comes to this love, which is to love God perfectly, with the same love wherewith He loves Himself,[21] but this cannot come to pass perfectly in this life, although in the estate of perfection, which is that of the Spiritual Marriage whereof we are speaking, it may come to pass after some manner.

4. And in this manner of perfect love there at once results in the soul[22] an intimate and substantial jubilation in God, since it appears, and is true in fact, that the whole substance of the soul, bathed in glory, magnifies God; and she is conscious of an intimate sweetness, after the manner of fruition, which makes her overflow in praising, reverencing, prizing and magnifying God, with great joy and with complete absorption in love. And this comes not to pass save if God has given to the soul in the said estate of transformation great purity, such as was that of the estate of innocence or baptismal cleanness, which the soul says likewise here that the Spouse was to give her immediately in the same transformation of love, saying:

And there at once, my life, wouldst thou give me   That which thou gavest me the other day.[23]

5. By 'the other day' she denotes the estate of original justness, wherein God gave to her, in Adam, grace and innocence; or the day of baptism, wherein the soul received total cleanness and purity, which the soul says here in these lines that He would give her at once in the same union of love. And this is that which is understood by what she says in the last line, namely: 'That which thou gavest me the other day'; for, as we have said, to this purity and cleanness the soul attains in this estate of perfection.[24]

---

[21] Md adds: 'in the sense aforementioned, concerning the living of Saint Paul' (see p. 213, n. 12, above).

[22] The Saint inserts the words 'in fruition' as a marginal note.

[23] The Saint inserts the word 'predestination' as a marginal note, which he expounds in the second redaction.

[24] Gr, Lch, Md modify this paragraph thus: 'By "the other day" she denotes the state of original justness, and the day of bap-

STANZA XXXVIII[1]

**The breathing of the air,[2]   The song of the sweet philomel,
The grove and its beauty in the serene night,   With a flame that
consumes and gives no pain.**

Exposition

We expound two things for which the Bride prayed in the
last stanza. The first was that which her soul desired; the second was that[3] which He had given her the other day, whereof,
since we have just now described it, there is no need to treat
further. But the first petition, wherein she speaks of that
which her soul desired, is now described in this stanza. For it
is not only[4] the perfect love which we mentioned above, but
likewise, as we there observed, all that is contained in this
stanza, which is the same love and that which by these means
is communicated to the soul; and thus in this stanza she sets
down five things, which are all the things that she wished
above to make clear that she desired. The first is the breathing of the air, which is the love whereof we have spoken, and
that which she principally desires. The second is the song of

---

tism wherein the soul receives purity, which the soul says will be
given her in this union of love; for, as we have said, to this the
soul attains in this estate of perfection.' The same reading is found
in Bz, Bj, 8,654, save that for 'wherein the soul receives purity'
they read: 'wherein the soul receives innocence and purity.'

[1] [For the versions of §§ 2, 3, 4, 5, 9, 10, 11 of this chapter,
as given in the Granada group of MSS., see Appendix, pp. 515–20,
below.]

[2] Br misreads *del aire* ('of the air') as *deleite* ('delight').

[3] [*Lit.*, 'was to pray for that . . .']

[4] Lch, 8,654, Gr, Bj, Md vary these lines thus: 'The first, that
which her soul desired. And the other, that which He had given her
the other day. Of this second there is no need to treat further, for
we have already described it; but that which she desired in the first
she now describes in this stanza; for it is not only . . .', etc.

the philomel, which is jubilation in praise of God. The third is the grove and its beauty, which is the knowledge of the creatures and their order. The fourth is pure and sublime contemplation. And the fifth—namely, the flame that consumes and gives no pain—is almost contained in the first, for it is a flame of sweet transformation of love in the possession of all these things.

The breathing of the air,

2. This breathing of the air is a property[5] of the Holy Spirit, for which the soul here prays so that she may love God perfectly. She calls it the breathing of the air, because it is a most delicate touch and feeling of love which habitually in this estate is caused in the soul by the communication of the Holy Spirit. Breathing with that His Divine breath,[6] He raises the soul most sublimely, and informs her, that she may breathe in God the same breath of love that the Father breathes in the Son and the Son in the Father, which is the same Holy Spirit that They breathe into her in the said transformation. For it would not be a true transformation if the soul were not united and transformed in the Holy Spirit as well as in the other two Divine Persons, albeit not in a degree revealed and manifest, by reason of the lowliness and the condition of this life. And this is for the soul so high a glory, and so profound and sublime a delight, that it cannot be described by mortal tongue, nor can human understanding, as such, attain to any conception of it.

3. But the soul that is united and transformed[7] in God breathes in God into God the same Divine breath[8] that God, being in her, breathes into her in Himself, which, as I understand, was the meaning of Saint Paul when he said: *Quoniam autem estis filii Dei, misit Deus Spiritum Filii sui in corda vestra clamantem: Abba, Pater.*[9] Which signifies: Because you are sons of God, God sent the Spirit of His Son into your

[5] [*habilidad; lit.,* 'talent,' 'capacity,' 'accomplishment.']
[6] [*aspiración.* See p. 475, n. 1, below.]
[7] G, V, Vd, Br omit the words 'and transformed.'
[8] [*aspiración.*]
[9] Galatians iv, 6.

hearts, crying in prayer to the Father, which, in the perfect, is according to the manner described. And there is no need to wonder that the soul should be capable of aught so high; for, since God grants her the favour of attaining to being deiform and united in the Most Holy Trinity, wherein she becomes God by participation, how is it a thing incredible that she should perform her work of understanding, knowledge and love in the Trinity, together with It, like the Trinity Itself, by a mode of participation, which God effects in the soul herself?

4. And how this comes to pass cannot be known, nor is it possible to express it, save by describing how the Son of God obtained for us this high estate and merited for us this high office, as Saint John says, of being able to become sons of God.[10] And thus He prayed to the Father, as says the same Saint John, saying: *Pater, volo ut quos dedisti mihi, ut ubi sum ego, et illi sint mecum: ut videant claritatem meam quam dedisti mihi.*[11] Which signifies: Father, I will that they whom Thou hast given Me may be also with Me where I am, that they may see the brightness which Thou gavest Me. That is to say, that they may work in Us by participation the same work which I do by nature, which is the breathing of the Holy Spirit. And He says further: 'I pray not, Father, only for these that are present, but for them also who, through their teaching, shall believe in Me, that they may all be one and the same thing; so that as Thou, Father, art in Me, and I am in Thee, even so may they be one and the same thing in Us; and I have given them the brightness which Thou hast given Me, that they may be one and the same thing, as We are one and the same thing; I in them, and Thou in Me, that they may be perfect in one; that the world may know that Thou hast sent Me, and hast loved them, as Thou hast loved Me';[12] namely, by communicating to them the same love as to the Son, though not naturally, as to the Son, but, as we have said, by unity and transformation of love. It is not to be understood here that the Son means to say to the Father that the saints

10 St. John i, 12.
11 St. John xvii, 24.
12 St. John xvii, 20–3.

are to be one thing in essence and nature, as are the Father
and the Son; but rather that they are to be so by union of
love, as are the Father and the Son in unity of love. Wherefore
souls possess these same blessings by participation as He possesses by nature; for the which cause they are truly gods by
participation, equals of God and His companions.[13] Wherefore Saint Peter said: 'Grace and peace be complete and perfect in you in the knowledge of God and of Christ Jesus our
Lord, according as all things are given to us of His Divine virtue for life and godliness, through the knowledge of Him that
has called us with His own glory and virtue; whereby He has
given unto us most great and precious promises, that by these
things we may be made companions of the Divine nature';[14]
which is for the soul to have participation in God, performing
in Him, in company with Him, the work of the Most Holy
Trinity, after the manner whereof we have spoken, by reason
of the substantial union between the soul and God. And,
though this can be perfectly fulfilled only in the next life,
nevertheless, in this life, when the estate of perfection is
reached, a clear trace and taste of it are attained, after the
manner that we are describing, albeit, as we have said, this
cannot be expressed.

5. O souls created for these grandeurs and called thereto!
What do ye do? Wherein do ye occupy yourselves? Your
desires[15] are meannesses, and your possessions miseries. O
wretched blindness of the eyes of your souls, which are blind
to so great a light and deaf to so clear a voice, seeing not that
for so long as ye seek grandeurs and glories ye remain miserable and deprived of so many blessings, and have become
ignorant and unworthy! There follows the second thing for
which the soul prays, namely:

The song of the sweet philomel,

6. That which is born in the soul from that breathing of
the air is the song of the sweet philomel; for, even as the song

---

[13] [*por lo cual verdaderamente son dioses por participación,
iguales y compañeros suyos de Dios.*]

[14] 2 St. Peter i, 2–4.

[15] [*pretensiones,* the substantive of *pretender;* see p. 212, n. 1,
above.]

of the philomel, which is the nightingale,[16] is heard in the spring, when the cold and the rains of the winter are all past, and makes melody to the ear and gives refreshment to the spirit, even so in this present communication and transformation of love the Bride is protected and freed from all temporal changes and disturbances, and detached and purged from all the imperfections and penalties and mists[17] of her nature, and feels the new spring in her spirit, wherein she hears the sweet voice of the Spouse, Who is her sweet philomel, refreshing and renewing the substance of her soul, saying: 'Arise, make haste, My friend,[18] My dove, My beautiful one, and come; for the winter is now past, the rains are now over and gone far away, the flowers have now appeared in our land, the time of pruning is come, and the voice of the little turtle-dove has been heard in our land.'[19]

7. In this voice of the Spouse, Who speaks to the Bride in the inmost part of the soul, she perceives the end of her ills and the beginning of her blessings; and in the refreshment and protection and delectable feeling which this causes her she likewise lifts up her voice, as does the sweet philomel, in a new song to God, which unites with the song[20] that causes it. For He gives her a voice, that[21] she may sing to God with Him, for that is His aspiration[22] and desire. This is also the desire of the same Spouse in the Songs, when He speaks with her and says: 'Arise, make haste, My friend, and come, My dove, into the clefts of the rock and the cavern of the enclosure; show Me thy face, let thy voice sound in Mine ears, for thy voice is sweet and thy face comely.'[23] By the ears of God are here meant the desires of God, that we may praise

---

[16] [The Saint uses the poetical word *filomena* throughout, except here, where he explains it by the popular word *ruiseñor*, nightingale.]

[17] [*nieblas*, see p. 135, n. 32, above.]

[18] [See p. 446, n. 27, below.]

[19] Canticles ii, 10–12.

[20] [Or: 'with Him.']

[21] Br: 'For, if He gives her a voice, it is that . . .' Vd: 'For He gives her a voice so that . . .' G, V: 'For He gives her His voice, so that . . .'

[22] [*pretensión.*]

[23] Canticles ii, 13.

Him perfectly; for the voice for which He here asks the Bride is perfect praise and jubilation in God, the which voice, that it may be perfect, the Spouse bids the soul to send forth and cause to sound in the caverns of the rock, which are the loving knowledge of the mysteries of Christ, wherein we said above that the soul was united with Him. For, because in this union the soul rejoices and praises God together with God Himself, as we said in speaking of their love, it is perfect praise, for the soul, being in perfection, performs works which are perfect. And thus this voice is very sweet to God and to the soul, wherefore there follow the words: 'for thy voice is sweet.' That is to say, not only for thee, but also for Me; for, being at one with Me, thou dost raise thy voice as a sweet philomel in unison with Me.

The grove and its beauty

8. The third thing which the soul says that they are to show her there, by means of love, is the grove and its beauty. By the grove is here understood God, together with all the creatures that are in Him; for, even as all the trees and plants have their life and root in the grove, so the creatures, celestial and terrestrial alike, have their root and their life in God. This, then, the soul says: that she will show herself there to God inasmuch as He is life and being to all the creatures, for she knows that in Him are the beginning and the duration of them and for them, for without Him naught is given to the soul, nor does she believe herself able to know them in the spiritual way. The soul also greatly desires to see the beauty of the grove; this is the grace and wisdom and beauty which not only does each of the creatures have from God, but which they cause among themselves in their wise and ordered mutual correspondence, both of the higher creatures and of the lower; this is to know the creatures by the contemplative way, which is a thing of great delight, for it is to have knowledge concerning God. And thus follows the fourth thing:

In the serene night,

9. This night, wherein the soul desires to see these things, is contemplation; for contemplation is dark, and for that rea-

son is called by its other name, 'mystical theology,' which signifies secret and hidden wisdom of God, wherein without
noise of words and without the service and aid of any bodily
or spiritual sense, as in the silence and quiet of the night,
hidden by darkness from all that is of the senses and of nature, God teaches the soul after a most hidden and secret
manner, without her knowing how; this is that which some
spiritual men call 'understanding yet understanding not.' For
this is not done by the active understanding, as the philosophers call it, which works in forms and fancies and apprehensions of things; but it is done in the understanding inasmuch as it is possible[24] and passive, when, without receiving
such forms, it passively receives substantial knowledge, which
is given to it without any active office or work of its own.

10. And for this cause, not only is this contemplation
called night, but likewise serene. For, even as the night is
called serene because it is free from clouds and vapours in
the air, which are the things that disturb the serenity of the
night, so this night of contemplation is, to the sight of the understanding, empty of and withdrawn from all clouds[25] of
forms and fancies and particular knowledge which may enter
by the senses, and is clean likewise of all kinds of vapour from
the affections and desires. Wherefore contemplation is serene
night to the natural understanding and sense, even as the
philosopher teaches, saying that even as the ray of the sun is
dark and black to the eye of the bat,[26] even so the lofty and
bright things of God are dark to our understanding.

With a flame that consumes and gives no pain.

11. All the last-named things the soul begs the Spouse
here in this line to give her, together with a flame that consumes and gives no pain; by the which flame is here understood the love of God now perfect in the soul. For, in order
to be perfect, it must have these two properties, namely that

---

[24] Cf. p. 107, above.

[25] [nubes.]

[26] Metaph., Bk. I, Chap. ii. Cf. also St. Thomas, Summa, Pt. I,
q. xii, a. I. This Aristotelian principle the Saint adduces on various
occasions in his writings.

it may consume and transform the soul in God and that the enkindling and transformation of this flame in the soul may give no pain; and thus this flame is sweet love; for in the transformation of the soul therein there is conformity and satisfaction on either side, and therefore there is no pain caused by difference between the greater and the less, as there was before the soul attained to the capacity of this perfect love. For, now that the soul has attained, it is as completely transformed and brought into conformity with God as is the burning coal with the fire, without that smoking and flaming[27] that it gave forth before it was in that condition, and without the darkness and accidents proper to it which it had before the fire had entered into it completely. These properties of darkness, smoking and flaming[28] the soul habitually has, with a certain pain and fatigue as concerning the love of God, until it arrive at such a degree of perfection of love that the fire of love, fully and completely,[29] possesses it, and that gently,[30] without the pain of smoke and of the natural accidents and passions, but transformed into a gentle[31] flame, which has consumed it with respect to all this, and has changed it into God, wherein its movements and actions are now Divine.

12. It is in this flame that the Bride desires the Spouse to give her, as we have said, all the things to which she aspires, for she desires neither to possess them nor to esteem nor to enjoy them without the perfect and sweet[32] love of God.

27 G, V: 'gleaming.'
28 *Ibid.*
29 Br: 'amply.'
30 [Or 'sweetly': *suavemente.*]
31 [Or 'sweet': *suave;* as in 'sweet love' above.]
32 [*suave.*] G, V, Vd, Br omit 'and sweet.'

STANZA XXXIX[1]

**For none saw it,   Neither did Aminadab appear,
And there was a rest from the siege,   And the cavalry came
down at the sight of the waters.**

Exposition

In this last stanza the soul desires to describe the preparation
which is now hers for receiving the favours which are enjoyed
in this estate and for which she has prayed the Spouse. Without such preparation she could not receive these favours, nor
preserve them within her, and thus she sets before the Beloved four kinds of preparation or things which are convenient and sufficient for the favours aforementioned, in order to constrain Him the more to give them to her, as has
been said.[2] The first thing is that her soul is detached and far
withdrawn from all things; the second, that the devil has now
been conquered and put to flight; the third, that the passions
of the soul and the spiritual and natural desires[3] are now
held in bondage; the fourth, that the sensual part of the soul
has now been reformed and purified in conformity with the
spiritual part, so that not only is it not disturbed by the spirit,
but it is rather united[4] therewith, and has become a partaker
of its blessings. And this she says in the stanza aforementioned, in these words:

For none saw it,[5]

2. This is as though she were to say: My soul is now so
completely alone and withdrawn and detached from all cre-

---

[1] [For the version of §§ 3, 4, 5, 6 of this chapter in the Granada
group of MSS. see Appendix, pp. 519–20, below.]

[2] Bj, Bz omit the words 'in order . . . has been said.'

[3] G, V, Vd, Br omit the words 'and the . . . desires.'

[4] G, V, Vd, Br: 'is rather one.'

[5] G, V omit this line and the commentary on it.

ated things, both above and below, and has entered so far
into recollection with Thee, that none of the said things can
come within sight of it—that is, they cannot move it by their
sweetness to desire them, nor by their wretchedness and misery to dislike and be troubled by them; for my soul is so far
from them that they remain far behind and are lost from sight.
Not only so, but

Neither did Aminadab appear,

3. This Aminadab, in Divine Scripture, signifies the devil,
who is the adversary of the Bride-Soul, and who was ever
giving her battle and disturbing her with the innumerable
munitions of his temptations and snares, that she might not
enter into this fortress and secret place of interior recollection
with the Beloved. The soul placed herein is so greatly favoured and so strong in virtues and victories that the devil
dares not appear before her. Wherefore, since she is in the
favour of such an embrace, and since she has also gained a
perfect victory over the devil in the exercise of the virtues, so
that he has now been put to flight through the strength of her
virtues, he no longer appears before her. Thus the Bride well
says that neither did Aminadab appear.

And there was a rest from the siege,

4. By this siege she here understands[6] the passions and desires of the soul, which, when they are not conquered and
mortified, besiege and give battle to it round about, wherefore
she calls them the siege. From this siege she says, too, that
there is now a rest; and begs that, since this is so, the Spouse
will not fail to communicate and grant her the favours for
which she has prayed Him, since the siege aforementioned
can no longer hinder the inward peace which she needs in
order to receive them, possess them and preserve them. This
she says because in this estate it is needful that the passions
of the soul should be set at rest, and the desires and affec-

---

[6] V, Vd: 'By which she here understands, as I think . . .', etc.
Br: 'By which I think she understands here . . .', etc. G: 'By
which she understands here, as I understand, those passions . . .',
etc.

tions mortified, so that they can neither disturb the soul nor make war upon it, but that this entire siege aforementioned, with its operations, may be in conformity with the inward spirit, and after this manner the soul[7] may be recollected and enjoy the delights which are enjoyed by the spirit. For this reason she says next:

And the cavalry came down at the sight of the waters.

5. By these waters she here understands the spiritual delights and blessings of God whereof in this estate the soul has fruition. By the cavalry are understood the faculties of the sensual part, both interior and exterior, which, says the Bride, come down in this estate at the sight of these spiritual waters. For the sensual part of the soul is so purified and spiritualized in this estate that the soul with its sensual[8] faculties and natural forces is recollected and has participation and fruition, after its manner, of the spiritual grandeurs which God is communicating to the spirit, even as David indicated when he said: *Cor meum et caro mea exultaverunt in Deum vivum.*[9] Which is to say: My spirit and my flesh have rejoiced and delighted in the living God.

6. And it is to be noted that the Bride says not here that the cavalry came down to taste of the waters, but that it came down at the sight of them. For this sensual part with its faculties cannot essentially and properly taste of spiritual blessings because they have not a proportionate capacity for this, either in this life or in the next; but through a certain overflowing of the spirit they receive therefrom refreshment and delight, whereby these faculties and senses of the body are attracted[10] into that interior recollection, wherein the soul is drinking of[11] spiritual blessings. This is to come down at the sight of them rather than to taste of them essentially,[12] though they taste,

---

7 [*Lit.,* 'they.']

8 Br omits 'sensual.'

9 Psalm lxxxiii, 3 [A.V., lxxxiv, 2].

10 G, V, Vd, Br read erroneously *atribuídas* ('attributed') for *atraídas* ('attracted').

11 G, V, Vd, Br: 'receiving.'

12 Br: 'to taste essence of them.'

as we have said, of the overflowing which is communicated
from the soul to them. And the soul says here that they came
down, and she uses no other word, in order to signify that all
these faculties descend and come down from their natural
operations, from which they cease, to interior recollection;
whereto may the Lord Jesus,[13] the sweetest Spouse, be pleased
to bring all such as invoke His Most Holy Name, to Whom
belong honour and glory together with the Father and the
Holy Spirit *in sæcula sæculorum*. Amen.[14]

[13] G, V, Vd, Br: 'the Lord Jesus Christ.'
[14] Bj, G, V, Vd, Br, Md add: 'Laus Deo.' Lch: 'Soli Deo honor
et gloria.' Gr, 8,654: 'Finis.'

SPIRITUAL CANTICLE

(Second Redaction)

Exposition of the stanzas which treat of the exercise of love between the Soul and Christ the Spouse, wherein are touched upon and expounded some points and effects of prayer, at the request of Mother Ana de Jesús, Prioress of the Discalced at San José of Granada. The year 1584.[1]

PROLOGUE[2]

Forasmuch as these stanzas, religious Mother,[3] appear to be written with a certain degree of fervour of love for God, Whose wisdom and love are so vast that, as is said in the Book of Wisdom,[4] they reach from one end to another, and the soul which is informed and moved by Him has to some extent this same abundance and impetus in its words, I do not now think of expounding all the breadth and plenteousness imbued in them by the fertile spirit of love—it would rather be ignorance to think that sayings of love understood mystically, such as those of the present stanzas, can be fairly explained by words of any kind. For the Spirit of the Lord, Who helps our infirmity, as Saint Paul says, dwells in us and makes intercession for us, with groanings unutterable, pleading for that which we cannot well understand or comprehend, so as to express it ourselves.[5] For who can write down that which He reveals to loving souls wherein He dwells? And who can set

[1] As to this title there are variants in the Codices, but all readings are substantially the same. A merely says: 'Illuminative Way. Prologue to M. Ana de Jesús, Discalced Carmelite Nun.'
[2] S omits the prologue and the forty stanzas which follow. Bg omits the prologue and puts the stanzas at the end. G, Ej omit the prologue.
[3] S omits 'religious Mother.'
[4] Wisdom viii, 1.
[5] [Romans viii, 26.]

forth in words that which He makes them to feel? And lastly, who can express that which He makes them to desire? Of a surety, none; nay, indeed, not the very souls through whom He passes. It is for this reason that, by means of figures, comparisons and similitudes, they allow something of that which they feel to overflow, and utter secrets and mysteries from the abundance of their spirits rather than explain these things rationally. These similitudes, if they be not read with the simplicity of the spirit of love and understanding embodied in them, appear to be nonsense rather than the expression of reason, as may be seen in the divine Songs of Solomon and in other books of Divine Scripture, where, since the Holy Spirit cannot express[6] the abundance of His meaning in common and vulgar terms, He utters[7] mysteries in strange figures and similitudes.[8] Whence it follows that no words of holy doctors, albeit they have said much and may yet say more, can ever expound these things fully, neither could they be expounded in words of any kind. That which is expounded of them, therefore, is ordinarily the least part of that which they contain.

2. Since these stanzas, therefore, have been composed under the influence of a love which comes from abounding mystical understanding, they cannot be fairly expounded, nor shall I attempt so to expound them, but only to throw upon them some general light[9] (since your Reverence has so desired).[10] And this I think to be best, for the sayings of love are better expounded[11] in their fullness, so that everyone may pluck advantage from them according to the manner and to the measure of his spirit, than abbreviated in a sense to which not every taste can accommodate itself. And thus, although they are expounded after a certain manner, there is no reason why anyone should be bound to this exposition. For mystical wisdom (which comes through love, whereof

[6] B: 'since the Holy Spirit desires not to express . . .'

[7] S: 'the Holy Spirit utters . . .'

[8] A abbreviates: 'in vulgar terms and similitudes, it follows thence that no words . . .', etc.

[9] A, Av, B, Bz, S: 'some light of a general kind.'

[10] S omits the words in parentheses.

[11] Bz, S: 'better left.'

the present stanzas treat) needs not to be understood distinctly in order to produce love and affection in the soul; it is like to faith, whereby we love God without understanding Him.[12]

3. I shall therefore be very brief, although I shall be unable to refrain from extending myself in certain places where the matter requires it, and where occasion offers to expound and treat certain points and effects of prayer, for since there are many such in the Stanzas I cannot refrain from treating of some. But I shall leave aside the commonest of them, and treat briefly the most extraordinary, which come to pass in those that, by the favour of God, have left behind the beginners' state. And this for two reasons: the one, that there are so many things written for beginners; the other, that I speak herein with your Reverence by your command, and to your Reverence Our Lord has granted the favour of drawing you forth from these beginnings and leading you[13] farther inward to the bosom of His Divine love. Thus I trust that, although I may write here of certain points of scholastic theology concerning the interior commerce of the soul with its God, it will not be in vain to have talked somewhat after the manner of pure spirit; for though your Reverence may lack[14] the practice of scholastic theology whereby are comprehended Divine verities, yet you lack not that of mystical theology, which is attained through love, and wherein these verities are not only known but also experienced.

4. And to the end that all I say (which I desire to submit to better judgment, and entirely so to that of Holy Mother Church) may be the better received, I think not to affirm aught that is mine,[15] trusting to my own experience, or to that of other spiritual persons[16] of which I have known, or to that which I have heard from them (although I purpose to profit by both) unless it be confirmed and expounded by

[12] S adds: 'clearly.'

[13] S modifies: 'that I speak herein with persons to whom Our Lord has granted the favour of having drawn them forth from these beginnings and led them farther inward . . .', etc.

[14] S: 'for though some may lack . . . they lack not . . .', etc.

[15] S omits 'that is mine.'

[16] Av, Bz: 'other particular spiritual persons.'

authorities from Divine Scripture, at the least in those things which appear to be[17] the most difficult of comprehension. Wherein I shall follow this manner—to wit, that first I shall set down the texts in their Latin and then shall expound them with respect to the subject which they illustrate. And first I shall set down all the Stanzas together, and then in order shall set down each one separately with intent to expound it; whereof I shall expound each line, setting it down at the beginning of its exposition.

END OF THE PROLOGUE

SONGS BETWEEN THE SOUL AND THE SPOUSE[1]

Bride[2]

1. Whither hast thou hidden thyself,   And hast left me, O Beloved, to my sighing?
   Thou didst flee like the hart, having wounded me:[3]   I went out after thee, calling, and thou wert gone.[4]

2. Shepherds, ye that go   Yonder, through the sheepcotes, to the hill,
   If perchance ye see him that I most love,   Tell ye him that I languish, suffer and die.

3. Seeking my loves,   I will go o'er yonder mountains and banks;
   I will neither pluck the flowers nor fear the wild beasts;   I will pass by the mighty and cross the frontiers.

[17] S: 'which are.'
[1] Thus Jaén, A, Av, B, Bz, S. The other versions differ very slightly.
[2] This word is found only in Jaén, A, S.
[3] Ej, G: 'leaving me wounded.'
[4] G, S: 'and thou wert already gone.' Ej: 'thou wert already gone.'

4. O woods and thickets   Planted by the hand of the Beloved![5]

O meadow of verdure, enamelled with flowers,   Say if
he has passed by you.

5. Scattering a thousand graces,   He passed through these
groves in haste,

And, looking upon them as he went,   Left them, by his
glance[6] alone, clothed with beauty.[7]

6. Ah, who will be able to heal me!   Surrender thou thyself
now completely.[8]

From to-day do thou send me now[9] no other messenger,
For they cannot tell me what I wish.

7. And all those that serve[10]   Relate[11] to me a thousand
graces of thee,

And all wound me the more   And something[12] that they
are stammering leaves me dying.

8. But how, O life,[13] dost thou persevere,   Since thou livest
not where thou livest,

And since the arrows make thee to die which thou receivest
From the conceptions of the Beloved which thou formest
within thee?

9. Since thou hast wounded this heart,[14]   Wherefore didst
thou not heal it?

And wherefore, having robbed me of it, hast thou left it thus
And takest not the prey that thou hast spoiled?

[5] Bg: 'of my Beloved.'
[6] [See p. 43, n. 7, above.]
[7] Ej, G: 'with his beauty.'
[8] [Cf. p. 43, n. 9.]
[9] A omits 'now.'
[10] A: 'that go down' [*bajan* for *vagan*]. Ej has *vacan*, on which
see the Saint's commentary, p. 278, below.
[11] [*Lit.*, 'are relating.']
[12] Av inserts *ya* ('already,' 'now').
[13] B: 'O soul.'
[14] G: 'this my heart.'

10.[15] Quench thou my griefs,   Since none suffices to remove them,

And let mine eyes behold thee,   Since thou art their light and for thee alone I wish to have them.

11. Reveal thy presence   And let the vision of thee and thy beauty slay me;

Behold, the affliction of love is not cured   Save by thy presence and thy form.

12. O crystalline fount,   If on that thy silvered surface

Thou wouldst of a sudden form the eyes desired   Which I bear outlined in my inmost parts!

13. Withdraw them, Beloved, for I fly away.

Spouse[16]

Return thou, dove,

For the wounded hart appears on the hill   At the air of thy flight, and takes refreshment.

14. My Beloved, the mountains,[17]   The solitary, wooded[18] valleys,

The strange islands, the sonorous rivers,   The whisper of the amorous breezes,

15. The tranquil night,   At the time of the rising of the dawn,

The silent music, the sounding solitude,   The supper that recreates and enkindles love.

16. Drive us away the foxes,   For our vineyard is now in flower,

While we make a bunch of roses,   And let none appear upon the hill.[19]

15 A omits this stanza.

16 This word is found only in Jaén and S. The latter repeats it [at intervals in the poem; cf. pp. 44–7, above], but we follow the Jaén readings in the text.

17 B has: 'Beholding the mountains,' and omits 'My Beloved.'

18 A has *tremerosos* ('trembling') for *nemorosos* ('wooded').

19 A, Bz: 'upon the countryside.'

17. Stay thee, dead north wind. Come, south wind, that
awakenest love;[20]

Breathe through my garden and let thy odours[21] flow,
And the Beloved shall pasture among the flowers.

18. O nymphs of Judaea, While mid the flowers and rose-trees
the ambar sends forth perfume,

Dwell in the outskirts And desire not to touch our thresholds.

19. Hide thyself, dearest one, And look with thy face upon
the mountains,

And desire not to speak, But look upon her companions[22]
who travels mid strange islands.

20. Birds of swift wing,[23] Lions, harts, leaping does,
Mountains, valleys, banks, waters, breezes, heats,[24] And
terrors that keep watch by night.

21. By the pleasant lyres And by the sirens' song, I conjure
you,

Cease your wrath[25] and touch not the wall, That the
Bride[26] may sleep more securely.

22. The Bride has entered Into the pleasant garden of her
desire,[27]

And at her pleasure rests, Her neck reclining on the gentle
arms of the Beloved.

23. Beneath the apple-tree, There wert thou betrothed to me;
There did I give thee my hand And thou wert redeemed
where thy mother had been corrupted.

---

20 [*Lit.,* 'loves.'] B, Bg: 'that recreatest loves.'
21 Thus Jaén, S. The other versions have 'its odours.'
22 Av, B, Bz: 'countries.'
23 [*Lit.,* 'the light birds.']
24 Av, Bz, G: 'breezes, waters, heats.'
25 [*Lit.,* 'Let your wraths cease.']
26 G: 'That the Spouse.'
27 [*Lit.,* 'pleasant desired garden.']

24. Our flowery bed,   Encompassed with dens of lions,

     Hung with purple[28] and builded in peace,   Crowned with a thousand shields of gold.

25. In the track[29] of thy footprint   The young girls run along by the way.[30]

     At the touch of a spark, at the spiced wine,   Flows forth[31] the Divine balsam.

26. In the inner cellar, of my Beloved have I drunk,   And, when I went forth over all this meadow,

     Then[32] knew I naught   And lost the flock which I followed aforetime.

27. There he gave me his breast;   There he taught me a science most delectable;

     And I gave myself to him indeed, reserving nothing; There I promised him to be his bride.

28. My soul has employed itself   And all my possessions in his service:

     Now I guard no flock nor have I now other office,   For now my exercise is in loving alone.[33]

29. If, then, on the common land,   From henceforth I am neither seen nor found,

     You will say that I am lost;   That, wandering love-stricken, I lost my way and was found.[34]

30. With flowers and emeralds[35]   Gathered in the cool mornings

     We will make the garlands flowering in thy love   And interwoven with one hair from my head.

---

[28] B, Bg: 'dyed in purple.'

[29] [Or simply 'behind,' 'after,' as in the current Spanish phrase.]

[30] Ej: 'The young girls discover [*or* reveal] the way.' G: 'The youths discover [*or* reveal] the way.'

[31] [*Lit.*, 'emissions of,' without a verb.]

[32] B, Bg substitute *yo* [emphatic form of 'I'] for *ya* ('then').

[33] A: 'is to fall in love.'

[34] [*ganada. Lit.*, 'gained.' Ej reads, however, *hallada*, 'found.']

[35] Bg reads: 'With enamelled flowers,' but is corrected in MS. to the reading in the text.

31. By that hair alone   Which thou regardedst fluttering on
    my neck,

    Beholding it upon my neck, thou wert captivated,   And
    wert wounded by one of mine eyes.

32. When thou didst look on[36] me,   Thine eyes imprinted
    upon me their grace;[37]

    For this cause didst thou love me greatly,   Whereby mine
    eyes deserved to adore that which they saw in thee.

33. Despise me not,   For, if thou didst find me swarthy,

    Now canst thou indeed look upon me,[38]   Since thou didst
    look upon me and leave in me grace and beauty.

34. The little white dove   Has returned to the ark with the
    bough,

    And now the turtle-dove   Has found the mate of her de-
    sire[39] on the green banks.

35. In solitude she lived   And in solitude now has built her
    nest,

    And in solitude her dear one alone guides her,   Who like-
    wise in solitude was wounded by love.

36. Let us rejoice, Beloved,   And let us go to see ourselves in
    thy beauty,

    To the mountain and the hill where flows the pure water;
    Let us enter farther into the thicket.

37. And then we shall go forth   To the lofty caverns of the
    rock which are well hidden,

    And there shall we enter   And taste the new wine of the
    pomegranates.

---

36 [The verb is *mirar,* more conveniently translated 'regard' in
Stanza XXXI and its commentary.]

37 Bg: 'thy grace.'

38 B: 'Now indeed wilt thou be able to look upon me.'

39 [*Lit.,* 'her desired mate.'] Bg has the slight variant *El ocio* for
Al socio and reads: 'Has found the desired peace.'

38. There wouldst thou show me   That which my soul de-
    sired,[40]

    And there at once, my life, wouldst thou give me   That
    which thou gavest me the other day.

39. The breathing of the air,   The song of the sweet philomel,
    The grove and its beauty in the serene night,   With a flame
    that consumes and gives[41] no pain.

40. For none saw it,   Neither did Aminadab appear,
    And there was a rest from the siege,[42]   And the cavalry
    came down[43] at the sight of the waters.

[40] [The verb is not *desear*, but *pretender*, to aim at, lay claim to,
strive for.]

[41] G has 'consumes' in the indicative and 'gives' in the subjunctive [thus making the latter verb more indefinite than the
former].

[42] Bg has (*ciervo* for *cerco*) 'And the hart was at rest.'

[43] [See p. 48, n. 38.] Av, Bz have: 'appeared.'

ARGUMENT[1]

The order which these Stanzas follow is from the time when a soul begins to serve God until it reaches the last estate[2] of perfection, which is the Spiritual Marriage; and thus there are touched upon in them the three estates or ways of spiritual exercise through the which the soul passes until it reaches the said estate; which are the Purgative, the Illuminative and the Unitive; and concerning each of these are expounded certain of its properties and effects.[3]

2. The earliest of these Stanzas treat of beginners—that is, of the Purgative Way. Those that come next treat of progressives,[4] where the Spiritual Betrothal[5] is made, and this is the Illuminative Way. After these, those that follow treat of the Unitive Way, which is that of the perfect, wherein is made the Spiritual Marriage. This Unitive Way, or that of the perfect, follows the Illuminative Way, which is that of progressives;[6] and the last stanzas treat of the beatific estate, to which only the soul in that perfect estate aspires.[7]

[1] G, Ej: 'Prologue to the reader.'

[2] G: 'degree.'

[3] S: 'of their properties and effects.'

[4] [aprovechados. This is sometimes translated 'adepts,' but 'progressives' is a more exact rendering when referring to the second of the three traditional mystical states.]

[5] G: 'matrimony.' [This is, of course, an error.]

[6] Sg omits the words: 'which . . . progressives.' Bg omits: 'which is that . . . Unitive Way,' an evident slip by the copyist, who skipped the words between two identical phrases.

[7] Ej reproduces the first of these two paragraphs almost as it stands above, but without the enumeration of the three Ways. The second paragraph it shortens considerably [without any great loss to the sense], and adds that in the stanzas relating to the Unitive Way 'are related many properties and praises of God' and that the Spiritual Marriage is 'that which one may reach in this life.'

BEGINNETH THE EXPOSITION OF THE STANZAS BETWEEN THE BRIDE AND CHRIST THE SPOUSE[1]

Annotation[2]

The soul, taking account of her obligations, seeing that life is short[3] and the path of eternal life[4] narrow,[5] that the just man is scarcely saved,[6] that the things of the world are vain and deceitful, that everything comes to an end and fails like running water,[7] that time is uncertain, the account strict, perdition very easy, salvation very difficult; knowing, on the other hand, the great debt that she owes to God for that He has created her for Himself alone, for which she owes Him the service of her whole life, and for that He has redeemed her for Himself alone, for which she owes Him all the rest of the love of her will,[8] and the return of His love to her, and for a thousand other benefits wherein she knows that she has been indebted to God since before her birth; and that a great part of her life has vanished,[9] and that for all this she must give an account and reason, for the first as for the last, even to the uttermost farthing,[10] when God shall search Jerusalem with lighted candles;[11] and that it is now late and perchance

---

[1] S: 'Beginneth the Exposition of the Stanzas.'

[2] S: 'Annotation to the stanza following, which is the first.' A, B, Bg do not copy the word 'Annotation.'

[3] Job xiv, 5.

[4] B: 'the eternal path.' A, Bg: 'the path [narrow].'

[5] St. Matthew vii, 14.

[6] 1 St. Peter iv, 18.

[7] 2 Kings [A.V., 2 Samuel] xiv, 14.

[8] A, Av, G, Sg omit: 'of the love.' Ej modifies: 'and for His having redeemed her, for the which she has still not the wherewithal to pay God, and a thousand other benefits.' [The text reads literally: 'the rest and return of the love of her will.']

[9] [*Lit.*, 'has gone away into the air.']

[10] St. Matthew v, 26.

[11] Sophonias i, 12.

the end of the day;[12] in order to remedy so much evil and
harm, especially as she feels God to be very far distant[13] and
hidden, since she has been content to forget Him so much
among the creatures, she is touched with fear and inward grief
of heart at so great perdition and peril, and renounces all
things, ceases from all business and delays not a day neither
an hour. Then, with yearning and sighs that come from the
heart, wounded now with love for God, she begins to invoke
her Beloved, and says:

STANZA THE FIRST

**Whither hast thou hidden thyself,   And hast left me, O Be-
loved, to my sighing?**
**Thou didst flee like the hart, having wounded me:[1]   I went
out after thee, calling, and thou wert gone.[2]**

Exposition

2. In this first stanza, the soul that is enamoured[3] of the
Word, the Son of God, her Spouse, desiring to be united with
Him through clear and essential vision,[4] sets forth her love's
anxieties, reproaching Him for His absence, the more so because, since He has pierced and wounded[5] her with love for
Him, for which she has abandoned all created things, yea even
herself, she has still to suffer the absence of her Beloved and
is not yet loosed[6] from her mortal flesh that she may be able

[12] St. Matthew xx, 6.
[13] J, S: 'to be very wroth.'
[1] G, Ej: 'leaving me wounded.'
[2] G: 'and thou wert already gone.' Ej, S: 'thou wert already
gone.'
[3] Ej, G, S: 'that is already wounded and enamoured.'
[4] Bg: 'union.'
[5] [*herido y llagado*. Cf. p. 75, n. 5 above and 277, below.] Jaén
alone omits *y llagado*. Bg has: '. . . and wounded her by His
hand.'
[6] Sg: 'is not yet killed, taken away and loosed.' Ej: 'is not yet
taken away and loosed.'

to have fruition of Him in the glory of eternity. And thus she says:

Whither hast thou hidden thyself?

3. It is as though she said: O Word, my Spouse, show me the place where Thou art hidden; wherein she begs Him to manifest His Divine Essence; for the place where the Son of God is hidden is, as Saint John[7] says, 'the bosom of the Father,' which is the Divine Essence, the which is removed from every mortal eye and hidden from all human understanding. For this cause Isaias, speaking with God, said: 'Verily Thou art a hidden God.'[8] Hence it is to be noted that, however lofty are the communications of a soul with God in this life, and the revelations of His presence, and however high and exalted is its knowledge of Him, they are not God in His Essence, nor have aught to do with Him. For in truth He is still hidden from the soul, and therefore it ever beseems the soul, amid all these grandeurs, to consider Him as hidden, and to seek Him as One hidden, saying: 'Whither hast Thou hidden Thyself?' For neither is a sublime communication of Him nor a sensible revelation of His presence a sure testimony of His gracious presence, nor is aridity or the want of all these things in the soul a testimony of His absence[9] from it. For which cause says the prophet Job: 'If He comes to me I shall not see Him; and if He departs, I shall not understand Him.'[10]

4. Wherein is to be understood that, if the soul should experience any great communication or spiritual knowledge or feeling it must not for that reason persuade itself that that feeling is to possess or see God clearly and essentially, or that it is to possess God more completely or be more deeply in God, however profound it may be;[11] and that, if all these sensible and spiritual communications fail, and it remains in

[7] St. John i, 18.

[8] Isaias xlv, 15.

[9] Sg had *presence*, which was emended to *absence*. Bz: '. . . in the soul the less clear testimony of His presence.'

[10] Job ix, 11.

[11] Bg: '. . . that that feeling is to possess God truly, or to be in God, however profound such experiences may be, to fear [*temer* for *tener*, an evident slip] God more.'

aridity, darkness and desolation, it must not think that for that reason God is failing it in one estate more than in another. For in reality the one estate can give no assurance to a soul that it is in His grace, neither can the other, that it is outside it. As the Wise Man says:[12] 'No man can know if he be worthy of love or of hatred before God.' So that the principal intent of the soul in this line is not merely to beg for sensible and affective devotion, wherein there is neither certainty nor clear evidence of the possession of the Spouse in this life, but principally to beg for the clear presence and vision of His Essence, wherewith it desires to be given assurance and satisfaction in the next.

5. This same thing was signified by the Bride in the Divine Songs when, desiring to be united with the Divinity of the Word her Spouse, she begged the Father for it, saying: 'Show me where Thou feedest, and where Thou liest in the midday.'[13] For to entreat Him to show her where He fed was to beg that she might be shown the Essence of the Divine Word, His Son, for the Father feeds not upon aught else than upon His only Son,[14] since He is the glory of the Father. And to beg Him to show her the place where He lay was to beg that selfsame thing, since the Son alone is the delight of the Father,[15] Who lies not, neither is present, in any place, save in His beloved Son, in Whom He lies wholly, communicating to Him all His Essence—'in the midday,' which is in Eternity, where He ever begets Him and has begotten Him. It is this pasture, then, of the Word-Spouse[16] where the Father feeds in infinite glory, and this flowery bed,[17] whereon with infinite delight of love He lies profoundly hidden from every mortal eye and from every creature, that the Bride-Soul entreats[18] when she says: 'Whither hast Thou hidden Thyself?'

[12] Ecclesiastes ix, 1.
[13] Canticles i, 6.
[14] G, S: 'only begotten Son.' Ej: 'on aught else save on the Word His Son.'
[15] A, without apparent motive, omits several lines here.
[16] S: 'This pasture, then, is the Word-Spouse.'
[17] S: '[which] is the flowery bed.'
[18] S: '. . . every creature, and this the Bride-Soul entreats.'

6. And, to the end that this thirsty soul may come to find her Spouse, and be united with Him through union of love in this life, so far as she may, and allay her thirst[19] with this drop that can be tasted of Him in this life, it will be well, since the soul asks this of her Spouse, that we should take her hand on His behalf and answer her by showing her the surest place where He is hidden, so that she may surely find Him there with the perfection and sweetness that is possible in this life,[20] and thus may not begin to roam about vainly in the tracks of her companions. To the which end it is to be observed that the Word, the Son of God, together with the Father and the Holy Spirit, is hidden, in essence and in presence, in the inmost being of the soul. Wherefore, the soul that would find Him must go forth from all things according to the affection and will, and enter within itself in deepest recollection,[21] so that all things are to it as though they were not. Hence Saint Augustine, speaking with God in the Soliloquies,[22] said: 'I found Thee not, O Lord, without, because I erred in seeking Thee without that wert within.'[23] God, then, is hidden within the soul, and there the good contemplative must seek Him with love, saying: 'Whither hast Thou hidden Thyself?'

7. Oh, then, thou soul, most beautiful of all the creatures, that so greatly desirest to know the place where thy Beloved is, in order to seek Him and be united with Him, now thou art told that thou thyself art the lodging wherein He dwells, and the closet and hiding-place wherein He is hidden, and that it is a matter of great contentment and joy for thee to see that all thy good and thy hope are so near thee as to

[19] Jaén reads 'being,' by a slight slip [ser for sed].

[20] Ej: 'so that she may there see that which is sure with the perfect possession and pleasure that is possible in this life.' G has 'read' [lea] for 'see' [vea].

[21] Bg: 'be united within itself in recollection.' A, B: 'enter within itself in recollection.'

[22] Soliloquies, Chap. xxxi: 'Misi nuntios meos omnes sensus exteriores, ut quærerem te; et non inveni, quia male quærebam. Video enim, lux mea Deus qui illuminasti me, quia male te per illos quærebam, quia tu es intus.'

[23] G, Ej, Sg end: 'wert within me.'

be within thee, or, to speak more exactly, so near that thou canst not be without them. Behold, says the Spouse, the kingdom of God is within you.[24] And His servant the apostle Saint Paul says: 'You are the temple of God.'[25]

8. A great contentment for the soul is it to understand that God is never absent from the soul,[26] even though it be in mortal sin,[27] and still less from the soul in grace. What more desirest thou, O soul, and what more seekest thou without thyself, since within thyself thou hast thy riches, thy delights, thy satisfaction, thy fullness and thy kingdom, which is thy Beloved, Whom thy soul desires and seeks? Rejoice thou and be glad in thy inward recollection with Him, since thou hast Him so near. There desire Him, there adore Him, and go thou not to seek Him outside thyself, for so shalt thou be wearied and distracted; and thou shalt neither find Him nor rejoice in Him more surely or more quickly or more intimately than within thyself. There is but one thing to be remembered—that, although He be within thee, He is hidden. But it is a great thing to know the place where He is hidden in order to seek Him there with certainty. And this is that which thou also entreatest here, O soul, when with affection of love thou sayest: 'Whither hast Thou hidden Thyself?'

9. But yet thou sayest: 'If He Whom my soul loves is within me, how is it that I neither find Him nor feel Him?' The reason is that He is hidden and that thou hidest not thyself likewise that thou mayest find Him and feel Him; for he that has to find some hidden thing must enter very secretly[28] even into that same hidden place where it is, and, when he finds it, he too is hidden like that which he has found. Since, then, thy beloved Spouse is the treasure hidden in the field of thy soul, for the which treasure the wise merchant gave all that he had,[29] it will be fitting that, in order to find it, thou forget

[24] St. Luke xvii, 21.

[25] 2 Corinthians vi, 16.

[26] A, Sg, G, Ej: 'from it.'

[27] Sg has a marginal addition: 'giving to it and preserving in it its natural being.'

[28] [Lit., 'very hiddenly.']

[29] St. Matthew xiii, 44.

all that is thine, withdraw thyself from all creatures, hide in the interior closet of thy spirit,[30] and, shutting the door upon thee (that is to say, shutting thy will upon all things), pray to thy Father Who is in secret.[31] Thus, remaining secretly with Him, shalt thou then experience His presence in secret, and shalt love Him and have fruition of Him in secret, and shalt delight in Him in secret—that is to say,[32] beyond all that is attainable by tongue and sense.

10. Come, then, beauteous soul, since now thou knowest that the Beloved of thy desire dwells hidden within thy bosom, strive to be securely hidden with Him, and in thy bosom thou shalt embrace Him and experience His presence with affection of love. And see, He bids thee to that hiding-place, through Isaias, saying: 'Come, enter thou into thy chambers, shut thy doors about thee (that is, shut all thy faculties upon all creatures), hide thyself a little for a moment'[33]—that is, for this moment of temporal life. For if in this brief space of life, O soul, thou keepest thy heart with all diligence, as says the Wise Man,[34] without any doubt God will give thee that which later He describes, through Isaias, in these words: 'I will give thee the hidden treasures and I will reveal to thee the substance and mysteries of the secrets.'[35] This substance of the secrets is God Himself, for God is the substance of faith and the conception thereof, and faith is the secret and the mystery. And when this that faith keeps secret and concealed from us is revealed and made manifest, which is, as Saint Paul says,[36]

[30] St. Matthew vi, 6.

[31] [*Lit.*, 'is hidden.' So, to the end of the sentence, the word (*escondido*) translated 'secret' for the sake of the English is that which above is rendered 'hidden,' because of its connection with *esconder*, 'to hide.']

[32] Av modifies: 'pray to thy Father Who is in secret, and thou shalt have delight in Him and shalt feel Him and love Him and have fruition of Him in secret, that is to say . . .' A reads similarly.

[33] Isaias xxvi, 20. [The word rendered 'chambers' is translated 'closet(s)' in the last paragraph.]

[34] Proverbs iv, 23.

[35] Isaias xlv, 3.

[36] 1 Corinthians xiii, 10.

the perfection of God,[37] then shall the substance and mysteries of the secrets be revealed to the soul; but, in this mortal life, although the soul will not attain to them as purely as in the next, however deeply it hide itself, yet if it hide itself, like Moses,[38] in the cavern of the rock, which is the true imitation of the perfection of the life of the Son of God, Spouse of the soul, protected by God[39] with His right hand, it will merit being shown the 'back parts' of God, which is to attain to such perfection in this life, as to be united and transformed through love in the said Son of God its Spouse. And this in such wise that it will feel itself so closely united with Him and so fully instructed and learned in His mysteries that, so far as the knowledge of Him in this life is concerned, it will no longer need to say: 'Whither hast Thou hidden Thyself?'

11. Thou hast been told, O soul, what method thou art to follow in order to find the Spouse in thy hiding-place; but, if thou wilt hear it again, hear a word full of substance and unapproachable truth: it is that thou seek Him in faith and in love, without desiring to find satisfaction in aught, or to taste or understand more than that which it is well for thee to know; for these two[40] are the guides[41] of the blind, which will lead thee, by a way that thou knowest not, to the hidden place of God. Because faith, which is the secret that we have mentioned, is like the feet wherewith the soul journeys to God, and love is the guide that directs it; and if it continues to discourse and meditate upon[42] these mysteries and secrets of

---

[37] A reads: 'for God is the substance of faith, which is the perfection of God,' omitting all that is between these two phrases in the text.

[38] Exodus xxxiii, 22.

[39] Ej, G: 'which is the true imitation of the Passion of Jesus Christ and perfection of His most holy life, protected by God . . . , etc.' Sg reads similarly.

[40] [I.e. faith and love.]

[41] [Lit., 'the blind man's youths,' los mozos del ciego.] B has los mozos de cielo, 'the youths of heaven,' and Bg, los modos del cielo, 'the manners of heaven,' substituting for the following phrase: 'whereby thou wilt not be able to find the hidden place of God.'

[42] [manoseando, lit., 'touching frequently.'] S has manejando, 'handling.'

faith it will merit the revelation to it by love of that which faith holds within itself, which is the Spouse Whom it desires in this life through especial grace[43] of Divine union with God, as we have said, and in the next life through essential glory, having fruition of Him face to face, and in no way secretly. But meanwhile, although the soul attains to this said union[44] (which is the loftiest estate that it can reach in this life), inasmuch as He is still hidden from it in the bosom of the Father, as we have said, which is the way in which it desires to have fruition of Him in the life to come, the soul says ever: 'Whither hast Thou hidden Thyself?'[45]

12. Right well doest thou, O soul, to seek Him ever in His hiding-place, for greatly dost thou magnify God, and closely dost thou approach Him, when thou holdest Him to be far more lofty and profound than all that thou canst reach; remain thou not, therefore, either partly or wholly, in that which thy faculties can comprehend. I mean, be thou never willingly satisfied with that which thou understandest of God,[46] but rather with that which thou understandest not of Him; and do thou never rest in loving and having delight in that which thou understandest or feelest concerning God, but do thou love and have delight in that which thou canst not understand and feel concerning Him; for this, as we have said, is to seek Him in faith. Since God is unapproachable and hidden, as we have likewise said, however much it seem to thee that thou findest and feelest and understandest Him, thou must ever hold Him as hidden, and serve Him, as One that is hidden, after a hidden manner. And be thou not like many ignorant persons who hold a low conception of God, understanding God to be farther off and more completely hidden when they understand Him not and have no consciousness or experi-

[43] Jaén, A, Sg, omit the following 'of.' S has 'through spiritual grace.' The remaining versions read as in the text.

[44] Thus Jaén, Av, Bz. The rest read: 'this Divine union.'

[45] Ej omits or alters a great part of the passage 'Because faith . . . hidden Thyself.' G also has some variations, but very slight ones.

[46] Ej omits the words 'of God . . . understandest not.' G reads: '. . . of God, but love and have delight in that which thou canst not understand or feel concerning Him; for this is . . .', etc.

ence of Him; the truth being rather the contrary, that, the less clearly[47] they understand Him, the nearer they are approaching to Him,[48] for, as says the prophet David,[49] He made darkness His hiding-place. Thus, when thou drawest near to Him, thou must perforce be conscious of darkness because of the weakness of thy sight. Well doest thou, then, at all times, whether of adversity or of temporal or spiritual prosperity, to hold God to be hidden and thus to cry to Him, saying: 'Whither hast Thou hidden Thyself?'

And hast left me, O Beloved, to my sighing?

13. The Bride calls Him 'Beloved,' in order the more to move and incline Him to her prayer, for, when God is loved, He responds to the petitions of His lover with great readiness.[50] And this He says through Saint John, in these words: 'If you abide in Me, you shall ask all that you will and it shall be done.'[51] Wherefore the soul can then in truth call Him Beloved when it is wholly with Him and has not its heart set on aught that is outside Him and thus has its thought habitually upon Him. For want of this Dalila asked Samson how he could say that he loved her when his spirit was not with her.[52] In this spirit are included the thought and the affection. Some, therefore, call the Spouse 'Beloved' when He is not in truth their Beloved because they have not their heart wholly with Him; and thus their petition is of less effect before God; wherefore they are not at once granted their petition until they persevere in prayer and, at the same time, come to have their spirit more continuously with God, and their heart more wholly with Him in affection of love, for naught is obtained of God save by love.

[47] S omits 'clearly.'
[48] This is the reading of G, Ej, Sg. Jaén, B, Bg, A, Av read thus: 'that, the more clearly they understand Him, the nearer they are approaching to Him'—a manifest error, since this is not the thought of the Saint.
[49] Psalm xvii, 12. [A.V., xviii, 11.]
[50] [*facilidad.*] Ej, Sg, *fidelidad*, 'fidelity.' G: 'with grace of fidelity.'
[51] St. John xv, 7.
[52] Judges xvi, 15.

14. In the words which she then says: 'And hast left me to my sighing,' it is to be observed that the absence of the Beloved causes in the lover a continual sighing, because apart from Him she loves naught, rests in naught and finds relief in naught; whence a man who indeed loves God will be known by this, namely, if he be content with naught that is less than God. But why do I say 'be content'? For although[53] he have all things at once he will not be content, but rather the more he has, the less satisfied will he be;[54] for satisfaction of the heart is not found in the possession of things, but in detachment from them all and in poverty of spirit. Since perfection of love wherein God is possessed with a very intimate[55] and individual grace consists in this, the soul in this life, when it has attained thereto, lives with a certain satisfaction, but not with fullness thereof, for David, with all his perfection, expected fullness only in Heaven, saying: 'When Thy glory shall appear I shall be satisfied.'[56] And thus the peace and tranquillity and satisfaction of heart to which the soul may attain in this life suffice not for it to have within it no more sighing (albeit peaceful and not painful sighing) in the hope of obtaining that which it lacks. For the sighing is connected with the hope.[57] Such sighing the Apostle declared that he and others had, though they were perfect, saying: 'We ourselves, who have the firstfruits of the Spirit, groan within ourselves, waiting for the adoption of sons of God.'[58] The sighing, then, the soul in this stanza has within herself, in the heart enkindled with love; for where love wounds, there is the sighing of the wounded soul, crying ever in sorrow for the absence of her Beloved,[59] above all when, having enjoyed some kind of sweet and delectable communion with the

[53] Ej, G, Sg: 'But why do I say "be content"? Rather he "occupies himself," for although . . .'

[54] A: 'but rather, the more he has [of] these, the more satisfied will he be.'

[55] Av, B, Bg, Bz, G, Ej, Sg: 'united.'

[56] Psalm xvi, 15. [A.V., xvii, 15.]

[57] A, B, Bg: 'with the hope of obtaining that which it lacks.'

[58] Romans viii, 23.

[59] [The text omits 'of her Beloved.']

Spouse, He absents Himself and she is left of a sudden dry
and alone. Wherefore she says next:

Thou didst flee like the hart,

15. Here it is to be observed that in the Songs the Bride
compares the Spouse to the hart and the mountain goat, saying: 'My Beloved is like to the goat, and to the young of
the harts.'[60] And this not only because He is strange and
solitary and flees from companions,[61] like the hart, but also
because of the swiftness wherewith He hides and reveals Himself, as He is wont to do in the visits which He makes to
devout souls, to refresh them and give them courage, and in
the withdrawals and absences which He makes them experience after such visits, in order to prove them[62] and humble
them and teach them. In this way He makes them to grieve
the more bitterly for His absence, as the soul now declares
in that which follows, saying:

Having wounded me:

16. And this is as though she had said: Not only were the
sorrow and grief which I suffer ordinarily in Thy absence in-
sufficient for me, but Thou didst wound me yet more, by love,
with Thine arrow; and, increasing my passion and desire for
the sight of Thee, Thou dost flee with the swiftness of the
hart and allowest not Thyself to be in the very smallest degree
comprehended.

17. For the further exposition of this line we must know
that, beside many other different kinds of visit[63] which God
makes to the soul, wounding it and upraising it in love,[64]
He is wont to bestow on it certain hidden touches[65] of love,
which like a fiery arrow strike and pierce the soul and leave

[60] Canticles ii, 9.

[61] Ej, B, G have *compañías*, 'those who keep Him company'; Bg:
campañas, 'countries.'

[62] Ej, G: 'to keep them.'

[63] Jaén: 'many other differences and visits.' Bg: 'many other
differences or visits.'

[64] S: 'wounding it with love.'

[65] A, Av, Bz, Bg, B, Sg: 'enkindling touches.'

it wholly cauterized[66] with the fire of love; and these are properly called the wounds of love, whereof the soul here speaks. So greatly do these wounds enkindle the will, and in affection, that the soul finds itself burning in the fire and flame of love, so much so that it appears to be consumed in that flame which causes it to go forth from itself and be wholly renewed and enter upon another mode of being; like the phœnix, that is burned up and re-born anew. Of this David speaks and says: 'My heart was kindled and my reins were changed and I brought myself to nothing and I knew not.'[67]

18. The desires and affections, which the Prophet here describes as reins, are all stirred, and in that enkindlement of the heart change into Divine affections, and the soul through love is reduced to naught, and knows naught save love. And at this season there takes place the stirring[68] of these reins, which is much like to a torture, and a yearning to see God—so much so that the rigour wherewith love treats the soul seems to it intolerable; not because it has been wounded thereby (for aforetime it held such wounds to be health),[69] but because it is left thus grieving in love, and has not been wounded more severely, even to the point of death, in the which case it would see and unite itself with Him[70] in a life of perfect love. Wherefore the soul magnifies or describes her pain, and says: 'Having wounded me.'

19. That is to say: Leaving me wounded thus, dying with wounds of love for Thee, Thou hast hidden Thyself with as great swiftness as that of the hart. This grief that is so great comes to pass thus because, when God inflicts that wound of love upon the soul, the affection of the will rises with sudden celerity to the possession of the Beloved, Whose touch it has felt. With equal celerity it feels His absence and its inability to possess Him here[71] as it desires, and thus it is conscious at one and the same time that it is sighing at

66 Sg: 'wholly as if taken captive.'
67 Psalm lxxii, 21. [A.V., lxxiii, 21–2.]
68 [conmutación.] G: comunicación, 'communication.'
69 Av, Ej, G, Sg, S: 'to be its health.'
70 S: 'would be united and joined with Him.'
71 Ej, G, Sg: 'to possess Him here in this life.'

this same absence, for these visits are not like others wherein
God refreshes and satisfies the soul, for these visits He makes
to wound rather than to heal, and to afflict rather than to
satisfy, since they serve to quicken the knowledge and increase
the desire, and, consequently, the pain and yearning to see
God. These are called spiritual wounds of love, and are to
the soul most delectable and desirable; for which cause
it would fain be ever dying a thousand deaths from these
lance-thrusts, for they cause it to issue forth from itself and
enter into God. This the Bride expresses in the line following,
saying:

I went out after thee, calling, and thou wert gone.[72]

20. There can be no medicine for the wounds of love save
that which comes from him that dealt the wounds. For this
cause this wounded soul went out, in the strength of the fire[73]
caused by her wound, after her Beloved that had wounded
her, calling to Him so that He should heal her. It must be
known that this going out is here understood spiritually according to two ways of going after God: the one, a going
forth from all things, which she does by abhorring and despising[74] them: the other, a going forth from herself, by forgetting herself, which she does for love of God; for, when
this love touches the soul with the efficacy whereof we are
here speaking, it raises her up in such wise that it makes her
to go out not only from herself through forgetfulness of herself, but even from her judgment[75] and the ways and inclinations natural to her, and she calls for God. And thus it is
as though she said:[76] By this Thy touch and wound of love,
my Spouse,[77] Thou hast drawn forth my soul, not only from
all things, but likewise hast drawn it forth and made it to

[72] Jaén has a slip here [*eres* for *eras,* reading] 'Thou art gone.'
[73] [In the context of the earlier version (p. 54, above) it was
necessary to translate 'the violence of the burning'; the Spanish
phrases are identical.]
[74] G: 'by knowing and despising.'
[75] See p. 55, n. 18, above.
[76] Ej omits: 'which she does for love of God . . . calls for God.'
[77] Bg: 'by this that is Thine and [this] wound of love.'

go out from itself (for truly it seems that He draws it from its very flesh) and hast raised it up to Thyself, so that it cries for Thee, loosed from all things that it may cling to Thee. 'And Thou wert gone.'

21. As though she had said: At the time when I desired to possess Thy presence I found Thee not, and I remained loosed from the one thing yet not clinging to the other, buffeted woefully by[78] the gales of love and finding support neither in myself nor in Thee. This going forth in order to go to seek the Beloved, as the soul here terms it, is called by the Bride in the Songs to 'rise,' where she says: 'I will rise and seek Him whom my soul loveth, going about the city, in the streets and the broad ways. I sought Him (she says) and I found Him not,[79] and they wounded me.'[80] The rising of the Bride-Soul is here understood, speaking spiritually, as of an ascent from the low to the high, which is the same as the going out from oneself, whereof the soul speaks here—that is, from one's own low way of life and love of self to the high love of God. But the Bride there says that she was wounded because she found Him not; and here the soul says likewise that she is wounded by love and has been left thus; wherefore one that is enamoured[81] lives ever in affliction during the absence of the Beloved, for he is already surrendered to Him, and has expectation to be paid for the surrender which he has made, which payment is the surrender to him of the Beloved, and this is not yet granted him; and being already lost to all things, and to himself, for the Beloved, he has found no gain to compensate him for his loss, for he lacks the possession of Him Whom his soul loves.[82]

22. This affliction and sorrow for the absence of God is wont to be so great in those that are approaching the estate of perfection, at the time of these Divine wounds, that if the Lord provided not for them they would die. For, as they have kept the palate of the will healthy and the spirit clean and

[78] See p. 55, n. 20, above.
[79] Canticles iii, 2.
[80] Canticles v, 7.
[81] S: 'And this is because he that is enamoured . . .'
[82] B adds: 'Such are the signs of him that goes about afflicted for God—that he has given himself to God and that he loves Him.'

well prepared for God, and as in that experience whereof we
have spoken He gives them to taste something of the sweetness
of Divine love, for which they yearn above all things, therefore do they likewise suffer above all things. For there is
shown to them in glimpses an immense good, and it is not
granted to them; wherefore their affliction and torment are
unspeakable.[83]

STANZA II

**Shepherds, ye that go   Yonder, through the sheepcotes, to the
hill,
If perchance ye see him that I most love,   Tell ye him that I
languish, suffer and die.**

Exposition

In this stanza the soul seeks to make use of intercessors and
intermediaries with her Beloved, begging them to tell Him of
her pain and affliction; for it is a characteristic of the lover,
when she cannot commune with her Beloved in His presence,
to do so by the best means that she may. And so at this point
the soul would fain use her desires, affections and sighs as
messengers, who are so well able to make known to her Beloved the secrets of her heart. And thus she exhorts them to
go, saying:

Shepherds, ye that go

2. Calling her desires, affections and sighs shepherds, inasmuch as they feed the soul on spiritual good things. For shepherd[1] signifies 'one who feeds,' and by their means God communicates Himself to her and gives her Divine pasture, which
without them He does but little. And she says: 'Ye that go.'

---

[83] Ej, G: 'therefore do they suffer very greatly; for in glimpses
there is shown to them an immense good and it is hidden from
them; wherefore exceeding great is their affliction and torment.'

[1] [The Spanish word is *pastor*, which is more appropriate here
than 'shepherd.']

Which is as much as to say, Ye that go forth from pure love; because not all the affections and desires go to Him, but those only that go forth from true love.

Yonder, through the sheepcotes, to the hill,

3. By the 'sheepcotes' she means the hierarchies and choirs of the angels, by whose ministry, from choir to choir, our sighs and prayers travel to God, Whom she here calls 'the hill,' because God is the greatest of all heights; and because in Him, as on the hill, are spied out[2] and seen all things, and the higher and the lower sheepcotes. To Him go our prayers, which the angels offer Him, as we have said; according as the angel said to holy Tobias, in these words: 'When thou didst pray with tears and didst bury the dead, I offered thy prayer[3] unto God.'[4] We can likewise understand by these shepherds the angels themselves, for not only do they bear our messages to God, but they also bring God's messages to our souls, feeding our souls, like good shepherds, with sweet communications and inspirations from God, which He also creates by means of them. And they protect and defend us[5] from the wolves, who are the evil spirits. Yet, whether these shepherds be taken to mean the affections, or whether they be taken to mean the angels, the soul desires them all to help her and be intermediaries for her with her Beloved, and thus she says to them all:

If perchance ye see . . .

4. This is as much as to say: If my good fortune and happiness are such that ye reach His presence so that He sees you and hears you. Here it is to be observed that, although it is true that God knows and understands all things, and sees and observes even the very thoughts of the soul,[6] as Moses says,[7] yet He is said to see our necessities and prayers, or to hear

[2] [See p. 57, n. 2, above.]
[3] S: 'thy prayers.' Sg: 'thy heart.'
[4] Tobias xii, 12.
[5] G, Ej, Sg add: 'like good shepherds.'
[6] Ej, G: 'even the thoughts and motions,' omitting 'of the soul.' Sg: 'even the motions and thoughts of the soul.'
[7] Deuteronomy xxxi, 21.

them, when He relieves them or fulfils them; for not all necessities and petitions reach such a point that God hears them in order to fulfil them, until in His eyes they arrive at a proper season and time and the number of them is sufficient.[8] And then He is said to see them or to hear them, as may be seen in the Book of Exodus, where, after the four hundred years during which the children of Israel had been afflicted in the bondage of Egypt, God said to Moses: 'I have seen the affliction of My people and I am come down to deliver them,'[9] though He had ever seen it. Even so said Saint Gabriel to Zacharias[10] that he was not to fear, since God had already heard his prayer in giving him now the son for which he had been begging Him many years;[11] yet He had ever heard him. And thus it is to be understood by every soul that, albeit God hearkens not at once to its necessity and prayer, yet it follows not that He will not so hearken at a fitting time—He Who is,[12] as David says, a helper in due time and in tribulation,[13] if the soul faint not and cease not from prayer.[14] This, then, is signified here by the soul when she says, 'If perchance ye see . . .' That is: If by good fortune the time has arrived at which He sees fit to grant my petitions.

. . . him that I most love,

5. That is to say: more than all things. Which is true when naught that presents itself to the soul daunts her from doing and suffering aught wherein she may serve Him; and when the soul can truly say that which she says here, in the line following, it is a sign that she loves Him above all things. The line, then, is:

Tell ye him that I languish, suffer and die.

[8] [*Lit.*, 'they arrive at a sufficient time and season and number.'] Ej, G: 'at a sufficient and just time and season.' Sg: 'at a sufficient and just season and time and number.'

[9] Exodus iii, 7, 8.

[10] St. Luke i, 13.

[11] Ej, G: '. . . heard his prayer which he had been making for many days.' So Sg, except that this has 'years' for 'days.'

[12] S: 'For He is.'

[13] Psalm ix, 10. [A.V., ix, 9.]

[14] [*Lit.*, 'and cease not.']

6. Herein the soul represents three kinds of need, to wit: languor, suffering and death; for the soul that truly loves God with a love[15] having any degree of perfection suffers ordinarily from His absence in three ways, according to the three faculties of the soul, which are understanding, will and memory. She says that she languishes in the understanding, because she sees not God, Who is the health of the understanding, even as God says, through David: 'I am thy health.'[16] She says that she suffers as to the will, because she possesses not God,[17] Who is the refreshment[18] and delight of the will, even as David says likewise, in these words: 'With the torrent[19] of Thy delight shalt Thou satisfy them.'[20] She says that she dies as to the memory, because, remembering that she lacks all the blessings of the understanding, which are the sight of God, and the delights of the will, which are the possession of Him, and that it is likewise very possible to be deprived of Him for ever among the perils and chances of this life, she suffers at this remembrance a grief after the manner of death, for she can see that she lacks the certain and perfect possession[21] of God, Who is the life of the soul, even as Moses says in these words: 'Of a surety He is thy life.'[22]

7. These three kinds of need Jeremias likewise represented to God in the Lamentations, saying: 'Remember my poverty, the wormwood and the gall.'[23] The poverty refers to the understanding, because to it belong the riches of the wisdom of the Son of God, in Whom, as Saint Paul says, are hid all the treasures of God.[24] The wormwood, which is a herb most bitter, refers to the will, for to this faculty belongs the sweetness of the possession of God; lacking which, the soul

---

[15] Ej, G, Sg: 'with a hunger.'
[16] Psalm xxxiv, 3. [A.V., xxxv, 3.]
[17] Sg omits: 'because she possesses not God.'
[18] Bz: 'refuge.'
[19] Ej, G, Sg: 'With the current.'
[20] Psalm xxxv, 9. [A.V., xxxvi, 8.] Jaén, Bg, B, Bz, Av, S have: 'satisfy us.'
[21] B, Bg: 'and direct possession.'
[22] Deuteronomy xxx, 20.
[23] Lamentations iii, 19.
[24] Colossians ii, 3.

is left with bitterness. And that the bitterness belongs spiritually[25] to the will is made clear in the Apocalypse, when the angel speaks to Saint John, saying that he should eat that book and it should make his belly bitter,[26] by the belly being understood the will. The gall refers not only to the memory, but to all the faculties and powers of the soul, for the gall signifies the death of the soul, even as Moses writes in Deuteronomy, when he speaks of the damned, saying: 'Their wine will be the gall of dragons and the venom of asps, which is incurable';[27] which signifies there the lack of God, which is the death of the soul. These three needs and afflictions are founded upon the three theological virtues—faith, charity and hope—which relate to the three faculties aforementioned in the order here set down: understanding, will and memory.

8. And it is to be observed that in the line aforementioned the soul does no more than represent her need and affliction to the Beloved. For one that loves discreetly has no care to beg for that which he lacks and desires, but only shows forth his need, so that the Beloved may do that which seems good to Him. As when the Blessed Virgin spake to the beloved Son at the wedding of Cana of Galilee, not begging Him directly for wine, but saying to Him: 'They have no wine.'[28] And when the sisters of Lazarus sent to Him, not to say that He should heal their brother, but to tell Him to see how he whom He loved was sick.[29] And this for three reasons. First, because the Lord knows better than we that which befits us; second, because the Beloved has the greater compassion when He sees the necessity of him that loves Him, and his resignation; third, because the soul is on surer ground with respect to self-love and love of possession if she represents her need than if she begs Him for that whereof she believes herself

---

[25] A: 'belongs especially.'

[26] Apocalypse x, 9.

[27] Deuteronomy xxxii, 33. Jaén, A, B, Bg have *insaciable* ('insatiable') for *insanable* ('incurable').

[28] St. John ii, 3. Av has: 'not begging Him but representing to Him the need: Wine they have not.'

[29] St. John xi, 3. Av: 'And the sisters of Lazarus said not: "Come Lord, to heal our brother," but only: "He whom Thou lovest is sick."'

to have need. It is precisely this that the soul does here, where
she represents her three necessities. And it is as though she
were to say: 'Tell my Beloved this: Since I languish, and He
alone is my health, may He give me my health; and since
I suffer, and He alone is my joy,[30] may He give me my joy;
and since I die, and He alone is my life, may He give me
life.'[31]

STANZA III

**Seeking my loves,   I will go o'er yonder mountains and banks;
I will neither pluck the flowers nor fear the wild beasts;   I will
pass by the mighty and cross the frontiers.**

Exposition

When the soul sees that, in order to find the Beloved, sighs
and prayers suffice her not, nor yet the making use of good
intercessors, as she did in the first and the second stanza, and
forasmuch as the desire wherewith she seeks Him is genuine
and her love is great, she is unwilling to leave unmade any
effort that is within her power; for the soul that of a truth
loves God is not slothful in doing its utmost to find the Son
of God, its Beloved; and even after it has done everything
it is still not satisfied and thinks it has done nothing. And
thus in this third stanza, wherein the soul desires to seek Him
in deed, she describes the method which she has to employ
in order to find Him,[1] namely this: she must practise the
virtues and perform the spiritual exercises of the active and
the contemplative life; and to this end she must accept no
comforts or delights; nor must all the powers and snares of
the three enemies of the soul—which are world, devil and flesh
—suffice to detain and hinder her. So she says:

Seeking my loves,

[30] A, B, Bg: 'glory.' Bz: 'and since He alone is my glory.'
[31] A, Av, Bz, Bg, B, G, Sg: 'may He give me my life.'
[1] Ej, G, Sg: 'in order to do it.'

2. That is, my Beloved. The soul clearly declares here that, to find God in truth, it suffices not to pray with the heart and with the tongue alone, nor yet to make use of the help of others; but, together with this, it is needful also to do ourselves that which is in our power; for God is wont to esteem more highly one thing done by a person himself than many things[2] done for that person by others. Wherefore the soul, remembering here the saying of the Beloved which runs 'Seek and you shall find,'[3] determines to go forth herself, after the manner that we have described above, to seek Him in very deed, and not to rest until she finds Him, as do many who desire not that God shall cost them more than words, and even those badly put together, and will scarcely do anything for Him if it costs them anything. And some, for His sake, would not even rise from a place which is to their pleasure and liking unless by their doing so the sweetness of God came to their mouths and hearts without their moving a step and mortifying themselves by losing any of their useless desires, consolations and pleasures. But, until they leave these in order to seek Him, they will not find Him, however much they cry to Him; for thus did the Bride seek Him in the Songs and found Him not until she went forth to seek Him. And this she says in these words:[4] 'In my bed by night I sought Him Whom my soul loveth: I sought Him, and found Him not. I will rise, and will go about the city; in the streets and the broad ways I will seek Him Whom my soul loveth.'[5] And after passing through certain trials she says here that she found Him.

3. He, therefore, who seeks God desiring to have pleasure and rest in Him seeks Him by night and so will not find Him. But he that seeks Him in the practice and performance of the virtues, having abandoned the bed of his pleasures and delights, such a one seeks Him by day and thus will find Him.

[2] Bg: 'than many things together.'
[3] St. Luke xi, 9.
[4] A: 'for thus did the Bride seek Him and found Him not, as is said in the Songs in these words.'
[5] Canticles iii, 1–2. Ej quotes the Latin text and not the vernacular version.

For that which cannot be found by night is visible by day. This is well expressed[6] by the Spouse Himself in the Book of Wisdom, where He says: 'Wisdom is bright and never fadeth away, and is easily seen by them that love her and is found by them that seek her. She preventeth them that covet her, so that she first sheweth herself unto them. He that seeketh her early in the morning shall not labour, for he shall find her sitting at the door of his house.'[7] In this passage he means that, when the soul leaves the house of her own will, and the bed of her own pleasure, having gone forth thence, she shall find the said Divine Wisdom, which is the Son of God, her Spouse; wherefore the soul says here: Seeking my loves,

I will go o'er yonder mountains and banks;

4. By the mountains, which are lofty, she here means the virtues: first, by reason of their loftiness; second, because of the difficulty and toil which are experienced in climbing them; and o'er these mountains she says that she will go, by practising the contemplative life. By the banks, which are low, she means mortifications, penances and spiritual exercises; and o'er these she says also that she will go, by practising in them the active life, together with the contemplative life whereof she has spoken,[8] for in order to seek God surely, and to acquire the virtues, there is need of both. This, then, is as much as to say: Seeking my Beloved, I will ever put into practice the lofty virtues and abase myself in lowly mortifications and exercises of humility. This she says, because the way to seek God is ever to be doing good in God, and mortifying evil in oneself, after the manner which she describes in the following verses, saying:

I will neither pluck the flowers . . .

[6] Bg omits 'well.' Ej, G: 'very well.'
[7] Wisdom vi, 13–15.
[8] G: '. . . active life, as in the virtues above-mentioned [she practises] the contemplative life.' So Ej, but with 'contemplation' for 'the contemplative life.'

5. Inasmuch as in order to seek God it is needful to have a heart that is detached and strong, free from all evil things and from good things that are not simply God, the soul speaks in this present line and in those which follow of the liberty[9] and the courage which she must have in order to seek Him. And herein she says that she will not pluck the flowers that she may find on the way, whereby she means all the pleasures and satisfactions and delights which may be offered her in this life and which might obstruct her road if she should desire to pluck or accept them. These things are of three kinds: temporal, sensual and spiritual. And because they all occupy the heart, and, if the soul should pay heed to them or abide in them, are an impediment to its attainment of such detachment of spirit as is needful in order to follow the straight road to Christ, she says that in seeking Him she will not pluck all these things[10] aforementioned. And thus it is as if she had said: I will not set my heart upon the riches and good things which the world offers, nor will I accept the satisfactions and delights of my flesh, neither will pay heed to the pleasures and consolations[11] of my spirit, in such manner as to be kept from seeking my loves over the mountains of virtues and trials. This she says because she has accepted the counsel which the prophet David has given to those that go by this road, saying: *Divitiæ si affluant, nolite cor apponere.*[12] That is: If riches abound, apply not your heart to them. This, too, she understands of sensual pleasures, as also of the majority of temporal blessings and spiritual consolations. Here it is to be observed that not only do temporal blessings and corporeal delights hinder and turn one aside from the road to God, but likewise spiritual delights and consolations, if we attach ourselves to them or seek after them, obstruct the road to the Cross of our Spouse Christ. Wherefore it behoves him that will go forward not to turn aside[13] and pluck these flow-

[9] B, Bg, Bz: 'of the virtue.'
[10] Ej, G, Sg: 'these flowers.'
[11] Av: 'to the joys, pleasures and consolations.'
[12] Psalm lxi, 11. [A.V., lxii, 10.]
[13] S: 'not to stop.'

ers. And not only so, but it behoves him also to have the courage and the fortitude to say:

> . . . nor fear the wild beasts;
> **I will pass by the mighty and cross the frontiers.**[14]

6. In these lines the Bride speaks of the three enemies of the soul, which are world, devil and flesh, and these are they that war upon her and make her way difficult. By the 'wild beasts' she understands the world; by the 'mighty,' the devil; and by the 'frontiers,' the flesh.

7. She calls the world[15] 'wild beasts' because to the imagination of the soul that sets out upon the road to God the world seems to be represented after the manner of wild beasts, which threaten her fiercely,[16] and this principally in three ways. First, the favour of the world will leave her, and she will lose friends, credit, reputation and even property. Secondly—a wild beast no less terrifying—she must be able to bear the renunciation for ever of worldly satisfaction and delight, and of all the world's comforts. Thirdly—and this is worse still—the tongues of men will rise up against her, and will mock her, and will proffer many sayings and gibes against her and will set her at naught. These things are wont to prejudice certain souls in such a way that it becomes supremely difficult for them, not only to persevere against these wild beasts, but even to be able[17] to set out upon the road at all.

8. But a few generous souls are wont to meet other wild beasts, which are more interior and spiritual—difficulties and temptations, tribulations and trials of many kinds through which they must needs pass. Such God sends to those whom He will raise to high perfection, by proving and examining them as gold in the fire, even as in one place David says: *Multæ tribulationes justorum.*[18] That is: Many are the afflictions of the just, but out of them all will the Lord deliver them. But the soul that loves indeed, that prizes her Beloved

---

[14] Ej, G, Sg omit the following paragraph.

[15] S: 'The world she calls.'

[16] Sg omits this phrase; Ej, G also omit it and substitute 'and spiritually' for 'and this principally.'

[17] Ej, G, Sg: 'but they even think they will be unable.'

[18] Psalm xxxiii, 20. [A.V., xxxiv, 19.]

above all things and that trusts in His love and favour, finds it not hard to say:[19] 'Nor will I fear the wild beasts.'

I will pass by the mighty and cross the frontiers.

9. Evil spirits, who are the second enemy, she calls 'the mighty,' because with a great display of strength they endeavour to seize the passes of this road; likewise because their temptations and wiles[20] are stronger and harder to overcome,[21] and more difficult to penetrate, than those of the world and the flesh, and furthermore because they reinforce themselves with these other two enemies, the world and the flesh, in order to make vigorous warfare upon the soul. Wherefore David, speaking of them, calls them mighty, saying: *Fortes quæsierunt animam meam.*[22] Which signifies: The mighty sought after my soul. Concerning their might, the prophet[23] Job says also: 'There is no power upon earth that can be compared with that of the devil, who was made to fear no one.'[24] That is, no human power can be compared with his; and thus, only the Divine power suffices to be able to conquer him and only the Divine light to penetrate his wiles. Wherefore the soul that is to overcome his might will be unable to do so without prayer, nor will it be able to penetrate his deceits without mortification and without humility; whence Saint Paul, in counselling the faithful, says these words: *Induite vos armaturam Dei, ut possitis stare adversus insidias diaboli, quoniam non est nobis colluctatio adversus carnem et sanguinem.*[25] Which signifies: Put on the armour of God, that you may be able to stand against the deceits of the devil, for our wrestling is not against flesh and blood. By blood he means the world; and by the armour of God,

[19] Bg: 'fears not greatly to say.'
[20] Bz: 'their wily temptations.' A: 'the temptations are stronger.'
[21] Ej, G, Sg omit: 'and harder to overcome.'
[22] Psalm liii, 5. [A.V., liv, 3.]
[23] Bg: 'the holy prophet.'
[24] Job xli, 24. [A.V., xli, 33.]
[25] Ephesians vi, 11. Ej, G neither copy the Latin text nor translate it. Bz omits the translation. B, Bg omit the Latin text after *Dei* but translate the whole Latin text as above, A has the translation and omits the text.

prayer and the Cross of Christ, wherein is the humility and mortification whereof we have spoken.[26]

10. The soul also says that she will cross the frontiers, whereby, as we have said, she indicates the repugnance which the flesh has of its nature to the spirit and the rebellions which it makes against it. As Saint Paul says: *Caro enim concupiscit adversus spiritum*.[27] That is: For the flesh lusteth against the spirit.[28] It sets itself, as it were, upon the frontier and resists those that travel on the spiritual road. And these frontiers the soul must cross, by surmounting these difficulties and, by the force and resolution of the spirit, overthrowing all the desires of sense and the natural affections; for, so long as these remain in the soul, the spirit is impeded[29] by their weight so that it cannot pass on to true life and spiritual delight. This Saint Paul sets clearly before us, saying: *Si spiritu facta carnis mortificaveritis, vivetis*.[30] That is: if by the spirit you mortify the inclinations of the flesh and the desires, you shall live.[31] This, then, is the procedure which the soul says in this stanza that she must needs follow in order to seek her Beloved along this road. Briefly, she must have constancy[32] and resolution not to stoop to pluck the flowers, courage not to fear the wild beasts and strength to pass by the mighty and cross the frontiers, and she must determine only to go over the mountains and banks, which are the virtues, after the manner already expounded.

[26] Av adds: 'with the which Divine armour we shall be able to conquer the mighty, who are the princes of darkness.'

[27] Galatians v, 17. Ej, G: 'As St. Paul says: *Concupiscit adversus spiritum*, which is to set itself as it were upon the frontier.'

[28] Sg: 'For the flesh kicks (*cocea*) against the spirit.' [*Cocear* is 'to kick against the goad.']

[29] Bg, Ej: 'is oppressed.'

[30] Romans viii, 13.

[31] Sg: 'the carnal desires and inclinations.' Ej, G add after the Latin text: '*Hoc est:* the carnal desires, inclinations and temptations.'

[32] [*Lit.*, 'which, in short, is constancy.'] Ej, G: 'wherein, in short, is constancy.' S: 'which, in short, is to have constancy.'

STANZA IV

O woods and thickets   Planted by the hand of the Beloved!
O meadow of verdure, enamelled with flowers,   Say if he has
passed by you.

Exposition

After the soul has described the way wherein she will prepare herself for setting out upon this road, in order not to
turn aside after delights and pleasures, and fortitude[1] to conquer temptations and difficulties, wherein consists the practice
of self-knowledge, which is the first thing that the soul must
achieve in order to come to the knowledge of God, she now,
in this stanza, sets out upon her road, through consideration
and knowledge of the creatures, to the knowledge of her Beloved, their Creator. For, after the practice of self-knowledge,
this consideration of the creatures is the first thing in order
upon this spiritual road to the knowledge of God; by means
of them the soul considers His greatness and excellence, according to that word of the Apostle where he says: *Invisibilia
enim ipsius a creatura mundi, per ea quæ facta sunt, intellecta, conspiciuntur.*[2] Which is as if she said: The invisible
things of God are known by the soul through the invisible
and created visible things.[3] The soul, then, in this stanza,
speaks with the creatures, asking them for news of her Beloved. And it is to be observed that, as Saint Augustine says,[4]
the question that the soul puts to the creatures is the medi-

[1] S: 'and the fortitude which she must have.' [This addition is
necessary to the sense, unless we read as in the first redaction, p. 66,
above.]

[2] Romans i, 20. Ej, G have only *'Invisibilia Dei,* the soul speaking then, etc.'

[3] Av: 'the created visible things.' Sg: 'the visible things, created
and sensible.'

[4] *Confessions,* Bk. X, Chap. vi.

tation that she makes by their means upon their Creator. And thus in this stanza is contained a meditation on the elements and on the other lower creatures, and a meditation upon the heavens and upon the other creatures and material things that God has created therein, and likewise a meditation upon the celestial spirits. She says:

O woods and thickets

2. She describes as 'woods' the elements, which are earth, water, air and fire; for, like the most pleasant woods, they are peopled thickly with creatures,[5] which here she calls 'thickets' by reason of their great number and the wide difference which there is between those in each element. In the earth, innumerable varieties of animals and plants; in the water, innumerable different species of fish; and in the air, a great diversity of birds; while the element of fire concurs with all in animating and preserving them; and thus each kind of animal lives in its element, and is set[6] and planted therein as in its own wood and region where it is born and nurtured. And in truth, God so commanded when He created them:[7] He commanded the earth to produce plants and animals; and the sea and the waters, fish; while He made the air the dwelling-place of birds. Wherefore, when the soul sees that thus He commanded and thus it was done, she says as in the line that follows:

Planted by the hand of the Beloved!

3. In this line is the following consideration[8]—namely, that these varieties and wonders could be made and nurtured only by the hand of the Beloved, God. Here it is to be observed that she says intentionally 'by the hand of the Beloved'; for albeit God performs many other things by the hands of others, as by angels and men, He never performed the act of creation,

[5] S: 'because even as the most pleasant woods are planted and peopled with thick plants and groves, even so are the elements [peopled] thickly with creatures.'

[6] Av: 'lodged'; S: 'placed.'

[7] Genesis i.

[8] S: 'In which line this is the consideration.'

neither performs it, save by His own hand. And thus the soul is greatly moved to love her Beloved, God, by the consideration of the creatures, seeing that these are things that have been made by His own hand. And she says furthermore:

O meadow of verdure,

4. This consideration is upon Heaven, which she calls 'meadow of verdure,' because the things that are created therein have ever unfading greenness and neither perish nor wither with time; and in them, as among fresh verdure, the just take their pleasure and delight;[9] in the which consideration likewise is comprehended all the diversity of the beauteous stars and other celestial planets.

5. This name of verdure the Church gives likewise to heavenly things when, praying to God for the souls of the faithful departed, and speaking to them, she says: *Constituat vos Dominus inter amœna virentia.* This signifies: May God set you among the delectable verdure.[10] And she says also that this meadow of verdure is likewise

Enamelled with flowers,

6. By these flowers she understands the angels and the holy souls, wherewith that place is adorned[11] and beautified like a graceful and costly enamel upon an excellent vase of gold.

Say if he has passed by you.

7. This question is the consideration spoken of above, and it is as if she said: Say what excellences He has created in you.

[9] S omits 'and delight.'
[10] S: 'Which signifies: May Christ, Son of the living God, set you among the ever delectable verdure of His Paradise. The soul says also that this meadow of verdure is . . .', etc. Ej, G give the text as: *Constituat vos Dominus in prata virentia,* and continues: 'Among the delectable verdure may God place you.'
[11] Jaén, A, B, Bz: 'is ordered.'

STANZA V

Scattering a thousand graces,   He passed through these groves
in haste,
And, looking upon them as he went,   Left them, by his glance
alone, clothed with beauty.[1]

Exposition

In this stanza the creatures make answer to the soul, which
answer, as Saint Augustine says also in that same place,[2] is
the testimony which in themselves they bear to the soul concerning the greatness and excellence[3] of God, and for which
the soul asks in its meditation. And thus that which is contained in this stanza is in substance that God created all things
with great facility and brevity[4] and in them left some trace
of Who He was; not only did He give them being out of nothing, but He even endowed them with innumerable graces and
virtues, making them beauteous with marvellous orderliness
and unfailing[5] interdependence,[6] and doing all this through
His Wisdom[7] whereby He created them, which is the Word,
His Only-begotten Son. She says, then, thus:

Scattering a thousand graces,

2. By these thousand graces which she says He scattered
as He went is understood the innumerable multitude of the
creatures. She sets down here the greatest number, which is a
thousand, in order to denote their multitude. She calls them
graces, by reason of the many graces wherewith He endowed

1 B, Ej, G, Sg: 'with his beauty.'
2 *Confessions*, Bk. X, Chap. vi.
3 B, Bg: 'beauty.'
4 Av omits 'with great facility and brevity.'
5 A, Ej, G, Sg: 'indifferent' [i.e. 'unchanging'].
6 Ej, G, Sg: 'mutual correspondence.'
7 S: 'with His wisdom.'

the creatures; and, scattering them—that is to say, peopling the whole world—,

He passed through these groves in haste,

3. To pass through the groves is to create the elements, which here she calls groves. Through these she says He passed, scattering a thousand graces, because He adorned them with all the creatures, which are full of grace. And, moreover, He scattered among them the thousand graces, giving them virtue that they might be able to contribute to the generation and conservation of them all. And she says that He passed, because the creatures are, as it were, a trace of the passing of God, whereby are revealed His greatness, power, wisdom and other Divine virtues. And she says that this passing was in haste, because the creatures are the lesser works of God, Who made them as it were in passing. The greater works, wherein He revealed Himself most clearly and which He wrought most lovingly, were those of the Incarnation of the Word and the mysteries of the Christian faith, in comparison wherewith all the rest were wrought as it were in passing, and in haste.

And, looking upon them as he went,   Left them, by his glance[8] alone, clothed with beauty.

4. According to Saint Paul, the Son of God is the brightness of His glory and the figure of His substance.[9] It must be known, then, that God looked at all things in this image of His Son alone, which was to give them their natural being, to communicate to them many natural gifts and graces, and to make them finished and perfect, even as He says in Genesis, in these words: 'God saw all the things that He had made and they were very good.'[10] To behold them and find them very good was to make them very good in the Word, His Son. And not only did He communicate to them their being and their natural graces when He beheld them, as we

[8] See p. 43, n. 7, above.
[9] Hebrews i, 3.
[10] Genesis i, 31. Ej, G: '. . . in these words: *Vidit Deus cuncta, etc.* And they were very good.'

have said, but also in this image of His Son alone He left
them clothed with beauty, communicating to them supernatural being. This was when He became man, and thus
exalted man in the beauty of God, and consequently[11] exalted
all the creatures in him, since in uniting Himself with man
He united Himself with the nature of them all. Wherefore
said the same Son of God: *Si ego exaltatus a terra fuero,
omnia traham ad me ipsum.*[12] That is: I, if I be lifted up
from the earth, will draw all things to Myself. And thus, in
this lifting up of the Incarnation of His Son, and in the glory of
His resurrection according to the flesh, not alone did the
Father beautify the creatures[13] in part, but we can say that
He left them all clothed with beauty and dignity.[14]

Annotation of the Stanza Following[15]

But, over and above all this, speaking now according to the
sense and the affection of contemplation, it is to be known
that in the vivid contemplation and knowledge of the creatures the soul sees that there is in them such abundance of
graces and virtues and beauty wherewith God endowed them,
that, as it seems to her, they are all clothed with marvellous
natural virtue and beauty, wondrously derived from and communicated by[16] that infinite supernatural beauty of the
image[17] of God, Whose beholding of them clothes the world
and all the heavens with beauty and joy; just as does also the
opening of His hand, whereby, as David says,[18] He fills every
animal with blessing. And therefore the soul, being wounded
in love by this trace of the beauty of her Beloved which she

[11] Bg: 'exalted the Humanity of Christ, and consequently . . .'
[12] St. John xii, 32. G copies the Latin text only. Ej omits the
Latin, and has 'bring' for 'draw.'
[13] Bg: 'not alone does the Father cause the creatures to be re-
born.'
[14] Sg: 'and divinity.'
[15] A, B, Bg, Bz omit this heading.
[16] Ej, G, Sg: 'supernatural and communicated by.' S: 'with
marvellous supernatural virtue and beauty, derived from and communicated by.'
[17] [*figura.*] Bg: 'beauty.' Ej, G, Sg: 'sight.'
[18] Psalm cxliv, 16. [A.V., cxlv, 16.]

has known through the creatures, yearns to behold that invisible[19] beauty which caused this visible beauty,[20] and speaks as in the stanza following.[21]

STANZA VI

Ah, who will be able to heal me!   Surrender thou thyself now completely.[1]
From to-day do thou send me now no other[2] messenger,   For they cannot tell me what I wish.

Exposition

2. As the creatures have given the soul signs of her Beloved by revealing to her in themselves traces of His beauty and excellence, her love has increased, and in consequence the pain which she feels at His absence has grown (for the more the soul knows God, the more grows her desire and anguish to see Him); and when she sees that there is naught that can cure her pain save the presence and sight of her Beloved, she mistrusts any other remedy, and in this stanza begs Him to surrender to her the possession of His presence, entreating Him from that day forth to entertain her with no other knowledge[3] and communications from Himself and traces of His excellence, since these increase her yearnings and pain, rather than satisfy her will and desire;[4] the which will is contented and satisfied with naught less than the sight and presence[5]

[19] A: 'insatiable.'
[20] Av: 'by that invisible beauty.' G: 'by this other visible [beauty].' S: 'to behold that beauty, which is the cause of this other visible beauty.' Ej omits 'which . . . beauty.'
[21] Av: 'wherefore she utters the present stanza.' Ej: 'and says thus.'
[1] B inserts an additional 'now.'
[2] Sg: 'no longer any other.'
[3] Bg: 'caresses.'
[4] S: 'increase her yearnings and the pain of being without the presence which satisfies her will and desire.'
[5] S omits 'and presence.'

of Him. Wherefore, she says, let Him be pleased to surrender Himself to her in truth, in complete and perfect love, and thus she says:

Ah, who will be able to heal me!

3. As though she had said: Among all the delights of the world[6] and the satisfactions of the senses, and the consolations and sweetness of the spirit, naught of a truth will be able to heal me, naught will be able to satisfy me. And since this is so:

Surrender thou thyself now completely.[7]

4. Here it is to be noted that any soul that truly loves cannot wish to gain satisfaction and contentment until it truly possess God. For not only do all other things fail to satisfy it, but rather, as we have said, they increase its hunger and desire to see Him as He is. And thus each sight[8] that the soul obtains of the Beloved, whether it be of knowledge, or feeling, or any other communication soever (which are like messengers that communicate to the soul some knowledge of Who He is, increasing and awakening the desire[9] the more, even as crumbs increase a great hunger) makes it grieve at being entertained with so little, and the soul says: 'Surrender thou thyself now completely.'

5. Since all that can be known of God in this life, much though it be, is not complete knowledge, for it is knowledge in part and very far off, while to know Him essentially is true knowledge, which the soul begs here, therefore she is not content with these other communications, and says next:

From to-day do thou send me now[10] no other messenger,

6. As though she were to say: Permit me not henceforward to know Thee thus imperfectly through these messengers—to

---

[6] Ej: 'of the Beloved.'

[7] [See p. 43, n. 9, above.]

[8] Av, B, Sg have 'visit [*visita*] . . . from' for 'sight [*vista*] . . . of.'

[9] Ej, G: 'the desire and yearning.'

[10] A omits 'now.'

wit, by the knowledge and the feelings that I am given of
Thee, so far distant and removed from that which my soul
desires of Thee. For to one who grieves for Thy presence,
well knowest Thou, my Spouse, that the messengers bring an
increase of affliction: for the one reason, because with the
knowledge of Thee that they give they re-open the wound;
for the other, because they seem but to delay Thy coming.
Wherefore from this day forth do Thou send me no more of
such far distant knowledge, for if until now I could make
shift with it, since I neither knew Thee nor loved Thee much,
now the greatness of the love that I have[11] cannot be satisfied with this earnest of knowledge: wherefore do Thou surrender Thyself completely. It is as if she said more clearly:
This thing, O Lord my Spouse, that Thou art giving of Thyself in part to my soul, do Thou now give completely and
wholly. And this thing that Thou art showing as in glimpses,
do Thou now show completely and clearly.[12] And this that
Thou art communicating through intermediaries, which is like
to communicating Thyself in mockery, do Thou now communicate completely and truly, giving Thyself through Thyself. For at times in Thy visits it seems that Thou art about
to give the jewel of the possession of Thyself, and, when my
soul regards herself well, she finds herself without it; for Thou
hidest it from her, which is as it were to give it in mockery.
Surrender Thyself, then, completely, giving Thyself wholly
to the whole of my soul, that it wholly may have Thee wholly,
and be Thou pleased to send me no other messenger.[13]

For they cannot tell me what I wish.

7. As though she were to say: I wish for Thee wholly, and
they are unable and know not how to speak to me of Thee
wholly; for naught on earth or in heaven can give the soul
the knowledge which she desires to have of Thee, and thus
they cannot tell me what I wish. In place of these messengers,
therefore, be Thou messenger and messages both.

[11] Ej, G, S, Sg add: 'to Thee.'
[12] Av lacks the sentences following ('And this . . . no other messenger').
[13] S adds: 'from to-day.'

STANZA VII

**And all those that serve[1]   Relate to me a thousand graces of
thee,**
**And all wound me the more   And something that they are
stammering leaves me dying.**

Exposition

In the last stanza the soul has described herself as being sick
or wounded with love for her Spouse, by reason of the knowledge of Him that the irrational creation has given her; and in
this present stanza she describes herself as wounded with love
by reason of a loftier knowledge of the Beloved that she receives through the rational creation—namely, angels and men,
who are nobler than the former. And, furthermore, she says
that not only is this so, but likewise that she is dying of love
because of a wondrous immensity that is revealed to her
through these creatures; yet she attains not to a complete
revelation thereof, for she calls it here a 'something,' since
she cannot describe it, save that it is such that it makes the
soul to be dying of love.[2]

2. From this we may infer that in this business of loving
there are three kinds of pain which come to the soul from
the Beloved, corresponding to three kinds of knowledge that
can be had of Him. The first is called a wound; this is the
slightest of the three and passes the most briefly, as does a
wound, because it is born of the knowledge that the soul
receives from the creatures, which are the lowest works of
God. And of this wound, which here we likewise call sickness,
the Bride speaks in the Songs, saying: *Adjuro vos, filiæ
Jerusalem, si inveneritis dilectum meum, ut nuntietis ei, quia
amore langueo.*[3] Which signifies: I adjure you, O daughters

---

[1] [*vagan.*] Ej has *vacan* [cf. § 6, below]; A, *bajan*, 'go down' [an
evident error, *b* and *v* being identically pronounced and frequently
confused in writing, in Spanish].

[2] S, Sg omit 'of love.'

[3] Canticles v, 8. Ej, G omit the translation which follows.

of Jerusalem, if you find my Beloved, that you tell him that I languish with love—meaning by the daughters of Jerusalem the creatures.

3. The second is called a sore, which takes firmer hold upon the soul than a wound, and for that reason lasts longer, for it is like a wound which has become a sore, wherewith the soul feels in truth that it goes about sorely wounded by love. And this sore is made in the soul by means of the knowledge of the works of the Incarnation of the Word and mysteries of the faith; which, being greater works of God and comprehending within themselves a greater love than those of the creatures, produce a greater effect of love upon the soul; so that, if the first is as a wound, this second is as a continuous sore. Of this the Spouse in the Songs, addressing the soul, says: 'Thou hast ravished My heart, My sister, thou hast ravished My heart with one of thine eyes, and with one hair of thy neck.'[4] Because the eye here signifies faith in the Incarnation of the Spouse, and the hair signifies the love of the same Incarnation.

4. The third kind of pain in love is like to dying, which is as though the soul had the sore festered, and the soul has become wholly festered.[5] The soul lives while yet dying, until love slays it and so makes it to live the life of love, transforming it into love. And this dying of love is effected in the soul by means of a touch of highest[6] knowledge of the Divinity, which thing is the 'something' whereof, as is said in this stanza, they are stammering. This touch is neither continuous nor long, for were it so the soul would loose itself from the body; but it passes quickly, and thus the soul remains dying of love, and dies the more seeing that it cannot wholly die of love. This is called impatient love, spoken of in Genesis, where the Scripture says that Rachel had such great desire to conceive that she said to her spouse Jacob: *Da mihi liberos, alioquin moriar.*[7] That is: Give me children or else I shall die. And the prophet Job said: *Quis mihi det, ut qui coepit*

---

[4] Canticles iv, 9. Av, Ej, G, Sg omit 'thou hast ravished My heart' the second time.

[5] B, Bg: 'become one whole fester.'

[6] A: 'of human.' S: 'of its.'

[7] Genesis xxx, 1.

ipse me conterat?[8] Which is to say: Who will grant me that
he that hath begun me, the same shall end me?

5. These twofold pains of love[9]—namely, the sore and the
dying—says the soul in this stanza, are caused in her by these
rational creatures. The sore, in that place which says that
they are relating to her a thousand graces of the Beloved
in the mysteries and Wisdom of God taught her by the faith.
The dying, in that place which says that they are 'stammering,' which is the sense and knowledge of the Divinity revealed
to the soul in things that she hears said of God. She says,
then:

And all those that serve[10]

6. She means here, as we have said, by 'those that serve,'
the rational creatures—angels and men—for these alone among
all the creatures serve God with understanding of Him. For
that is the meaning of this word (*vagan*) which in Latin
is *vacant*. Thus it is as much as to say: all those that serve
God. Some do this by contemplating[11] Him in Heaven and
having fruition of Him, as do the angels; others, by loving
and desiring Him upon earth, as do men. And because through
these rational creatures the soul knows God more keenly (now
by considering their excellence, which is greater than that of
all things else created, now by that which they teach us of
God: the ones inwardly by secret inspirations, like those of
the angels, the others outwardly through the truths of Scripture), she says:

Relate[12] to me a thousand graces of thee,

7. That is: they reveal to me wondrous things of Thy grace
and mercy in the works of Thy[13] Incarnation and truths of
faith which they expound to me concerning Thee, and relate
to me more and more; for the more they desire to say, the

[8] Job vi, 8–9.
[9] Av: 'These two manners of love.'
[10] [See p. 77, n. 15, above.]
[11] Ej, G, Sg: 'by confessing.'
[12] [Cf. p. 233, n. 11, above.]
[13] S has 'the' for 'Thy.'

more graces will they be able to reveal concerning Thee.[14]

And all wound me the more

8. For the more the angels inspire me and the more men teach me concerning Thee, the more do they make me to be in love with Thee, and thus the more do all wound me with love.

And something that they are stammering leaves me dying.

9. As if she had said: But beyond the fact that these creatures wound me in the thousand graces which they reveal to me concerning Thee, there is a something which, I feel, still remains to be said; a thing which I know has yet to be said;[15] a clearly imprinted trace of God which is revealed to the soul, and which it has to follow; a most lofty understanding of God, which cannot be expressed, and for that reason is called a 'something'; and if the other thing that I understand[16] inflicts upon me the wound and the sore of love, this that I cannot wholly understand, yet feel most deeply, slays me. This happens at times to souls that are already adept, to whom God grants the favour of giving, through that which they hear or see or understand, and sometimes without any of those means, a sublime knowledge, wherein it is granted them to understand or to perceive the loftiness and greatness[17] of God; and in this perception the soul experiences such lofty feelings of God that it understands clearly that all has yet[18] to be understood; and that understanding and feeling that the Divinity is so vast that it cannot be perfectly understood is a most sublime understanding. And thus one of the great favours that God grants fleetingly in this life is to give it to understand so clearly and to feel so deeply concerning God, that it is able to understand clearly that it cannot understand or feel at all; for in some manner the soul is like those who

[14] [*de ti.*] Jaén, A, B, Bg have *de sí* ['of themselves'].
[15] The MSS., except Jaén, read: 'which I know not has yet to be revealed.' S: 'which I know not has yet to be said.'
[16] Bg: 'that I have.'
[17] Av, Ej, G, Sg omit 'and greatness.'
[18] Av: 'all has yet clearly.' Jaén: 'all gives itself.'

see Him in Heaven, where those that know Him the best understand the most distinctly the infinitude that they still have to understand, while those that see Him least perceive less clearly than those that see most how much they have yet to see.

10. This, I think,[19] one who has not experienced it will not succeed in understanding; but the soul that experiences it, seeing that it has yet to understand that which it feels so profoundly, calls it a 'something'; for, as it is not understood, so neither can it be expressed—although, as I have said, it can be felt. Wherefore the Bride says that the creatures are stammering to her because they cannot perfectly explain themselves; for that is the meaning of 'stammer'—namely, to talk as do children, and not to convey and express perfectly that which they have to say.

Annotation for the Stanza Following

Likewise, with respect to the other creatures, there come to the soul certain enlightenments in the way that we have described (albeit they are not always so sublime) when God grants the soul the favour of unfolding to it the knowledge and perception of the spiritual power which is in them. They seem to be expressing grandeurs of God which they are unable to express perfectly, and it is as if they are going to express them, but fall short of making them understood,[20] and thus it is a 'something that they are stammering.' And thus the soul proceeds with her complaint, and in the stanza following addresses her own life, saying:

[19] S: 'This, I understand.'
[20] Sg: '. . . of God, and are unable to express them perfectly, and they remain without being able to do so.' ['Remain' has here the force of little more than 'be.'] Ej: '. . . of God, and cannot express them perfectly, and they fall short of making them understood. It is as if they are going to express them, and remain without doing so.' A, B omit: 'and it is as if they are going to express them.'

STANZA VIII

But how, O life,[1] dost thou persevere,   Since thou livest not
where thou livest,
And since the arrows make thee to die which thou receivest
From the conceptions of the Beloved which thou formest
within thee?

Exposition

2. As the soul sees herself to be dying of love, even as she
has just said, and sees also that she is not dying wholly, in
such a way as to be able to have the fruition of love[2] freely,
she makes complaint of the duration of her bodily life, by
reason of which her spiritual life is delayed. And thus in this
stanza she addresses the very life of her soul, laying stress
upon the pain which it causes her. The sense of this stanza is
as follows: Life of my soul, how canst thou persevere in this
fleshly life, since it is death to thee and privation of that true
spiritual life[3] of God, wherein in essence, love and desire
thou livest more truly than in the body? And albeit this were
no cause for leaving and freeing thyself of the body of this
death in order to enjoy and live the life of thy God, how canst
thou still persevere in the body so frail, since, besides this,
the wounds which thou receivest from the love of the grandeurs that are communicated to thee from thy Beloved are
alone sufficient to end thy life, all of which wounds leave
thee vehemently wounded with love; so that the things that
thou feelest and understandest concerning Him are so many
touches and wounds which thou receivest, and which slay
with love? The lines continue:

But how, O life,[4] dost thou persevere,   Since thou livest not
where thou livest,

[1] B: 'O soul.'
[2] Ej, G: 'in order to have fruition of the Beloved.'
[3] A: 'since it is true death to thee of that true spiritual life.'
[4] B: 'O soul.'

3. For the understanding hereof[5] it is to be known that the soul lives where it loves rather than in the body which it animates, because it has not its life in the body, but rather gives it to the body, and lives through love in that which it loves. But over and above this life of love, whereby the soul that loves God lives in Him, the soul has its natural and radical life, as have likewise all created things, in God, according to that word of Saint Paul, who says: 'In Him we live and move and are.'[6] Which is to say: In God we have our life and our movement and our being. And Saint John says that all that was made was life in God.[7] And as the soul sees that she has her natural life in God, through the being that she has in Him, and likewise her spiritual life, through the love wherewith she loves Him, she complains and bewails that a life so frail in a mortal body can do as much as to impede her from enjoying a life so real, true and delectable as that which she lives in God through nature and love. The insistence that the soul lays upon this is great, for she here declares that she is suffering in two contrary ways—namely, in her natural life in the body and in her spiritual life in God, which in themselves are contrary, because the one wars against the other; and since she lives in both she has perforce to suffer great torment, for the one life, which is grievous, hinders the other, which is delectable, so much so that natural life is to her as death, since through it she is deprived of the spiritual life wherein she has all her being and life through nature, and all her operations and affections through love. And to explain more clearly the rigour of this frail life she next says:

Since the arrows make thee to die which thou receivest

4. As if she had said: And, apart from what I have said, how canst thou persevere in the body, since the touches of love (for this she means by 'arrows') which the Beloved inflicts upon thy heart suffice alone to deprive thee of thy life? These touches make the soul and the heart so fruitful in

[5] S: 'For the understanding of these lines.'
[6] Acts xvii, 28.
[7] St. John i, 4. See p. 80, n. 5, above.

understanding and love of God that it may well be said that she has conception of God, according to what is said in the line which follows, namely:

From the conceptions of the Beloved which thou formest within thee?

5. That is to say, of the greatness, beauty, wisdom, grace and virtues that thou understandest of Him.

Annotation for the Stanza Following

As the hart, when it is wounded with a poisoned arrow,[8] has no ease and rest, but seeks remedies here and there,[9] now plunging into these waters, now into those; and as, each time, notwithstanding all the remedies that it applies, the poison[10] takes ever stronger hold upon it, till it seizes upon the heart and causes death; even so the soul that goes about pierced by the poisoned arrow[11] of love,[12] as does she of whom we are here treating, never ceases to seek remedies for her pain, and not only does she not find them, but rather all that she thinks, says and does becomes to her an occasion of[13] further pain. And she, knowing that this is so, and that she has no other remedy, save to come and place herself in the hands of Him that wounded her, that He may give her relief[14] and slay her outright through the power of love, turns to her Spouse, Who is the cause of all this,[15] and addresses to Him the following stanza.[16]

[8] [*Lit.*, 'wounded with poison.']
[9] Ej, G, Sg: 'seeks remedies in this place and in that.'
[10] Ej, G: 'the wound.'
[11] [*Lit.*, 'the poison.'] Ej, G: 'the wound.'
[12] Av: 'of the love of God.' Bg: 'of the touch of love.'
[13] B, Bg, Ej, G, Sg: 'serves her for.'
[14] Ej, G: 'that He may wound her.'
[15] A: 'of all her pain.' Av omits 'Who is the cause of all this.'
[16] A: 'and says [as in] the following stanza.'

STANZA IX

**Since thou hast wounded this heart,[1] Wherefore didst thou
not heal it?
And wherefore, having robbed me of it, hast thou left it thus
And takest not the prey that thou hast spoiled?**

Exposition

2. In this stanza, then, the soul speaks yet once more with
the Beloved, making complaint of her pain,[2] for love that
is impatient, such as the soul here reveals, allows itself no
rest nor gives any respite to its grief, setting forth its yearnings
in every wise until it find a remedy. And as the soul sees
herself wounded[3] and alone, having no healer, nor any other
medicine, save her Beloved, Who it was that wounded her,
she asks Him why, since He wounded her heart with the love
that comes from knowledge of Him, He has not healed her
with the vision of His presence. And why (she asks further),
since He has robbed her of her heart, through the love wherewith He has enamoured her, drawing her forth from her own
power, has He left her thus, namely, drawn forth from her
power,[4] (for one that loves possesses his heart no longer, but
has given it to the Beloved) and has not placed her truly in
His power, taking her to Himself in complete and perfect
transformation of love in glory.[5] She says, then:

**Since thou hast wounded this heart,[6] Wherefore didst thou
not heal it?**

3. She makes not complaint because He has wounded her,
for the more deeply the enamoured soul is wounded, the

---

[1] Ej, G: 'this heart of mine.'
[2] Bg: 'of her love.'
[3] Sg: 'favoured.'
[4] B, Ej, G, Sg omit the words 'has He left . . . her power.'
[5] Av: 'and perfect transformation of glory.'
[6] Ej, Sg: 'this heart of mine.'

greater is her joy; but because, having wounded her heart, He did not heal it, by slaying it wholly; for so sweet and so delectable are the wounds of love that if they succeed not in slaying they cannot satisfy, but they are so delectable[7] that she would fain have them wound her even till they have wholly slain her,[8] wherefore she says this: 'Since Thou hast wounded this heart, wherefore didst Thou not heal it?' As though she had said: Wherefore, since Thou hast wounded it even to the point of leaving a sore in it, dost Thou not heal it by slaying it outright with love? Since Thou art the cause of its wound in affliction of love, be Thou the cause of its health in death of love;[9] for after this manner the heart that is wounded with the pain of Thy absence will be healed with the delight and glory of Thy sweet presence. And she adds:

And wherefore, having robbed me of it, hast thou left it thus

4. To rob is naught else than for a robber to dispossess an owner of that which is his and to take possession thereof himself. This plaint, then, the soul sets forth here to the Beloved, enquiring of Him why, since out of love He has robbed her heart and taken it out of her power and possession, He has abandoned it thus, without taking it truly into His own possession and keeping it for Himself, as the robber does to the spoils that he has robbed, by carrying them off with him.

5. Wherefore he that has fallen in love is said to have his heart robbed or raped[10] from him by the object of his love, because it wanders far away from him and is set upon the object of his love, and thus he has no heart of his own, for it belongs to the person whom he loves. Wherefore the soul may know well[11] if it loves God purely or no; for, if it loves Him, it will have no heart for itself, nor for regarding

---

[7] Sg omits the words 'that if they . . . so delectable.'

[8] Ej, G, Sg: 'till they had ended her life.' Bg reads [*llegar* for *llagar*, an almost certain error]: 'she would fain have them attain even to slaying her wholly.'

[9] Av omits: 'be Thou . . . love.' Bg reads: 'certain is the cause . . .'

[10] Av, Bz, Ej, Sg omit 'or raped.' [Cf. also p. 83, n. 6, above.]

[11] S: 'very well.'

its pleasure and profit, but only for the honour and glory of God and for giving Him pleasure, for, the more of its heart it has for itself, the less it has for God.

6. And whether or no the heart has indeed been stolen by God can be determined by one of two things: by whether it has yearnings for God, and cares for naught else save for Him, as the soul here declares. The reason is because the heart cannot be in peace and rest without some kind of possession, and, when its affections are well set, it has possession neither of itself nor[12] of aught beside; and if,[13] furthermore, it possesses not completely that which it loves, its weariness[14] cannot fail to be as great as its loss until it possess it and be satisfied; for until then the soul is like to an empty vessel waiting to be filled, like to the hungry man that desires food, like to the sick man sighing for health, and like to one that is suspended in the air and has no place whereon to find a foothold. In that case is the heart of one that has truly fallen in love, and it is this that the soul by experience feels[15] here, saying: 'Wherefore hast Thou left it thus?' Which is to say, empty, hungry, lonely, wounded, in pains of love, suspended in the air.

And takest not the prey that thou hast spoiled?

7. Which is to say: Why takest Thou not the heart that Thou hast spoiled through love, in order to fill it and satisfy it and accompany it and heal it,[16] giving it perfect rest and a perfect abode in Thyself? However complete the agreement between it and the Beloved, the loving soul cannot fail to desire the recompense and wages of its love, for the sake of which recompense it serves the Beloved; and otherwise its love would not be true; for the wages and recompense of love are naught else, nor can the soul desire[17] aught else, than greater

12 A reads: 'without some kind of possession, either of itself or,' etc.

13 Thus Ej, G, Sg. The other MSS. and editions read: 'And so.'

14 A, S: 'wherefore its weariness.'

15 Sg reads 'understands,' and Ej, G read 'understands well' for 'feels.'

16 Sg: 'and satisfy it and protect it and love it.'

17 B reads 'ask' for 'desire.'

love, until it attains to perfection of love; for love confers no payment save of itself, according as the prophet Job declared, when, speaking with the same yearning and desire which the soul here possesses, he says: 'Even as the servant[18] desireth the shade, and as the day-labourer looketh for the end of his work, so I had empty months and counted the nights wearisome for myself. If I sleep, I shall say: "When will come the day when I shall arise?" And then I shall await the evening once again, and shall be filled with sorrows till the darkness of night.'[19] So, then, the soul that is enkindled in the love of God desires the fulfilment and perfection of love in order to find complete refreshment there; as the servant wearied with the summer desires the refreshment of the shade, and as the hireling awaits the end of his work, so does the soul await the end of hers. Here it is to be noted that the prophet Job said not that the hireling awaited the end of his labour, but the end of his work, in order to convey the idea that we are expressing—namely, that the soul that loves awaits not the end of its labour, but the end of its work. For its work is to love, and of this work, which is to love, the soul awaits the end and termination, which is the perfection and fulfilment of loving God. Until this is fulfilled for it, the soul is ever in the form described by Job in the passage aforementioned, holding the days and the months as empty and counting the nights as wearisome and tedious for itself. In that which has been said it is signified how the soul that loves God must not claim[20] or hope for any other guerdon for its services save the perfection of loving God.

Annotation of the Stanza Following[21]

The soul, then, being at this stage of love, is like a sick man greatly wearied, who, having lost taste and appetite, is nauseated by all food and troubled and annoyed by everything;

[18] Bz and S follow the Scriptural authority correctly thus. The other MSS. and editions read *ciervo* ('hart') for *siervo* ('servant').

[19] Job vii, 2–4.

[20] S reads 'wish,' and A 'ask,' for 'claim.'

[21] Ej includes the preceding sentence in this Annotation.

but in all that presents itself to his thought or sight[22] he has
before him one longing[23] and desire alone, which is for
health; and all that conduces not thereto is wearisome and
oppressive to him. Wherefore this soul, having reached this
pain[24] of love for God, has these three characteristics,
namely: that, in all things which present themselves to her and
with which she has to do, she has ever before her that concern[25] for her health, which is her Beloved; and thus, although she may occupy herself with these things, because she
cannot do otherwise, she has her heart ever in Him. Hence
comes the second characteristic, which is that she has lost her
taste for all things. And hence likewise follows the third, that
all these things are wearisome to her and every kind of thing
that she does is oppressive and grievous.

2. The reason for all this, deduced from that which we have
said, is that, since the palate of the will of the soul has tasted
and savoured this food of the love of God, therefore, whatsoever thing or treatment is offered to it, the will is immediately inclined, without taking into account any other liking
or consideration, to seek and to enjoy its Beloved therein.
Even so was it with Mary Magdalene, when with ardent love
she went about the garden in search of Him, and, thinking
that He was the gardener, said to Him, without any reason
or reflection: 'If thou hast taken Him hence, tell me, and I
will take Him away.'[26] Since this soul has a similar yearning
to find Him in all things, and finds Him not as soon as she
desires—but rather quite the contrary—not only do these things
not please her, but they are even a torment to her, and sometimes a very great one; for such souls suffer much in their
commerce with men and in other business, since they are disturbed rather than helped thereby in their aspiration.

3. These three characteristics the Bride clearly declares that
she possessed when she sought her Spouse in the Songs, say-

[22] A, S: 'thought and feeling or sight.'
[23] [Lit., 'appetite.']
[24] Ej, G: 'sickness and pain.'
[25] [Most expressively in the original: 'that "ah!" concerning her
health.']
[26] St. John xx, 15.

ing: 'I sought him, and found him not. But they that go about
the city found me and wounded me, and the keepers of the
walls took away my cloak from me.'[27] For they that go about
the city are the affairs of the world, who, when they find the
soul that seeks God, deal her many wounds, which are sorrows, pains and displeasures;[28] for not only does she fail to
find in them that which she seeks, but they even hinder her.
And they that guard the wall of contemplation that the soul
may not enter therein, which are the evil spirits and the affairs
of the world, take away the cloak of the peace and tranquillity
of loving contemplation. From all this the soul that is enkindled in love for God receives a thousand displeasures and an-
noyances; and seeing her, for as long as she is in this life
without sight of God, she cannot free herself[29] from them
either to a great or to a small degree, she continues her entreaties with her Beloved, and says as in the stanza following:

STANZA X

**Quench thou my griefs,   Since none suffices to remove them,
And let mine eyes behold thee,   Since thou art their light and
for thee alone I wish to have them.**

Exposition

4. The soul continues, then, in the present stanza, entreating
the Beloved to be pleased now to set an end to her yearnings
and afflictions, since there is none other that suffices to do
this save only Himself; and she entreats Him to do it in such
a way that her eyes may behold Him, since He alone is the
light by which they see and she desires to use them for naught
else save for Him only. She says:[1]

Quench thou my griefs,

[27] Canticles v, 6–7.
[28] Jaén: 'wounds, pains, sorrows and displeasures.'
[29] S: 'she cannot find alleviation.'
[1] Ej, G, Sg: 'to use them for naught else, and thus says:'

5. The concupiscence of love,[2] then, has this one property, as has been said, that all that is not done and said in agreement with that which the will loves wearies, fatigues and grieves it, and makes it fretful, when it sees not the fulfilment of that which it desires; and this, and the weariness which she has to see God, the Bride here calls 'griefs,' to remove which naught else suffices but the possession of the Beloved. Wherefore she entreats Him to quench them with His presence, and to refresh them all, as cool water refreshes one that is wearied with the heat. For this reason she here uses this word 'quench,' to signify that she is suffering from the fire of love.

Since none suffices to remove them,

6. In order the better to move and persuade the Beloved to fulfil her petition, the soul says that, since none other than He suffices to satisfy her need, it must be He that shall quench her griefs. Whence it is to be noted that God is very ready to comfort the soul and satisfy her in her needs and afflictions, when she neither has nor seeks to have any other satisfaction and comfort than Himself; and thus the soul that can find pleasure in naught apart from God cannot remain for long without a visitation from the Beloved.

And let mine eyes behold thee,

7. That is, let me see Thee[3] face to face with the eyes of my soul.

Since thou art their light

8. Over and above the fact that God is supernatural light to the eyes of the soul, without which she is in darkness, she calls Him here, through her affection, 'light of her eyes,' in the way wherein the lover is wont to call the person whom he loves the 'light of his eyes,' to show the affection which he bears to her. And thus it is as if he had said in the two lines above mentioned: Since the eyes of my soul have no other light, either of their nature or of love, save Thee, let

---

[2] Ej, G, Sg: 'of the soul.'
[3] A: 'That is, let mine eyes see Thee.'

mine eyes behold Thee, for in every way Thou art their light.
Of this light David felt the loss when with grief he said: 'The
light of mine eyes, even that is not with me.'[4] And Tobias
when he said: 'What joy can be mine, since I am sitting in
the darkness and see not the light of Heaven?'[5] Wherein he
desired the bright vision of God, because the light of Heaven
is the Son of God, according as Saint John says, in these
words: 'The heavenly city has no need of the sun, nor of
the moon, to shine in it; for the brightness of God lightens
it, and the lamp thereof is the Lamb.'[6]

And for thee alone I wish to have them.

9. Herein the soul seeks to constrain the Spouse to let her
see this light of her eyes, not only because, having no other
light, she will be in darkness, but also because she wishes to
have them for naught else than for Himself.[7] For even as
that soul is justly deprived of the Divine light who desires
to set the eyes of her will on the light of possession[8] of any
other thing beside God, inasmuch as the sight is occupied
thereby and cannot receive the light of God, even so also,
in the same way, a soul merits[9] that this be given her, if she
closes her eyes aforementioned[10] to all things, to open them
to her God only.

Annotation for the Stanza Following

But it must be known that the loving Spouse of souls cannot
see them grieve for long alone, as He sees this soul of whom
we are speaking, for, as He says through Zacharias, her griefs
and complaints touch Him in the apple of His eye[11]; above
all when the griefs of such souls are for love of Him, as are
those of this soul. Wherefore He says also through Isaias as

4 Psalm xxxvii, 11. [A.V., xxxviii, 10.]
5 Tobias v, 12.
6 Apocalypse xxi, 23.
7 [*que para él.*] A has *que parece* ['that appears'].
8 G: 'light of prosperity.'
9 Ej, G: 'even so also a soul merits abundantly.'
10 G, Sg: 'she closes the door and her eyes.'
11 Zacharias ii, 8.

follows: 'Before they call, I will hear; even when the word is in their mouth I will hear them.'[12] The Wise Man says of Him that if the soul seeks Him as it seeks money it will find Him.[13] And thus it seems that this enamoured soul which seeks Him more covetously than it seeks money, since it has left all things—even itself—for Him, has been granted by God, after these exceeding fervent entreaties, a certain spiritual presence of Himself, wherein He shows it certain profound glimpses of His divinity and beauty, wherewith its desire to see Him and its fervour[14] are greatly increased. For even as men are wont to throw water on a forge to increase the heat and intensity of the fire, even so is the Lord wont to do with certain of these souls, which experience these calms of love,[15] by giving them certain signs of His excellence, in order to make their love more intense,[16] and thus to prepare them ever more for the favours which He desires afterwards to grant them. And even as, in that dark presence, the soul has seen and experienced that supreme good and beauty that is hidden therein, dying with desire[17] to see it, the stanza which follows says:[18]

STANZA XI

Reveal thy presence   And let the vision of thee and thy beauty slay me;
Behold, the affliction of love is not cured   Save by thy presence and thy form.

Exposition

2. The soul, then, desires to see herself possessed by this great God, by Whose love the heart feels itself to be stolen

[12] Isaias lxv, 24.
[13] Proverbs ii, 4.
[14] Sg: 'its favour and desire to see Him.'
[15] Ej: 'these yearnings of love.'
[16] Ej, G, Sg: 'to make their affection greater.'
[17] Sg: 'burning with desire.'
[18] Ej, G abbreviate: 'that supreme good and hidden beauty, she says thus:'

away and wounded; and, being unable to suffer it any longer, she begs Him expressly in this stanza to reveal and show His beauty, which is His Divine Essence, and to slay her with the vision thereof, and thus to loose her from the flesh (since she cannot see Him in the flesh and have fruition of Him as she desires). She sets before Him the grief and yearning of her heart, which she feels continually as she suffers for love of Him and is unable to find any remedy less than this glorious vision of His Divine Essence. The line follows:

Reveal thy presence

3. For the exposition hereof it must be known that there are three ways wherein God may be present in the soul. The first is in essence, and in this way He is present, not only in the best and holiest souls, but also in evil and sinful souls and in all other creatures; for by this presence He gives them life and being, and if they were to lack this essential presence they would all be annihilated and would cease to be: this presence is never lacking in the soul. The second presence is by grace, wherein God dwells in the soul, pleased and satisfied with it. And not all have this presence, for those that fall into mortal sin[1] lose it; and the soul cannot know naturally if it has it.[2] The third presence is by spiritual affection, since in many devout souls God is wont to create many kinds of spiritual presence wherewith He recreates, delights and gladdens them; but these methods of spiritual presence, like the rest, are all hidden, because God shows not Himself in them as He is, since the nature[3] of this life suffers it not; and thus of any of these may be understood the above-mentioned verse, namely: 'Reveal Thy presence.'

4. Inasmuch as it is certain that God is ever present in

[1] Jaén, A, Av: 'fall into sin.'

[2] Sg modifies thus: 'and if this [presence] were lacking they would all be annihilated, and thus this essential presence which has been spoken of is never lacking in the soul. The second presence is spiritual by grace, wherein God dwells, pleased and satisfied with it. And not all souls have this presence, for those that are born in mortal sin lose it, and souls cannot know naturally if they have it.' Substantially identical with Sg are Ej and G.

[3] A: 'stanza' [canción for condición: an error]; B, Bg: 'capacity.'

the soul, at least in the first way, the soul entreats Him, not
to present Himself to her, but to reveal and manifest to her
this hidden presence, which He grants to her, whether naturally or spiritually or affectively, in such a way that she may
see Him in His Divine Being and beauty. She begs Him that,
as with His present Being He gives natural being to the soul,
and with His present grace He perfects it, so with His glory
made manifest He will glorify it. But, forasmuch as this soul
is full of fervours and affections of love for God, we have
to understand that this presence which here she begs the
Beloved to reveal to her principally denotes a certain affective
presence which the Beloved has communicated, of Himself,
to the soul. This was so lofty that it seemed to the soul that
there was an immense hidden being there, of which she was
conscious, and out of which God communicates to her certain
half-obscure glimpses of His Divine beauty; and these produce
such effect upon the soul that they cause her to conceive a
great aspiration and to faint in desire for that which she feels
to be hidden there[4] in that presence, which is like to that
which David felt when he said: 'My soul longeth and fainteth
for the courts of the Lord.'[5] For at this time the spirit faints
with the desire to immerse itself in that supreme good which
it feels to be present and hidden; although it be hidden, the
soul is very deeply conscious of the good and the delight that
are therein. And therefore the soul is attracted to this good,
and carried away by it, with greater violence than that wherewith a natural object is attracted to its centre. And the soul,
having that great longing and heartfelt desire, can no longer
contain herself,[6] and says: 'Reveal Thy presence.'

5. The same thing happened to Moses on Mount Sinai. Being there in the presence of God, he was enabled to obtain
such lofty and profound glimpses of the loftiness and beauty
of the hidden divinity of God[7] that, being unable to bear it,

[4] G omits the passage: 'of which she was conscious . . . hidden
there.'

[5] Psalm lxxxiii, 1. [A.V., lxxxiv, 2.]

[6] Av: 'can no longer stop.' A, B: 'can no longer be content.'

[7] Ej: 'profound glimpses of the loftiness and dignity of God.'
So Sg, but with 'divinity' for 'dignity.'

he twice entreated God to reveal His glory to him, saying
to God: 'Thou sayest that Thou knowest me by my own name
and that I have found grace in Thy sight. Now, therefore,
if I have found grace in Thy presence, show me Thy face,[8]
that I may know Thee and may find in Thine eyes the perfect
grace that I desire'[9] (which is, to attain to the perfect love
of the glory of God). But the Lord answered him, saying:
'Thou wilt not be able to see My face, for man shall not see
Me and live.'[10] Which is as if He were to say: It is a difficult
thing that thou askest of Me, Moses, for such is the beauty
of My face and the joy of the vision of My Being that thy
soul will be unable to bear it in this manner of life that is
so weak. And thus the soul, knowing this truth (whether because of the words wherein God here answered Moses, or
whether also because, as we have said, she feels that there
is something hidden in the presence of God), that she will
not be able to see Him in His beauty in this manner of life,
since she faints at the mere glimpse thereof, as we have said,
anticipates the answer that may be given to her, as it was
given to Moses, and says:

And let the vision of thee and thy beauty slay me;

6. Which is as if she were to say: Since the joy of the
vision of Thy Being and beauty is so great that my soul cannot
bear it, but that I must die upon seeing it,[11] let the vision
of Thee and Thy beauty slay me.

7. It is known that there are two visions which are fatal
to man because he cannot bear the strength and the efficacy
of them. The one is that of the basilisk, at whose sight, it
is said, men die immediately; the other is the vision of God.
But the causes are very different; for the vision of the one
slays with grievous poison and the other by boundless health
and blessing of glory. Wherefore the soul acts not strangely
here in desiring to die at the vision of the beauty of God,

---

[8] Av: 'show me Thy glory.'
[9] Exodus xxxiii, 12–13.
[10] Exodus xxxiii, 20.
[11] Av: 'is so great that my soul will be unable to see it without
dying upon seeing it.'

in order to enjoy it for ever; for if the soul had a single glimpse of the loftiness and beauty of God it would not only desire one death, as it does here, in order to see it for ever, but it would very gladly suffer a thousand most bitter deaths in order to see it for one single moment, and, after seeing it, it would beg that it might suffer as many more deaths in order to see it for a moment more.[12]

8. For the further exposition of this line, it must be known that here the soul speaks conditionally, when she prays that the vision and the beauty of God may slay her, assuming that she cannot see it without dying; for, if it might be so otherwise, she would not beg that it might slay her. For to desire to die is an imperfection of nature; but it is because she assumes that this corruptible life of man cannot co-exist with the other and incorruptible[13] life of God that she says: 'Let the vision of Thee and Thy beauty slay me.'

9. This doctrine Saint Paul declares to the Corinthians, saying: 'We would not be unclothed, but we would be clothed upon, that that which is mortal may be swallowed up by life.'[14] Which is to say: We desire not to be 'unclothed' of the flesh, but to be 'clothed upon' with glory. But, seeing that it is impossible to live in glory and in mortal flesh together, as we say, he says to the Philippians that he desires to be loosed and to see himself with Christ.[15] But here there arises one question, and it is this: Why did the children of Israel in olden times flee from God and fear to see Him lest they should die, as Manue said to his wife,[16] and yet this soul desires to die at the sight of God? To this the answer is that the causes are two. The one, because, at that time, even though they died in the grace of God, they would not see Him until Christ came, and it was far better for them to live in the flesh, increasing their merits and enjoying their natural life, than to be in limbo, incapable of earning merit, and suf-

[12] Ej, Sg: 'to see it again for another moment'; G: 'to see it again for a moment more.'

[13] A, B, Bz: 'inaccessible.'

[14] 2 Corinthians v, 4.

[15] Philippians i, 23.

[16] Judges xiii, 22. Bg adds: 'Manue is the name of the father of Samson.'

fering from darkness and the spiritual absence of God; for the which cause they held it then to be a great favour and benefit of God to live many years.

10. The second cause arises from love; for, since in those days men were not so completely confirmed in love, neither had they attained so nearly to God by love, they feared to die at the vision of Him; but now that, under the law of grace, when the body dies the soul may see God, it is healthier[17] to desire to live but little and to die at the vision of Him. And, even were this not so, the soul that loves God as this soul loves Him would not fear to die at the vision of Him, for true love receives all that comes to it from the Beloved, be it adversity or prosperity, and even chastisements, as that which He wills to work in it, with complete indifference, and in one and the same manner, and they become to it joy and delight. For, as Saint John says, perfect love casteth out all fear.[18] To the soul that loves, death cannot be bitter, for it finds therein all the sweetnesses and joys of love; the thought thereof cannot cause it sadness, since it finds joy therein; nor can it be heavy and grievous, since it is the termination of all its griefs and afflictions and the beginning of all its good. Death it holds as its friend and bride, and with the thought thereof it joys as upon the day of its betrothal and marriage; and it desires that day and that hour, wherein its death is to come,[19] more than the kings of the earth desired kingdoms and principalities.[20] For of this kind of death the Wise Man says: 'O death! Good is thy sentence for the man that feels himself needy.'[21] If this is good for the man who feels in need of things here below, when it supplies not his needs, but rather strips him of that which he had, how much better will its sentence be for the soul that (like this soul) is in need of love, and is calling for more love, since not only will it not strip it of that which it had, but it will also be to it a cause of the fulfilment of the love which it desired, and

[17] A: 'may see God by love, I say that it is healthier . . .'
[18] 1 St. John iv, 18.
[19] A: 'wherein it has to live its death.'
[20] Ej, G, Sg: 'kingdoms and primacies.'
[21] Ecclesiasticus xli, 2.

satisfaction for all its needs? The soul, then, acts rightly in venturing to say without fear: 'Let the vision of Thee and Thy beauty slay me'; since she knows that, at that same moment when the vision comes to her, she will be rapt away by the same beauty and absorbed in the same beauty, and transformed in the same beauty, and will become beautiful like the same beauty, and will be provisioned and enriched by the same beauty.[22] For this reason David says that the death of the saints is precious in the sight of the Lord.[23] Which would not be if they had not a part in His own grandeurs; for before God there is naught precious save that which He is in Himself; wherefore the soul, when it loves, fears not to die, but rather desires to do so. But the sinner ever fears to die, for he suspects that death will take from him all good things and will give him all evil things; for, as David says, the death of sinners is very evil.[24] Wherefore, as the Wise Man says, the remembrance thereof is bitter to them,[25] for, because they have a great love for the life of this world, and they love that of the next but little, they fear death greatly. But the soul that loves God lives in the next life rather than in this, for the soul lives where it loves rather than where it breathes, and thus it holds this temporal life as of small account. Wherefore the Bride says: 'Let the vision of Thee and Thy beauty slay me.'

Behold, the affliction of love is not cured   Save by thy presence and thy form.

11. The reason that love's sickness has no other cure save the presence and the form of the Beloved, as is here said, is that, even as the pain of love differs from other sicknesses, so its medicine differs likewise. For in other sicknesses, according to sound philosophy, contraries are cured by contraries; but love is not cured save by things that are in har-

[22] Ej, G abbreviate this passage thus: 'she will be rapt away and absorbed in the same beauty, and transformed therein, and will be like the same beauty.'
[23] Psalm cxv, 15. [A.V., cxvi, 15.]
[24] Psalm xxxiii, 22. [A.V., xxxiv, 21.]
[25] Ecclesiasticus xli, 1.

mony with love. The reason is that the health of the soul is
the love of God, and thus, when it has not perfect love, it
has not perfect health, and is therefore sick, for sickness is
naught else than lack of health; so that, when the soul has
no degree of love, it is dead; but, when it has any degree
of love for God,[26] howsoever small this may be, it is at least
alive, though very weak and infirm by reason of the little
love[27] that it has; and the more its love continues to increase,
the more health it will have; so that, when it has perfect love,
its health will be complete.

12. Here it must be known that love never attains to a state
of perfection until the lovers are on so complete a level of
equality that they are transformed the one in the other, and
then love has perfect health. And because the soul here feels
herself to have, as it were, the shadow of love,[28] which is
the affliction whereof she here speaks, desiring that it may
be perfectly formed, by means of the Form to Whom the
shadow belongs, which is her Spouse, the Word, the Son of
God, Who, as Saint Paul says, is the brightness of His glory
and the form of His substance,[29] because this form is that
which the soul here understands, and wherein she desires to
be transformed through love, she says: 'Behold, the affliction
of love is not cured, save by Thy presence and Thy form.'

13. Rightly is love that is not perfect called affliction, since,
even as the sick man is too enfeebled to work, even so the
soul that is weak in love is also too weak to work the heroic
virtues.[30]

14. Likewise it may here be understood that in one that
feels in himself affliction of love—that is, lack of love—it is
a sign that he has some love, for it is by comparison with
that which he has that he is able to realize that which he

---

[26] S omits the words 'degree of love for God.'

[27] S: 'the little love for God.'

[28] [*Lit.*, 'feels herself with a certain outline (*dibujo*) of love.'
The related verb *dibujar* is translated 'outlined' in the final line of
the following stanza.]

[29] Hebrews i, 3.

[30] Bg: 'is not also weak in loving the heroic virtues.' [This should
probably read: 'is also too weak,' etc. The change involves only the
substitution of *lo* for *no*.]

lacks; but the fact that one feels not this is a sign either that he has none or that he has perfection thereof.

Annotation for the Stanza Following

At this season, the soul feels within itself such a vehement desire to journey to God that it is like a stone that is approaching ever nearer to its centre. Or, again, it feels like the wax that has begun to receive the impression of the seal and has not perfectly received its form. Again, it knows itself to be like the image of a first sketch and outline,[31] and cries out to Him that outlined it that He will complete its painting and formation. For its faith is so enlightened here that it causes it to trace[32] very clearly a certain Divine likeness[33] of the majesty of its God. It knows not what to do save to turn to faith itself, as to that which encloses and conceals within itself the form and beauty of its Beloved, from which it likewise receives the said shadows[34] and pledges of love. The soul, then, speaks to faith, and says as in the next stanza.

STANZA XII

O crystalline fount,   If on that thy silvered surface[1]
Thou wouldst of a sudden form the eyes desired   Which I bear outlined in my inmost parts![2]

Exposition

2. As with so great a desire the soul desires union with the Spouse, and sees that in all the creatures there is no means to that end, neither any relief, she speaks again to faith as

31 [dibujo. Cf. n. 28, p. 299.]
32 Av, G: 'to seek.' Bg: 'to make out.'
33 [semblantes. See p. 88, n. 2, above.]
34 dibujos.
1 semblantes.
2 See p. 88, n. 2, above.

to the one who shall give her the most vivid light from her Beloved,[3] considering faith as a means to that end; for indeed there is no other way whereby a soul may come to the true union[4] and spiritual betrothal with God, according as He declares through Osee, saying: 'I will betroth thee to Me in faith.'[5] And with the desire[6] wherein she burns she says as follows, which is the sense of the stanza: O faith of Christ my Spouse! If thou wouldst but show forth clearly the truths concerning my Beloved which, obscurely and darkly concealed, thou hast infused into my soul[7] (for faith, as the theologians say, is an obscure habit), so that that which thou communicatest to me in obscure and unformed knowledge thou mightest discover and reveal in a moment, withdrawing thyself from those truths (since faith is the covering and veil[8] of the truths of God), suddenly, formally and completely, and turning them into a manifestation of glory! The line, then, says:

O crystalline fount,

3. She calls faith 'crystalline' for two reasons: the first, because it is from Christ[9] her Spouse, and the second, because it has the properties of crystal in being pure in its truths, and strong, and clear and free from errors[10] and natural forms. And she calls it 'fount,' because from it there flow to the soul the waters of all spiritual blessings. Hence Christ our Lord, speaking with the Samaritan woman, called faith a fount, saying that in those that believed in Him He would make a fount whose water should spring up into everlasting life.[11] And this water was the spirit which they that believed on Him should receive in their faith.[12]

[3] Ej, G, Sg: 'shall speak to her most vividly of her Beloved.'
[4] Ej, G, Sg: 'to perfect union.'
[5] Osee ii, 20.
[6] A: 'with the so great desire'; B, Bg: 'with the great desire.'
[7] Ej, G, Sg: 'wherewith . . . thou hast informed my soul.'
[8] A: 'the curtain and veil.'
[9] [See p. 88, n. 5, above.]
[10] Sg: 'free from truths and errors.'
[11] St. John iv, 14.
[12] St. John vii, 39.

If on that thy silvered surface

4. The propositions and articles which faith sets before us she calls a silvered surface. For the understanding of this and of the other lines it must be known that faith is compared to silver with respect to the propositions it teaches us, and the truths and substance which they contain in themselves are compared to gold; for that same substance which now we believe, clothed and covered with the silver of faith, we shall behold and enjoy in the life to come, fully revealed, with the gold of the faith laid bare. Wherefore David, speaking thereof, says thus: 'If you sleep between the two lots, the feathers of the dove shall be silvered, and the hinder parts of her back shall be of the colour of gold.'[13] He means: If we close the eyes of the understanding to things above and below (which he calls to 'sleep between') we shall remain in faith, which he calls a dove, whose feathers, which are the truths that it tells us, will be silvered, because in this life faith sets them forth to us obscurely and veiled, for which reason the Bride here calls them a silvered surface. But when this faith shall have come to an end, which will be when it is perfected through the clear vision of God, then the substance of the faith will remain, stripped of this veil of silver, and in colour as gold. So that faith gives and communicates to us God Himself, but covered with the silver of faith; but it fails not for that reason to give Him to us in truth, even as one may give a silvered vessel, which is also a vessel of gold, for, though covered with silver, it is none the less a golden vessel that he gives. Wherefore, when the Bride in the Songs desired this possession[14] of God, He promised it to her, so far as in this life may be, saying that He would make her earrings of gold, but enamelled with silver.[15] In these words He promised to give Himself to her, veiled by faith. The soul, then, now says to faith: 'Oh if on that thy silvered surface . . . ,' by which she means the articles aforementioned wherewith thou hast

13 Psalm lxvii, 14. [A.V., lxviii, 13. Cf. p. 89, n. 11, above.]
14 Ej, G, Sg: 'this presence.'
15 Canticles i, 10.

covered the gold of the Divine rays, which are the 'eyes desired,' whereof she next speaks, saying:

Thou wouldst of a sudden form the eyes desired

5. By the eyes she means, as we said, the Divine truths and rays; the which, as we have likewise said, are set forth to us by faith in its formless and hidden articles. And thus it is as if she were to say: Oh that Thou wouldst but give me these truths which Thou teachest me formlessly and darkly, and which are veiled in Thy articles of faith clearly and formally revealed in them according to the entreaty of my desire! And she calls these truths 'eyes' by reason of the greatness of the presence of the Beloved which she feels, so that it seems to her that she is ever gazing at it. Wherefore she says:

Which I bear outlined in my inmost parts!

6. She says that she bears these truths outlined in her inmost parts—that is to say, in her soul, according to the understanding and the will; for according to the understanding she has these truths infused into her soul by faith. And, because her knowledge of them is not perfect, she says that they are outlined; for, even as an outline is not a perfect painting, so the knowledge of faith is not perfect knowledge. Wherefore the truths that are infused into the soul through faith are as it were in outline, and when they are in clear vision they will be in the soul as a perfect and finished painting, according to the words of the Apostle, where he says: *Cum autem venerit quod perfectum est, evacuabitur quod ex parte est.*[16] Which signifies: When that which is perfect is come (namely, clear vision), then that which is in part[17] (namely, the knowledge of faith) shall be done away.

7. But besides this outline of faith there is another outline in the soul of the lover, which is of love, and this is according to the will; wherein the image of the Beloved is outlined in such manner, and so completely and vividly pictured, when there is union of love, that it is true to say that the Beloved

---

[16] 1 Corinthians xiii, 10.
[17] Sg: 'that which is temporal.'

lives in the lover and the lover in the Beloved; and such manner of likeness does love make in the transformation of the two that are in love that it may be said that each is the other and that both are one. The reason for this is that in the union and transformation of love the one gives possession of itself to the other, and each one abandons itself[18] to the other and exchanges itself for the other. Thus each lives in the other, and the one is the other, and both are one through the transformation of love. It is this that Saint Paul meant when he said: *Vivo autem, jam non ego, vivit vero in me Christus.*[19] Which signifies: I live, yet not I,[20] but Christ liveth in me. For in saying 'I live, yet not I,'[21] he meant that, although he lived, his life was not his own, because he was transformed in Christ and his life was divine rather than human. Wherefore he says that it is not he that lives but Christ that lives in him.

8. So that, according to this likeness of transformation, we can say that his life and the life of Christ were one life through union of love, which in Heaven will be perfectly accomplished in the Divine life in all those who shall merit being in God; for, being transformed in God, they will live the life of God, and not their own life, and yet it will be their own life, for the life of God will be their own life. And then they will say in truth: We live, yet not we, for God liveth in us. This may come to pass in this life, as in the case of Saint Paul—not, however, in a complete and perfect way, although the soul may reach such a transformation of love as is in the Spiritual Marriage, which is the highest estate that can be attained in this life; for everything may be called an outline of love by comparison with that perfect image of transformation in glory. But when this outline of transformation is attained in this life it is a great and good happiness, because the Beloved is greatly pleased with it. For this reason, desiring that the Bride should grave Him upon her soul as an outline, He said to her in the Songs: 'Set Me as a seal upon thy heart, as a

18 A, Av, B, Bg, Bz, Sg: 'abandons and gives itself.'
19 Galatians ii, 20.
20 S: 'but yet not I.'
21 S: 'but yet not I.'

seal upon thine arm.'[22] The heart here signifies the soul,
whereupon God is set in this life as the seal of an outline of
faith, even as was said above; and the arm signifies the strong
will, wherein it is as the seal of an outline of love,[23] as we
have just now said.

9. After such manner walks the soul at this time that, albeit
briefly, I will not fail to say something thereof, although by
words it cannot be explained. For it appears to the soul that
its bodily and its spiritual substance are dried up by thirst
after this living fount of God; for its thirst is like to that which
David had when he said: 'As the hart desireth the fountains
of waters, so my soul desireth Thee, O God.[24] My soul was
thirsty for God, the living fount. When shall I come and appear before the face of God?'[25] And this thirst so wearies it
that it would think naught of breaking through the midst of
the Philistines, as did the mighty men of David to fill his vessel
of water at the well[26] of Bethlehem,[27] which was Christ; it
would think naught of enduring all the difficulties of the
world and the furies of evil spirits and the pains of hell in
order to immerse itself in this fathomless[28] fount of love.
For with respect to this it is said in the Songs: 'Love is strong
as death and its importunity is hard as hell.'[29] For it cannot
be believed how vehement is the yearning and the grief which
the soul feels when it sees that it is gradually approaching
the fruition of that blessing, and yet that this is not granted
to it; for the nearer one sees that which one desires and yet
is denied, the greater are the grief and the torment caused
thereby.[30] Wherefore Job says with this spiritual intent: 'Before I eat, I sigh, and the roaring and raging of my soul are

[22] Canticles viii, 6. Av, Bz omit: 'as a seal upon thine arm.' Ej,
G: 'Set me as a seal of the outline of faith.'

[23] S: 'as a seal outlined with love.' Sg: '. . . the soul, for in this
life God is a seal of the outline of love.'

[24] A, Av, Ej, S: 'my God.'

[25] Psalm xli, 3. [A.V., xlii, 1–2.]

[26] Ej, G, Sg: 'to take his vessel of water to the well.'

[27] 1 Paralipomenon xi, 18. [A.V., 1 Chronicles xi, 18.]

[28] Sg: 'voluminous.'

[29] Canticles viii, 6.

[30] Sg: 'so great is the pain and greater is the torment caused
thereby.'

like the overflowing of the waters'[31]—that is, through my longing for food, by food being here understood God. Because, according to the yearning of the soul for this food, and the knowledge which it has thereof, even so is the grief which it has on account of it.

Annotation for the Stanza Following

The reason that the soul suffers so much at this time is that, the nearer it comes to union with God, the more keenly it feels within itself its emptiness of God, and[32] the direst[33] darkness, together with spiritual fire which dries and purges it so that, when it is purified, it may be united with God. For, inasmuch as God sends not into it[34] any ray of supernatural light from Himself, God is intolerable darkness to it, when He is near it according to the spirit, since supernatural light darkens natural light with its excess.[35] All this David expressed when he said: 'Clouds and darkness are round about Him; fire goeth before His presence.'[36] And in another psalm he says: 'He made darkness His covert and secret place, and His tabernacle round about Him was dark water in the clouds of the air; through His great brightness in His presence there are clouds, hailstones and coals of fire,'[37] that is to say, to the soul that is attaining. For the nearer the soul attains to Him, the more it feels within itself all that has been said, until God draws it into His Divine brightness through transformation of love. And meanwhile[38] the soul is ever like to Job, saying: 'Who will grant me that I might know Him and find Him and come even to His throne?'[39] But through the

---

[31] Job iii, 24.

[32] [*Lit.*, 'and within its soul.']

[33] Bz, Ej, G: 'greatest.'

[34] A, Av, Bz, Sg [use a stronger word, very similarly pronounced and written—*derriba* for *deriva*—best translated] 'overcomes it not with.'

[35] G: 'any ray of supernatural light, He darkens the natural light with its excess.'

[36] Psalm xcvi, 2–3. [A.V., xcvii, 2–3.] Sg has 'snow' [*nieve*] for 'cloud' [*nube*].

[37] Psalm xvii, 12–13. [A.V., xviii, 11–12.]

[38] S omits: 'And meanwhile.'

[39] Job xxiii, 3.

boundless pity[40] of God the consolations and favours that He gives are proportionate to the darknesses and emptinesses of the soul, for *sicut tenebræ ejus, ita et lumen ejus;*[41] for in exalting and glorifying souls He humbles and fatigues them.[42] And in this way He has sent the soul, even while it is thus fatigued, certain Divine rays[43] from Himself, with such glory and strength of love[44] that He has stirred up its whole being and changed its whole nature;[45] and thus with great natural fear and affright the soul speaks to the Beloved at the beginning of this following stanza, while the Beloved Himself[46] continues for the remainder of it.

STANZA XIII

Withdraw them, Beloved, for I fly away.

Spouse:

Return thou, dove,
For the wounded hart appears on the hill   At the air of thy flight, and takes refreshment.

Exposition

2. In the great desires and fervent affections of love which the soul has expressed in the preceding stanzas, the Beloved is wont to visit His Bride, in a way most chaste, most delicate[1] and most loving and with great strength of love. For

[40] Bg, S: 'the boundless goodness.' Ej, G: 'the goodness and pity.'

[41] Psalm cxxxviii, 12. [A.V., cxxxix, 12.]

[42] S adds 'likewise.'

[43] B: 'certain rays of glory.'

[44] B: 'with such strength of love.'

[45] [The Spanish word, *desencajó*, means literally 'disjointed,' 'disarticulated.']

[46] Bz: 'the Lover Himself.'

[1] A, B, Bg, Bz, Sg, S: 'in a way most lofty, most delicate.' Ej, G abbreviate: 'in a way most lofty and most loving, according to the greatness of the fervours, etc.'

ordinarily the favours and visits of God to the soul are wont to be great in proportion to the fervours and yearnings of love which have preceded them. And, as the soul has just now desired these Divine eyes with such great yearning, even as she has just said in the foregoing stanza, the Beloved has revealed to her some rays of His greatness and divinity, as she has desired. These rays were communicated with such loftiness and such power that the soul was made to issue forth from herself in rapture and ecstasy, which at the first is accompanied by great suffering and natural fear. And thus the soul, being unable to suffer excess in so frail a mortal form, says in the present stanza: 'Withdraw them, Beloved.' That is to say: Withdraw these Thy Divine eyes, for they make me to soar aloft, issuing forth from myself in highest contemplation above that which my physical nature can bear. This she says because it seemed to her that her soul was flying out of her body, which is what she desired: for this reason she begged Him to withdraw His eyes—that is, to communicate them no longer to her in the flesh, since in this wise she could neither bear them nor enjoy them as she would desire, but to communicate them to her in the flight which she was about to make from out of the flesh. But this desire and flight the Spouse prevented, saying: Return, dove, for the communication which thou art now receiving from Me belongs not yet to that estate of glory to which thou now aspirest. But return thou to Me, for it is I Whom thou seekest, wounded as thou art by love. And I also, Who am like to the hart wounded by thy love, now begin to reveal Myself to thee in thy lofty contemplation, and take recreation and refreshment in the love of thy contemplation. Wherefore the soul says to the Spouse:

Withdraw them, Beloved,

3. According as we have said, the soul, as befitted the great desires which she had[2] for these Divine eyes, which signify Divinity, received inwardly from the Beloved such communication and knowledge of God that it compelled her to say:

[2] Ej, G, Sg: 'according to the degrees of love and desire which it had.'

'Withdraw them, Beloved.' For such is the wretchedness of our physical nature in this life that that which is truest life to the soul and which she desires with such great desire—namely, the communication and knowledge of her Beloved, when they come and are given to her—she cannot receive without its almost costing her her life, so that when those eyes which she sought with so much solicitude and yearning, and by so many ways, are revealed to her, she may come to say:[3] 'Withdraw them, Beloved.'

4. For at times the torture felt[4] in such visits of rapture is so great that there is no torture which so wrenches asunder the bones and straitens the physical nature—so much so that unless God provided for the soul its life would come to an end. And in truth, to the soul which experiences it, it seems indeed to be ended, because it feels as though the soul is detached from the flesh and the body is unprotected. The reason for this is that such favours cannot be received by one that is wholly in the flesh, because the spirit is raised up to commune with the Divine Spirit which comes to the soul, and thus it has perforce in some manner to abandon the flesh.[5] And hence it is that the flesh has to suffer, and, consequently, the soul that is in the flesh, through the unity which they have in one being. Wherefore the great torture which the soul feels at the time of this kind of visit, and the great terror which comes to it as it sees itself treated in supernatural wise cause it to say: 'Withdraw them, Beloved.'

5. But it is not to be understood that, because the soul entreats Him to withdraw them, she desires their withdrawal, for that saying comes from natural fear, as we have said. Rather, though it should cost her far more, she would not willingly lose these visits and favours of the Beloved, because, although the physical nature suffers therein, the spirit soars to supernatural recollection, in order to have fruition of the Spirit of the Beloved, since it is this that she has desired and

---

[3] A: 'so that, when she finds those eyes . . . yearning, she may come to say.'

[4] Sg: 'the torture experienced.' Bz, B: 'the torture which she feels.'

[5] Ej, G omit: 'The reason . . . abandon the flesh.'

entreated. Yet she would not desire to receive it in the flesh, where it is impossible for it to be received[6] perfectly, but only to a slight extent and with difficulty; she would rather receive it in the flight of the spirit from out of the flesh, where she can have fruition of it freely. For this cause she said: 'Withdraw them, Beloved.' Which is to say: Cease to communicate them to me in the flesh.

For I fly away.

6. As though she said: I fly away from the flesh that Thou mayest communicate them to me apart from it, since they are the cause making me fly from out of it. And that we may the better understand what flight is this, it is to be noted that, as we have said, in that visitation of the Divine Spirit the spirit of the soul is enraptured with great force, to communicate with the Spirit, and destroys the body,[7] and ceases to experience feelings and to have its actions in the body, since it has them in God. For this cause said Saint Paul, with respect to that rapture of his, that he knew not if his soul was receiving it in the body or out of the body.[8] It is not for this reason to be understood that the soul destroys and forsakes the body[9] of natural life, but that it has not its actions in it. And it is for this reason that in these raptures and flights the body remains without its senses, and, although the greatest pains be inflicted upon it, it feels them not; for this is not like other swoons and trances, which are natural, so that their subjects return to themselves with the first touch of pain. And these feelings are experienced in such visitations by those who have not yet arrived at the estate of perfection, but who are travelling along the road in the estate of progressives, for those who have already attained receive all these communications in peace and gentle love, and these raptures cease, since they were commu-

[6] [The words 'for it to be received' are not in the original.] Some MSS., to fill the gap, read: 'where it is impossible to have fruition of it perfectly.'

[7] Sg: 'and makes the body destitute.' S: 'to commune with the Divine and become destitute.'

[8] 2 Corinthians xii, 2.

[9] S: 'that the soul makes the body destitute and forsakes it.' Av, Bg, Sg read: 'makes the body destitute' for 'forsakes the body.'

nications and preparation for the communication which crowns all.[10]

7. This would be a convenient place for treating of the different kinds of rapture and ecstasy and of other issuings forth and subtle flights of the spirit, which are accustomed to befall spiritual persons. But, since my intent is but to expound these stanzas briefly, as I promised in the prologue,[11] these other things must remain for such as can treat them better than I. And I pass over the subject likewise because the Blessed Teresa of Jesus, our mother,[12] left notes admirably written upon these things of the spirit, the which notes I hope in God will speedily be printed and brought to light.[13] That, then, which the soul says here concerning flight is to be understood of rapture and ecstasy of the spirit in God. And next the Beloved says:

Return thou, dove,

8. Very willingly was the soul leaving the body upon that spiritual flight, thinking that its life was coming to an end, and that it would be able to have fruition of its Spouse for ever and remain with Him unhindered by a veil. But the Spouse prevented its flight, saying: 'Return thou, dove.' As though He had said: O dove, in the quick and lofty flight of thy contemplation, and in the love wherewith thou burnest, and the simplicity wherein thou goest (for the dove has these three properties[14]), return thou from this lofty flight wherein thou aspirest to attain to possession of Me in truth, for not yet has the time arrived for such lofty knowledge. And adapt thyself to this lower knowledge that I now communicate to thee in this thy excess.[15]

For the wounded hart . . .[16]

[10] [Lit., 'the total communication.'] Av, B, Bz: 'communications which prepared for the total communication.' A, Bg [substituting la tal for la total, read]: 'for that [or 'the said'] communication.'
[11] Ej, G omit 'as I . . . prologue.'
[12] A, B, Bg, Ej, G, Sg omit: 'our mother.'
[13] B, Bg, Ej, G omit: 'the which . . . to light.'
[14] Jaén, Ej omit: 'three.'
[15] Ej, G omit: 'in this thy excess.'
[16] Sg omits the commentary on this line.

9. The Spouse compares Himself to the hart, for by the hart He here means Himself. It must be known that the characteristic of the hart is to mount up to high places, and when wounded it goes with great haste to seek refreshment in the cool waters; and if it hears its mate complain and perceives that she is wounded it goes straightway to her and fondles and caresses her. Even so does the Spouse now, for, seeing that the Bride is wounded for love of Him, He comes when she sighs, wounded in like manner with love of her, for in those that are in love with each other the wound of one is the wound of both and the two have one and the same feeling. And thus it is as if He had said: Return thou, My Bride, for if thou goest wounded with love for Me, I also, like the hart, come to thee wounded in this thy wound, Who am as the hart; and I also appear on the heights. For which reason He says:

. . . appears on the hill[17]

10. That is, through the loftiness of the contemplation which thou hast in this flight. For contemplation is a lofty height, from which in this life God begins to commune with the soul and reveal Himself to it, but not completely. For this reason He says not that He has appeared completely, but that He 'appears,' for, however sublime the degrees of knowledge of God which are given to the soul in this life, they are all as very devious[18] appearances. There follows the third characteristic of the hart, whereof we spoke, which is that contained in the line following:

At the air of thy flight, and takes refreshment.

11. By flight He means contemplation in that ecstasy whereof we have spoken, and by the air He means that spirit of love which this flight of contemplation produces in the soul. And this love which is produced by the flight He here most appropriately calls 'air,' for the Holy Spirit, Who is love, is also compared to air in the Divine Scripture, since He is the

---

17 B omits the commentaries on this and the next line.

18 [*muy desviadas asomadas*] Av has 'divided' [*divisas*] for 'devious.'

breath of the Father and the Son. And, even as there He is the air of the flight—that is, He proceeds from the contemplation and wisdom of the Father and the Son,[19] and is breathed—so here the Spouse calls this love of the soul air, because it proceeds from the contemplation and knowledge which at this time the soul has of God. And it is to be noted that the Spouse says not here that He is coming at the flight, but at the air of the flight, for properly speaking God communicates not Himself to the soul through the flight of the soul—which is, as we have said, the knowledge that it has of God—but through the love which comes from that knowledge; for, even as love is union of the Father and the Son, even so also is it union of the soul with God. Hence it comes that, although a soul have the loftiest knowledge of God, and contemplation, and knowledge of all mysteries, if it have not love it profiteth it nothing, as Saint Paul says,[20] towards union with God. As likewise that same Apostle said: *Charitatem habete, quod est vinculum perfectionis.*[21] That is to say: Have charity, which is the bond of perfection. This charity, then, and love of the soul, brings the Spouse running to drink of this fount of the love of His Bride, even as the fresh water-brooks bring the thirsting and wounded hart to taste their coolness. Wherefore the line continues: 'And takes refreshment.'

12. For even as the air brings coolness and refreshment to him that is fatigued with the heat, so does this air of love refresh and recreate him that burns with the fire of love. For this fire of love has such properties that the air which affords it coolness and refreshment is an increased fire of love; for, in the lover, love[22] is a flame which burns with the desire of burning more, as does the flame of natural fire. Wherefore He here describes as refreshment the fulfilment of this desire of His to burn more in the ardour of love for His Bride, which is the air of her flight. And thus it is as though He said: It burns more at the ardour of thy flight, for one love enkindles another. Here it is to be noted that God sets not His grace and

---

[19] S adds: 'through the will.'
[20] 1 Corinthians xiii, 2.
[21] Colossians iii, 14.
[22] B, Bg have 'the fire of love' for 'love.'

love in the soul save according to the will and love of the soul; for which cause he that is truly in love must see that this love fail not, for by this means, as we have said, it will (if we may so say) move God the more to have more love for the soul[23] and to find more refreshment in it. And, in order to follow after[24] this charity, it must practise that which the Apostle says thereof, where he writes: 'Charity is patient, is kind; envieth not, doeth no evil,[25] is not puffed up, is not ambitious, seeketh not her own, is not provoked, thinketh no evil, rejoiceth not in iniquity but rejoiceth in the truth;[26] beareth all things which have to be borne; believeth all things (that is, those which ought to be believed); hopeth all things; endureth all things'—namely, those which are in accord with charity.[27]

Annotation and Argument of the Two Stanzas Following[28]

Now as this little dove, which is the soul, was flying on the breezes of love above the waters of the flood (namely, those her fatigues and yearnings of love which she has described up to this point) and found no rest for her foot, upon this last flight which we have described, the compassionate father Noe put forth the hand of his mercy, and caught her, and brought her into the ark of his charity and love;[29] and this was at the time when, in the stanza that we have just expounded, the Spouse said: 'Return thou, dove.' In the which recollection the soul, finding all that she has desired and more than she can express, begins to sing praises to her Beloved, relating the great things which she feels and enjoys in this union in Him in the two following stanzas, saying:

23 [*a que Dios le tenga más amor.*]
24 [*seguir.*] Ej, S have *conseguir*, 'to attain to.'
25 B, Bg omit the rest of the paragraph.
26 Ej, G omit the rest of the paragraph.
27 1 Corinthians xiii, 4–6. Bz abbreviates the last phrase: 'that is, those which have to be believed and are in accord with charity.'
28 Thus S. Jaén and Sg have: 'Annotation for the stanza following.'
29 Ej, G: 'into the ark of his breast and love.' [Genesis viii, 9.]

STANZAS XIV AND XV

My Beloved, the mountains,   The solitary, wooded valleys,
The strange islands, the sonorous rivers,   The whisper of the
   amorous breezes,

The tranquil night,   At the time of the rising of the dawn,
The silent music, the sounding solitude,   The supper that recreates and enkindles love.

Annotation

2. Before we enter upon the exposition of these stanzas it
is necessary to explain, for the better intelligence thereof and
of the stanzas which follow them, that by this spiritual flight
which we have just described is denoted a lofty estate and
union of love wherein after much spiritual exercise God is
wont to place the soul,[1a] which is called spiritual betrothal
with the Word, the Son of God. And at the beginning, when
this is done for the first time, God communicates to the soul
great things concerning Himself, beautifying it with greatness
and majesty, decking it with gifts and virtues, and clothing it
with knowledge and honour of God, just as if it were a bride
on the day of her betrothal. And upon this happy day, not
only is there an end of the soul's former vehement yearnings
and plaints of love, but, being adorned with the good things
which I am describing, she enters into an estate of peace and
delight and sweetness of love, as is described in the present
stanzas,[1b] wherein she does naught else but relate and sing
the wonders of her Beloved, which she knows and enjoys in
Him, by means of the aforementioned union of the betrothal. And thus, in the remainder of the stanzas following,[1c]

[1a] A, B, Bg abbreviate: 'that in this spiritual flight God is wont
to place the soul.'
[1b] Av: 'in the following stanzas.'
[1c] A omits 'following.'

she speaks not of pains or yearnings as she did aforetime, but of the communication and exercise of sweet and peaceful love with her Beloved, since in this estate all those other things are now ended. And it is to be noted that in these two stanzas is contained the most that God is wont to communicate to a soul[1d] at this time; but it is not to be understood that to all such as arrive at this estate He communicates all that is expounded in these two stanzas, nor that He does so according to one single way and degree of knowledge and feeling. For to some souls He gives more and to others less; to some after one manner and to others after another; though souls belonging to either category can be in this estate of the Spiritual Betrothal. But we set down here the highest that is possible because in this is comprehended all else. And the exposition follows.

Exposition of the Two Stanzas

3. And it is to be noted that, even as in the Ark of Noe, as the Divine Scripture tells us, there were many mansions for many different kinds of animal, and every kind of food which they could eat, even so, in this flight[1] which it makes to this Divine Ark of the bosom of God, the soul not only sees therein the many mansions which His Majesty described in Saint John,[2] saying that they were in His Father's house, but sees and knows that all kinds of food are there—that is, all the grandeurs which can please the soul, which are all the things that are contained in the two stanzas above-mentioned, and are signified by those words used in common parlance, the substance of which is as follows.

4. In this Divine union the soul sees and tastes abundance, inestimable riches, finds all the rest and the recreation that it desires and understands strange kinds of knowledge and secrets of God, which is another of those kinds of food that it likes best. It feels likewise in God an awful power and

---

[1d] Ej, G, Sg add: 'by way of betrothal.'
[1] Ej, G, Sg: 'in this Divine flight.'
[2] St. John xiv, 2.

strength which transcends all other power and strength: it
tastes a marvellous sweetness[3] and spiritual delight, finds true
rest and Divine light and has lofty experience of the knowledge of God, which shines forth in the harmony of the creatures and the acts of God. Likewise it feels itself to be full of
good things and far withdrawn from evil things and empty
of them; and, above all, it experiences, and has fruition of,
an inestimable feast of love, which confirms it in love, and
this is the substance of that which is contained in the two
stanzas aforementioned.

5. In these stanzas the Bride says that her Beloved is all
these things, both in Himself and also for her;[4] for in that
which God is wont to communicate in such excesses[5] the soul
feels and knows the truth of that saying which Saint Francis[6]
uttered, namely: 'God mine, and all things.' Wherefore, since
God is all things to the soul, and the good of them all, the
communication of this excess is explained by the similitude of
the goodness of the things in the said stanzas,[7] which we shall
expound line by line. Herein must be understood that all that
is expounded here is in God in an eminent and an infinite
manner, or, to express it better, each of these grandeurs which
are spoken of is God, and they are all of them God; for, inasmuch as in this case the soul is united with God,[8] it feels that
all things are God, even as Saint John felt when he said:
Quod factum est, in ipso vita erat.[9] That is to say: That which
was made in Him was life. It is not to be understood that, in
that which the soul is here said to feel, it is, as it were, seeing
things in the light, or creatures in God, but that in that possession the soul feels that all things are God to it.[10] Neither
is it to be understood that, because the soul has such lofty

[3] Sg: 'marvellous subtlety.'

[4] [*y lo es para ella.*] Jaén, A, Av, Bg, Bz, Sg read: *y lo espera
ella* ['and she awaits Him' (or 'it'). Cf. p. 101, n. 6, above].

[5] A: 'in such exercises.'

[6] Av: 'which the seraphic father St. Francis.'

[7] Ej, G, Sg: 'by the similitude of the will of the things and of
their goodness in these stanzas.'

[8] Ej, G, Sg: 'is united with God in one simple being.'

[9] St. John i, 4. Cf. p. 80, n. 5, above.

[10] Ej, G, Sg omit: 'but that . . . to it.'

feelings concerning God in that which we are saying, it sees God essentially and clearly, for this is no more than a powerful and abundant communication, and a glimpse of that which He is in Himself, wherein the soul feels this goodness concerning the things which we shall expound in these lines, as follows:

My Beloved, the mountains,[11]

6. The mountains have height; they are abundant, extensive and beautiful, graceful, flowery and fragrant. These mountains my Beloved is to me.

The solitary, wooded valleys,

7. The solitary valleys are quiet, pleasant, cool, shady, abounding in fresh water; and with the variety of their groves and the sweet song of the birds they greatly recreate and delight the senses, in their solitude[12] and silence giving refreshment and rest. These valleys my Beloved is to me.

The strange islands,

8. The strange islands are girt around by the sea, and are far away over the sea, withdrawn and aloof from communication with men. Thus there are produced and bred in them things very different from those in our own experience, of very strange kinds and with virtues never seen by men, so that they cause great surprise and wonder in those that see them. And thus, by reason of the great and marvellous wonders and the strange knowledge, far removed from the knowledge of every day, that the soul sees in God, He is here called strange islands. There are two reasons for calling a man strange: either because he lives in retirement from men or because he is excellent and singular among other men in his deeds and works. For both these reasons the soul here speaks of God as strange; for not only has He all the strangeness of islands which have never been seen, but likewise His ways, coun-

---

[11] G, Sg: 'My beloved to the mountains.'
[12] Bg: 'in gentleness.' Ej, G, Sg omit 'and rest.' Bz omits 'and silence.'

sels[13] and works are very strange and new and marvellous to
men. And it is no marvel if God is strange to men who have
never seen Him, since He is strange also to the holy angels
and the souls who see Him; for they cannot see Him perfectly,
nor shall they so see Him, and until the last day of judgment
they will continually be seeing in Him so many things that
are new according to His profound judgments, concerning
the works of mercy and justice, that they will wonder continually and marvel ever more. So that not men alone, but
likewise angels, can speak of Him as of strange islands; only
to Himself is He not strange, neither to Himself is He new.

The sonorous rivers,

9. Rivers have three properties: the first is that they assail
and submerge all that they meet;[14] the second, that they fill
up all the low and hollow places that are in their path; the
third, that their sound is such as to drown and take the place
of all sounds else. And because in this communication of God
which we are describing the soul feels in herself these three
properties most delectably, she says that her Beloved is the
sonorous rivers. With respect to the first property that the soul
feels, it must be known that she feels herself to be assailed by
the torrent of the Spirit of God in this case, in such a manner,
and taken possession of thereby with such force, that it seems
to her that all the rivers of the world are coming upon her and
assailing her, and she feels that all her actions are whelmed
thereby, and all the passions which she had aforetime. Yet
though this is an experience of such violence, it is not for that
reason an experience of torment; for these rivers are rivers of
peace, even as God declares through Isaias, saying, concerning this assault upon the soul: *Ecce ego declinabo super eam
quasi fluvium pacis, et quasi torrentem inundantem gloriam.*[15]
Which is to say: Take note and be warned that I will come
down upon her (that is to say, upon the soul) and assail her
like a river of peace and like a torrent which overflows with
glory as it advances. And thus this Divine assault which God

[13] Bg: 'His ways, His rich counsels.'
[14] S: 'all into which they enter.'
[15] Isaias lxvi, 12.

makes[16] upon the soul, resembling the assault of sonorous rivers, fills it wholly with peace and glory. The second property which the soul feels is that this Divine water at this time fills up the low places of its humility and also fills the empty places of its desires, even as Saint Luke says: *Exaltavit humiles. Esurientes implevit bonis.*[17] Which is to say: He hath exalted the humble, and hath filled the hungry with good things. The third property that the soul feels in the sonorous rivers of its Beloved is a spiritual voice and noise[18] which is above all sounds and voices, the which voice drowns every other voice and its sound exceeds all the sounds in the world. And in the exposition hereof we must occupy ourselves for some little space.

10. This voice or sonorous sound of these rivers which the soul here describes is a fulfilment[19] so abundant that it fills the soul with good things, and a power so powerful that it possesses the soul and appears to her not merely as the sound of rivers but as most powerful thunderings. But this voice is a spiritual voice and is unaccompanied by those physical sounds, and by the pain and trouble of them, but is accompanied rather by grandeur, strength, power, delight and glory; and thus it is as an immense and inward sound and voice, which clothes the soul with power and strength. This spiritual voice[20] and sound was heard in the spirits of the Apostles at the time when the Holy Spirit, in a vehement torrent (as is said in the Acts of the Apostles), descended upon them; when, in order that the spiritual voice[21] that was speaking to them from within might be made manifest, this sound was heard from without as a vehement wind, in such wise that it was heard by all who were in Jerusalem:[22] whereby, as we say, was denoted that which the Apostles received inwardly,

[16] Bz: 'Thus at this time this assault of God fills the low and empty places—[this assault] which God makes, etc.'

[17] St. Luke i, 52–3.

[18] Ej, G: 'is a spiritual voice and sonorous sound.' Sg: 'is a spiritual voice and sound.' Bz: 'is a spiritual voice and river.'

[19] Ej, G: 'is an accumulation.'

[20] A has *gozo* ['joy'] for *voz* ['voice'].

[21] Ej, G, Sg have 'the interior voice' and omit 'from within.'

[22] Acts ii, 2.

which was, as we have said, a fulfilment of power and
strength. And likewise, when the Lord Jesus was praying to
the Father in the peril and anguish which were caused Him
by His enemies, as is said in Saint John,[23] there came to Him
an inward voice from Heaven, strengthening Him according
to His humanity, which sound the Jews heard from without,
and so solemn was it, and so mighty, that some said it had
thundered, and others, that some angel from Heaven had
spoken to Him; and by that voice which was heard from
without was denoted and signified the strength and power
given to Christ, according to His humanity, from within; yet
by this it is not to be understood that the soul fails to receive
in the spirit the sound of the spiritual voice. It must be noted
that the spiritual voice is the effect[24] which the voice makes
upon the soul, even as the physical voice impresses its sound
upon the ear and its intelligence upon the spirit. This was in
the mind of David when he said: *Ecce dabit voci suæ vocem
virtutis.*[25] Which signifies: Behold, God will give to His voice
a voice of virtue, the which virtue is the voice within. When
David said that He would give His voice a voice of virtue he
meant that[26] to the outward voice, which is heard in outward
wise, He would give a voice of such virtue that it would be
heard within. By this it must be understood that God is an
infinite voice, and that, communicating Himself to the soul
after the said manner, He produces the effect of an immense
voice.

11. This voice Saint John heard in the Apocalypse, and he
says of the voice that he heard from Heaven: *Erat*[27] *tanquam
vocem aquarum multarum,* and, *tanquam vocem tonitrui
magni.*[28] Which is to say, That the voice which he heard was
as a voice of many waters and as the voice of a great thunder.
And that it may not be inferred that this voice, because it was
so great, was harsh and disagreeable, he adds at once that this

[23] St. John xii, 28.
[24] Bg: 'is the fruit.'
[25] Psalm lxvii, 34. [A.V., lxviii, 33.]
[26] Av abbreviates: '. . . the voice within; which is as much as
to say that, etc.'
[27] S: 'that he heard from Heaven, that it was,' etc.
[28] Apocalypse xiv, 2.

same voice was so soft that *erat sicut citharedorum citharizantium in citharis suis.*[29] Which signifies: It was as of many
harpers who harped upon their harps. And Ezechiel says that
this sound as of many waters was *quasi sonum sublimis Dei,*[30]
which is to say, as a sound of the Most High God. That is,
that He communicated Himself therein after a manner most
high and likewise most gentle. This voice is infinite, for, as
we said, it is God Himself Who communicates Himself, speaking in the soul: but He limits Himself by the capacity of each
soul, uttering a voice of such virtue as befits its limitations;
and He produces in the soul great delight and grandeur. And
for this cause the Bride said in the Songs: *Sonet vox tua in
auribus meis, vox enim tua dulcis.*[31] Which signifies: Let
Thy voice sound in my ears, for Thy voice is sweet. The line
continues:

The whisper of the amorous breezes,

12. Of two things the soul makes mention in this present
line, namely, of breezes and of a whisper. By the amorous
breezes are here understood the virtues and graces[32] of the
Beloved, which, by means of the said union of the Spouse,
assail the soul, communicate themselves most lovingly and
touch it in its substance. And by the whisper of these breezes
is meant a most lofty[33] and most delectable knowledge of
God, and of His virtues, the which overflows into the understanding at the touch which these virtues of God effect in
the substance of the soul: and this is the supreme delight
which is contained in all things that the soul here experiences.

13. And in order that what has been said may be the better
understood, it must be noted that even as two things are perceived in the air—namely, the touch thereof and the sound or
whisper—so in this communication of the Spouse two other
things are perceived—namely, feeling of delight, and knowledge. And even as the touch of the air is felt with the sense of

29 *Ibid.*
30 Ezechiel i, 24.
31 Canticles ii, 14. Ej, G omit the rest of the paragraph.
32 Bg: 'and grandeurs.'
33 Ej, G: 'a most abundant'; Sg: 'a most loving.'

touch and the whisper of the same air is heard by the ear,
even so likewise the touch of the virtues of the Beloved is felt
and enjoyed with the sense of touch[34] of this soul which is in
its substance;[35] and the knowledge of these virtues of God is
felt in the ear of the soul, which is the understanding. And it
must be known likewise that the amorous breeze is said to
have come when it strikes delectably, satisfying the appetite
of him that so greatly desired this refreshment, for then the
sense of touch is soothed and refreshed, and with this soothing of the sense of touch the ear experiences great soothing
and delight in the sound and whisper of the air, much more
than does the sense of touch in the touch of the air;[36] for the
sound in the ear is more spiritual, or, to speak more exactly,
comes nearer to the spiritual, than the sense of touch; wherefore the delight which it causes is more spiritual than that
which is caused by the sense of touch.[37]

14. Precisely because this touch of God brings great satisfaction and comfort to the substance of the soul, and sweetly
fulfils its desire, which was to be in this union, the said union,
or touch, is spoken of as 'amorous breezes'; for, as we have
said, in it are communicated to the soul, lovingly and sweetly,
the virtues of the Beloved, whence is derived in the understanding the whisper of knowledge. And it is called a whisper
because, even as the whisper which is caused by the air enters
subtly[38] into the organ of hearing, even so this most subtle
and delicate knowledge enters with marvellous sweetness and
delight into the inmost substance of the soul, which is a far
greater delight than any other. The reason is that substance
of understanding is given to it, stripped of accidents and

[34] [*con el tacto*. To distinguish *tacto* from *toque*, both of which
words are normally translated 'touch,' the former is rendered 'sense
of touch' in this paragraph.] A has *contacto* for *con el tacto* [read-
ing: 'the touch of the virtues feels and enjoys contact with this
soul'].

[35] S adds: 'by means of the will.'

[36] Av: 'than does the [sense of] touch of the air in the touch
(*toque*) which it receives.'

[37] A modifies: 'has come nearer to the spiritual than that which
is caused by the sense of touch.' Ej, G read very similarly.

[38] B, Bg: 'enters lovingly and subtly.'

imaginary forms, for it is given to the understanding that is called by philosophers 'passive' or 'possible,' because it receives it passively, doing naught on its own behalf; which is the principal delight of the soul, because it is in the understanding, wherein, as theologians say, consists fruition, which is to see God. Since this whisper signifies the said substantial knowledge, some theologians think that our father[39] Elias saw God in that gentle whisper of the breeze which he felt on the mount at the mouth of his cave. The Scripture calls it a gentle whisper of the breeze, because from the subtle and delicate communication of the Spirit knowledge[40] was born to it in the understanding; and the soul here calls it a 'whisper of amorous breezes,'[41] because from the amorous communication of the virtues of her Beloved it overflows into her understanding, wherefore she calls it a 'whisper of amorous breezes.'

15. This Divine whisper, which enters by the ear of the soul, is not only substance which I have called that of understanding, but likewise it is the manifestation of truths concerning the Divinity and the revelation of His hidden secrets; for ordinarily, when[42] some communication of God is found in the Divine Scriptures, and is said to enter by the ear, it is found to be a manifestation of these naked truths in the understanding, or a revelation of secrets of God, which are purely spiritual visions or revelations, given to the soul alone, without the help and aid of the senses, and so, when it is said that God communicates by the ear, that expression describes a very sublime and certain fact. Thus when Saint Paul wished to describe the loftiness of his revelation he said not, *Vidit arcana verba*, still less *Gustavit arcana verba*, but *Audivit arcana verba, quæ non licet homini loqui*.[43] Which is as though he had said: I heard secret words which it is not lawful for a man to utter. As to this, it is thought that he saw God as did our father[44] Elias in that whisper. For even as

[39] A, B, Bg omit 'our father.'
[40] A has 'the communication' for 'knowledge.'
[41] Ej omits the rest of the paragraph.
[42] A, Av, B, Bg, Bz, Ej, G, Sg, S: 'whensoever.'
[43] 2 Corinthians xii, 4.
[44] A, B, Bg omit 'our father.'

faith, as Saint Paul says likewise, comes by bodily hearing, even so that which faith teaches us, which is the substance of understanding, comes by spiritual hearing. This was clearly expressed by the prophet Job, when he spoke with God, Who had revealed Himself to him, saying: *Auditu auris audivi te, nunc autem oculus meus videt te.*[45] That is to say: With the hearing of the ear I heard Thee, but now mine eye seeth Thee. Wherein it is clearly declared that to hear Him with the ear of the soul is to see Him with the eye of passive understanding whereof we spoke. Wherefore he says not: I heard Thee with the hearing 'of my ears,' but 'of my ear'; nor: I saw Thee 'with mine eyes,' but 'with mine eye,' which is the understanding. Wherefore this hearing of the soul is seeing with the understanding.

16. And it is not to be understood that, because this which the soul understands is naked substance, as we have said, it is perfect and clear fruition, as in Heaven; for, although it is free from accidents, it is not for that reason clear, but rather it is dark, for it is contemplation, which, as Saint Dionysius says, is in this life a ray of darkness;[46] wherefore we can say that it is a ray and image of fruition,[47] inasmuch as it is in the understanding, wherein consists fruition. This substance of understanding, which the soul here calls a whisper, is the 'desired eyes,' whereof the soul said, when the Beloved revealed them to her (because she could not bear the perception of them): 'Withdraw them, Beloved.'

17. And, as I think that in this place a passage in Job is very much to the point, as confirming a great part of that which I have said of this rapture and betrothal, I will relate it here,[48] although it may delay us a little longer, and I will expound the parts of it that are to our purpose. And first I will give it wholly in Latin and then wholly in the vulgar tongue, and afterwards I will briefly expound that part of it

[45] Job xlii, 5.
[46] *De Mystica Theologia:* Migne, *Patrologia Græca,* Vol. III, p. 999.
[47] Jaén has: 'ray of image of fruition.' [P. Silverio adopts this reading.]
[48] B, Bg omit the following passage: ('although . . . next stanza').

which concerns our purpose;[49] and having ended this I will continue the exposition of the lines of the next stanza. Eliphaz the Themanite, then, in the Book of Job, speaks after this manner: *Porro ad me dictum est verbum absconditum, et quasi furtive suscepit auris mea venas susurri eius. In horrore visionis nocturnæ, quando solet sopor occupare homines, pavor tenuit me, et tremor, et omnia ossa mea perterrita sunt: et cum spiritus, me præsente, transiret, inhorruerunt pili carnis meæ: stetit quidam, cujus non agnoscebam vultum, imago coram oculis meis, et vocem quasi auræ lenis audivi.*[50] Which in the vulgar tongue signifies: In truth a hidden word was spoken to me, and mine ear received as it were by stealth the veins of its whisper. In the horror of the vision by night, when sleep is wont to occupy men, I was occupied by fear and trembling, and all my bones shook; and, as the spirit passed before my presence, the skin[51] of my flesh shrank; and there came before me One Whose countenance I knew not, an image before mine eyes, and I heard a voice of a gentle breeze. In this passage is contained almost all that we have here said concerning this rapture, from the twelfth stanza,[52] which says: 'Withdraw them, Beloved,' down to this point. For in that which Eliphaz the Themanite says, namely, that a hidden word was spoken to him, is signified that hidden thing which was given to the soul, the greatness whereof it could not suffer, so that it said: 'Withdraw them, Beloved.'

18. In this saying that his ear received, as it were by stealth, the veins of its whisper, is signified the naked substance which, as we have said, is received by the understanding: for veins here denote inward substance, and the whisper signifies that communication and touch[53] of the virtues from which the said substance of understanding is communicated to the un-

---

[49] Av, Sg omit 'And first . . . concerns our purpose.'

[50] Job iv, 12–16. Ej, G, Sg, omitting the Latin text, have: 'Leaving aside the Latin, that which he means in the vulgar tongue is.' Av substitutes for the Latin text *'Porro a me dictum est usque lenis audivi.'*

[51] S: 'the hairs.' [Cf. Job iv, 15, A.V.]

[52] It is really from the thirteenth stanza, but only Ej, G, Sg give it correctly.

[53] A has for 'touch' (*toque*) 'intercourse,' 'commerce' (*trato*).

derstanding. And the soul here calls it a whisper, because such a communication is very gentle, even as in that other place she calls it 'amorous breezes,' because it communicates itself amorously. He says that he received it as it were by stealth, because even as that which is stolen belongs to another, even so that secret did not belong to man, speaking after the manner of nature: for he received that which was not according to his nature, wherefore it was not lawful for him to receive it,[54] as it was not lawful for Saint Paul to repeat that which he had heard. Wherefore the other Prophet said twice: 'My secret to myself.'[55] And when Eliphaz speaks of the horror of the vision by night, when sleep is wont to occupy man, and says that he himself has been occupied by fear and trembling, he refers to the fear and trembling which is caused naturally in the soul by that communication of rapture which we said human nature could not suffer in the communication of the Spirit of God. For this Prophet declares here that, as at the time when men go to rest they are wont to be oppressed and terrified by a vision which they call a nightmare, which comes to them between sleep and waking—the point when sleep begins—even so at the time of this spiritual transit from the sleep of natural ignorance to the waking of supernatural knowledge, which is the beginning of rapture or ecstasy, the spiritual vision which is then communicated to them fills them with fear and trembling.[56]

19. And he adds further that all his bones were terrified, or shaken. Which is as though he had said that they were moved and dislocated[57] from out of their places; wherein is described the great dislocation of the bones which, as we have said, is suffered at this time. This was clearly expressed by Daniel, when he saw the angel, and said: *Domine, in visione tua dissolutæ sunt compages meæ.*[58] That is: Lord, in Thy

[54] Above these words, in Av, a corrector has written: 'to say it.'
[55] Isaias xxiv, 16. Ej, G actually give the phrase twice.
[56] A: 'the spiritual union which is then communicated to them makes them to tremble and fear.'
[57] [The word used here, *desencajaron,* is rather stronger than that of] Av and the first redaction: *descasaron.* A has *descansaron* ('rested') [an evident slip].
[58] Daniel x, 16.

vision the joints of my bones have become loosed. And in that which he then says, which is: 'And as the spirit passed before my presence'—that is to say, when He made my spirit pass beyond its limits and natural ways by means of the rapture whereof we have spoken—'the skin[59] of my flesh shrank,' he describes that which we have said concerning the body, which in this transit is frozen so that the flesh shrinks like that of a dead man.

20. The passage continues: 'There was One Whose countenance I knew not, an image before mine eyes.' This One Who he says was present was God, Who communicated Himself after the manner aforementioned. And he says that he knew not His countenance, in order to indicate that in this communication and vision, most lofty though it be, the face and the Essence of God are neither known nor seen. But he says that it was an image before his eyes: for, as we have said, that knowledge of the hidden word was most sublime, as it were the image and trace[60] of God, but it is not to be understood that such knowledge is the essential vision of God.

21. The passage then concludes, saying: 'And I heard a voice of a gentle breeze.' By this is understood the whisper of the amorous breezes, to which the soul here[61] likens her Beloved. It is not to be understood that they always come to pass[62] in these visits with these natural distresses and fears, which, as has been said, are the lot of those that are beginning to enter the estate of illumination and perfection, and to experience this kind of communication; for in others these things are accompanied rather by great sweetness. The exposition continues:

The tranquil night,

22. This spiritual sleep which the soul has in the bosom of its Beloved comprises enjoyment of all the calm and rest and quiet of the peaceful night, and it receives in God together with this a profound and dark Divine intelligence; and for

[59] S: 'the hairs.'

[60] [rastro.] Thus Jaén and Ej. The other authorities have rostro ('face').

[61] A adds: 'in this present stanza.'

[62] Sg: 'come.'

this reason the Bride says that her Beloved is to her 'the tranquil night.'

At the time of the rising of the dawn,

23. But this tranquil night, she says, is not as the dark night, but as the night which is already near the rising of the morning; that is, it appears together with the rising because this calm and quiet[63] in God is not complete darkness to the soul, as is the dark night, but it is tranquillity and quiet in the Divine light, in a new knowledge of God, wherein the spirit is most gently tranquil, being raised to the Divine light. And here she very fitly calls this Divine light the rising of the dawn, which means the morning; for, even as the rising of the morning dispels the darkness of the night and reveals the light of the day, even so this spirit that is tranquil and quiet in God is raised from the darkness of natural knowledge to the morning light of the supernatural knowledge of God—not brightly, but, as we say, darkly, like the night at the time of the rising of the dawn; for even as the night at the time of such rising is neither wholly night nor wholly day, but, as men say, 'between two lights,' so this Divine tranquillity and solitude is neither informed with the Divine light in all its clearness nor does it fail in some measure to participate thereof.

24. In this tranquillity the understanding sees itself raised up in a new and strange way, above all natural understanding, to the Divine light, much as one who, after a long sleep, opens his eyes to the light which he was not expecting. This knowledge, as I understand, was indicated by David when he said: *Vigilavi, et factus sum sicut passer solitarius in tecto.*[64] Which signifies: I awakened and became like to the sparrow all alone on the house-top. As though he had said: I opened the eyes of my understanding and I found myself above all kinds of natural knowledge, all alone, without them, upon the house-

---

[63] Thus Jaén, Ej, G: '. . . the rising of the dawn of the morning; because it appears with the rising; this calm and quiet,' etc. Sg: '. . . the rising of the dawn, which is the morning; because, that is, this calm and quiet in Divine light appear with the rising.' A, Av, B, Bg, Bz, S: '. . . the rising of the morning, because this calm and quiet,' etc.

[64] Psalm ci, 8. [A.V., cii, 7.]

top—that is, above all things here below. And he says that
he became like to the sparrow that is all alone, because in
this manner of contemplation the spirit has the properties of
this sparrow, which are five. First, it ordinarily perches upon
the highest places, even as the spirit, in this experience, engages in the highest contemplation. Second, it ever keeps its
beak turned towards the direction of the wind, even as the
spirit here turns the beak of its affection towards the direction
whence comes the spirit of love, which is God. Third, it is
ordinarily alone and will have no other bird whatsoever near
to it, so that, when any other settles[65] beside it, it flies away.
Even so the spirit in this contemplation is withdrawn from
all things, detached from them all and[66] consenting to naught
save solitude in God. The fourth property is that it sings very
sweetly; even so does the spirit sing to God at this time, for
the praises which it makes to God are of sweetest love, most
delectable to itself and most precious to God. The fifth is that
it is of no definite colour; even so is the perfect spirit, which
in this excess not only has no colour[67] of sensual affection
and love of self, but has not even any particular consideration
of things above or below, neither can it speak thereof in any
method or manner, for that which possesses it is the fathomless knowledge of God, even as we have said.

The silent music,[68]

25. In that aforesaid tranquillity and silence of the night,
and in that knowledge of the Divine light, the soul is able
to see a marvellous fitness and disposition of the wisdom of
God in the diversities of all His creatures and works, all and
each of which are endowed[69] with a certain response to God,
whereby each after its manner testifies to that which God is
in it, so that it seems to hear a harmony of sublimest music

[65] Ej, G, Sg have 'arrives,' and S has 'stops,' for 'settles.'

[66] S: 'from all things of the world, flees from them all and
is,' etc.

[67] So Av, Ej, G, Sg, S. Jaén and certain other authorities omit
'no,' thus clearly reversing the Saint's meaning.

[68] Ej, G, Sg omit the commentary on this line.

[69] Thus Av, Bg. Other versions read: de todas ('of all') for
dotadas ('endowed').

surpassing all concerts and melodies of the world. The Bride calls this music silent because, as we have said, it is a tranquil and quiet intelligence, without sound of voices; and in it are thus enjoyed both the sweetness of the music and the quiet of the silence. And so she says that her Beloved is this silent music, because this harmony of spiritual music is known and experienced in Him. Not only so but likewise He is

The sounding solitude,

26. This is almost the same as silent music; for, although that music is silent to the senses and the natural faculties, it is a most sounding solitude to the spiritual faculties; for when these are alone and empty of all natural forms and apprehensions they can readily and most sonorously receive in the spirit the spiritual sound[70] of the excellence of God, in Himself and in His creatures, according to that which, as we said above, Saint John saw in spirit in the Apocalypse— namely, when he heard the voice of many harpers who harped upon their harps.[71] This was in the spirit: he speaks not of material harps, but of a certain knowledge which he had of the praises of the blessed, which each one, according to his own degree of glory, makes to God continually. And this is like music, for as each one possesses the gifts of God in a different degree, even so does each one sing the praises of God in a different degree, yet all make one harmony of love, just as in music.

27. After this same manner the soul is able to see, in that tranquil wisdom, how of all the creatures—not the higher creatures alone, but also the lower, according to that which each of them has received in itself from God—each one raises its voice in testimony to that which God is. She sees that each one[72] after its manner exalts God, since it has God in itself according to its capacity;[73] and thus all these voices make one voice of music, extolling the greatness of God and His

[70] Thus B, Bz, Ej, G. Jaén, A, Av, Bg, S read: 'the spiritual sense.'

[71] [See p. 106, § 11, above.]

[72] Ej, G, Sg: '. . . each one raises its voice as to that which God is. And in testimony hereof each one,' etc.

[73] Ej, G, Sg add: 'and virtue.'

marvellous knowledge and wisdom. And it is this that the Holy Spirit signifies in the Book of Wisdom, where He says: *Spiritus Domini replevit orbem terrarum, et hoc quod continet omnia, scientiam habet vocis.*[74] Which is to say: The Spirit of the Lord hath filled the round world, and this world, which containeth all things that He hath made, hath knowledge of the voice. This is that sounding solitude which, as we say, the soul knows here, which is the testimony that all things give in themselves concerning God. And inasmuch as the soul receives this sounding music, not without solitude and withdrawal from all outward things, she calls them the silent music and the sounding solitude. This, she says, is her Beloved. And He is further

The supper that recreates and enkindles love.

28. To those that are loved[75] suppers bring recreation, satisfaction and love. And because these three things are caused by the Beloved in the soul in this sweet communication, the Bride here calls Him the supper that recreates and enkindles love. It is to be known that in Divine Scripture this word 'supper' is understood of the Divine vision; for, as supper is the end of the day's work and the beginning of the night's rest, so this knowledge which we have called tranquil gives to the soul a realization of the sure termination of things evil and the possession[76] of things that are good, whereat it is more enkindled with love for God than it was before. Wherefore God is to the soul the supper which recreates it by being the termination of its evils, and enkindles it in love by being to it the possession[77] of all things that are good.

29. But in order that it may be the better understood of what kind is this supper of the soul—the which supper, as we have said, is her Beloved—it is fitting here to observe that which the same Beloved, the Spouse, says in the Apocalypse, namely: 'I stand at the door and knock; if any man open to Me, I will come in, and will sup with him and he with

[74] Wisdom i, 7.
[75] S: 'that are in love.'
[76] Sg: 'position.'
[77] S: 'the beginning of possession.'

Me.'[78] Whereby He indicates that He brings with Him the supper, which is naught else than His own sweetness and the delights whereof He Himself has fruition; which, when He unites Himself with the soul, He communicates to her, so that she has fruition thereof likewise; for this is what is meant by: 'I will sup with him and he with Me.' And thus in these words is described the effect of the Divine union of the soul with God, in the which union God shares with the Bride-Soul the same good things which are proper to Him, for, as we have said, He communicates them to her, graciously and bounteously. And thus He is Himself for her the supper which recreates and enkindles love, for by His bounteousness to her He recreates it and by His graciousness to her He enkindles it within her.

30. Before we enter into the exposition of the other stanzas it is meet to observe here that, although we have said that the soul in this estate of betrothal enjoys all tranquillity, and that all the other things that are possible in this life are communicated to her, it is not for that reason to be understood that the tranquillity is only according to the higher part,[79] because the sensual part never, until the estate of the Spiritual Marriage, completely loses its imperfections, neither is its strength completely subdued, as will be said hereafter. That which is here communicated to it is the most that is possible in the estate of the Betrothal; for in the Spiritual Marriage its profit is much greater. In the Betrothal, although in the visits of the Spouse the Bride-Soul enjoys these great blessings which we have described, she nevertheless suffers from His absences, and from perturbations and disturbances coming from her lower part and from the devil, all of which things cease[80] in the estate of the Marriage.

[78] Apocalypse iii, 20. Sg omits the following sentence.

[79] S: 'all the other things that it is possible to communicate in this life are communicated to her, it is not for that reason to be understood that it is in her whole being, but that this tranquillity is according to the higher part.' The Toledo edition follows this reading [which it seems to me almost obligatory to follow on grounds of sense].

[80] A: 'all of which things she uses.'

Annotation of the Stanza Following

The virtues of the Bride having now reached the point of perfection in her soul, so that she is enjoying habitual peace in the visits which the Beloved pays her, she has at times a fruition of their sweetness and fragrance which is most sublime, because the Beloved has touched them, even as one enjoys the sweetness and beauty of lilies and other flowers when they are open and one handles them. In many of these visits the soul becomes conscious within her spirit of all her virtues,[81] by reason of the light which He has given her; and then with the wondrous delight and sweetness of love she gathers them all together and offers them to the Beloved, as it were a bunch[82] of beautiful flowers. Then the Beloved, when He accepts them (for He does indeed accept them), accepts therein a great service. All this comes to pass within the soul, at which time she feels the Beloved to be within her as upon His own bed, for the soul offers herself, together with the virtues, which is the greatest service that she can render Him; and this delight that the soul receives from this kind of gift which she makes to the Beloved is one of the greatest delights that she is wont to receive in her interior intercourse with God.

2. And the devil, becoming aware of this prosperity of the soul (for in his great malice he envies all the good that he sees in her), makes use of all his skill at this time and exercises all his arts so that he may be able to distract the soul from even the least part of this blessing; for he sets greater store upon keeping back from the soul a fraction of this her wealth and glorious delight than upon causing many other souls to fall into many other sins and very grave ones; for those other souls have little or naught to lose, whereas this soul has much, that which it has gained being very great and exceeding precious, just as the loss of the smallest quantity of finest gold is worse than that of a great quantity of base metals. Here the devil profits by the desires of the senses, al-

---

[81] S adds here: 'which God has given her.'
[82] [piña. See p. 162, n. 2, above.]

though as a rule he can do very little, or nothing, in this estate, since they are already mortified; and, since he is powerless in this respect, he presents many distractions[83] to the imagination. And sometimes he stirs up many motions in the sensual part of the soul, as will afterwards be said, and causes other vexations, both spiritual and sensual, from which it is not in the power of the soul to free herself until the Lord sends His angel (as is said in the Psalm) round about them that fear Him, and delivers them,[84] and makes peace and tranquillity alike in the sensual part of the soul and in the spiritual part. This soul, in order to make this manifest and to entreat this favour, being fearful, from the experience which she has of the wiles used by the devil to work the aforementioned harm in her at this time, addresses the angels, whose office is to show her favour at this time[85] by putting the evil spirits to flight, and speaks as in the following stanza:

STANZA XVI

Drive us away the foxes,   For[1] our vineyard is now in flower,[2] While we make a bunch[3] of roses,   And let none appear upon the hill.

Exposition

3. The soul, then, desiring that naught may keep from her the continuance of this interior delight of love, which is the flowering of the vineyard of her soul[4]—neither the envious

---

[83] Bg: 'vanities.'

[84] Psalm xxxiii, 8. [A.V., xxxiv, 7.]

[85] Ej, G, Sg: 'favour in this necessity'; B, Bg: 'favour on these occasions.'

[1] Sg: 'Because.'

[2] B, Bg, Ej, G, Sg: 'flowering.'

[3] [On the word translated 'bunch,' 'nosegay,' see p. 162, n. 2, above.]

[4] [sic.]

and malicious evil spirits, nor the raging desires of sensuality, nor the various comings and goings of imaginations,[5] nor any other awareness of things and their presence—invokes the angels, adjuring them to drive away all these things,[6] and to keep them back, lest they themselves keep back the soul from the exercise of interior love, in the delight and savour whereof the virtues and graces are being communicated and enjoyed by the soul and the Son of God. And thus she says:

Drive us away the foxes,   For[7] our vineyard is now in flower,[8]

4. The vineyard here spoken of is the nursery of all the virtues which is in this holy soul, the which virtues give it a wine of sweet savour. This vineyard of the soul is flowering thus when the soul is united with the Spouse according to the will and in the same Spouse is rejoicing according to all these virtues together. At certain times, as we have said, there are wont to resort to the memory and fancy many and various[9] forms of imagination, and in the sensual part of the soul there rise up many and various[10] motions and desires. These are of so many and such various kinds that, when David was drinking this delectable wine of the spirit with great thirst for God, feeling the hindrance and vexation which they caused him, he said: 'My soul thirsted for Thee, in how many ways has my flesh thirsted for Thee!'[11]

5. All this chorus[12] of desires and motions of the senses the soul here calls foxes, because of the great similarity which at this time they have to them. For, even as the foxes feign sleep that they may capture their prey when they go hunt-

[5] S: 'of the imagination.'
[6] Ej, G, Sg: 'all these foxes.'
[7] Sg: 'Because.'
[8] Bg, Ej, Sg: 'is now flowering.'
[9] Ej, G, Sg: 'and very various.'
[10] Ej, G, Sg: 'and very various.'
[11] Psalm lxii, 2. [A.V., lxiii, 1.] [The second 'thirsted' is omitted in Spanish, which follows the Vulgate: *Sitivit in te anima mea; quam multipliciter tibi caro mea!*] Av has: 'in how many ways does my flesh desire Thee!' Ej, G add the Latin text.
[12] [*Lit.*, 'harmony.']

ing,[13] so all these desires and powers of the senses are at rest and asleep until these flowers of the virtues spring up in the soul and open and burst forth; and then it seems that, in its sensual part, its flowers, of the desires and powers of the senses, awaken and spring up in their attempt to resist the spirit and to reign. Even to this point comes the lust which, as Saint Paul says, the flesh has against the spirit;[14] for, its inclination towards the senses being strong, that which is wholly carnal finds weariness and distaste when it tastes of the spirit; wherein these desires cause great vexation to the sweetness of the spirit; wherefore the Bride says: 'Drive us away the foxes.'

6. But the malicious evil spirits for their part trouble the soul here in two ways. For they excite and stir up these desires with vehemence,[15] and with them, and with other imaginations, etc., they make war upon this flourishing[16] and peaceful kingdom of the soul. And in the second place (and this is worse) when they cannot act in this way they assail the soul with bodily noises and torments in order to cause it distraction. And, what is worse, they do battle against it with spiritual horrors and fears, amounting at times to terrible torment; which they can do very effectively at this time, if they are given permission, for, when the soul becomes very greatly detached in spirit in order to perform this spiritual exercise, the devil can readily appear to it, since he is a spirit likewise. At other times he makes other assaults upon the soul by means of horrors before it begins to enjoy these sweet flowers, when God is beginning to draw it forth to some extent from the house of its senses so that it may enter upon the said inward exercise in the garden of the Spouse; for he knows that, if once the soul enters into this recollection, it is so well protected that, do what he may, he cannot harm it. And often, when the devil goes out to intercept the soul, it will very

[13] S: 'when the game comes out.' [The two expressions are very similar in Spanish, *caza* meaning either 'hunting' or 'game.']

[14] Galatians v, 17.

[15] A, Ej, G, Sg: 'with great vehemence.'

[16] [The Spanish word is *florido,* translated 'flowering' in the text and notes above.]

quickly become recollected in the deep hiding-place of its inmost being, and then those terrors[17] which it suffers are so far away and so greatly removed that not only do they cause it no fear, but they make it to be glad and to rejoice.

7. Of these terrors the Bride made mention in the Songs, saying: 'My soul troubled me by reason of the chariots of Aminadab.'[18] By Aminadab she there means the devil, and she calls his assaults and attacks upon the soul 'chariots,' because of the great vehemence and the confusion and noise that accompany them. Afterwards the soul says here:[19] 'Drive us away the foxes.' This the Bride also entreats in the Songs, to the same purpose, saying: 'Drive us away the little foxes that spoil the vineyards, for our vineyard hath flourished.'[20] And she says not: 'Drive me away,' but, 'Drive us away,'[21] for she is speaking of herself and of the Beloved, since they are at one and are enjoying the flower of the vineyard. The reason for which she says here that the vineyard is in flower, and not in fruit, is that the fruition of the virtues in the soul in this life, although it be in such perfection as in this soul of whom we speak, is, as it were, of flower; only in the next life will it be as of fruit. And she says next:

While we make a bunch of roses,

8. For at this season, when the soul is enjoying the flower of this vineyard and taking her delight upon the breast of her Beloved, it comes to pass that the virtues of the soul stand out clearly to view, as we have said, and are at their best, revealing themselves to her and bestowing upon her great sweetness and delight. These virtues the soul feels to be in herself and in God, so that they seem to her to be a pleasant vineyard, full of flower, belonging to them both, wherein both of them pasture and have their delight. Then the soul gathers together all these virtues, and in each one of them and in

[17] Ej, G, Sg: 'torments.'
[18] Canticles vi, 11. [A.V., vi, 12.]
[19] S: 'And the soul says, even as here.'
[20] Canticles ii, 15. Sg has *ha fallecido* ('has failed,' 'has died') for *ha florecido* ('hath flourished').
[21] Ej, G: 'but says it in the plural.'

all of them together makes most delectable acts of love; all these she offers to the Beloved with great tenderness of love and sweetness; and the Beloved Himself aids her herein, for without His favour and aid she could not thus gather together and offer the virtues to her Beloved. Wherefore she says: 'We make a nosegay'—that is to say, the Beloved and I.

9.[22] She calls this gathering together of virtues a cone or nosegay,[23] because even as a pine-cone is strong, and contains within itself many pieces, strong and strongly bound together,[24] which are the pine-kernels, even so this cone or nosegay of virtues which the soul makes for her Beloved is one single piece of the soul's perfection, which firmly and in an ordered manner[25] embraces and contains within itself many perfections and virtues which are very strong, and gifts which are very precious, for all the perfections and virtues are ordered[26] and contained in one firm perfection of the soul. Inasmuch as this perfection is being formed through the practice of the virtues, and, when formed, is being offered to the Beloved by the soul[27] in the spirit of love after the manner which we are describing, it is fitting, then, that the foxes aforementioned be driven away so that they hinder not the said interior communication between the two. And not only does the soul in this stanza make this request alone that she may be able to fashion the nosegay well, but likewise she desires[28] that which ensues in the line following, namely:

And let none appear upon the hill.[29]

10. This Divine interior exercise also requires withdrawal and detachment from all things that might present themselves

[22] [This paragraph and the preceding are both numbered '8' by P. Silverio, and paragraphs 10 and 11 are numbered by him 9 and 10.]

[23] [See p. 162, n. 2, above.]

[24] S adds: 'among themselves.'

[25] A, Ej, G, Sg have: *ordinariamente* ['habitually'] for *ordenadamente* ['in an ordered manner'].

[26] Av omits several lines here [destroying the sense].

[27] Jaén reads: 'to the Beloved by the Beloved'—an evident error.

[28] Av: 'desires to do.'

[29] Av, Bz: 'upon the countryside.'

to the soul, whether from the lower part of a man, which is that of the senses, or[30] from the higher part, which is that of the reason, in the which two parts are comprised the entire harmony of the faculties and senses of a man, which harmony the Bride here calls a hill, because all the knowledge and the desires of nature dwell and are situated thereon, as quarry on the hill, and the devil is wont to pursue and capture these desires and this knowledge to the detriment of the soul. She begs that none may appear on this hill—that is to say, that no representation and form of any object that pertains[31] to any of these faculties or senses whereof we have spoken may appear before the soul and the Spouse. It is thus as though she were to say: In all the spiritual faculties of the soul—namely the understanding, the memory and the will—let there be no other knowledge or private affections or considerations of any kind; and in all the senses and faculties of the body, both inward and outward, such as the imagination, the fancy, etc., and seeing, hearing, etc., let there be no other digressions and forms,[32] and images and figures, neither representations of objects to the soul, nor other natural operations.

11. This the soul says here since, in order to have perfect fruition of this communication with God, it is fitting that all the senses and faculties, whether interior or exterior, be empty, idle and at rest from their own operations and objects; for, at such a time, the more they exercise themselves of their own accord, the more they disturb the soul. For, when the soul attains to some manner of interior union of love, the spiritual faculties no longer work in it, still less do the bodily faculties, inasmuch as the work of the union of love is already wrought and done, and the soul is moved in love, and thus the faculties have ceased to work, for when they reach their goal all medial operations come to an end. Thus that which the soul does at this time is to wait lovingly upon God, which is to love in continuation of unitive love. Let none, then, ap-

[30] Av omits: 'from the lower . . . senses or.'

[31] Ej, Sg: 'that is pertinent'; G: 'that is impertinent.'

[32] A, B, Bg modify thus: '. . . and faculties of the body, such as the imagination, fancy, etc.; seeing and hearing, both inward and outward, let there be no other digressions and forms.'

pear upon the hill; let the will alone appear, waiting upon
the Beloved in the surrender of itself and of all the virtues
after the manner which has been described.

Annotation for the Stanza Following

For a further knowledge of the stanza which follows, it is
meet here to observe that the absences of her Beloved which
the soul suffers in this estate of spiritual betrothal are very
afflicting,[33] and some are of such a kind that there is no grief
to be compared with them. The cause of this is that, since
the love which the soul has to God in this estate is great and
vehement, she is greatly and vehemently tormented in His absence. And to this grief is added the vexation[34] which comes
to the soul at this time from any kind of intercourse or communication with the creatures, which is very great. For, as
she is experiencing the great vehemence of her fathomless desire for union with God, any kind of intercourse is most
grievous and vexatious to her; just as, when a stone with great
impetus and velocity goes rushing towards its centre, anything
which it might meet and which detained it in that void would
cause it a most violent shock.[35] And, as the soul has already
experienced the taste of these sweet visits, they are more desirable to her than gold and all beauty.[36] Wherefore the soul,
greatly fearing to be deprived of so precious a presence, even
for a moment, addresses herself to aridity,[37] and to the spirit
of her Spouse, saying in this stanza:[38]

[33] B, Bg, Ej, Sg have *afectivas* ('affective') for *aflictivas* ('afflicting').
[34] Bg: 'the absence.'
[35] B, Bg: 'will be very vexatious to it.'
[36] A: 'and all other beauties.'
[37] [*sequedad*: translated 'dryness' in the following paragraphs.]
[38] S: 'says the words of the following stanza.'

STANZA XVII

**Stay thee, dead north wind.   Come, south wind, that awakenest
love;**

**Breathe through my garden and let its odours[1] flow,   And the
Beloved shall pasture[2] among the flowers.**

Exposition

2. In addition to that which we have said in the last stanza,
spiritual dryness is a cause whereby is kept from the soul the
substance[3] of inward sweetness whereof we have spoken[4]
above; and the soul, fearing this, does two things in this
stanza. First, she keeps out dryness, shutting the door upon
it by means of continual prayer and devotion. The second
thing that she does is to invoke the Holy Spirit, for it is He
that has to drive out this dryness from the soul, that sustains
and increases her love for the Spouse, and that will lead[5] the
soul to the interior practice of the virtues—all this to the end
that the Son of God, her Spouse, may have greater rejoicing
and delight in her, for her whole aim[6] is to please the Beloved.

Stay thee, dead north wind.

3. The north wind is a very cold wind[7] which dries up
and withers the flowers and plants, or at least makes them
to shrink and close up[8] when it strikes them. And because
spiritual dryness and the realization of the Beloved's absence[9]

---

[1] [P. Silverio here takes the reading of p. 235, n. 21, above.]

[2] A: 'shall appear.' [*parecerá* for *pacerá*.]

[3] [*jugo*, the sap or pith of a plant.]

[4] S: 'have treated.'

[5] [The Spanish text changes abruptly here from indicative to subjunctive in a way that cannot be exactly expressed in English.]

[6] Sg: 'her whole perfection.'

[7] A: 'is a dry and cold wind.'

[8] Bg: 'and dry up.'

[9] [*Lit.*, 'and the affective absence of the Beloved.']

cause this same effect in the soul which experiences them, quenching in her[10] the substance and savour and fragrance of the virtues which she tasted, she calls it the north wind; because all the virtues and the affective exercises which the soul practised are mortified in her, wherefore the soul says: 'Stay thee, dead north wind.' This saying of the soul is to be understood of an act and deed of prayer, and of spiritual exercises,[11] which shall stay this dryness. But, because in this estate the things that God communicates to the soul are so intimate that by no exercise of her faculties can the soul of herself put them into practice and experience them if the Spirit of the Spouse cause not this motion of love within her, she next invokes Him, saying:

Come, south wind, that awakenest love;

4. The south wind is another wind, which is commonly called *ábrego;*[12] this peaceful breeze causes rain and makes grass and plants to grow and flowers to open and scatter their fragrance; its effects are contrary to those of the north wind.[13] And thus by this breeze the soul denotes the Holy Spirit, Who, as she says, awakens love; for, when this Divine breeze assails the soul, it enkindles it wholly and refreshes it and revives it and awakens the will and upraises[14] the desires which aforetime had fallen and were asleep, to the love of God, in such manner that it may well be said thereof that it awakens the love both of the Spouse and of the Bride; and that which she begs of the Holy Spirit[15] is that which she says in the line following:

Breathe through my garden

5. This garden is the soul; for, just as the soul called herself above a vineyard in flower, because the flower of the virtues

---

[10] S: 'exhausting in her.'

[11] S omits: 'prayer, and of.'

[12] [See p. 167, n. 9, above.]

[13] S modifies: 'and scatter their fragrance; and in fact this breeze has the contrary effects to those of the north wind.'

[14] Sg: 'and awakens.'

[15] Ej, G: 'of the Spouse.'

which are in her gives her a wine of sweet savour, so here she calls herself a garden,[16] because there are planted within her, and are born and grow, the flowers of perfections and virtues whereof we have spoken. And here it is to be noted that the Bride says not 'Breathe in my garden,' but 'Breathe through my garden,' for there is a great difference between the breathing of God into the soul and His breathing through the soul.[17] To breathe into the soul is to infuse into it grace, gifts and virtues; and to breathe through the soul is for God to touch and set in motion the virtues and perfections which have already been given to it, refreshing them and moving them so that they may diffuse into the soul wondrous fragrance and sweetness. This is just as when aromatic spices are shaken; for, as soon as they are set in motion, they shed the abundance of their odour, which formerly was not present or was not perceived to so high a degree. For the virtues that the soul has in itself, whether acquired or infused, it is not always actually feeling and enjoying; because, as we shall say later, they are present in the soul during this life like flowers enclosed in the bud,[18] or like aromatic spices covered over, the fragrance whereof is not perceived until they are opened and shaken, as we have said.[19]

6. But at times God grants to the Bride-Soul such favours that, breathing with His Divine Spirit through this her flowering garden, He opens all these buds, or virtues, and uncovers these aromatic spices which are the gifts and perfections and riches of the soul, and, by manifesting this inward wealth and treasure, reveals all her beauty. And then it is a wondrous thing to see, and sweet to feel, the riches of the gifts which are revealed to the soul and the beauty of these flowers of the virtues which are now all opened in the soul; and the sweetness of the fragrance which each one diffuses, according to its nature, is inestimable. This the Bride here calls the flow-

---

[16] A omits the next four lines, continuing: 'for there is . . .'

[17] S: 'the breathing of God into the soul or through the soul'; Ej, Sg: '. . . into the soul and the breathing of God through the soul.'

[18] S: 'in the shoot or in the bud.'

[19] Ej, G omit the following paragraph.

ing of the odours of the garden, and she says in the line following:

And let its odours flow,

7. These odours are at times so abundant that the soul thinks herself to be clothed with delights and bathed in inestimable glory—so much so that not only is she conscious of them within, but they are also wont to overflow from her, without, to such an extent that all who are able to discern such things recognize it,[20] and the soul in this case seems to them to be like a delectable garden, full of the delights and riches of God. And not only when these flowers are opened can this be observed in these holy souls, but they bear within them habitually something of greatness and dignity which causes others to stop and respect them by reason of the supernatural effect produced in them through their close and familiar intercourse with God, even as it is written of Moses, in the Book of Exodus,[21] that they could not look upon his countenance by reason of the honour and glory which remained upon it[22] because he had spoken with God face to face.

8. In this breathing of the Holy Spirit through the soul, which is His visitation of her in love,[23] the Spouse, Who is the Son of God, communicates Himself to her after a lofty manner. To this end He first sends His Spirit, Who is His forerunner, as He did to the Apostles, to prepare for Him a dwelling for the soul His Bride, raising her up in delight, setting her garden in order, causing its flowers to open, revealing its gifts, adorning her with the tapestry of His graces[24] and riches. And thus with great desire the Bride-Soul desires all this—namely, that the north wind may depart, that the south wind may come and that it may breathe through the garden, for herein[25] the soul gains many things together. She gains the fruition of the virtues which have been brought

[20] Ej, G, Sg: 'feel and recognize it.'
[21] Exodus xxxiv, 30.
[22] So Jaén. The other MSS. read: 'upon his person.'
[23] S: '. . . His visitation, enamoured of her.'
[24] Ej, Sg: 'with His tapestries and graces.' G: 'embellishing her with His tapestries and graces.'
[25] So all the MSS. except Jaén, which reads: 'for then.'

to the highest point of delectable exercise, as we have said. She gains the fruition of the Beloved in them, since by their means, as we have just said, He communicates Himself within her in more intimate love, granting her more special favours than before. She also gains this, that the Beloved delights in her far more through this actual exercise of the virtues, and it is this that pleases her most, namely that her Beloved is pleased with her. She also gains the continuance and duration of this fragrance and sweetness of the virtues, which continues in the soul for as long as the Spouse is present within her after this manner, and the Bride is giving Him sweetness in her virtues, even as she says in the Songs after this wise: 'While the King was in his reclining-chamber—that is to say, in the soul—my flowering and fragrant little tree gave forth fragrance of sweetness.'[26] By this fragrant little tree is here understood[27] the soul itself, which from the flowers of the virtues that it has within itself gives forth fragrance of sweetness to the Beloved, Who dwells within it in this kind of union.

9. Wherefore this Divine breath of the Holy Spirit is greatly to be desired, and likewise that every soul should pray that He may breathe through its garden so that the Divine odours of God may flow. And because this is so necessary, and of such great glory and good for the soul, the Bride desired it and prayed for it in the Songs in the same terms as here, saying: 'Rise up hence, north wind, and come, southwest wind,[28] and breathe through my garden; and its fragrances and precious spices shall flow.'[29] And all this the soul desires, not for the delight and glory which come to her thereby, but because she knows that her Spouse delights therein. This is[30] a preparation and prediction for the Son of God to come and take His delight in her; wherefore she says next:

And the Beloved shall pasture among the flowers.

10. The soul here refers to this delight that the Son of God has in her at this time, and she gives it the name of pasture,

---

[26] Canticles i, 11. [A.V., i, 12.]
[27] S: 'she here gives to be understood.'
[28] [ábrego.]
[29] Canticles iv, 16.
[30] S adds: 'all.'

which describes it with the greatest fitness, since pasturing or feeding[31] is a thing that gives not only pleasure, but likewise sustenance; and even so the Son of God delights in the soul, and in these the soul's delights, and takes sustenance from her—that is, He continues in her, as in a place wherein He has great delight, since the place itself truly delights in Him. And it is this, as I understand, that He Himself meant when He said, through the mouth of Solomon, in the Proverbs: 'My delights are with the sons of men'[32]—that is to say, when their delights are to be with Me, Who am the Son of God.[33] And it is fitting to note here that the soul says not that the Beloved will pasture 'upon' the flowers, but 'among' the flowers; for, since His communication (that is to say, that of the Spouse) is in the soul itself, by means of the adornment of the virtues aforementioned, it follows that it is upon the soul itself that He pastures, transforming it into Himself, when it is prepared and seasoned and made fragrant with the aforementioned flowers of virtues and gifts and perfections, which are the things[34] whereby and among which He pastures upon the soul. These things, by the power of His forerunner aforementioned, are rendering the soul pleasing and sweet to the Son of God, to the end that by this means He may pasture the more upon her love; for this is the habit[35] of the Spouse, to unite Himself with the soul amid the fragrance of these flowers. This habit the Bride observes very well[36] in the Songs, as one who well knows it, when she speaks in these words: 'My Beloved is gone down into His garden, to the beds and breezes of the fragrant spices, to pasture in the gardens and to gather lilies.'[37] And again she says: 'I for my Beloved and my Beloved for me: He feedeth among the lil-

[31] Bg: 'since pasturing that is supplied.'
[32] Proverbs viii, 31.
[33] Av omits: 'Who am the Son of God.'
[34] [*Lit.*, 'the sauce.']
[35] S: 'this is the love.'
[36] S: 'observes well.'
[37] Canticles vi, 1. [A.V., vi, 2–3.] For 'beds and breezes' [which in the Spanish is singular in form, though plural in meaning] Bg has: 'to the manner and breeze,' and A: 'to the fragrance and breeze.'

ies.'[38] That is to say: He pastures upon my soul and delights in it, and it is His garden, among the lilies of my virtues and perfections and graces.

Annotation for the Stanza Following

In this estate of spiritual betrothal the soul can see her excellences and great riches, but perceives that she possesses them not and enjoys them not as she would desire, because she still has her abode in the flesh. Oftentimes, therefore, she suffers greatly, especially when her realization of this becomes more vivid.[39] For she is able to see that, while in the body, she is like to a great lord in prison, subject to a thousand miseries, with his kingdoms confiscated and all his dominion and wealth taken away from him; of all his possessions allowed to have nothing but food, and that very sparingly. Anyone will be well able to see how he suffers,[40] especially since the very domestics in his house no longer render him due obedience, but at every opportunity his servants and slaves set themselves up against him, and treat him with no respect, even to the point of trying to take the very food[41] from his dish.[42] And when God[43] grants the soul the favour of giving it to taste some of[44] the good things and riches which He has prepared for it, immediately there rises up in its sensual part some evil servant of desire, or perchance some slave of disorderly motions, or other rebellious elements[45] in this its lower nature, to prevent its attaining this good.

2. Herein the soul feels as though it were in the country

[38] Canticles vi, 2. [A.V., vi, 3.] Ej, G, Sg read: 'among the flowers—that is to say, in my soul—and delights in it, which is His garden,' etc.

[39] B, Bg, by reading *acaba* for *aviva,* modify thus: 'especially when her realization of this comes to an end.'

[40] Ej, Sg read: 'Anyone will be able to judge what this great lord of whom we have spoken will feel.'

[41] [*Lit.,* 'to take the morsel.']

[42] Av: 'from his mouth.'

[43] S: 'Thus, then, is the soul in the body, when God, etc.'

[44] [*Lit.,* 'some morsel of.']

[45] [*Lit.,* 'or other rebellions.'] A, Bz: 'revelations.'

of enemies and as though tyrannized over among strangers, and as one dead among dead men—feeling indeed that which is expressed by the prophet Baruch, when he dwells upon this misery in describing the captivity of Jacob, saying: 'Who is Israel,[46] that it should be in its enemies' land? Thou art grown old in a strange country; thou art defiled with the dead and they have counted thee with them that go down to hell.'[47] And Jeremias, feeling the wretchedness of this treatment[48] that the soul suffers from the captivity of the body, speaking with Israel according to the spiritual sense, says: 'Is Israel perchance a servant or a slave that he is thus taken prisoner? The lions roared upon him,' etc.[49] He means here by the lions the desires and the rebellious elements, to which we are referring, of this tyrant king of sensuality. And to the end that she may describe the trouble that comes to her, and the desire which she has that this kingdom of sensuality, with all its armies[50] and troubles, may now come to an end or be wholly subjected to her, the soul raises her eyes to the Spouse as to Him that is to do all this, and, speaking against the said motions and rebellious elements, says as in this stanza:

STANZA XVIII

**O nymphs of Judaea,   While mid the flowers and rose-trees
  the ambar sends forth perfume,
Dwell in the outskirts   And desire not to touch our thresholds.**

Exposition

3. In this stanza it is the Bride that speaks, who, seeing herself adorned, according to her higher and spiritual part, with such rich and excellent gifts and delights, which come

[46] S reads, more correctly: 'How happeneth it, O Israel, etc.'
[47] Baruch iii, 10–11.
[48] A, B, Bg: 'feeling this same treatment.'
[49] Jeremias ii, 14–15.
[50] Bz, Sg have 'exercises' (*ejercicios*) for 'armies' (*ejércitos*).

from her Beloved, desires to preserve herself in the security and continual possession thereof, which, in the two preceding stanzas, the Spouse has granted her. She sees that in her lower part—namely, sensuality—there may be impediments, as in fact there are, which disturb so great a blessing. She therefore bids the operations and motions of that her lower part to be stilled in her faculties and senses, and not to pass beyond the limits of their own region, that of the senses,[1] nor to trouble and harass the higher and spiritual part of the soul, lest it should be kept, by any motion, howsoever small, from the blessing and sweetness which it enjoys. For if the motions of the sensual part and its faculties take place when the spirit is in fruition, they trouble and harass it all the more when they are busier and more active. She says, then, thus:

O nymphs of Judaea,

4. By Judæa she means the lower part of the soul, which is that of the senses. And she calls it Judæa, because it is weak and carnal and of itself blind, even as are the Jewish people. And by nymphs she means all the imaginations, fancies and motions and affections of this lower part. All these she calls nymphs because, even as the nymphs attract lovers to themselves by[2] their affectionate nature and their grace, so these operations and motions of sensuality contrive to attract the will pleasantly to themselves from the rational part of the soul, in order to take it from that which is inward, and so making it to love that which is outward, which they themselves love and desire, and likewise moving the understanding and attracting it to be married and united with them after their base, sensual manner, contriving to bring into conformity and to unite[3] the rational part with the sensual. You sensual motions and operations, then, she says:

While mid the flowers and rose-trees . . .

[1] Thus Jaén, Sg, S. Av, Bz: 'the limits of their sensual region.' A, B, Bg: 'the limits of their sensuality.' G: 'the limits of their religion, sensuality.'

[2] Thus Ej, G, Sg, S. Jaén, A, Av, B, Bg, Bz: 'all these she calls nymphs, who by,' etc.

[3] S has 'attract' for 'unite.'

5. The flowers, as we have said, are the virtues of the soul.
The rose-trees are the faculties of the same soul:[4] memory,
understanding and will; these bear and nurture flowers of Divine conceptions and acts of love[5] and of the said virtues.
While, then, amid these virtues and faculties of my soul, etc.,

. . . the ambar sends forth perfume,

6. By the ambar is here understood the Divine spirit of
the Spouse which dwells in the soul; and for this Divine ambar
to send forth perfume amid the flowers and rose-trees is for
it to scatter and communicate itself most sweetly in the faculties and virtues of the soul, thereby giving the soul a perfume
of Divine sweetness.[6] For so long, then, as this Divine spirit
is giving spiritual sweetness to my soul,

Dwell in the outskirts

7. In the outskirts of Judæa, which, we said, are the inferior or sensual portion of the soul. Its outskirts are the inward sensual senses, such as the memory,[7] the fancy, the
imagination, wherein meet and gather the forms and images
and phantasms of objects, by means whereof sensuality moves
its desires and longings. It is these forms, etc., which are here
called nymphs; and while these are quiet and at rest the desires also sleep. These nymphs enter these outskirts of the
inward senses through the gates of the outward senses, which
are hearing, sight, smell, etc.; so that we may term all these
faculties and senses, whether inward or outward,[8] of this
sensual part, outskirts, because they are the suburbs which
are without the walls of the city. For that which is called
city in the soul is that most inward part—that is to say, the
rational part, which has capacity for communion with God,
and the operations of which are contrary to those of sensuality. But since there is natural communication between the
dwellers in these outskirts (which are the sensual part of the

[4] S: 'The rose trees are its faculties.'
[5] Ej, G, Sg: 'Divine contentments and acts of love of God.'
[6] Ej, G, Sg: 'perfume of sweetest odour.'
[7] Sg adds: 'and understanding.'
[8] S: 'and inward and outward senses.'

soul, these dwellers being the nymphs) and the higher part, which is the city,[9] so that that which is done in this lower part is habitually felt in the other inward part, and in consequence causes itself to be noticed and disturbs that spiritual work and presence which it has in God; therefore she tells them to dwell in her outskirts—that is, to be stilled in the outward and inward senses of her sensual part.

And desire not to touch our thresholds.

8. That is, touch not the higher part[10] even in your first motions, for the first motions of the soul are the entrances and the thresholds to an entrance therein, and, when they pass from being first motions into the reason, they are crossing the thresholds; but, when they are naught but[11] first motions, they are said only to touch the thresholds or to knock at the door, which happens when attacks upon the reason are made by sensuality with regard to some disorderly act. The Bride here not only bids these not to touch the soul; she even says that no considerations must come near which make not for the tranquillity and blessing whereof the soul has fruition.

Annotation for the Stanza Following

The soul in this estate has become so great an enemy of the lower part and its operations that it would have God communicate to that part naught that is spiritual, when He communicates such a thing to the higher part. If He communicates aught to the lower part, it must be very little or the soul will be unable to bear it by reason of the weakness of its condition, without its natural forces failing and consequently its spirit suffering and being afflicted, in which case it will be unable to rejoice in peace. For, as the Wise Man says, the body presses down the spirit, because it is corruptible.[12] And as

[9] Ej abbreviates and modifies: 'in these outskirts and those that dwell in the city.'

[10] A: 'touch not the higher door.'

[11] Jaén omits the words: 'into the reason . . . first motions.'

[12] Wisdom ix, 15.

the soul desires the sublimest[13] and most excellent communications of God, and cannot receive these in company with its sensual part, it desires God to grant them apart therefrom. For with regard to that sublime vision of the third heaven which Saint Paul saw,[14] wherein he says that he saw God, he himself says that he knows not if he received it in the body or out of[15] the body. But after whatsoever manner it may have been it was without[16] the body, for if the body had had a part therein he could not have failed to know it, nor could the vision have been as sublime as he says it was, when he says that he heard words so secret that it is not lawful for a man to utter them.[17] Wherefore the soul, knowing full well that such great favours cannot be received in so strait a vessel, desires the Spouse to grant them outside of[18] it, or, at the least, without[19] it, and, speaking to the Spouse Himself, entreats Him thus in this stanza.

STANZA XIX

Hide thyself, dearest one,   And look with thy face upon the mountains,
And desire not to speak,   But look upon her companions who travels mid strange islands.

Exposition

2. Four things begs the Bride-Soul of the Spouse in this stanza. The first, that He will be pleased to have communion with her most inwardly in the hidden part of her soul. The

---

[13] Jaén has 'the sublime'; A: 'desires the holy souls.' All the other authorities read as in the text.

[14] 2 Corinthians xii, 2.

[15] [*fuera de:* outside—i.e. the soul is in a state of ecstasy.]

[16] [*sin:* independent of—the body has no share in the Divine communications.]

[17] 2 Corinthians xii, 4.

[18] [*fuera de.*]

[19] [*sin.*]

second, that He will illumine and inform her faculties with the glory and excellence of His Divinity. The third, that He will deal with her so sublimely and profoundly that none may be able or may wish to describe it, and that the outward and sensual part of her soul may be unable to apprehend it. And the fourth, that He will fall in love with the many virtues and graces that He[1] has placed in her, in company whereof she is going and soaring aloft to God through high and noble knowledge of the Divinity, and through excesses of love most strange and singular, surpassing such as she habitually experiences.

Hide thyself, dearest one,

3. As though she were to say: Dear Spouse of mine, withdraw Thee into[2] the inmost part of my soul, communicating Thyself to it after a secret fashion, and manifesting to it Thy hidden wonders,[3] which are far removed from all mortal eyes.[4]

And look with thy face upon the mountains,

4. The face of God is His Divinity and the mountains are the faculties of the soul—memory, understanding and will. Thus it is as though she were to say: Assail my understanding with Thy Divinity, giving it Divine intelligence; and my will, giving and communicating to it Divine love; and my memory, with Divine possession of glory. Herein the soul prays Him for all that for which she may pray, since she is not now being content with knowledge and communication of God from behind, such as God granted to Moses—that is, with a knowledge of Him by His effects and works;[5] but she desires to see the face of God, which is essential communication[6] of His Divinity, without any kind of intermediary in the soul, through certain contact[7] thereof with the Divinity. This is a

[1] Ej, G, Sg: 'with her many virtues, that He,' etc.

[2] S: 'Hide Thyself in.'

[3] Ej, G, Sg: 'Thy secret places and wonders.'

[4] In the margin of Sg, P. Manuel de Santa María wrote (in the eighteenth century): 'Here are missing two folios.'

[5] Exodus xxxiii, 22–3.

[6] Ej: 'essential knowledge.' G: 'especial knowledge.'

[7] S: 'certain knowledge.' Av has here a folio missing.

thing far removed from all sense and accidents, inasmuch as it is the touch of pure substances—that is, of the soul and the Divinity. Wherefore she says next:

And desire not to speak,

5. That is to say: And desire not to speak as Thou didst aforetime, when the communications that Thou workedst in me were such that Thou didst utter them to the outward senses, since they concerned things whereof these were capable, and were not so sublime and profound that the senses could not attain to them. But now let these communications be so sublime and substantial, and so intimate, that naught may be said of them to the outward senses—that is, that these may be unable to attain to a knowledge thereof; for substance of the spirit cannot be communicated to sense, and whatsoever is communicated to sense, especially in this life, cannot be pure spirit, for sense is incapable thereof. The soul, then, desiring here this communication of God, which is so substantial and essential as not to be apprehended by sense, prays the Spouse not to speak thereof, which is as much as to say: Let the depth of this hiding-place of spiritual union be of such a kind that sense may not succeed either in speaking of it or in feeling it; may it be like the secrets which Saint Paul heard, whereof it was not lawful for man to speak.[8]

But look upon her companions

6. For God to look is for Him to love and to grant favours;[9] and the companions upon whom the soul here begs God to look are the multitude of virtues and gifts and perfections and other spiritual riches which He has set within her, like pledges, tokens and jewels of an affianced bride. And thus it is as though she were to say: But first turn Thou, Beloved, to my inmost soul, and fall in love with the company of riches which Thou hast set therein; so that, having come to love my soul through them, Thou mayest hide Thyself in her and

---

[8] 2 Corinthians xii, 4.

[9] Jaén has: 'to look and to grant favours.' [P. Silverio considers this a slip, but it seems to me quite an intelligible variant.]

remain in her;[10] for in truth, although they be Thine, yet, since Thou hast given them to her, they are hers likewise.

Who travels mid strange islands.

7. That is to say, they belong to my soul, which travels to Thee through strange knowledge of Thee and by ways and in manners that are strange, and far removed from all the senses, and from common natural knowledge. This is as though she were to say, desiring to constrain Him: Since my soul travels to Thee through strange and spiritual knowledge that is far removed from the senses, do Thou communicate Thyself to her likewise to so inward and sublime a degree that Thy communication may be far removed from them all.

Annotation for the Stanzas[11] Following

In order to reach so lofty an estate of perfection as that to which the soul here aspires, which is the Spiritual Marriage, it suffices her not[12] to be clean and purified from all the imperfections and rebellious ways and imperfect habits of the lower part, wherein, the old man being stripped off, she is subjected and surrendered to the higher part; but she needs also to have great strength and a love most sublime for so firm and so close[13] an embrace of God. For not only does the soul in this estate attain to a very high degree of purity and beauty, but she likewise acquires a terrible strength, by reason of the close and firm knot that is made by means of this union between God and the soul.

2. Wherefore, in order to come to this estate, the soul has need to have reached a point of purity, strength and sufficient love; for which reason the Holy Spirit (Who it is that intervenes and brings about this spiritual union), desiring that the soul should attain to the possession of these qualities in order to merit it, speaking with the Father and the Son in the Songs,

[10] S: 'having fallen in love with them, Thou mayest hide Thyself in her and remain in her.'

[11] So S, for there are actually two stanzas. Jaén reads: 'the stanza.'

[12] The majority of the MSS. wrongly omit 'not.'

[13] Ej, G: 'so strange,' 'so rare.'

said: 'What shall we do for our sister in the day when she shall come out to the presence of her lover[14] and to speak? For she is very little and her breasts have not grown. If she be a wall, let us build upon it bulwarks and defences of silver; and, if she be a door, let us join it together with boards of cedar.'[15] Here, by the bulwarks and defences of silver are meant the strong and heroic virtues, contained in faith, which is signified by the silver; the which heroic virtues are those of the Spiritual Marriage, which are builded upon the soul that is strong, here signified by the wall, upon the strength whereof the peaceful Spouse will repose undisturbed by any weakness. And by the boards of cedar are meant the affections and accidents of sublime love, the which sublime love is signified by the cedar-tree; and this is the love of the Spiritual Marriage. And, that the Bride may be joined together with these boards, it is needful that she be a door—in order, that is to say, that the Spouse may enter, she holding open for Him the door of the will with the true and complete consent of love, which is the consent of the betrothal that is given before the Spiritual Marriage. And, further, by the breasts of the Bride is meant that same perfect love that it befits her to have in order that she may appear before Christ the Spouse, and her estate be consummated.

3. But the text quoted above says that, desiring as she did to go out to His presence,[16] the Bride answered, saying: 'I am a wall, and my breasts are as a tower.'[17] Which is to say: My soul is strong and my love most sublime—so that He may not for that reason draw back. This the Bride-Soul, moved by the desire that she has for this perfect union and transformation, has likewise been explaining in the preceding stanzas, especially in that which we have just expounded, wherein she sets before the Spouse the virtues and rich dispositions[18] which she has received from Him, in order to con-

---

[14] [*salir a vistas*. On the mystics' allegorical use of this phrase, see *Studies of the Spanish Mystics*, Vol. I, pp. 183–4: 2nd ed., I, 147.]

[15] Canticles viii, 8–9.

[16] [*salir a estas vistas*. See n. 14, above. The translation repeats the phrase used above.]

[17] Canticles viii, 10.

[18] Bz, Ej, G, S: 'virtues, riches and dispositions.'

strain Him the more. And therefore the Spouse, desiring to make an end of this matter, replies in the two following stanzas, wherein He completes the purification of the soul, and makes it strong, and prepares it for this estate according to the sensual part as well as according to the spiritual, speaking in these stanzas against all contrarieties and rebellions, as well of the sensual part as of the part of the devil.

STANZAS XX AND XXI

**Birds of swift wing,   Lions, harts, leaping does,
Mountains, valleys, banks, waters, breezes, heats,   And terrors
    that keep watch by night.**

**By the pleasant lyres   And by the sirens' song, I conjure you,
Cease your wrath[1] and touch not the wall,   That the Bride may
    sleep more securely.**

Exposition

4. In these two stanzas the Spouse, the Son of God, sets the Bride-Soul in possession of peace and tranquillity, in the conformity of the lower part of her nature with the higher, cleansing her of all her imperfections and bringing into control[2] the natural reasoning powers and faculties of the soul, according as is said in these two stanzas, the sense whereof is as follows. First,[3] the Spouse conjures and commands the useless digressions of the fancy and the imagination from henceforth to cease; and furthermore, He brings into control the two natural faculties, which formerly to some extent afflicted the soul, the irascible and the concupiscible; and, in so far as may be in this life, He brings to the perfection of their objects the three faculties of the soul—memory, under-

---

[1] [Cf. p. 235, n. 25, above.]
[2] Ej, G: 'into perfection.'
[3] Sg recommences here.

standing and will. Besides this, He conjures and commands
the four passions of the soul—namely: joy, hope, grief and
fear—which from henceforth are mitigated and brought into
control. All these things are signified by all those names which
are set down in the first stanza, whose troublesome operations
and motions the Spouse causes to cease in the soul by means
of the great sweetness and delight and fortitude which she
receives in the spiritual communication and surrender of Himself which God grants her at this time. Wherein, since God
quickly transforms the soul into Himself, all the faculties, desires and motions of the soul lose their natural imperfection
and become Divine. And thus the stanza says:

Birds of swift wing,

5. He calls the digressions of the imagination birds of swift
wing, since they are light and subtle in their flight first in
one direction and then in another. When the will, in quietness,
is enjoying the delectable communication of the Beloved, they
are apt to cause it displeasure, and, by their subtle flights,
to quench its joy. These the Beloved says that He conjures
by the pleasant lyres, etc. That is to say that, since the sweetness and delight of the soul[4] are now so abundant and frequent that they will be unable to hinder it as they were wont
to do aforetime when it had not reached so high an estate,
they are to cease their restless flights, their impetuosities and
their excesses. This is to be understood after the same manner
in the other parts of this stanza which we have here to expound, as for example:

Lions, harts, leaping does,

6. By the lions He means the acrimonies and impetuosities
of the irascible faculty, which faculty is as bold[5] and daring
in its acts as are lions. And by the harts and the leaping does
is understood the other faculty of the soul, which is the con-

---

[4] Bz, S: 'the sweetness of delight of the soul'; Ej, G, Sg: 'the
sweetness of delight of the Beloved.'
[5] S: 'which is as it were bold.'

cupiscible[6]—that is, the power of the desire,[7] which has two effects: the one of cowardice[8] and the other of boldness. It produces the effects of cowardice[9] when it finds that things are inconvenient to itself, for at such times it withdraws and retires within itself and behaves timidly, and in these effects it is compared to the hart; for even as harts possess this concupiscible[10] faculty to a higher degree than many other animals, so, too, they are very timid and retiring. The effects of boldness[11] it produces when it finds that things are convenient to itself, for then it retires not any more, neither behaves timidly, but comes forth boldly to desire[12] them and accept them with its desires and affections. And as concerns these affections of boldness this faculty is compared to the does, which have such concupiscence toward that which they desire that not only do they run towards it, but they even leap after it, for which reason they are here called 'leaping.'[13]

7. So that, in conjuring the lions, the Spouse restrains the impetuosities[14] and excesses of wrath; and in conjuring the harts, He strengthens[15] the concupiscible faculty with respect to the cowardice and feebleness of mind which aforetime caused it to shrink; and in conjuring the leaping does, He satisfies it and subdues the desires and appetites which aforetime roamed restlessly about, leaping like does from one thing to another in order to satisfy that concupiscence which is now satisfied by the pleasant lyres, whose sweetness it enjoys, and by the sirens' song, upon the delight whereof it pastures. And it is to be noted that it is not wrath and concupiscence which the Spouse conjures here, for these faculties are never wanting in the soul, but their troublesome and disorderly acts, which

[6] S: 'is understood the concupiscible.'
[7] [apetecer.]
[8] Ej, G, Sg omit several words here.
[9] S: 'It produces that of cowardice.'
[10] S omits 'concupiscible.'
[11] S: 'The affection of boldness.'
[12] [apetecer.]
[13] S: 'and for this reason He calls them "leaping."'
[14] Ej, G, Sg: 'the appetites.'
[15] Ej, G: 'He restrains.'

are denoted by the lions, harts and leaping does; it is necessary in this estate that these should cease.

Mountains, valleys, banks,

8. By these three names are denoted the vicious and disorderly acts of the three faculties of the soul, which are memory, understanding and will, which acts are disorderly and
vicious when they are carried to a high extreme, and likewise
when they are at a low and defective extreme, or even when
they are not at either extreme, but tend thereto in one direction. And thus by the mountains, which are very high, are
signified acts which are extreme in being over-disorderly.[16]
By the valleys, which are very low, are signified the acts of
these three faculties, which are less extreme than is fitting.
And by the banks, which are neither very high nor very low,
yet, since they are not flat,[17] participate somewhat of the one
extreme and of the other, are signified the acts of the faculties
when these to some extent exceed or fail to reach that mean
and level height of what is just. These acts, though not disorderly in the extreme,[18] as they would be if they amounted
to mortal sin, are nevertheless partially so, since they are
either venial sins or imperfections,[19] however slight, in the
understanding, the memory and the will. All these acts which
exceed what is just He conjures likewise, by the pleasant lyres
and the aforementioned song, that they cease; the which lyres
and song have brought the three faculties of the soul to such
perfection of efficiency that they are completely occupied in
the just operation which pertains to them, and this to such
an extent that they avoid not only every extreme but also
every tendency thereto. There follow the remaining lines:

Waters, breezes, heats,   And terrors that keep watch by night.

9. By these four things, again, are understood[20] the affections of the four passions, which, as we said, are grief, hope,

[16] S: 'which are at an excessive extreme. And by,' etc.
[17] S: 'not very flat.'
[18] Ej, G: 'though not to a disorderly extent extreme.'
[19] S: 'partially so, fringing venial sins or imperfections.'
[20] S: 'are signified.'

joy and fear. By the waters are understood the affections of
grief which afflict the soul; for they enter the soul like water,
wherefore David said to God in speaking of them: *Salvum
me fac, Deus, quoniam intraverunt aquæ usque ad animam
meam.*[21] That is: Save me, my God, for the waters are come
in even unto my soul. By the breezes He understands the affections of hope, for like the breezes they fly to desire that which
is absent and is hoped for. Wherefore David says likewise:
*Os meum aperui, et attraxi spiritum, quia mandata tua de-
siderabam.*[22] As though he were to say: I opened the mouth
of my hope and drew in the breath of my desire, for I desired
and hoped for Thy commandments. By the heats are understood the affections of the passion of joy, which enkindle the
heart like fire; wherefore the same David says: *Concaluit cor
meum intra me, et in meditatione mea exardescet ignis.*[23]
Which signifies: My heart grew hot within me and in my
meditation fire shall be enkindled; which is as much as to
say: In my meditation shall joy be enkindled. By the terrors
that keep watch by night are understood the affections of the
other passion, which is fear; which affections, in spiritual persons that have not yet reached this estate of the Spiritual Marriage whereof we are speaking, are wont to be very great.
At times they come from God, when He desires to grant such
persons certain favours, as we have said above, and is wont
to bring fear and affright to their spirits, and likewise[24] a
shrinking to their flesh and senses, since they have not fortified and perfected their nature and habituated it to these favours. At times, again, they come from the devil, who, when
God grants the soul recollection and sweetness in Himself,
becomes very envious and greatly afflicted because of that
blessing and peace which have come to the soul, and contrives
to set horror and fear in its spirit, to hinder it from obtaining
that blessing; sometimes he even threatens it within its very
spirit. And when he sees that he cannot reach the inmost part

[21] Psalm lxviii, 1. [A.V., lxix, 1.]
[22] Psalm cxviii, 131. [A.V., cxix, 131.]
[23] Psalm xxxviii, 4. [A.V., xxxix, 3.]
[24] S omits 'likewise.'

of the soul, since it is deeply recollected and closely united with God, he then attacks it from without, in its sensual part, and sets[25] there distraction and inconstancy and sensible afflictions and pains and horror,[26] if haply by this means he may harry the Bride in her marriage-chamber. These things the Spouse calls[27] terrors of the night,[28] because they all come from evil spirits, and because by their means the devil tries to diffuse darkness in the soul, that he may obscure the Divine light wherein it is rejoicing. He says of these fears that they keep watch, because their effect is to cause the soul to watch and to awaken it from its sweet[29] inward sleep, and likewise because the evil spirits that cause them are ever watching to produce them. These fears, coming from God, or from the devil, as I have said, are infused passively into the spirits of those[30] who are already spiritual; and I treat not here of other fears which are temporal or natural, because it is not for spiritual people to have such fears, whereas to have the spiritual fears aforementioned is proper to spiritual people.[31]

10. So the Beloved likewise conjures all these four manners of affection of the four passions of the soul, making them to cease and be at rest, since He now gives to the Bride in this estate riches and strength and satisfaction in the pleasant lyres of His sweetness and the sirens' song of His delight, so that not only can these things not reign within her but they cannot even cause her the least degree of dispeace. For the grandeur and stability of the soul in this estate are so complete that, if formerly there reached the soul the waters of any grief soever, even those of its own sins or of the sins

[25] S: 'he contrives to [*procura*] set.' Cf. also p. 184, n. 14, above.
[26] Sg: 'inconstancy and appetites and sensible horror.'
[27] S: 'And the Spouse calls them.'
[28] Ej, G, Sg: 'calls terrors that keep watch.'
[29] Ej, G, Sg: 'its sublime.'
[30] S modifies thus: '. . . watching to produce them. These fears, which come passively from God or from the devil, as I have said, are infused into the souls—I mean into the spirits—of those . . .', etc.
[31] S modifies thus: 'because to have them belongs not to spiritual people, as it does to have the other fears aforementioned.'

of some other person, which is what spiritual persons habitually feel the most, now,[32] although it still realizes their importance, they cause it neither pain nor sorrow;[33] and it no
longer feels compassion,[34] though it performs the works of
compassion and has the perfection thereof; for in this estate
the soul has no longer that part of its virtues which was weak;
but there remains to it that which was strong, constant and
perfect in them; for in this transformation of love the soul[35]
acts as do the angels, who apprehend perfectly things that
are grievous without feeling grief, and practise works of mercy
without feeling compassion;[36] although occasionally and at
certain seasons God bestows a favour upon the soul, making
it to feel things and suffer that it may grow in merit, and
become more fervent in love, even as He did with the Virgin
Mother, and with Saint Paul and others;[37] but the estate[38]
does not imply this condition necessarily.

11. Neither is the soul afflicted by the desires of hope, for,
being now satisfied with this union of God, in so far as is
possible in this life, it has naught to hope for with respect
to the world, and naught to desire with respect to that which
is spiritual, since it sees and feels itself to be full of the riches
of God, and thus, in life and in death, is conformed and reconciled[39] to God's will, saying, according to the sensitive and
the spiritual part: *Fiat voluntas tua,* without being impelled
by any other desire and appetite; and thus the desire to see
God which it experiences is without affliction. Likewise the
affections of joy, which were wont to be felt by the soul, to
a greater or a lesser degree, seem to be in no way diminished,

[32] [The MSS. here read *y* ('and') for the *ya* ('now') of the first
redaction. P. Silverio follows them, but, as the sense of the passage
is destroyed by this reading, I prefer the other.]

[33] S: 'neither grief nor anguish of sorrow.'

[34] Sg: 'composition.'

[35] Sg: 'the Beloved.'

[36] Sg: 'composition.'

[37] Sg: 'with the Magdalen and with Saint Paul and others.'

[38] Sg: 'but the affection.'

[39] S modifies: '. . . riches of God, although it may grow in
charity, and thus in death and life it is conformed and reconciled.'
Sg reads: *ajuntada* ['united'] for *ajustada* ['reconciled'].

nor does their abundance cause it surprise. For its rejoicing is habitually so great[40] that, like the sea, it[41] is not diminished by the rivers that flow from it, neither is it increased by those that enter it; for it is within this soul that there is made that spring, the water whereof, as Christ says, through Saint John, springs up to eternal life.[42]

12. And since I have said that the soul in this case receives nothing new in this estate of transformation, wherein it seems to lose accidental joys, which are granted even to the glorified, it must be known that, although such a soul is not without those accidental sweetnesses and joys[43]—nay, rather, those which it habitually has are innumerable—it has no increase[44] as to the substantial communication of the spirit, for the reason that all that is capable of coming to it anew it has already had; and thus that which it has in itself is greater than that which comes to it anew. Therefore, whenever things of joy and gladness[45] present themselves to such a soul—be they exterior, or spiritual and interior—the soul at once turns to enjoy the riches that it already has in itself, and has far greater joy and delight in them than[46] in those which come to it anew, because in some manner it has gained herein possession of God; Who, though He delights in all things, delights in them less than in Himself, because in Himself He has good which is eminent above them all. And thus all new joys and pleasures which this soul receives serve it rather as reminders[47] to rejoice in what it already has and feels within itself

[40] S: 'for, so great is the abundance which it habitually enjoys.'

[41] S: 'that it is like the sea, which.'

[42] St. John iv, 14.

[43] Ej, G, Sg: 'although such a soul be not without these accidental joys.'

[44] S adds: 'of joy.' A reads: 'it rises for naught.'

[45] Ej reads: 'of joy and riches—I mean delight,' and omits several clauses following. G reads: 'whenever things of joy and riches —I mean delight therein—present themselves to such a soul, those which come to it anew . . .' [Neither reading preserves the sense, or the thought, of the text above.]

[46] [The original has 'and,' but the sense is clearly as in the text above.]

[47] Sg reads *serían* for *sirven*: 'would rather be to it reminders.'

than in these new acquisitions,[48] for, as I say, it is greater than they.

13. And it is natural that, when a thing causes the soul joy and contentment, if the soul has something else that it prizes more highly and that gives it more pleasure, it should remember this immediately and set its pleasure and joy upon it.[49] And thus the accidental character of these new spiritual acquisitions, and the new experiences that they bring to the soul, are so little by comparison with that substantial communication which it already has within itself that we may truly describe it as being nothing, for the soul that has reached this fullness[50] of transformation, wherein it is full-grown, continues not to grow[51] by reason of new spiritual acquisitions, as do others who have not attained to this estate. But it is a wondrous thing to see that while the soul receives no new delights it always seems to be doing so, and also to have been in possession of them. The reason is that it is ever tasting them anew, because the good which they bring is ever new; and thus it seems continually to be receiving new acquisitions without having any need to receive them.

14. But if we could wish to speak of the illumination of glory which God[52] sometimes bestows upon the soul in this habitual embrace that He has given to it, which is, as it were, a spiritual turning[53] to it, wherein He makes it at the same time to behold and to enjoy this abyss of delights and riches which He has set within it, there is naught that could be said which would express any part of it. For, as the sun when it shines fully upon[54] the sea illumines even its profoundest

[48] S: 'than in the same new acquisitions.'

[49] Ej modifies: '. . . that when the soul has in itself something of joy and contentment that it greatly prizes, if another and a lesser thing comes to it, it should remember this immediately and set its pleasure upon it.'

[50] Ej, Sg: 'this point.'

[51] S adds: 'with respect to the estate.'

[52] The word 'God' occurs only in S, though in all the versions it is clearly implied by the context.

[53] [Lit., 'conversion.'] S reads: 'conversation.'

[54] [Lit., 'fully assails.']

depths[55] and caverns, and reveals the pearls and richest veins of gold and other precious minerals, etc., so this Divine Sun, the Spouse, turns to the Bride and, as it were, brings to light the riches of the soul, so that even the angels marvel and repeat those words of the Songs which say: 'Who is she that cometh forth as the morning rising, fair as the moon, choice as the sun, terrible in her array[56] as the ranks of armies?'[57] In this illumination, great as is its excellence, the soul has no increase, but there is simply revealed that which she already has, to the end that she may rejoice therein.

15. Finally, the terrors that keep watch by night come not nigh her, since she is so pure and so strong,[58] and her repose is so firmly fixed upon God that the evil spirits can neither enfold her in[59] their darkness nor affright her with their terrors, nor awaken her with their violence; wherefore naught can approach her or trouble her, since she has left all things else and entered into her God, where she has fruition of all peace, tastes all sweetness, and delights in all delight, in so far as the condition and estate of this life allow. For of the soul in such a case is understood that which the Wise Man says, namely: 'The peaceful and quiet[60] soul is as a continual feast.'[61] For, even as at a feast there is the savour of all kinds of meat and the sweetness of all kinds of music, even so in this feast which the soul now enjoys in the bosom of the Spouse, she rejoices in all delight and tastes all sweetness. And what we have said, and indeed all that words can express, is so small a part of what comes to pass here that no more than the smallest part could ever be described of the experience of the soul that reaches this happy estate. For, if the soul is enabled to reach the peace of God, which, as the Church says,[62] surpasses all that is of sense,[63] then all

[55] [senos, lit., 'cavities,' 'holes,' translated above as 'recesses.' Cf. p. 210, n. 11.]
[56] [Lit., 'terrible and ordered.']
[57] Canticles vi, 9. [A.V., vi, 10.]
[58] A: 'so pure [clara] and so perfect.'
[59] [Lit., 'darken her with.']
[60] Ej, G, Sg read: 'secure' for 'quiet.'
[61] Proverbs xv, 15.
[62] S: 'as St. Paul says.'
[63] [I.e., 'passeth all understanding.'] Philippians iv, 7.

that is of sense will remain bereft and mute in speaking thereof. There follows the first line of the second stanza.

By the pleasant lyres   And by the sirens' song, I conjure you,

16. We have already explained that by the pleasant lyres the Spouse here signifies the sweetness diffused by the soul in this estate, whereby He causes all its troubles whereof we have spoken to cease. For, even as the music of the lyres fills the soul[64] with sweetness and refreshment, and absorbs and enraptures it so as to transport it far from distresses and afflictions, even so this sweetness keeps the soul so completely within itself that no grievous thing reaches it.[65] And thus it is as though He were to say: By the sweetness that I set in the soul, let all things that are not sweet to the soul cease. It has likewise been said that the sirens' song signifies the habitual delight which the soul possesses. And this delight He calls the sirens' song because, even as (so they say) the sirens' song is so delectable and delicious as to enrapture and enamour one who hears it and thus to make him as forgetful as one that is borne away from all things, even so the delight of this union absorbs[66] the soul in itself and refreshes it, in such a way as to give it a charm against all the troubles and disturbances[67] caused by the things aforementioned; which are understood in this line:

Cease your wrath[68]

17. Indicating by wrath the said disturbances and troubles of the disorderly affections and operations whereof we have spoken. And because, even as wrath is a certain impetuosity that disturbs peace, going beyond the limits thereof, even so

---

[64] A number of authorities read: 'the spirit.'

[65] Bg: 'so as to detach it from itself, without savour of distresses or troubles; thus this distress [*sic*] keeps the soul within itself so completely that no grievous thing wounds it.'

[66] B, Bg: 'darkens.'

[67] Sg: 'against all other things and troubles and tribulations.'

[68] Ej, G, Sg: 'Cease your wrath.' [Cf. p. 188, n. 31, above. The 'and' is found here, though not in the poem.]

all the affections, etc.,[69] aforementioned transgress the limits
of the peace and tranquillity of the soul, disquieting it when
they touch it. Wherefore He says:

And touch not the wall,

18. By the wall is meant the fence of peace and the rampart
of virtues and perfections wherewith the same soul is now
fenced around and guarded; for she is the garden whereof
mention has been made above, where her Beloved pastures on
the flowers, and which is fenced around and guarded for Him
alone. Wherefore He speaks of her in the Songs as of a garden enclosed, saying: 'My sister is a garden enclosed.'[70] And
thus He says that they are not to touch even the fence and the
wall of this His garden.

That the Bride may sleep more securely.

19. That is to say, that she may delight[71] the more according to her pleasure in the quiet and sweetness whereof she has
fruition in the Beloved. Whence it must be known that there
is now no door closed to the soul, but that it is in her power
to enjoy this sweet sleep of love every time and whensoever she
desires, according as the Spouse declares in the Songs, saying:
'I adjure you, daughters of Jerusalem, by the roes and the
harts of the fields, that ye stir not up nor awake the beloved
till she please.'[72]

Annotation for the Stanza Following

So great was the desire of the Spouse to complete the libera-
tion and ransoming of this His Bride from the hands of sensuality and the devil that, having done so, as He has done

[69] G: 'all the disorderly operations and affections.'

[70] Canticles iv, 12. Av and Bz omit the quotation.

[71] Ej, G: 'The Bride having already endeavoured this, namely, to
delight . . .'

[72] Canticles iii, 5.

here, He rejoices[73] as the good Shepherd rejoices, bearing upon His shoulders[74] the sheep which He had lost and sought by many devious paths, and as the woman, when she has in her hands the piece of silver to find which she had lighted the candle, and turned all the house about, delights, calls her friends and neighbours[75] and gives thanks with them, saying: 'Rejoice with me, etc.'[76] Even so it is a wonderful thing to see this loving Shepherd and Spouse of the soul and the pleasure and the joy which He has when He sees the soul, now won and perfected in this way, lying upon His shoulders and held by His own hands in this longed-for embrace and union. And not only does He Himself rejoice, but He likewise makes the angels and holy souls participators of His gladness,[77] saying, as in the Songs: 'Go forth, ye daughters of Sion, and see King Solomon with the crown wherewith his mother crowned him in the day of his betrothal, and in the day of the joy of his heart.'[78] In these words aforesaid He calls the soul His crown, His Bride,[79] and the joy of His heart, carrying her at last in His arms, and dealing with her as the Spouse of her bride-chamber. All this He declares in the following stanza.

[73] S: 'that having done to this point as has been seen, now also He rejoices.'

[74] St. Luke xv, 5.

[75] S has these two substantives in their feminine form; the other authorities use the masculine or common gender.

[76] St. Luke xv, 9.

[77] S: 'of His glory.'

[78] Canticles iii, 11.

[79] Ej, G: 'In these words spoken to her heart, He calls the soul Bride.'

STANZA XXII

**The Bride has entered   Into the pleasant garden of her desire,[1]
And at her pleasure rests,   Her neck reclining[2] on the gentle
arms of the Beloved.[3]**

Exposition

2. The Bride having now done all in her power that the
foxes may be driven away and the north wind may depart,
and the nymphs be stilled, since these have been hindrances
and inconveniences impeding the perfect delight of the estate
of the Spiritual Marriage; and having likewise invoked and
obtained the breeze of the Holy Spirit (as has been described
in the preceding stanzas), which is the proper disposition and
means for the perfection of this estate: it now remains to
treat, in this stanza, of this estate, wherein the Spouse now
speaks to the soul, calling her His Bride, and says two things.
He says, first, that the soul, having issued forth victoriously,
has now attained to this delectable estate of the Spiritual Marriage which both He and she had so greatly desired. The
second thing that He does is to enumerate the properties of
the said estate, of which properties the soul now has fruition
in Him, and these are for her to rest at her pleasure and for
her neck to recline upon the gentle arms of the Beloved, even
as we shall now go on to show in our exposition.

The Bride has entered

3. In order that we may expound the arrangement of these
stanzas the more exactly, and describe the soul's habitual progress ere it reach this estate of the Spiritual Marriage, which is
the highest estate that, by Divine favour, we have now to de-

---

[1] [*Lit.*, 'pleasant desired garden.']
[2] Ej, G: 'declining' [i.e. 'leaning'].
[3] A: 'of her Beloved.'

scribe, it is to be noted that, ere the soul reaches this estate, it exercises itself first of all in the trials and bitternesses of mortification and in meditation upon spiritual things, as the soul said at the beginning from the first stanza down to that which says: 'Scattering a thousand graces.' And afterwards it enters upon the contemplative way,[4] wherein it passes through the ways and straits of love which have been described in the stanzas following,[5] as far as that which says 'Withdraw them, Beloved,' wherein was made the Spiritual Betrothal. And beyond this point it goes along the unitive way, wherein it receives many and very great communications and visits and gifts and jewels from the Spouse, even as does an affianced bride, and continually increases in knowledge and perfection in His love,[6] as it has described from the said stanza wherein this betrothal was made and which says 'Withdraw them, Beloved,' even to this present one which begins: 'The Bride has entered. . . .' It now remains for the said Spiritual Marriage to be made between the soul aforementioned and the Son of God. This is without comparison far greater than the Spiritual Betrothal[7] because it is a total transformation[8] in the Beloved, wherein on either side there is made surrender by total possession of the one to the other with a certain consummation[9] of union of love, wherein the soul is made Divine and becomes God by participation, in so far as may be in this life. And thus I think that this estate is never attained without the soul being confirmed in grace therein; for the faithfulness of both is confirmed, that of God being confirmed in the soul; wherefore this is the highest estate which in this life is attainable. For, even as in the consummation[10] of marriage according to the flesh the two become one flesh, as says the Divine Scrip-

---

[4] B, Bg, Ej, G have: *vida* ['life'] for *vía* ['way'].

[5] S: 'in the progress of the stanzas.'

[6] Bz, Ej, Sg: 'and is continually entering into His love and increasing in perfection thereof.'

[7] B, Bg omit the words: 'between the soul . . . Spiritual Betrothal.'

[8] A: 'a total spiritual transformation.'

[9] B: 'with a certain communication.'

[10] B, Bg: 'in the communication.'

ture,[11] even so, when this Spiritual Marriage between God
and the soul is consummated, there are two natures in one
spirit and love, even as says Saint Paul, making this same comparison and saying: 'He that is joined unto the Lord is made
one spirit with Him';[12] even as when the light of the star or
of the candle is joined and united with that of the sun, so
that that which shines is not the star or the candle but the
sun, which has absorbed the other lights in itself. And of this
estate the Spouse treats in the present line, saying: 'The Bride
has entered'—that is to say, has gone out from all that is temporal and from all that is natural,[13] and from all spiritual
manners and modes and affections, and, having left behind
and forgotten all temptations, disturbances,[14] griefs, anxiety[15] and cares, is transformed in this sublime embrace. Of
this the following line goes on to treat, namely:

Into the pleasant garden of her desire,

4. This is as though she were to say: She has been transformed in God, Who it is that is here called a pleasant garden, by reason of the delectable and sweet repose which the
soul finds in Him. The soul does not come to this garden of
complete transformation (which is the joy and delight and
glory of the Spiritual Marriage) without first passing through
the Spiritual Betrothal[16] and through the mutual and loyal
love of those that are betrothed. For, after the soul has been
for some time the Bride of the Son of God, in love which is
sweet and perfect, God calls her and sets her in this His
flowering garden for the consummation of this most happy
estate of marriage with Him, wherein is effected such union of
the two natures and such communication[17] of the Divine
nature to the human, that, while neither of them changes its
being, each of them appears to be God. Although in this life

[11] Genesis ii, 24.
[12] 1 Corinthians vi, 17.
[13] Ej, G, Sg omit: 'and from all that is natural.'
[14] Ej, G, Sg omit: 'disturbances.'
[15] [*sic.* Cf. p. 175, n. 12.]
[16] Ej, G, Sg: 'through the Betrothal.'
[17] Ej, G, Sg: 'and such consummation.'

this thing cannot come to pass perfectly, yet it surpasses everything that can be described or conceived.

5. This is very clearly expressed by the Spouse Himself in the Songs, where He invites the soul, now made His Bride, to this estate, saying: *Veni in hortum meum, soror mea sponsa, messui myrrham meam cum aromatibus meis.*[18] Which signifies: Come and enter into My garden, My sister, My spouse, for I have now gathered My myrrh with My fragrant spices.[19] He calls her sister and spouse because this she was in the love and surrender of herself which she had made to Him before He called her[20] to this estate of the Spiritual Marriage, where He says that He has now gathered[21] His fragrant myrrh and aromatic spices, which are the fruits of the flowers, now ripe and made ready for the soul, the which fruits are the delights and grandeurs[22] that He Himself communicates to her in this estate—that is, He communicates them to her in Himself; for the which cause He is to her the pleasant garden of her desire. For the whole desire and aim of the soul, and that of God in all the works[23] of the soul, is the consummation[24] and perfection of this estate, wherefore the soul never rests until she reaches Him; for in this estate she finds much greater abundance and fullness of God and a peace[25] more sure and stable, and a sweetness more perfect[26] without compare than in the Spiritual Betrothal, since she is now placed in the arms of such a Spouse, Whose close spiritual embrace she habitually feels—a true embrace, by means whereof the soul lives the life of God. For in this soul is fulfilled that which Saint Paul says: 'I live, yet not I, for Christ liveth in me.'[27]

---

18 Canticles v, 1.

19 Ej omits the vernacular of this quotation.

20 Ej, G: 'before He brought her near.'

21 Ej: 'watered' [*regada* for *segada*].

22 G: 'delights and graces'; Sg: 'delights and graces and grandeurs.'

23 Ej, G: 'in all the things and works.'

24 B, Bz, G: 'is the communication.'

25 [P. Silverio has the incorrect reading *haz* ('face') for *paz* ('peace').]

26 A: 'more secure.'

27 Galatians ii, 20. S has: '*I* live, but yet . . .' [with the emphatic form of the pronoun].

Wherefore, since the soul now lives a life so happy and glorious as this life of God, let each one consider, if he can, how
delectable a life will be that which the soul lives, wherein
neither can God perceive aught that is displeasing to Him, nor
does the soul perceive it, but the soul enjoys and perceives
the delight of the glory of God in its very substance, which is
now transformed in Him. Wherefore the next line continues:

And at her pleasure rests,   Her neck reclining[28] . . .

6. Here the neck signifies the strength of the soul, by means
whereof, as we have said, is wrought this embrace and union
between the soul and the Spouse; for the soul could not bear
so close an embrace if it were not already very strong. And
because in this strength the soul laboured, and practised the
virtues, and conquered the vices, therefore it is just that, after
it has conquered and laboured, it should take its repose with
its neck reclining

. . . on the gentle arms of the Beloved.

7. For the neck to recline on the arms of God is for it to
have its strength now united—or rather, its weakness—in the
strength of God;[29] for the arms of God signify the strength of
God;[30] wherein our weakness, reclining upon Him and transformed in Him; has now the strength of God Himself. Wherefore it is very convenient to denote this estate of the Spiritual
Marriage by this reclining of the neck on the gentle arms of
the Beloved, since God is now both the strength and the
gentleness of the soul, in Whom it is defended and protected
from all evils and in Whom it savours all good things.[31]
Hence the Bride in the Songs, being desirous of this estate,
said to the Spouse: 'Who would give Thee to me, my brother,
that Thou mightest suck the breasts of my mother, so that I
might find Thee alone without and might kiss Thee,[32] and

[28] Ej, G omit the commentary on these lines.
[29] Bg: 'its weakness—upon the arms of God and upon His
strength.'
[30] S omits this clause.
[31] Ej, G, Sg: 'and favoured in all good things.'
[32] Bg: 'and might care for thee.'

none would then despise me?'[33] By calling Him her brother, she denotes the equality which there is in the betrothal of love between the two before they attain to this estate. By saying 'that Thou mightest suck the breasts of my mother,' she means, that Thou mightest quench and dry up in me the desires and passions, which are the breasts and the milk of Mother Eve[34] in our flesh, and are a hindrance to this estate. And thus, she continues, when this is done, 'I might find Thee alone without'—that is: I might go out from all things, even from myself, in solitude and detachment of spirit, when once the aforementioned desires are dried up; and there I, being alone, 'might kiss Thee,' Who art alone—that is to say: My nature, now that it is alone and detached from all impurity, temporal, natural and spiritual, might be united with Thee alone,[35] with Thy nature alone, and without any other intermediaries,[36] which alone comes to pass in the Spiritual Marriage,[37] which is the kiss of God by the soul, where none despises it or assaults it; for in this estate neither devil nor flesh nor world nor desires molest it. For herein is fulfilled that which is said in the Songs: 'Winter is now past and the rain has gone and the flowers have appeared in our land.'[38]

Annotation of the Stanza Following

In this high estate of the Spiritual Marriage the Spouse reveals His wondrous secrets to the soul, as to His faithful consort, with great readiness and frequency, for true and perfect love[39] can keep nothing hidden from the person loved. He communicates principally to it sweet mysteries[40] concerning His Incarnation and the modes and ways of human redemp-

---

[33] Canticles viii, 1.
[34] S: 'of our mother Eve.'
[35] S adds: '—that is.'
[36] S adds: 'save love.'
[37] Sg omits: 'and without any . . . Marriage.'
[38] Canticles ii, 11–12.
[39] Ej, G, Sg: 'because in truth true love.'
[40] Ej: 'great mysteries and sweet.'

tion, which is one of the highest works of God, and is thus most delectable to the soul. For this reason, although He communicates to it many other mysteries, the Spouse makes mention in the stanza following of His Incarnation only, as being the most important of all; and thus He speaks to her and says:

STANZA XXIII

Beneath the apple-tree,[1]   There wert thou betrothed to me; There did I give thee my hand[2]   And thou wert redeemed where thy mother had been corrupted.[3]

Exposition

2. The Spouse sets forth to the soul in this stanza the wondrous manner and plan of His redemption of her and of His betrothal of her to Himself, using the same terms as to describe the corruption and ruin of the human race, and saying that, even as by means of the forbidden tree of Paradise she was ruined and corrupted in her human nature through Adam, even so upon the Tree of the Cross she was redeemed and restored, by His giving her the hand of His favour and mercy,[4] through His death and passion, and raising the barriers[5] that came from[6] original sin between the soul and God. And thus she says:

Beneath the apple-tree,

3. That is, beneath the favour of the Tree of the Cross, which is here understood by the apple-tree, whereon the Son of God redeemed human nature, and, in consequence, be-

[1] Bg has 'an' for 'the.'
[2] A: 'There did I stretch forth my hand.'
[3] Bg has 'was' for 'had been.'
[4] Ej, G: 'favour and friendship.'
[5] [*Lit.*, 'the truces.'] Av: 'the surrenders.' A note by the copyist indicates that he was doubtful as to the true form of the word. A: 'attaining the truces.'
[6] Ej, G, Sg have 'through' for 'from.'

trothed it to Himself,[7] and consequently betrothed to Himself every soul, giving to each soul in token thereof grace and pledges in the Cross. And thus He says:

> **There wert thou betrothed to me;**
> **There did I give thee my hand**

4. This is to say, the hand of My favour and help, raising thee up from thy low estate[8] to be My companion and My betrothed.

And thou wert redeemed where thy mother had been corrupted.

5. For thy mother, human nature, was corrupted in thy first parents beneath the tree, and there likewise wert thou redeemed—namely, beneath the Tree of the Cross. So that, if thy mother gave thee death beneath the tree, I gave thee life beneath the Tree of the Cross. After this manner God continues to reveal to the soul the ordinances and dispositions of His wisdom; since He is able so wisely and beauteously to bring good from evil, and to ordain to our greater good that which was the cause of evil. That which is literally contained[9] in this stanza is said by the same Spouse to the Bride in the Songs, where He says: *Sub arbore malo suscitavi te: ibi corrupta est mater tua, ibi violata est genitrix tua.*[10] Which signifies: Under the apple-tree I raised thee up; there thy mother was corrupted,[11] and there was she violated that bore thee.

6. This betrothal that was made upon the Cross is not that whereof we are now speaking; for that is a betrothal which is made once for all[12] when God gives to the soul the first grace, which comes to every soul in baptism. But this betrothal is after the way of perfection, which takes place only gradually and by stages; and, although they are both one, the difference is that the one[13] is wrought at the soul's pace, and so is grad-

[7] S: '. . . the Son of God won victory, and, in consequence, betrothed human nature to Himself.'

[8] S: 'from [a] miserable and low estate.'

[9] Ej, G, Sg: 'literally understood.'

[10] Canticles viii, 5.

[11] Jaén, A, B, Bg: *extraída* [see p. 180, n. 5, above]. Av: 'corrupt.' S, Sg: 'corrupted.' Bz: 'destroyed.' Ej, G omit the translation of this Latin text.

[12] S: 'for that is made once for all.'

[13] S: 'is that the latter.'

ual, while the other is according to God's pace, and thus is wrought once and for all. For this betrothal whereof we are treating is that which God describes through Ezechiel, speaking with the soul after this manner: 'Thou wast cast out upon the earth, in despite of thy soul, on the day that thou wast born. And, passing by thee, I saw thee trodden under foot in thy blood, and I said unto thee when thou wast in thy blood: "Live";[14] and I caused thee to multiply like the grass of the field; thou didst multiply and grow great, and didst enter in and come to the greatness of woman; and thy breasts grew and thy hair was multiplied, and thou wast naked and full of confusion. And I passed by thee and looked upon thee, and I saw that thy time was the time of lovers, and I spread my mantle over thee and covered thy ignominy. And I made an oath to thee and entered into a covenant with thee and made thee mine. And I washed thee with water, and I washed away the blood from thee, and I anointed thee with oil, and clothed thee with colours and shod thee with hyacinth, and girded thee with fine linen and clothed thee with fine garments. And I decked thee with ornaments, put bracelets on thy hands and a chain on thy neck. And upon thy mouth I put a jewel,[15] and in thy ears earrings and a crown of beauty upon thy head. And thou wert decked with gold and silver, and clothed in fine linen and broidered silks and many colours; bread very choice and honey and oil didst thou eat, and thou becamest of mighty[16] beauty, and camest even to reign and be a queen, and thy name went forth among the peoples because of thy beauty.'[17] Thus far go the words of Ezechiel. And this is the condition of the soul of whom we are here speaking.

Annotation for the Stanza Following

But after this delectable surrender of the Bride and the Beloved, that which then follows immediately is the bed of them

[14] Ej, G, Sg: 'And, passing that way, I saw thee trodden under foot in thy blood; I lived.' Bz omits: 'when thou wast in thy blood.'

[15] *zarcillo*. The word [also means earrings, and] is used by A, B, Bg five words later [where Jaén has *cerquillos*, 'earrings'].

[16] Sg: 'fit,' 'due.'

[17] Ezechiel xvi, 5–14.

both, wherein the Bride tastes the aforementioned delights of the Spouse very much more abidingly; and thus the following[18] stanza treats of His bed and hers, which is divine, pure and chaste, wherein the soul is divine, pure and chaste. For the bed is naught else than her very Spouse, the Word, Son of God, as will presently be said, wherein, by means of the said union of love, she takes her rest. This bed she calls flower-like,[19] because not only is her Spouse flower-like,[20] but, as He Himself says of Himself in the Songs, He is the very flower of the field and the lily of the valleys.[21] And thus the soul rests, not only in the flowery bed, but in the flower itself, which is the Son of God, the which flower has in itself divine odour and fragrance and grace and beauty, as He says also through David, in these words: 'The beauty of the field is with me';[22] wherefore the soul sings the properties and graces of her bed, and says:

STANZA XXIV

**Our flowery bed,   Encompassed[1] with dens of lions,
Hung with purple[2] and builded in peace,   Crowned with a
thousand shields of gold.**

Exposition

2. In two earlier[3] stanzas the Bride-Soul has sung of the graces and wonders of her Beloved, the Son of God. And in

---

[18] Ej, G, Sg: 'the present.' Stanza XXIV is in either case referred to.

[19] *florido* [translated 'flowery' in the stanza below].

[20] See preceding note.

[21] Canticles ii, 1.

[22] Psalm xlix, 11. [A.V., l, 11.]

[1] A: 'exalted.'

[2] Bg, G: 'dyed in purple.'

[3] The text [which P. Silverio follows] has: 'In the last two stanzas,' referring to Stanzas XIII and XIV in the Sanlúcar Codex (cf. p. 117, above), which numbers this stanza XV. [In the present redaction the two stanzas referred to are numbered XIV and XV.]

this stanza she not only continues the recital thereof, but likewise sings of the happy and high estate wherein she sees herself set, and of its security. And thirdly she sings of the riches
of the gifts and virtues wherewith she sees herself endowed[4]
and adorned, in the nuptial chamber of her Spouse. For she
says that she is already in union with God, and possesses the
virtues in strength. Fourthly, that she now has perfection of
love.[5] Fifthly, that she has perfect spiritual peace,[6] and that
she is wholly enriched and beautified with gifts and virtues,
such as it is possible to possess and enjoy in this life, as will be
explained progressively in the lines of the stanza. The first
theme, then, of which she sings is the delight[7] that she enjoys
in the union of the Beloved, saying:

Our flowery bed,

3. We have already said that this bed of the soul is the
Spouse,[8] the Son of God, Who is flower-like[9] to the soul; for
now that she is united with Him, and reposes in Him, and has
become His Bride, there are communicated to her the breast
and the love of the Beloved, which is for the wisdom and
secrets and graces and virtues and gifts of God to be communicated to her, wherewith she becomes so greatly beautified,
so rich and so full of delights, that she thinks herself to be
upon a bed made of a variety of sweet and divine flowers,
which delight her as she touches them and refresh her with
their fragrance; for the which cause she very properly[10] calls
this bond of love with God a flowery bed; for so the Bride
calls it, where she speaks to the Beloved in the Songs, saying:
Lectulus noster floridus,[11] that is: Our flowery bed. And she
calls it 'ours,' because the same virtues and the same love
(namely, those of the Beloved) are common to both, and the

[4] Ej, G, Sg: 'ornamented.'
[5] Ej, G, Sg: 'she now has perfected love.'
[6] Av: 'that she has spiritual peace, perfected and beautified . . .'
[7] A, B, Bg: 'is the desire.'
[8] S: 'is the breast and love of the Spouse.'
[9] [*florido*.]
[10] Ej, G, Sg omit: 'very properly.'
[11] Canticles i, 15 [A.V., i, 16]. Ej, G, Sg omit the following
words: 'that is: Our flowery bed.'

same delight is common to both, even as the Holy Spirit says in the Proverbs, in these words: 'My delights are with the sons of men.'[12] She calls it flowery also, because in this estate the virtues are now perfect and heroic in the soul, the which thing could not be until the bed had become flowery in perfect union[13] with God. And so she next sings of the second theme, in the line following, saying:

Encompassed with dens of lions,

4. Meaning by dens of lions the virtues which the soul possesses in this estate of union with God. The reason is that the dens of lions are most secure and protected[14] from all other beasts, since these fear the strength and boldness of the lion that is within, and hence not only dare not to enter, but dare not even to tarry near.[15] And thus each of the virtues, when the soul at last possesses them in perfection, is to her like a lion's den, wherein Christ the Spouse dwells and is present, united with the soul in that virtue and in each of the other virtues, like a strong lion. And the soul herself, united with Him in these same virtues, is also like a strong lion, for there she is given[16] the properties[17] of God. And thus in this case the soul is so well protected and so strong[18] in each of the virtues and in all of them together, reposing on this flowery bed of union with her God, that not only do the evil spirits not presume to attack her, but they dare not even appear before her, by reason of the great fear which they have of her, when they see her so greatly exalted, encouraged and emboldened with the perfect virtues in the bed of the Beloved. For, since she is united in transformation of union,[19] they fear her as much as they fear God Himself and dare not even look upon her: greatly does the devil fear the soul that has perfection.

[12] Proverbs viii, 31.
[13] Ej, G, Sg: 'in perfection and union.'
[14] Ej, G, Sg omit: 'and protected.'
[15] A: 'even to pass near.'
[16] Ej, G, Sg: 'she resists her opponents and is given.'
[17] A: 'the same virtues and properties.'
[18] Bg: 'so pure and strong.'
[19] Av, Bz, Ej, G, Sg, S: 'transformation of love.'

5. She says likewise that the bed is encompassed with these dens—namely, the virtues[20]—because in this estate the virtues are linked among themselves, united and strengthened mutually and ordered in the soul's complete perfection, each being supported by others,[21] in such a way that there is no weak or exposed part of it where the devil can enter, neither can aught in the world, high or low, cause her unrest, disturb her or even move her; for being now free from all disturbance of the natural passions, and withdrawn and detached from the torture and diversity[22] of temporal cares, as she is here, the soul has fruition, in security and tranquillity, of the participation of God. This very thing is that which was desired by the Bride in the Songs, where she says: 'Would that Thou mightest be given to me, my brother, to suck the breasts of my mother,[23] so that I might find Thee alone without, and that I might kiss Thee and that no man might now despise me!'[24] This kiss is the union whereof we are speaking, wherein[25] the soul is made equal with God through love. Wherefore she has this desire, asking to be given the Beloved that He may be her brother, which phrase signifies and makes equality; and that He may suck the breasts of her mother, which signifies the consuming of all the imperfections and desires of her nature which she has from her mother Eve; and that she may find Him alone without, that is, may be united with Him alone, far away from all things, detached, according to the will and the desire, from them all; and thus none will despise her, that is to say, neither world nor flesh nor devil[26] will attack her; for, when the soul is free and purged from all these things and united with God, none of them can annoy her. Hence it is that the soul in this estate enjoys an habitual sweetness and tranquillity which is never lost to her and never fails her.

6. But, over and above this habitual satisfaction and peace,

---

[20] Ej, G, Sg: 'with these virtues.'
[21] Ej, G omit: 'and ordered . . . by others.'
[22] Ej, G, Sg omit: 'and diversity.'
[23] Ej, G omit all the rest of this paragraph save the last sentence.
[24] Canticles viii, 1.
[25] S adds: 'in a certain manner.'
[26] S: 'neither world, devil nor flesh.'

the flowers, or virtues, of this garden whereof we speak are wont to open in the soul and diffuse their fragrance in it after such manner that the soul seems to be, and in fact is, filled with delights from God. And I said[27] that the flowers, or virtues, which are in the soul are wont to open, because, although the soul is full of virtues in perfection,[28] it is not always actually enjoying them (although, as I have said, it does habitually enjoy the peace and tranquillity which they cause it); for we can say that in this life[29] they are in the soul as flowers in bud, tightly closed, in a garden—it is a marvellous thing at times to see them all opening, by the work of the Holy Spirit, and diffusing marvellous scent and fragrance in great variety. For it will come to pass that the soul will see in itself the flowers of the mountains whereof we spoke above, which are the abundance and greatness and beauty of God; with these will be intertwined the lilies of the wooded valleys, which are rest, refreshment and protection; and then there will be placed among them the fragrant roses[30] of the strange islands, which, as we say, are the strange kinds of knowledge concerning God; and likewise it will be assailed by the fragrance of the water-lilies from the sounding rivers,[31] which we said were the greatness of God that fills the entire soul; and intertwined and enlaced with these is the delicate scent of the jasmine (which is the whisper of the amorous breezes), whereof we said likewise that the soul has fruition in this estate; and furthermore all the other virtues and gifts[32] which come, as we said, from tranquil knowledge and silent music and sonorous solitude[33] and the delectable supper of love. And the enjoyment and perception by the soul of these flowers is at times of such a kind that the soul can say with complete truth: 'Our flowery bed, encompassed with dens of lions.'

[27] S: 'And I say.'
[28] Ej, G: 'in perfection in possession.'
[29] Ej, G, Sg: 'that in this estate.'
[30] A, Ej, Sg: 'the roses.'
[31] A has *lirios* ['lilies'] for *ríos* ['rivers'].
[32] B, Jaén omit: 'and gifts.'
[33] Ej, G: 'and sonorous sweetness.'

Happy the soul that in this life merits at times to taste[34] the
fragrance of these Divine flowers. She says also that this bed is

Hung with purple[35]

7. By purple, in the Divine Scripture, is denoted charity;
kings[36] are clad in it and use it. The soul says[37] that this
flowery bed is hung with purple, because all virtues, riches and
good things are sustained by it, flourish[38] in it and have fruition only in the charity and love of the King of Heaven, without which love the soul could not enjoy this bed and its
flowers. And thus all these virtues in the soul are, as it were,
hung with the love of God, as with a substance which preserves them well; and they are, as it were, bathed in love,[39]
because all and each of them are ever enkindling the soul
with love for God, and in all things and works they are moved
by love to greater love of God. This is to be hung with purple.
This is well expressed in the Divine Songs; for there it is said
that the seat or bed that Solomon made for himself he made
of the woods of Libanus, and the pillars of silver, the couch
of gold and the hangings[40] of purple; and it says that he
ordered it all by means of charity.[41] For the virtues and
gifts[42] which God places in the bed of the soul, which are
denoted by the woods of Libanus, and the pillars of silver,
have their couch and resting-place of love, which is the
gold,[43] for, as we have said, the virtues are grounded and
preserved in love; and all of them, by means of the charity
of God and of the soul, are ordered and practised, as we have
just said. And she says that this bed is likewise[44]

. . . builded in peace,

[34] Ej, G, Sg, S: 'to enjoy.'
[35] Bg: 'dyed in purple.'
[36] Sg: 'princes and kings.'
[37] S: 'And therefore the soul says.'
[38] [Or 'flower.'] Ej, G, Sg omit: 'flourish in it.'
[39] Ej, G, Sg: 'as it were hung in the love of God.'
[40] [Lit., subida, 'the going up,' as in D.V.]
[41] Canticles iii, 9.
[42] Bz omits: 'and gifts.'
[43] S: 'and resting-place of gold, which is the love.'
[44] S: 'And she likewise says that this bed is.'

8. She here sets down the fourth excellence[45] of this bed, which depends in order upon the third, that has just been mentioned; for the third was perfect love, the property whereof is to cast out all fear, as says Saint John;[46] and from this issues the perfect peace of the soul,[47] which is the fourth property of this bed, as we said. For the better understanding of this it must be known that each of the virtues is of itself peaceful, meek and strong; and consequently in the soul that possesses them are produced these three effects, namely: peace, meekness and strength. And because this bed is flowery, composed of the flowers of virtues, as we have said, which are all peaceful, meek and strong, hence it comes to pass that the bed is builded in peace, and the soul is peaceful, meek and strong; which are three properties that can be attacked in no war, whether of world, devil or flesh. And the virtues keep the soul so peaceful and secure that it seems to her that she is wholly builded in peace. And she describes the fifth property of this flowering bed, which, besides what has been said, is likewise[48]

Crowned with a thousand shields of gold.

9. The which shields are here the virtues and gifts of the soul, which, although, as we have said, they are the flowers, etc., of this bed, serve it likewise as a crown and prize, for its work in having gained them. And not only so, but they likewise serve it as a defence, and as strong shields against the vices which by the practice of them it conquered; wherefore this flowery bed of the Bride[49] (that is, the virtues, the

[45] A: 'the fourth difference.' S begins: 'It is the fourth excellence.'

[46] 1 St. John iv, 18. All the MSS. have: 'as says Saint Paul.'

[47] Jaén omits: 'from this' [and is therefore not quite clear]. Ej, G: 'was perfect love, and from this, as says Saint Paul, issues . . .' S: 'was perfect love, and from perfect love, as says Saint Paul, issues . . .'

[48] S: 'The fifth property of this flowering bed, beyond what has been said, is explained in the line following as being . . .'

[49] G, Sg: 'but likewise, as strong shields against the vices, the virtues are a crown and defence, which [vices] it conquered by the practice thereof, and therefore this flowery bed of the Bride . . .'

crown and the defence)[50] is crowned with them as with the prize of the Bride and defended by them as by a shield. And she says they are of gold, to denote the great worth of these virtues. This very thing was said by the Bride in the Songs in other words, in this wise: 'Behold the bed of Solomon, how threescore mighty men of the most valiant of Israel are about it; the sword of each upon his thigh[51] as a defence against the fears of night.'[52] And she says that there are a thousand of them,[53] in order to denote the multitude of the virtues, graces and gifts wherewith God endows the soul in this estate; for He too used the same term in order to signify the number of the virtues of the Bride, which cannot be numbered, saying: 'Like the tower of David is thy neck, which is builded with defences; a thousand shields hang upon it, and all the arms of mighty men.'[54]

Annotation for the Following Stanza

But the soul that reaches this point[55] of perfection is not content to magnify and praise the excellences of her Beloved,[56] the Son of God, nor to sing and give thanks for the favours that she receives in Him and the delights which she enjoys in Him, but relates also that which He does to other souls; for both these things the soul is able to see in this blessed union of love. Wherefore, praising Him and giving Him thanks for the said favours[57] which He grants to other souls, the soul recites this stanza.

[50] Av, Bz omit this parenthesis.
[51] Ej, G, Sg: 'upon his hand.'
[52] Canticles iii, 7.
[53] S: 'And the Bride says here in this line that there are a thousand shields.'
[54] Canticles iv, 4.
[55] Ej, G, Sg: 'this estate.'
[56] Ej, G, Sg have 'grandeurs' for 'excellences' and omit 'the Son of God.'
[57] S: 'and magnifying the many favours.'

STANZA XXV

In the track of[1] thy footprint   The young girls[2] run along by
  the way.[3]
At the touch of a spark, at the spiced wine,   Flows forth the
  Divine balsam.

Exposition

2. In this stanza the Bride praises the Beloved for three
favours which devout souls receive from Him, whereby they
are the more incited[4] and exalted to love God; of these, having experienced them in this estate, she here makes mention.
The first, she says, is sweetness which He gives them of Himself, and which is of such efficacy that it makes them to run
very quickly upon the way of perfection. The second is a visit
of love whereby they are suddenly enkindled in love. The
third is abundance of charity infused into them, wherewith
they are inebriated after such manner that their spirit is as
greatly exalted with this inebriation as with the visit of love,
so that they send forth praises to God, together with the delectable affections of love, saying as follows:

In the track of thy footprint

3. The footprint is the trace of Him Whose the footprint
is, whereby the soul goes tracking and seeking out Him that
made it. The sweetness and knowledge concerning Himself
which God gives to the soul that seeks Him is the trace and
footprint whereby it knows and seeks Him increasingly.
Wherefore the soul says here to the Word[5] its Spouse: 'In

---

[1] See p. 236, n. 29, above.

[2] Bg, Sg: 'The youths.'

[3] Ej, G: 'The youths discover [or "reveal"] the way.'

[4] Ej, G, Sg: 'the more enamoured.'

[5] Ej, G, Sg: 'Wherefore the soul here says to the Word, the Son
of God.'

the track of Thy footprint'—that is, in the traces of sweetness which Thou imprintest upon them and wherewith Thou inspirest them, and in the fragrance of Thyself which Thou scatterest—

The young girls[6] run along by the way.[7]

4. This is to say that devout souls, with the youthful strength which they have received from the sweetness of Thy footprint, 'run along'—that is, run in many places and after many manners (for this is the meaning of the phrase),[8] each one in the place and after the manner which God grants to it, according to its spirit and to the estate which it has reached, by means of a great variety of spiritual works and exercises, along the road of eternal life, which is evangelical perfection, on the which road they meet the Beloved in union of love after attaining detachment of the spirit from all things. This sweetness and this trace of Himself which God leaves in the soul lighten it[9] greatly and make it to run after Him; for then the work done by the soul itself towards its journey along this road counts for very little or nothing;[10] rather it is moved and attracted by this Divine footprint of God, not only to set forth, but to run along that road after many manners, as we have said. Wherefore the Bride in the Songs entreated the Spouse for this Divine attraction,[11] saying: *Trahe me: post te curremus in odorem unguentorum tuorum.*[12] That is: Draw me after Thee and we will run to the fragrance of Thine ointments. And, after He has given her this Divine fragrance, she says: *In odorem unguentorum tuorum currimus: adolescentulæ dilexerunt te nimis.*[13] Which is to say: At the fragrance of Thine ointments we run; the young girls loved Thee

---

[6] A, Bg: 'The youths.'
[7] Ej, G, Sg: 'The youths discover [or "reveal"] the way.'
[8] [See p. 123, n. 2, above.]
[9] A, B, Bg: 'gladden it.' Ej, G, Sg: 'alleviate it.'
[10] Av: '. . . this road is [done] very gradually or not at all.'
[11] Ej, G: 'this Divine prayer.'
[12] Canticles i, 2–3.
[13] *Ibid.*

greatly. And David says: 'I ran the way of Thy commandments when Thou didst enlarge my heart.'[14]

**At the touch of a spark, at the spiced wine,   Flows forth the
Divine balsam.**

5. In the first two lines we have explained how souls in
the track of the footprint of the Beloved run along by the
way by means of exercises and outward works; now in these
last lines the soul describes the exercise which these souls perform inwardly with the will, moved by two other favours and
inward visits which the Beloved grants them, which she here
calls the touch of a spark and spiced wine; and the inward
exercise of the will which results from these two visits and
is caused by them she calls the flowings forth of Divine balsam. With respect to the first point, it must be known that
this touch of a spark which she mentions here is a most subtle
touch which the Beloved inflicts upon the soul at times, even
when she is least expecting it,[15] so that her heart is enkindled
in the fire of love just as if a spark of fire[16] had flown out
and kindled it. Then, with great rapidity, as when one suddenly awakens, the will is enkindled in loving, desiring, praising, giving thanks, doing reverence, esteeming and praying to
God with savour of love. These things she calls the flowings
forth of Divine balsam, which, at the touch of the sparks,
issue forth from the Divine love[17] which struck the spark,
which is the Divine balsam, that comforts and heals the soul
with its fragrance and substance.

6. Concerning this Divine touch the Bride speaks in the
Songs after this manner: *Dilectus meus misit manum suam
per foramen, et venter meus intremuit ad tactum ejus.*[18]
Which is to say: My Beloved put his hand through the opening and my bowels were moved at his touch. The touch of
the Beloved is that touch of love which, as we here say, is

[14] Psalm cxviii, 32 [A.V., cxix, 32].
[15] Sg: '. . . is a most subtle touch; at times when she is least
expecting it the Beloved inflicts it upon the soul.'
[16] Ej, G, Sg: 'a spark of living fire.'
[17] S: 'the burning Divine love.'
[18] Canticles v, 4.

inflicted upon the soul; the hand is the favour which He grants
it therein; the opening whereby this hand has entered is the
manner[19] and mode and degree of perfection[20] which the
soul possesses; for in this wise is the touch wont to be heavier
or lighter according to this manner or that of the spiritual
quality of the soul. The moving of the bowels whereof she
speaks is that of the will whereupon the said touch is inflicted;
and the moving thereof is the rising within her of her desires
and affections towards God, the desiring, loving and praising
of Him, and the other things whereof we have spoken, which
are the flowings forth of balsam produced by this touch, even
as we said.

. . . the spiced wine,

7. This spiced wine is another and far greater favour[21]
which God grants at times to souls that have made progress,
inebriating them in the Holy Spirit with a wine of love that
is sweet, delectable and strong, for the which cause she calls
it spiced wine. For even as such wine is prepared[22] with many
and divers spices that are fragrant and strong, so this love,
which is the love that God gives to those that are already
perfect, is prepared and made ready in their souls, and spiced
with the virtues which the soul has already gained. Seasoned
with these precious spices, this love infuses into the soul such
strength and abundance of sweet inebriation,[23] in the visits
that God makes to her, that with its great efficacy and strength
it causes her to send forth to God these emissions or outflowings,[24] wherein she praises, loves and reverences Him, and

[19] [On the word-play here, see p. 125, n. 8, above.]
[20] S: 'is the manner and way and perfection, at least, the degree
thereof.'
[21] Ej: 'which are the flowings forth of the balsam produced by
this touch, even as we say. With respect to the second [part of the
line], this is another and far greater kind of favour.'
[22] [Cf. p. 125, n. 9, above.] Sg: 'For even as the spiced wine is
spiced and prepared.' Ej: 'For even as the spiced wine is prepared.'
[23] Bg: 'Spiced with the virtues, this love gives them strength of
sweet inebriation.'
[24] Bg, S: 'or inebriations.' G: 'or envyings.' Ej omits: 'or outflowings.'

so forth, as we are saying here, and this with wondrous desires to work and[25] suffer for Him.

8. And it must be known that this favour of sweet inebriation[26] passes not as quickly as the spark, for it is of greater duration. The spark touches and is gone,[27] though its effect lasts for some time and occasionally for a very long time, but the spiced wine and its effect are both accustomed to last long,[28] and this, as I say, is love's sweetness in the soul. Sometimes it lasts for a day, or for two days; at other times, for many days, though not always at the same degree of intensity, since it weakens or increases, and the soul is unable to control it. Sometimes, when the soul has done nothing to produce it, it feels this sweet inebriation of its spirit and the enkindling[29] of this Divine wine,[30] within its inmost substance,[31] even as David says in these words: 'My heart grew hot within me and in my meditation fire will kindle.'[32] Sometimes the flowings forth of this inebriation of love last for as long as the inebriation; at other times, although the inebriation persists in the soul, it does so without the flowings forth aforementioned, and these, when they occur, are of greater or less intensity, according as the inebriation is of greater or less intensity. But the flowings forth or the effects of the spark habitually last longer than the spark itself; it leaves them in the soul, and they are more ardent than those which come from the inebriation, for at times this Divine spark leaves the soul consuming and burning away in love.

9. And, as we have spoken of wine that has been prepared by fermentation, it will be good[33] at this point to note briefly[34] the difference between fermented wine, which is

[25] Ej omits: 'work and.'
[26] S: 'that this sweet inebriation and favour which He works within her.' Ej, G, Sg have 'delectable' for 'sweet.'
[27] A: 'passes not as quickly as the spark touches and is gone.'
[28] S has: [for 'for a very . . . last long'] 'the spiced wine is wont to last rather longer and its effect a long time.'
[29] Sg: 'the inebriation.'
[30] S: 'of this Divine love.'
[31] Ej, G, Sg: 'its last substance.'
[32] Psalm xxxviii, 4 [A.V., xxxix, 3].
[33] Sg, S: 'well' for 'good.'
[34] Ej, G: 'it will be well here to speak briefly of.'

called old,[35] and new wine, which will be the same as that
between old and new lovers,[36] and will provide a little instruction for spiritual persons. In new wine the lees have not
yet been thrown off, and are not settled, wherefore the wine
ferments, and its goodness and worth cannot be known until
it has well settled on the lees and the fermentation has
ceased.[37] Until that time there is great likelihood of its going
bad; it has a rough and sharp taste, and to drink much of
it is bad for the drinker; its strength is chiefly in the lees.[38]
In old wine the lees are digested and settled, so that there
is no longer any fermentation going on in it as there is in
new wine; it is quite evidently good, and quite safe from going
bad, for that fermentation and bubbling which might cause
it to do harm is all over; and thus well fermented wine very
rarely goes bad or is spoiled. It has a pleasant flavour, and
the strength is in the substance of the wine and no longer
in the taste, wherefore a draught of it gives the drinker good
health and makes him strong.

10. New lovers are compared to new wine: these are they
that are beginning to serve God, for the fermentations of the
wine of their love are taking place wholly without, in their
senses, since they have not yet settled on the lees of weak
and imperfect sense, and the strength of their love resides only
in its sweetness. These lovers ordinarily derive the strength
to work from sweetness of sense, and by this sweetness they
are moved, so that such love as theirs cannot be trusted until
its fermentations and coarse tastes of sense are over. For, even
as these fermentations and heats of sense can incline the soul
to good and perfect love and serve it as a good means thereto,
when the lees of its imperfection have settled, even so it is
very easy in these beginnings, when these tastes are still new,
for the wine of love to fail and for the fervour and sweetness[39] of new things to be spoiled. And these new lovers

[35] Ej, G, Sg: 'spiced' for 'old.'

[36] S reads: 'new wines and old' for 'old and new lovers' [destroy-
ing the sense].

[37] [*Lit.*, 'until it has well digested the lees and fury of them.']

[38] S omits this sentence.

[39] A: 'the sweetness and favour.' Sg: 'the fervour.' Ej, G: 'for
the wine of love to be corrupted and spoiled in the fervour for new
things.'

always have yearnings and fatigues caused by love, which
come from the senses; it is meet for them to temper their
draught,[40] for, if they are very active while the wine is still
fermenting,[41] their natures will be ruined, with these yearnings and fatigues of love—namely, of the new wine, which,
as we said, is rough and sharp, and not sweetened as yet by
perfect preparation, after which these yearnings of love will
cease,[42] as we shall shortly say.

11. This same comparison is made by the Wise Man in
the Book of Ecclesiasticus, where he says: 'The new friend
is as new wine; it shall grow old and thou shalt drink it with
pleasure.'[43] Wherefore old lovers, which are they that are
practised and proved in the service of the Spouse, are like
old wine which has settled on the lees, and has not those fermentations of the senses, or those fires and storms of fermentation[44] from without; the sweetness of the wine of love can
be tasted now that it is substantially fermented, and has not
that savour[45] of sense as has the love of new lovers, but is
settled within the soul in the substance and savour of the spirit
and truth[46] in its works. And such souls desire not to cling
to those savours and fermentations of the senses, neither do
they desire to experience them, lest they suffer disgust and
weariness; for he that gives rein to the desire for any pleasure
of sense[47] has perforce many times to suffer pains and displeasures of sense and of spirit. Wherefore since these old
lovers lack the spiritual sweetness which has its roots in
sense,[48] they have no more yearnings or pains of love in sense
and spirit; and therefore it is a marvel if these old friends

[40] Av: 'to temper the sweetness.' [There are various other readings, of which this alone preserves any sense.]

[41] Av, Sg: 'while the wine still has strength.'

[42] Ej: 'and not sweetened nor perfectly digestible until these
yearnings of love cease.'

[43] Ecclesiasticus ix, 15 [A.V., ix, 10].

[44] ['Storms' is literally 'furies.']

[45] Ej, G, Sg: 'that fervour.'

[46] Ej, G, Sg: 'spirit and fervour.'

[47] Ej: 'for he that gives rein to any pleasure of the sensual appetite.' G: 'for he that gives rein to the pleasure, whatever it be, of
the sensual appetite.'

[48] Ej, G: 'which has furies [or 'storms'] in the sense.'

fail God,[49] for they are already far above that which might
make them fail, namely, above sensuality, and in them the
wine of love is not only fermented and purged of its lees,
but is also (as is said in the line) seasoned with the spices,
which, as we said, are virtues in perfection, and allow it not
to go bad like new wine. For this reason the old friend is
of great esteem in the sight of God and thus the author of
Ecclesiasticus says of him: 'Forsake not the old friend, for
the new will not be like to him.'[50] In this wine of love, then,
well proved and spiced in the soul, the Divine Beloved[51] produces the Divine inebriation which we have mentioned, in the
strength whereof the soul causes sweet and delectable outflowings to go forth to God. And so the sense of the last lines
is as follows: At the touch of the spark wherewith Thou awakenest my soul, and at the spiced wine wherewith Thou lovingly
inebriatest me, my soul sends to Thee its outflowings of the
movements and acts of love occasioned by Thee within it.

Annotation for the Stanza Following

So, then, we shall understand the happy soul to be in this
flowery bed, where all these things aforementioned and many
more come to pass, wherein for a couch[52] she has the Spouse,
the Son of God, and for covering and hangings the charity
and love of the same Spouse. In such wise can she of a surety
pronounce the words of the Bride, who says: 'His left hand
under my head.'[53] Wherefore it will be possible to say with
truth that this soul is here clothed in God and bathed in Divinity. And, not superficially, but in the inward parts of her spirit,
being filled with Divine delights, and having the fullness[54]

---

[49] S: 'in sense or spirit, and thus it is a marvel if they fail God.'
[50] Ecclesiasticus ix, 14 [A.V., ix, 10].
[51] G, Sg: 'Divine love.'
[52] [*reclinatorio:* the word used in Chap. xxiv, § 7, above.]
[53] Canticles ii, 6.
[54] Thus Jaén. B, Bg: 'being clothed in delights of wine [*de vino*,
for "divine"—*divino*], having the fullness . . .' The other authorities also have *revestida* ['clothed'] for *revertida* ['filled,' or, more

of the spiritual waters of life, she experiences that which David says of those that have drawn near to God, namely: 'They
shall be inebriated with the plenty of Thy house, and of the
torrent[55] of Thy delight shalt Thou give them to drink; for
with Thee is the fountain of life.'[56] What fullness, then, will
be this that is in the being of the soul, since the draught that
they give it is nothing less than a torrent of delight, which
torrent is the Holy Spirit; for, as Saint John says, He is the
resplendent river of living water that proceeds from the seat
of God and of the Lamb.[57] The waters of this river, since
they are the inmost love of God, flow into the inmost soul[58]
and give her to drink this torrent of love which, as we say,
is the spirit of her Spouse[59] which is infused into her in this
union, and therefore with great abundance of love she sings
this stanza.

STANZA XXVI

**In the inner cellar, of my Beloved have I drunk,   And, when I
    went forth over all this meadow,
Then knew I naught   And lost the flock which I followed afore-
    time.**

Exposition

2. In this stanza the soul describes the sovereign favour
which God has granted her by gathering her into the depth
of His love, which is the union or transformation of love in

---

exactly, 'having overflowed'], except Ej and G, which read
recocida [best translated 'consumed'].

[55] Ej, G, Sg: 'of the current.'

[56] Psalm xxxv, 9 [A.V., xxxvi, 8–9].

[57] Apocalypse xxii, 1.

[58] G: 'flow most abundantly into the soul.'

[59] Ej, G, Sg: 'is the Holy Spirit her Spouse.'

God; and she notes two effects[1] which she has derived there-from—namely, forgetfulness and withdrawal from all the things of the world, and the mortification of all its tastes and desires.

In the inner cellar,

3. In order that I might say aught concerning this cellar, and explain that which the soul desires to say or denote by it, it would be needful that the Holy Spirit should take my hand and move my pen. This cellar whereof the soul here speaks is the last and most intimate degree[2] of love to which the soul may attain in this life, wherefore she calls it the inner cellar—that is to say, the innermost. From this it follows that there are others less interior, which are the degrees of love whereby the soul rises to this, the last of all. And we may say that there are seven of these degrees or cellars of love,[3] all of which the soul comes to possess when she possesses in perfection the seven gifts of the Holy Spirit, in the manner wherein she is able to receive them. And thus, when the soul attains to perfect possession of the spirit of fear, she has like-wise in perfection the spirit of love, since that fear, which is the last of the seven gifts, is filial,[4] and the perfect fear[5] of a son proceeds from the perfect love of a father. Hence, when[6] the Divine Scripture desires to call a man perfect in charity,[7] it speaks of him as fearing God. Wherefore Isaias, prophesying the perfection of Christ, said: *Replebit eum spiritus timoris Domini.*[8] Which signifies: He shall be filled with the spirit of the fear of God. Saint Luke also described

---

[1] Ej, G, Sg: 'into the inner place of His love, which is union or transformation in God, and she relates two things, and these are two effects, etc.'

[2] [*Lit.,* 'most narrow degree.'] G, Sg: 'strange degree.' Ej: 'intimate degree.'

[3] Ej, G abbreviate thus: '. . . the degrees of love; and these cellars of love are seven.'

[4] Av: 'is most filial.'

[5] G, Sg: 'the perfect love.'

[6] Av modifies and adds: 'When fear is most perfect, love is most perfect, and thus when . . .'

[7] Ej, G: 'in holiness.'

[8] Isaias xi, 3 [A.V., xi, 2].

the holy Simeon as full of fear, saying: *Erat vir justus, et timoratus*.[9] And this is also true of many others.

4. It must be known that many souls attain to the first cellars and enter therein, each according to the perfection of love which he possesses, but few in this life attain to this last and innermost perfection, for in this there comes to pass that perfect union with God which they call the Spiritual Marriage, whereof the soul speaks in this place. And that which God communicates to the soul in this most intimate union is completely ineffable, so that naught can be said thereof, even as naught can be said concerning God Himself which may describe Him; for it is God Himself Who communicates this to the soul and transforms her into Himself with marvellous glory, so that they are both as[10] we should say the window is with the sun's ray, or coal with the fire, or the light of the stars with that of the sun—yet less essentially and completely so than will come to pass in the next life. And thus, in order to describe that which she receives from God in that cellar of union,[11] the soul says naught else, nor do I believe that she could say aught more appropriate to express some part thereof, than the following line:

Of my Beloved have I drunk,

5. For, even as a draught is diffused and shed through all the members and veins of the body, even so is this communication from God diffused substantially in the entire soul, or, to express it better, the soul is more nearly transformed into God, according to which transformation the soul drinks of its God according to its substance and its spiritual faculties. For, according to the understanding, it drinks wisdom and knowledge; according to the will, it drinks sweetest love; and, according to the memory, it drinks recreation and delight in the remembrance and sense of glory. With respect to the first point, that the soul receives and drinks delight substantially, the Bride herself says this, in the Songs, after this manner:

[9] St. Luke ii, 25.
[10] S: 'transforming her with marvellous glory. And in this estate they are both in one, as . . .'
[11] Ej, G, S: 'cellar of wine.' Bg: 'cellar of good.'

Anima mea liquefacta est, ut sponsus locutus est.[12] That is:
My soul delighted when the Spouse spake. The speaking of
the Spouse signifies here[13] His communicating Himself to the
soul.

6. And that the understanding drinks wisdom is declared
in the same book by the Bride, where, desiring to attain to
this kiss of union and entreating the Spouse for it, she says:
'There Thou shalt teach me (namely, wisdom and knowledge
in love); and I will give Thee a draught of spiced wine'[14]—
that is to say, of my love spiced with Thine,[15] or, in other
words, transformed into Thine.

7. With respect to the third point, which is that the will
drinks there of love, the Bride says this also in the said Book
of the Songs, in these words: 'He introduced me into the
secret cellar and ordained charity in me'; which is as much
as to say: He gave me to drink love introduced into His love,
or more clearly and properly speaking: He ordained in me
His charity, accommodating His own[16] charity to me and
making it mine: this is the drinking by the soul of the very
love of its Beloved, which its Beloved infuses into it.[17]

8. Here it is to be known, with respect to the saying of
some that the will cannot love, save what the understanding
first understands, that this has to be understood after a natural
manner; for in the way of nature it is impossible to love if
one understands not first that which one is to love; but in
the supernatural way God can readily infuse love and increase
it without infusing or increasing distinct knowledge, as is given
to be understood in the passage quoted. And this is the experience of many spiritual persons, who oftentimes find themselves burning in the love of God without having a more
distinct knowledge of Him than aforetime; for they can understand little and love much, and they can understand much

[12] Canticles v, 6.
[13] S: '. . . when the Spouse spake to her, the which speaking
here signifies.'
[14] Canticles viii, 2.
[15] S omits the words which follow ('or . . . Thine').
[16] Ej, G, Sg omit: 'own.'
[17] Sg: 'this is the drinking by the soul of its Beloved.' Ej, G omit:
'this is . . . into it.'

and love little. But habitually those spiritual persons who have
not a very excellent understanding concerning God are wont
to excel in will; and infused faith suffices them in the stead
of intellectual knowledge; by means of which faith God infuses into them charity, and increases it within them, together
with the act thereof, which is to love more, even though their
knowledge be not increased, as we have said. And thus the
will can drink of love without the understanding drinking
anew of knowledge, although in the case of which we are
speaking, wherein the soul says that she drank of her Beloved,
inasmuch as there is union in the inner cellar, which is according to the three faculties of the soul, as we have said,
all of them drink together.

9. And with respect to the fourth point—namely, that the
soul drinks of its Beloved there according to the memory—it
is clear that the soul is enlightened with the light of the
understanding in remembering the good things which it is
possessing and enjoying in the union of its Beloved.

10. This Divine draught[18] so greatly deifies and exalts the
soul and immerses it in God that when it goes forth—

When I went forth

11. That is to say, this favour has completely passed away,[19]
for although the soul be for ever in this high estate of marriage[20] after He has placed it therein, yet it is not for ever in
actual union according to the said faculties, although it is so
according to the substance of the soul. But in this substantial
union of the soul the faculties are also very frequently[21] in
union, and drink in this cellar; the understanding by knowledge, the will by love, etc. So, when the soul now says 'When
I went forth,' she understands not this of the essential or
substantial[22] union which she now possesses, which is the
estate aforementioned, but refers to the union of the faculties,

[18] Bg has: 'This Divine wisdom,' and omits the following words:
'deifies and.'
[19] S: 'That is to say, when this favour had just passed away.'
[20] Ej, G, Sg: 'in this spiritual estate.'
[21] Ej, G: 'very perfectly.'
[22] Ej, G, Sg omit: 'or substantial.'

which is not continuous in this life, neither can be so. She says, then, that when she went forth

Over all this meadow,

12. That is to say, over all this expanse of the world,

Then knew I naught

13. The reason is that that draught of the highest wisdom[23] of God which there she drank makes her forget all the things of the world, and it seems to the soul that its former knowledge, and even the knowledge of the whole world, is pure ignorance by comparison with that knowledge. And in order to understand this better it must be known that the most usual cause of this ignorance of the soul things of the world, when it is in this estate, is that it has been informed by supernatural knowledge,[24] beside which all the natural and political knowledge of the world is not so much knowledge as ignorance. Wherefore the soul that is led into this highest knowledge knows thereby that all that other knowledge which has naught in common with this knowledge is not knowledge but ignorance; and that there is no knowledge to be had from it; and the soul declares the truth of the saying of the Apostle, namely, that that which is greatest wisdom in the sight of men is foolishness in God's sight.[25] And therefore the Bride says that she knew naught after drinking of that Divine wisdom; and this truth—namely, that the wisdom of men and of the whole world is pure ignorance, and that it merits unknowing —cannot be known save when God grants to the soul the favour of being Himself within it,[26] communicating His wisdom to it, and strengthening it with this draught of love so that it may see it clearly, according as Solomon says, in these words: 'This is the vision that was seen and spoken of by the man with whom God is, who, being strengthened by the dwelling of God within him, said: "I am most foolish above

---

[23] Ej, G: 'highest sweetness.'
[24] Av, Bz: 'supernatural essence.'
[25] 1 Corinthians iii, 19.
[26] [*Lit.*, 'save by this favour of God's being in the soul.'] S: 'save by this truth of God's being in the soul.'

all men, and the wisdom of men is not with me." '[27] This is because the soul is in that exceeding high wisdom of God and therefore the lowly wisdom of men is ignorance to it; for the natural sciences themselves, and the very works that are done by God, are as ignorance compared with knowing God, for, where God is not known, naught is known. Wherefore the high places of God are ignorance and foolishness to men, as Saint Paul says likewise.[28] Hence the divinely wise and the worldly wise are each ignorant in the other's estimation; for the latter cannot apprehend the wisdom and science of God, neither can the former apprehend those of the world; inasmuch as the wisdom of the world, as we have said, is ignorance with respect to the wisdom of God, and that of God with respect to that of the world.

14. But over and above this, that deification and exaltation of the mind in God wherein the soul is as if enraptured, immersed in love and wholly one with God,[29] allows it not to take notice of anything soever in the world; and it is withdrawn not only from all other things, but even from itself, and is annihilated, as though it were transformed and dissolved in love, which transformation consists in passing from itself to the Beloved. And thus the Bride in the Songs, after having treated of this her transformation of love in the Beloved, describes this unknowing which was hers, in this word: *Nescivi;* which means: I knew not.[30] The soul in such a condition is in a certain manner as Adam was in the condition of innocence, when he knew not what evil was; for it is so innocent that it understands not evil nor judges aught as evil; and it will hear things that are very evil, and will see them with its eyes, and will be unable to understand that they are so,[31] because it has no habit of evil whereby to judge it, God having rooted out its imperfect habits and ignorance (including the evil of sin), with the perfect habit of true wisdom; and thus, with respect to this also, it 'knew naught.'

[27] Proverbs xxx, 1–2.
[28] 1 Corinthians ii, 14.
[29] S: 'and made one God.'
[30] Canticles vi, 11 [A.V., vi, 12].
[31] S: 'to understand what they are.'

15. The soul in such case will intervene little in things of others, since it remembers not even its own things. For the Spirit of God has this characteristic in the soul wherein He dwells, that He forthwith inclines it towards ignorance and unwillingness to know the things of others, especially things that are not to its profit. For the Spirit of God is recollected within the soul itself, and turns toward it, rather that He may draw it forth from extraneous things than in order to lead it among them. And thus the soul remains in a complete unknowing with respect to the things that it knew formerly.

16. It is not to be understood that, even if the soul continues in this state of unknowing, it loses therein the habits of the acquired sciences[32] which it had; it is rather that they are perfected with that most perfect habit—namely, the habit of supernatural science—which has been infused within it, although these habits no longer dominate the soul in such a way as to make it necessary that knowledge should come through them, albeit there is no obstacle to this happening occasionally. For in this union of Divine wisdom these habits are united with the highest wisdom of the other sciences,[33] just as, when a small light unites with another that is great, it is the greater that overwhelms the lesser and gives light, and the smaller is not lost, but rather is perfected, although it gives not the chief light. And this, I suppose, will be the position in Heaven, where the habits of acquired knowledge which the just bring there will not be destroyed, though they will be of no great importance to the just,[34] for they will know more in the Divine wisdom than these habits can teach them.

17. But the kinds of knowledge and the particular forms of things and acts of the imagination, and every other apprehension that has form and figure, are all lost and no longer known in that absorption of love, and this for two reasons. First, because, as the soul is actually absorbed and immersed in that draught of love, it cannot actually be in aught else

[32] Sg: 'the acquired essences.'
[33] Sg: 'with the highest wisdom of God, through which the soul chiefly understands the virtues of the other sciences.' So, too, Ej and G, except that they read 'truths' for 'virtues.'
[34] S: 'to them.'

neither take notice thereof. Secondly and chiefly, because that transformation in God makes it conform to the simplicity and purity of God (whereinto enters no imaginary figure or form) after such manner as to leave it clean and pure and empty of all forms and figures which it had aforetime, purged and enlightened with simple contemplation. It is like the sun upon a window, infusing itself therein, and making it bright, so that all the stains and spots which formerly appeared upon it are lost from sight; but when the sun departs again the obscurities and stains appear upon it once more. In the soul, however, since the effect of that act of love to some extent remains with it and endures, there likewise endures that unknowing, so that it cannot take note of anything in particular until the affection of that act of love passes.[35] For this act, which has inflamed it and changed it in love, has also annihilated it and destroyed it as to all that which was not love. This agrees with what we said above concerning David, namely: 'For my heart was inflamed and together with it my reins also were changed, and I was dissolved into nothing and I knew naught.'[36] For the reins to be changed by reason of this inflaming of the heart signifies that the soul is changed in God, as to all its desires and operations, into a new manner of life, and that it is destroyed and annihilated, concerning all those old things which it used aforetime; for which reason the Prophet says that he was dissolved into nothing, and that he knew naught, which, as we said, are the two effects caused by the draught from this cellar of God. For not only is all that first knowledge which the soul possessed annihilated, so that everything seems to it as nothing, but likewise all its former life and imperfections are annihilated and renewed in the new man; which is this second effect whereof we are speaking, and which is contained in this line:

And (I) lost the flock which I followed aforetime.

18. This signifies that, until the soul attains to this state of perfection whereof we are speaking, however spiritual it may

[35] Ej, G, Sg omit: 'there likewise . . . act of love passes.'
[36] Psalm lxxii, 21 [A.V., lxxiii, 21–2].

be, there ever remains to it a little flock, as it were, consisting of some of its desires and petty tastes and other of its imperfections—sometimes natural, sometimes spiritual[37]—after which it goes, endeavouring to pasture them while following them and satisfying them. For with respect to the understanding there are wont to remain to such a soul certain imperfections concerning the desire to know. With respect to the will, such souls permit themselves to be carried away by certain petty tastes and desires of their own. These may be temporal, like the possession of certain small things, preference for one thing over another, and certain kinds of presumption, esteem and punctilio to which they pay heed, and other little things which still reek and savour of the world. Or they may be natural, like food, drink and a taste[38] for this rather than for that, and a choosing and desiring of the best. Or, again, they may be spiritual, like the desire for consolations from God and other irrelevances which I might never cease retailing, which things are wont to cling to spiritual men who are not yet perfect. And, with respect to the memory, there are many varieties of things and cares and irrelevant reflections, which draw the soul after them.

19. Sometimes, again, with respect to the four passions of the soul, there are many useless hopes, joys, griefs and fears, after which the soul goes in pursuit. As to this flock aforesaid, some are attracted by more of such things and others by less; but they continually pursue them, until they enter this inner cellar to drink and lose their flock entirely, becoming, as we have said, wholly turned into love, wherein these flocks—that is, these imperfections of the soul—are consumed more easily than rust[39] and mould upon metals are consumed in the fire. So the soul feels itself to be free from all childish likes and dislikes and follies which it pursued, and it can indeed say: 'I lost the flock which I followed aforetime.'

[37] A, B, Bg: 'sometimes spiritual, sometimes temporal.'
[38] B, Bg, S: 'and a liking.'
[39] S: 'more easily, after the manner wherein rust.'

Annotation for the Stanza Following

With such great reality[40] of love does God communicate Himself to the soul in this interior union that no affection of a mother who so tenderly caresses her daughter, nor love of a brother, nor affection of a friend is comparable to it. For so great is the tenderness and reality of the love wherewith the boundless Father caresses and exalts this humble and loving soul—oh, marvellous thing and worthy of all awe and wonder![41]—that in very truth He subjects Himself to it in order to exalt it, as though He were the servant and the soul were His master; and He is as solicitous in granting it favours as though he were the soul's slave and the soul were His God. So profound is the humility and the sweetness of God! For in this communication of love He renders the soul in some degree that same service which He says in the Gospel that He will render to His elect in Heaven—that is to say that He will gird Himself, and, passing from one to another, will serve them.[42] And even so He is here employed in cherishing and caressing[43] the soul, as is the mother in serving and caressing her child, and nursing it at her own breasts; wherein the soul knows the truth of the saying of Isaias, where he says: 'To the breast of God you shall be brought and upon His knees shall you be caressed.'[44]

2. What, then, will the feelings of the soul be here among such sovereign favours?[45] How it will melt in love! How thankful will it be when it sees this breast of God opened to it with such wide and sovereign love! Conscious of being set among so many delights, it surrenders itself to Him wholly and gives Him also the breasts of its own will and love, for it feels

[40] Ej, G, Sg: 'With such great truths.'
[41] Ej, G, Sg: 'and exalts this soul, which is a thing worthy of all power and wonder.'
[42] St. Luke xii, 37.
[43] Ej, G: 'in cherishing, caressing and refreshing.' Sg: 'in cherishing, refreshing and caressing.'
[44] Isaias lxvi, 12. S has: 'and upon His knees will He fondle you.'
[45] Ej, G: 'such delectable favours.'

it passing in its soul, in the same way as the Bride[46] felt it in the Songs, where she speaks with her Spouse after this manner: 'I to my Beloved and His turning is toward me. Come, my Beloved, let us go forth into the field, let us lodge together in the villages; let us get up early in the morning to the vineyards and see if the vineyard has flourished and if the flowers are bringing forth fruits; if the pomegranates have flourished. There will I give Thee my breasts'[47]—that is, I will employ the delights and strength of my will in the service of Thy love. And as these two surrenders of the soul and God have thus come to pass in this union, she describes them in the following stanza, saying:

STANZA XXVII

There he gave me his breast;   There he taught me a science most delectable;
And I gave myself to him indeed, reserving nothing;   There I promised him to be his bride.

Exposition

3. In this stanza the Bride describes the surrender which was made upon either side in this spiritual betrothal, namely, that betwixt herself and God; saying that, in that inner cellar of love, they were united through the communication of Himself to her, when He gave her freely the breast of His love, showing her therein wisdom and secrets; and likewise through the communication of herself to Him, when she surrendered herself to Him indeed and wholly, without reserving aught either for herself or for another, and declaring herself His for ever. The line follows:

There he gave me his breast;

46 S: 'and feeling it and passing by it thus, says to her Beloved that which the Bride felt.'
47 Canticles vii, 10–12.

4. For one to give the breast to another signifies to give that one his love and friendship and to reveal to him his secrets as to a friend. Thus, when the soul says that He gave her His breast there, she means that He communicated to her there His love and His secrets, which God grants to the soul in this estate. Further, there is that which she says also in this line following:

There he taught me a science most delectable;

5. The delectable science which she says here that He taught her is mystical theology[1]—the secret science of God,[2] which spiritual men call contemplation—this is most delectable, since it is science through love, the which love is its master and that which makes it to be wholly delectable. And inasmuch as God communicates to the soul this science and knowledge in the love wherewith He communicates Himself to her, it is delectable to her understanding, since it is a science which pertains thereto; and likewise it is delectable to her will, since it consists in love, which pertains to the will.[3] She says next:

And I gave myself to him indeed, reserving nothing;

6. In that sweet draught of God, wherein, as we have said, the soul is immersed in God, it surrenders itself, most willingly and with great sweetness, to Him wholly, desiring to be wholly His and never again to have aught in itself that is alien from Him. God grants it, in the said union, the purity and the perfection which are necessary for this; for, inasmuch as He transforms the soul into Himself, He makes it to be wholly His and empties it of all that it possessed and that was alien from God. Wherefore the soul is indeed completely given up to God, reserving naught, not only according to its will, but also according to its works, even as God has given Himself[4]

[1] S begins: 'This delectable science is mystical theology.'

[2] Ej, G, Sg: 'which is very delectable and is the secret science of God.'

[3] S: 'because it is a science that pertains to Him, and is delectable to the will, since it consists in love, which pertains to the will.'

[4] A, G, Sg insert here: 'wholly.'

freely to the soul. So these two wills[5] are surrendered, satisfied
and given up the one to the other, so that neither shall fail
the other, as in the faithfulness and stability of a betrothal.
Wherefore the Bride adds these words:

There I promised him to be his bride.

7. For even as a maiden that is betrothed sets not her love
upon another than her spouse, nor directs her thoughts[6] or
her actions to any other, even so the soul in this estate has no
longer any affections of the will or acts of knowledge of the
understanding, nor any care or action which is not wholly
turned to God, together with its desires. It is, as it were,
Divine, deified, so that[7] in even its first movements it has
naught whereto the will of God is opposed, in so far as it can
understand. For even as in an imperfect soul its first movements at least, according to the understanding and according
to the will and memory and desires, are as a general rule[8]
inclined to evil[9] and also to imperfections, even so, the soul
in this estate, according to the understanding, will and memory and desires,[10] in its first movements, is as a general rule
moved and inclined to God, through the great help and stability which it already has in God and through its perfect
conversion to that which is good. All this David clearly explained when he said, speaking of his soul in this estate:
'Shall not my soul perchance be subject to God? Yea, for
from Him cometh my salvation, and He is my God, and my
Saviour; my Receiver, I shall not be any more moved.'[11]
By saying: 'my Receiver,' he means that, because his soul is

5 S: 'both these wills.'

6 [Lit., 'her care.']

7 S: 'It is, as it were, immersed in God, and thus it behaves so
that.'

8 A omits: 'as a general rule.' Jaén, Av, Bz read as in the texts;
the remaining authorities: 'as a rule.'

9 Ej, G, Sg omit: 'inclined to evil and also to.'

10 Sg omits several lines preceding this word. A adds: 'and imperfections.'

11 Psalm lxi, 2 [A.V., lxii, 1–2].

received in God and united in Him, as we say here, he could not be moved against God any more.[12]

8. From what has been said it is to be clearly understood that the soul which has reached this estate of spiritual betrothal knows naught save to love and ever to enjoy the delights of love with the Spouse. For, as it has now reached perfection, the form and being whereof, as Saint Paul says,[13] is love—for the more a soul loves the more perfect is it in that which it loves—therefore this soul that is now perfect is wholly love, if it may thus be expressed, and all its actions are love and it employs all its faculties and possessions[14] in loving, giving all that it has, like the wise merchant,[15] for this treasure of love which it has found hidden in God. And this treasure is of such great price[16] in His sight that, when the soul sees that its Beloved prizes nothing and is pleased with nothing beside love, it employs everything, in its desire to serve Him perfectly, in the pure love of God. And not only because He wills it thus,[17] but likewise because the love wherein it is united inclines it, in and through all things, to the love of God. For, even as the bee extracts from all plants[18] the honey that is in them, and has no use for them for aught else save for that purpose, even so the soul with great facility extracts the sweetness of love that is in all the things that pass through it; it loves God in each of them,[19] whether pleasant or unpleasant; and being, as it is, informed and protected by love, it has neither feeling nor taste nor knowledge of such things, for, as we have said, the soul knows naught but love, and its pleasure in all things and occupations

---

[12] In Ej and G follows here the word 'Annotation.' S has 'Annotation for the stanza following.' All three omit this heading at the beginning of the next paragraph but one.

[13] Colossians iii, 14.

[14] So S. The other authorities have: 'all the possessions of its soul.'

[15] St. Matthew xiii, 45–6.

[16] The MSS., except Jaén, read: 'is so precious.'

[17] Ej, G, Sg: 'because she wills it thus.' S: 'because she employs it thus.'

[18] B, Bg: 'from all flowers.' Bz, Ej, G, Sg: 'from all things.'

[19] [Lit., 'it loves God in them.'] Ej: 'it loves Him in them.' Ej, G, Sg add: 'and thus all things induce love in it.'

is ever, as we have said, the delight of the love of God. And to indicate this the soul utters the following stanza.

Annotation for the Stanza Following

Since, however, we said that God is pleased with naught save love, it will be well before we expound this stanza to state here the reason for this, which is that all our works and all our labours, though they be as numerous as is possible, are nothing in God's sight, for in them we can give Him nothing, neither can we fulfil His desire, which is solely to exalt the soul. He[20] desires nothing of this for Himself, since He has no need thereof; and thus, if anything pleases Him, it is that the soul may be exalted; and since there is no way wherein He can exalt it so much as by making it equal[21] with Himself, for that reason alone He is pleased when the soul loves Him. For the property of love is to make the lover equal with the object of his love. Wherefore, since its love is now perfect, the soul is called Bride of the Son of God, which signifies equality with Him; in the which equality of friendship all things of both are common to both, as the Spouse Himself said to His disciples, in these words: 'But I have called you friends; for all that I heard of My Father I have manifested to you.'[22] The stanza, then, says:

STANZA XXVIII

My soul has employed itself   And all my possessions in his service:
Now I guard no flock nor have I now other office,   For now my exercise is in loving alone.

Exposition

2. Inasmuch as the soul has said in the last stanza (or, rather, the Bride has said) that she has given herself wholly

[20] S: 'Because He.'
[21] S adds: 'after a certain manner.'
[22] St. John xv, 15.

to the Spouse, and has reserved naught for herself, she now, in this stanza, sets forth the manner and mode[1] wherein she accomplishes this. She says that her soul and her body and her faculties and all her abilities are occupied, no longer in other things,[2] but in those which pertain to the service of her Spouse.[3] And that for this reason she no longer goes about seeking her own gain, nor pursues her own tastes,[4] nor busies herself in other things, and in intercourse that has naught to do with God, and is alien to Him.[5] And that even with God Himself she has no other style or manner of intercourse save the exercise of love, inasmuch as she has changed and bartered that earlier mode of intercourse which she had with Him into love,[6] as she will now say.

My soul has employed itself

3. In saying that her soul has employed itself, the Bride refers to the surrender of herself which she made to the Beloved in that union of love[7] wherein her soul, with all its faculties, understanding, will and memory, was dedicated and subjected[8] to His service. Her understanding she employs in the understanding of those things that pertain most nearly to His service in order to do them; her will, in loving all that pleases God and in having affection of the will for God in all things; and her memory and care in[9] that which pertains to His service and will be most pleasing to Him. And she says further:

And all my possessions in his service:

[1] S: 'she now, in this stanza to the Beloved, sets forth the manner.'

[2] [*Lit.*, 'in the things.'] S: 'in all things.'

[3] Ej, G: 'and her faculties with all sweetness [*sc.*, are occupied] not in aught else save only in those things which are for the service of her Spouse.' Sg: 'and all her abilities [*sc.*, are occupied] no longer in aught else save in those things which belong to the service of her Spouse.'

[4] Ej, G, Sg: 'her own tastes and appetites.'

[5] Ej, G: 'and in commerce alien to God.'

[6] A, Bz, S: 'into loving.'

[7] Sg: 'in that surrender of love in the union of love aforementioned.'

[8] S omits: 'and subjected.'

[9] S: 'and her memory in care for . . .'

4. By all her possessions she here understands all that pertains to the sensual part of the soul. In this sensual part[10] is included the body with all its senses and faculties,[11] both interior and exterior, and all its natural ability—namely, the four passions, the natural desires, and the other possessions of the soul, all of which things, she says, are now employed in[12] the service of her Beloved, even as is the rational and spiritual part of the soul whereof we have just spoken in the last line. For the body now works according to God; the inward and outward senses are directed towards Him in all their operations; and all the four passions of the soul she likewise keeps bound to God, because she neither has enjoyment save from God,[13] neither has hope in aught save in God, nor fears any save only God, neither does she grieve save according to God; and likewise all her desires and cares are directed to God alone.

5. And all these possessions are now employed in God and directed toward God, in such manner that all the parts thereof which we have described tend,[14] in their first movements, without the soul's being conscious of it, to work in God and for God. For the understanding, the will and the memory go straightway to God;[15] and the affections, the senses, the desires and appetites, hope, joy and all the rest of the soul's possessions are inclined to God from the first moment, even though, as I say, the soul may not realize that it is working for God. Wherefore the soul in such case very frequently works for God, and is intent upon Him and the things that pertain to Him, without thinking or remembering that it is doing aught for Him; for the use and habit which it has acquired in this manner of procedure causes it neither to observe nor to have any care, and even takes from it the fervent acts which it was wont to have at the beginning. And since all these possessions are employed in God after the manner aforesaid, the soul

10 Ej, G, S: 'in the which part.'
11 B, S: 'with all its faculties.'
12 S: 'all of which she says has now returned to.'
13 Sg omits: 'because she . . . save from God.'
14 Ej, G: 'are moved.'
15 Ej, G: 'because the understanding moves the will and they go straightway to God.'

must needs likewise have that which it describes in the line following, namely:

Now I guard no flock

6. Which is as much as to say: Now I go no longer after my tastes and desires; for, having set them upon God and given them to Him, the soul no longer pastures them nor guards them for herself.[16] And not only does she say that she no longer guards this flock, but she says further:[17]

Nor have I now other office,

7. Many offices, and unprofitable ones, has the soul before she goes so far as to make this gift and surrender to the Beloved of herself and of her possessions, wherewith she sought to serve her own desire and that of others; for all the habits[18] of imperfections[19] that she had may be described as so many occupations, the which habits may be likened to the characteristic or office which she had of saying useless things, and also of thinking and acting them, instead of behaving herein as is fitting to the soul's perfection. A soul may also have other desires wherewith it serves the desires of others, such as desires for ostentatious actions, compliments, acts of adulation, paying respect, endeavouring to appear well and giving pleasure to people by what it does, and many other useless things, whereby it tries to please people,[20] employing therein its care and its desire[21] and its work,[22] and, in short, all its possessions. All these offices, she says, she has no longer, because all her words and her thoughts and actions are now of God and are directed toward God, and have no longer the imperfections[23] which they were wont to have. And thus it is as though she were to say: I seek not now to give pleasure to my

[16] Ej, G, Sg omit: 'nor guards them for herself.'
[17] S: 'guards it, but that she has no other office.'
[18] G: 'all the acts.'
[19] Sg: 'habits and imperfections.'
[20] Ej, G, Sg omit: 'and many . . . please people.'
[21] A, B, Bg, S: 'the care for the desire.'
[22] Sg: 'and its work and thought.'
[23] Jaén reads here, by an error, 'the perfections.'

own desire, nor to that of others, nor do I occupy or busy myself in other useless pastimes[24] or in things of the world.

For now my exercise is in loving alone.

8. This is as though she had said: For now all these offices are devoted to the practice of the love of God—namely, all the ability wherewith my soul and my body are provided: memory, understanding and will, inward and outward senses, desires of the sensual part and of the spiritual part. All these work in love and for the sake of love, so that all that I do I do with love and all that I suffer I suffer with the pleasure of love. This is what David meant when he said: 'I will keep my strength for Thee.'[25]

9. Here it is to be noted that, when the soul attains to this estate, all its exercise, both of its spiritual part and of its sensual part, be it in doing or in suffering, after whatsoever manner it be, causes it ever greater love and greater delight in God, as we have said; and even the very exercise of prayer and converse with God, which it was frequently wont to have in considerations of a different kind and in other ways, is now wholly the exercise of love. So that, whether its commerce be with temporal things or whether its exercise be concerning spiritual things, a soul in this case can ever say that its exercise is now in loving alone.

10. Happy life and happy estate and happy the soul that arrives thereat, where all is now substance of love to it and joy and delight[26] of betrothal; wherein the Bride may indeed say to the Divine Spouse those words which she addresses to Him out of pure love in the Songs: 'All the new and the old apples I have kept for Thee.'[27] Which is as if she should say: My Beloved, I desire for Thy sake to have all that is hard and wearisome, and all that is sweet and delectable I desire for

24 [Bz: 'in thoughts or other pastimes which are useless.' Av: 'nor do I occupy myself in other useless thoughts or devote myself to them.' Bg: 'in other useless thoughts.' Ej, G, Sg: 'pastimes or business.'

25 Psalm lviii, 10 [A.V., lix, 9].

26 S: 'joy of delight.'

27 Canticles vii, 13. A omits the following words: 'Which is . . . desire for Thee.'

Thee. But the sense of this line, as we have interpreted it, is that the soul in this estate of the Spiritual Betrothal walks habitually in union and love of God, which is the common and habitual presence of the loving will in God.

Annotation for the Stanza Following

Truly this soul is lost to all things and is gained only to love, its spirit being now occupied in naught else. For this reason it fails even in that which belongs to the active life and in other outward exercises, in order really to fulfil the one thing that the Spouse said was needful, which is to abide with God and to be continually exercised in His love.[28] This He prizes and esteems to such a high degree that He reproved Martha because she desired to withdraw Mary from His feet, so as to occupy her in other activities in the Lord's service,[29] considering that she was doing everything and Mary was doing nothing, since Mary was resting with the Lord, the truth being just the contrary, for there is no better or more necessary work than love. Thus, again, in the Songs He defends the Bride, conjuring all creatures in the world (who are understood here by 'daughters of Jerusalem') not to stir the Bride from her spiritual sleep of love, nor to waken her or let her open her eyes to aught else, till she please.[30]

2. Here it is to be noted that, for so long as the soul has not reached this estate of union of love, it must needs practise love, both in the active life and in the contemplative; but when it reaches that estate it befits it not to be occupied in other outward acts and exercises[31] which might keep it back, however little, from that abiding[32] in love with God, although they may greatly conduce to the service of God; for a very little of this pure love is more precious, in the sight of God

[28] St. Luke x, 42.

[29] Sg substitutes: 'to the Lord's detriment' [*perjuicio*, an apparent error].

[30] Canticles iii, 5.

[31] S adds: 'not being of obligation.'

[32] A, Av, Bz, S have: *existencia* ['being,' 'existence'] for *asistencia* ['abiding,' 'presence'].

and the soul, and of greater profit to the Church, even though the soul appear to be doing nothing, than are all these other works together. For this reason Mary Magdalene, although she wrought great good with her preaching, and would have continued to do so, because of the great desire that she had to please her Spouse and to profit the Church, hid herself in the desert for thirty years in order to surrender herself truly to this love, since it seemed to her that in every way she would gain much more by so doing, because of the great profit and importance that there is to the Church in a very little of this love.

3. Therefore if any soul should have aught of this degree of solitary love, great wrong would be done[33] to it, and to the Church, if, even but for a brief space, one should endeavour to busy it in active or outward affairs, of however great moment; for, since God adjures the creatures not to awaken the soul from this love, who shall dare to do so and shall not be rebuked? After all, it was to reach this goal of love that we were created. Let those, then, that are great actives, that think to girdle[34] the world with their outward works and their preachings, take note here that they would bring far more profit to the Church and be far more pleasing to God (apart from the good example which they would give[35] of themselves) if they spent only half as much time in abiding with God in prayer, even had they not reached such a height as this. Of a surety they would accomplish more with one piece of work than they now do with a thousand, and that with less labour, since their prayer would be of such great deserving and they would have won such spiritual strength by it. For to act otherwise is to hammer vigorously and to accomplish little more than nothing, at times[36] nothing at all; at times, indeed, it may even be to do harm. May God forbid that your salt should begin to lose its savour;[37] since, although in such a case it may seem superficially that it has some effect, it will

33 Jaén reads: 'was done'; but all the other MSS. as in the text.
34 Ej: 'to convert.'
35 S: 'which would be given.'
36 S: 'even at times.'
37 [Lit., 'to become vain.']

have no substantial effect, for it is certain that good works cannot be done save in the strength[38] of God.

4. Oh, how much could be written here about this matter! But this is not the place for it. I have said what I have in order to explain this next stanza, for therein the soul herself makes reply to all those that impugn[39] this her holy leisure and that desire her to be ever working, and making great display and attracting the eye superficially, since they know nothing of the hidden root and source whence the water springs and whence comes all fruit. And thus the stanza says:

STANZA XXIX

If, then, on the common land, From henceforth I am neither seen nor found,
You will say that I am lost; That, wandering love-stricken, I lost my way and was found.[1]

Exposition

5. The soul, in this stanza, makes answer to a tacit reproach uttered by those of the world,[2] which they are wont to direct to such as give themselves truly to God; for they consider them extravagant in their queerness and aloofness[3] and in their general behaviour, and also say that they are useless in important matters and are lost with respect to all things that the world prizes and esteems. This reproach the soul meets in an excellent way, facing it very boldly and daringly, as it faces all else that the world can impute to it, for, having attained to a living love of God, it takes little heed thereof. And not only

---

[38] Ej, G, Sg: 'in the truth.'

[39] S omits 'all.' Jaén, A, B, make 'those' feminines [with evident reference to 'creatures,' 'daughters'].

[1] [*Lit.*, *ganada*, 'gained.' Bz, Ej and G, however, read *hallada*, 'found.']

[2] A: 'by the worldly.'

[3] Sg: 'and recollectedness and aloofness.'

so, but the Bride herself confesses it in this stanza, and glories
and boasts of having done such things and become lost to
the world and to herself for the sake of her Beloved. And
thus[4] her meaning in this stanza, where she speaks to those
of the world, is that, if they no longer see her in the places
which she frequented formerly, following the pastimes which
she was wont to follow in the world, they are to say and to
believe that she has become lost to them and is withdrawn
from them, and that she considers this so great a gain[5] that
she has herself desired thus to be lost in going after her Beloved and seeking Him, enkindled as she is with love for
Him. And, that they may see how great a gain to her is this
loss, and may not consider it to be folly or delusion, she says
that this loss was her gain and that she became lost of set
purpose.

**If, then, on the common land,   From henceforth I am neither
seen nor found,[6]**

6. By 'common land' is ordinarily meant a place common
to all, where people are wont to come together to have solace
and recreation, and where likewise shepherds pasture their
flocks; and thus the soul here understands by this common
land the world, where worldly folk pursue their pastimes and
converse, and pasture the flocks of their desires. Herein the
soul says to those of the world that if she is not seen or found
as she was before she became wholly God's, they are to consider her, by reason of this very fact, as lost; and that they
may say this, since she rejoices in it and desires them to say it.
She adds:

You will say that I am lost;

7. He that loves is not abashed before the world concerning
the works which he does for God, neither does he hide them

4 S inserts 'now.'
5 S omits: 'and that . . . a gain.' Av, Bz, Ej, G, Sg read: 'and let
them understand also.' Jaén: 'and that she considers this so well.'
B, Bg: 'and that she considers this well.'
6 Ej, G, Sg omit the commentary on these lines.

with shame, even though the whole world condemn them. For he that is ashamed to confess the Son of God before men, and ceases to do His works, the same Son of God, as He says through Saint Luke, will be ashamed to confess him before His Father.[7] Wherefore the soul, with the courage of her love, takes pride in having been seen doing such work to the glory of her Beloved and having become lost therein to all things of the world. Wherefore she says: 'You will say that I am lost.'

8. Few spiritual persons attain to this perfect boldness and determination in their works; for, although some attempt to do so and carry on this practice, and some consider themselves to be very far advanced therein, they never completely lose themselves with respect to certain points, whether connected with the world or with their own natures, nor do they do work for Christ which is perfect and completely detached, looking not at what will be said of them or at what will appear. Such as these will be unable to say, 'You will say that I am lost,' for they are not lost to themselves in their works; they are still ashamed to confess Christ in their works before men; they have respect for things of the world; they live not[8] truly in Christ.

That, wandering love-stricken,

9. This is to say that, wandering stricken with love for God, and practising the virtues,

I lost my way[9] and was found.[10]

10. Knowing the words of the Spouse in the Gospel, namely, that no man can serve two masters, but that he must needs fail one,[11] the soul here says that, in order not to fail God, she has failed all that is not God—that is, all other things and her very self, losing all this for love of Him. He that is

---

[7] St. Luke ix, 26. The MSS. add 'Saint Matthew' after 'Saint Luke.'
[8] S: 'wherefore they live not.'
[9] [Or 'I became lost,' as sometimes below.]
[10] [*Lit.*, 'gained,' and so throughout the paragraph. The play of words (see n. 15, p. 421) has greater point on that account.] Ej has *hallada* [see p. 418, n. 1, above.]
[11] St. Matthew vi, 24.

indeed in love allows himself to be lost to all things else, that he may have the greater gain as to that which he loves; wherefore the soul says here that she became lost—that is, that she allowed herself to be lost of set purpose. And this is after two manners, as follows. First, she is lost to herself; she takes no thought for herself in any way, but only for the Beloved, surrenders herself to Him freely, and disinterestedly,[12] and in this wise becomes lost to herself, desiring no gain for herself in any way soever. Secondly, she is lost to all things,[13] and takes no heed of aught[14] pertaining to herself, but only of those things that concern the Beloved; and this is to become lost, namely, to desire that others may gain her.[15]

11. Such is he that walks love-stricken for God, and that aspires to no gain or prize, but only to lose all things and to be lost to himself in his will for God's sake, which he holds as gain. And gain it is, even as Saint Paul declares, when he says: *Mori lucrum*.[16] That is: My dying for Christ is my spiritual gain as to all things and to Himself. And therefore the soul says:[17] 'I was found'; for he that cannot be lost to himself is not found, but is indeed lost, even as Our Lord says in the Gospel, in these words: 'He who will gain his life for himself, the same shall lose it; and he who loses his life for My sake, the same shall gain it.'[18] And if we desire to understand this said line more spiritually and more to the purpose for the which it is here used, it must be known that when a soul on the spiritual road has reached such a point that it has become lost to all natural roads[19] and ways of progress in converse with God, so that it seeks Him no longer by meditations or forms or feelings or any other means which belong to crea-

[12] Cf. p. 146, n. 8, above.

[13] [*Lit.*, 'the second, to all things'] except in S, which reads as in the text.

[14] So S. The other authorities have: 'of all things.'

[15] [*que es tener gana que la ganen.* Cf. p. 146, n. 10, above.]

[16] Philippians i, 21.

[17] S: 'My dying is to profit spiritually, and gain for Christ. Therefore the soul says.'

[18] St. Matthew xvi, 25.

[19] Ej, G, Sg: 'natural manners.'

tures and to senses, but has passed beyond all this and beyond all modes and manners of its own, having converse with God and fruition of Him in faith and love:[20] then it says that it has indeed gained God, for indeed it has become lost to all that is not God and to that which is in itself.

Annotation for the Stanza Following

Now, therefore, that the soul has been gained in this manner, all that it does is gain; for all the strength of its faculties is converted into spiritual intercourse, with the Beloved, of most delectable interior love, wherein the interior communications that pass between God and the soul are of such delicate and sublime delight that there is no mortal tongue which can express it, nor human understanding that can understand it. For even as the betrothed maiden, on the day of her betrothal, is aware of naught save that this is love's delight and festival, and cares only to bring out all her jewels and her adornments, to give pleasure and delight therewith to her spouse, and the spouse shows her nothing less than all his riches and excellences, to give her joy and solace, so here, in this spiritual betrothal, where the soul indeed feels that which the Bride says in the Songs, namely: 'I to my Beloved and my Beloved to me,'[21] the virtues and adornments of the Bride-Soul and the magnificences and adornments of the Spouse, the Son of God, come to light and are displayed, so that the feast of this betrothal may be celebrated, and the good things and delights of each of the two may be communicated to the other with the wine of delectable love in the Holy Spirit. To express this the soul addresses the Spouse and says in this stanza:

[20] S: 'but, passing only beyond all this and beyond all methods of its own and beyond all manners, has converse with God and fruition of Him in faith and love.'
[21] Canticles [vi, 3,] vii, 10.

STANZA XXX

With flowers and emeralds   Gathered in the cool mornings
We will make the garlands flowering in thy love   And inter-
woven with one hair from my head.

Exposition

2. In this stanza the Bride[1] speaks again with the Spouse
in the communion and refreshment of love, and that which
she does therein is to treat of the solace and delight that the
Bride-Soul and the Son of God have in the possession of the
riches of each other's virtues and gifts and in the mutual
exercise of these, having fruition thereof between themselves
in communion of love.[2] Therefore, in speaking with Him,
she says that they will make rich garlands of gifts and virtues,
acquired and gained in a pleasant and convenient season,
beautified and made graceful in the love which He has for her
and sustained and preserved in the love which she has for
Him. Wherefore she calls this fruition of the virtues making
garlands of them; because in all of them, as in flowers that are
in garlands, they both have joy in the mutual love which each
bears to the other.

With flowers and emeralds

3. The flowers are the virtues of the soul and the emeralds
are the gifts which it has of God.[3] These flowers and emeralds
are

Gathered in the cool mornings[4]

[1] S: 'the Bride-Soul.'
[2] Ej, G: 'in communion of love and of union.' Sg: 'in communion of union of love.'
[3] S: 'which it has in God.'
[4] G: 'cool mountains.'

4. This signifies that they are gained and acquired in youth, which is life's cool morning.[5] She says they are 'gathered,' because the virtues that are acquired in this time of youth are choice[6] and most acceptable to God, since in the season of youth there is[7] more resistance on the part of the vices to their acquisition, and a greater inclination and readiness to lose them on the part of nature; and also because, since the soul begins to pluck them from this season of her youth onward, the virtues which she acquires are more perfect and more choice.[8] She calls these times of youth the cool mornings, because even as the cool of the morning is more pleasant in spring than are other parts of the day, even so is the virtue of youth before God. And these cool mornings may also be interpreted as the acts of love wherein the virtues are acquired, which are more pleasing to God than are cool mornings to the sons[9] of men.

5. Likewise are understood here by the cool mornings works which are performed at times of spiritual aridity and hardship, which are denoted by the coolness of winter mornings;[10] and these works, performed for God's sake at times of spiritual aridity and hardship, are greatly prized by God, because the virtues and gifts are richly acquired therein. And those which are acquired after this manner and with labour are for the most part choicer, rarer and more lasting than if they were acquired only at times of spiritual sweetness and delight; for in aridity and hardship and labour[11] virtue takes root, even as God said to Saint Paul, in these words: 'Virtue is made perfect in weakness.'[12] Wherefore, in order to extol the excellence and the virtues whereof garlands are to be made for the Beloved, it is well said: 'Gathered in the cool mornings,' because the Beloved has great joy only in those flowers and emeralds—which are virtues and gifts—that

[5] [*Lit.*, 'mornings.'] G: 'mountains.' Cf. p. 148, n. 3.
[6] [On this word, see p. 148, n. 4.]
[7] S: '. . . to God, this being the season when there is.'
[8] A, S omit: 'and more choice.'
[9] Ej, G: 'to the eyes' [*ojos* for *hijos*].
[10] Ej, G, Sg: 'by the cool winter mornings.'
[11] Ej, Sg: 'labour and temptation.' G: 'hardship and temptation.'
[12] 2 Corinthians xii, 9.

are choice and perfect,[13] and not in those which are imperfect. Wherefore the Bride-Soul says here that for Him, and of these flowers and emeralds,

We will make the garlands

6. For the understanding hereof it must be known that all the virtues and gifts which the soul, and God in the soul, acquire, are in the soul as a garden of various flowers wherewith it is marvellously beautified, even as with a vesture of rare variety. For the better comprehension hereof it must be known that, even as the material flowers are gathered one by one and made into the garland (which is gradually formed from them), so, after the same manner, as the spiritual flowers of virtues and gifts are acquired one by one, they are gradually set in order in the soul.[14] And, when they have all been acquired, the garland of perfection is then completed in the soul, so that both the soul and the Spouse[15] rejoice, when they are beautified and adorned with this garland, even as in the estate of perfection. These are the garlands which the Bride says have to be made, and this is to gird and surround[16] oneself with a variety of flowers and emeralds, which are perfect gifts and virtues, in order to appear worthily with this beauteous and precious adornment before the face of the King, and to merit being placed on an equality with Him even as a queen by His side, which the soul merits through the beauty of its variety. Thus David, speaking with Christ in such a case, said: *Astitit Regina a dextris tuis in vestitu deaurato, circumdata varietate.*[17] Which signifies: Upon thy right hand did stand the queen in vesture of gold, surrounded with variety. Which is as much as to say: Upon Thy right hand did she stand vested in perfect love and surrounded with a variety of perfect virtues and gifts. She says not: 'I alone will make the garlands,' nor yet 'Thou alone wilt make them,'

[13] Ej, G, Sg omit: 'and gifts.' G, Sg read: 'and perfections' for 'and perfect.'

[14] Sg: 'they gradually enter the soul.'

[15] S: '. . . in the soul, where she and the Spouse.'

[16] Ej, G, Sg: 'and adorn.'

[17] Psalm xliv, 10 [A.V., xlv, 9].

but 'We will make them, both of us together';[18] for the virtues cannot be wrought by the soul alone, nor can she attain to them alone, without the help of God, neither does God work them alone in the soul without her co-operation; for, although it is true that every good gift and every perfect gift cometh from above, descending from the Father of lights, as Saint James says,[19] yet no such thing as this is received apart from the capacity[20] and without the co-operation of the soul that receives it. The Bride, in the Songs, speaks of this with the Spouse, saying: 'Draw me, we will run after Thee.'[21] So the movement towards goodness must come from God, and from God alone, as is here declared; but the writer says not that he alone will run, or she alone, but that they will run both of them together—that is, that God and the soul will work together.[22]

7. This short line is understood with great propriety of the Church and of Christ, wherein His Bride, who is the Church, speaks with Him, saying: 'We will make the garlands.' By garlands are here understood all the holy souls begotten by Christ in the Church, each one of whom is as a garland adorned with flowers of virtues and gifts, and all of whom together are a garland for the head of Christ the Spouse. And likewise by the beauteous garlands can be understood the laurel-crowns[23] (which is another name for them) made likewise by Christ and the Church. These are of three kinds. The first is of the beauteous white flowers[24] of all the virgins, each with its crown[25] of virginity, and all of them together will be a crown to be placed upon the head of Christ the

---

[18] S abbreviates: 'And she says not "I will make," nor "Thou wilt make" the garlands alone, but "both [of us] together."'

[19] St. James i, 17.

[20] Sg: 'the humility.'

[21] Canticles i, 3 [A.V., i, 4].

[22] Ej, G, Sg omit: 'that God and the soul.' S re-arranges the clauses of the last sentence without changing the meaning.

[23] [Lit., lauréola, 'laurel-crown,' differing only by one letter from auréola, halo.] Bg has 'roses' for 'laurel-crowns.'

[24] S: 'of beauty and white flowers.'

[25] [Throughout this paragraph, except where otherwise stated, the word rendered 'crown' is lauréola.]

Spouse. The second crown is that of the resplendent flowers of the holy doctors,[26] and all of them together will be a crown to place upon the head of Christ above that of the virgins.[27] The third is composed of the crimson carnations of the martyrs,[28] each one likewise with his martyr's crown, all of which together will be one crown forming as it were a crown[29] to add to that of Christ the Spouse. So greatly beautified and so gracious to the sight with these three garlands[30] will be Christ the Spouse that there will be said in Heaven that which the Bride says of Him in the Songs, namely: 'Go forth, daughters of Sion, and see King Solomon with the crown wherewith his mother crowned him on the day of his betrothal, and on the day of the joy of his heart.'[31] We will make these garlands, then she says:

Flowering in thy love

8. The flower which belongs to the works and virtues[32] is the grace[33] and virtue which they derive from the love of God, without which not only would they not be flowering but they would all be dry and worthless before God, even though humanly they were perfect. But because He gives His grace and love these works flower in His love.

And interwoven with one hair from my head.

9. This hair of hers is her will and the love which she has for the Beloved, the which love possesses and performs the same office as the thread in the garland;[34] for even as the

---

[26] Ej, G, Sg add: 'each with his crown as a doctor.'

[27] Bg, Ej, G omit: 'above that of the virgins.' Bg also omits: 'to place.'

[28] Ej, G, Sg: 'the third [is] of the martyrs, which is of crimson carnations.'

[29] [In the last line 'crown' is *lauréola;* here it is *remate.*]

[30] Ej, G, Sg have 'laurel-crowns' [*lauréolas*] for 'garlands.'

[31] Canticles iii, 11.

[32] Ej, G, Sg: 'to the virtues.'

[33] Av: 'is the gain.'

[34] Av: 'the same office that He performed in the garland.' [Only one letter is different from that of Jaén here, Av reading: *él hizo* for *el hilo.*]

thread binds[35] and ties the flowers in the garland, so the
love of the soul binds and ties the virtues in the soul and
sustains them within her. For, as Saint Paul says,[36] charity
is the bond and link of perfection. So that in this love of the
soul the supernatural gifts and virtues are so essentially bound
together that, if it were to break by failing God, then all the
virtues of the soul would become unbound[37] and would fail,
even as the flowers would fall apart if the thread of the
garland were to be broken. So that it suffices not for God to
have love towards us that He may give us virtues; we too
must have love towards Him that we may receive and keep
them. She says 'one hair' of her head, and not 'many hairs,'[38]
in order to convey the fact that her will is now alone,[39] detached from all other hairs, which are strange affections for
others. Herein she markedly insists upon the worth and price
of these garlands of virtues; for, when love is single and
firmly fixed upon God, in the way that is here described, the
virtues are likewise perfect and complete, and flower freely
in the love of God; for then the love which He has toward
the soul is inestimable, even as the soul feels also.

10. Now if I desired to explain the beauty of the interweaving which characterizes these flowers of virtues and emeralds,[40] or to say aught of the strength and majesty with
which the order and arrangement of them endow the soul
and the fairness and grace wherewith this vesture of variety
adorns it, I should find no words and terms wherein to
express myself. Of the devil, God says in the Book of
Job[41] that his body is like shields of molten metal, garnished
with scales knit together among themselves so closely that
each is joined to another in such a way that the air cannot
pass between them. Now if the devil has such strength in

---

[35] S: 'even as in her He binds.'

[36] Colossians iii, 14.

[37] Ej, G, Sg: 'become loosed' [see p. 152, n. 17].

[38] S: 'and not "many."'

[39] Ej, G, Sg: 'is now set upon Him alone.'

[40] Ej: 'of virtues and garlands.' G, Sg: 'of virtues and garlands
with the emeralds.'

[41] Job xli, 6–7.

himself, through being clothed with scales of malice[42] all compact and interwoven one with another (all of which is signified[43] by the scales), that his body can be described as being like shields of molten metal, the scales of malice being in themselves weakness, how great will be the strength of this soul clothed entirely in strong virtues, so compacted and intertwined among themselves that there is room between them for no foulness or imperfection! Each one with its strength adds strength to the soul,[44] with its beauty it adds beauty, with its valour and price it makes it rich, and with its majesty it adds to it dominion and greatness. How marvellous, then, to the spiritual sight will be this Bride-Soul with the adornment[45] of these gifts at the right hand of the King her Spouse! 'Beautiful are thy steps in shoes,[46] O Prince's daughter,' says the Spouse of her in the Songs.[47] And he says 'Prince's daughter' to denote the princely character which she possesses here. And if he calls her beautiful in her shoes, what will she be in her vesture!

11. And because not only has she wondrous beauty in the vesture of these flowers but she also derives a fearful strength and power from the arrangement and order of them, and also from the intertwining[48] of the emeralds of innumerable Divine gifts, the Spouse says of her likewise in the said Songs: 'Thou art terrible, arrayed like the armies[49] of the camps.'[50] For these virtues and gifts of God, while they refresh with their spiritual fragrance, minister strength also with their substance when they are united in the soul. For this cause, when the Bride in the Songs was weak and sick of love, because she had not succeeded in binding and entwining these flowers and emeralds with the hair of her love, and when she desired to

---

[42] [*Lit.*, 'with malices.']
[43] S: 'is denoted.'
[44] Jaén, A, Av, Bz, Ej, G: 'adds to the soul.'
[45] Ej, G: 'with the manner and adornment.'
[46] Ej, G, Sg have: *con el calzado* [for *en los calzados:* the variant is best translated 'with shoes,' 'shod'; cf. Canticles vii, 1, A.V.].
[47] Canticles vii, 1.
[48] G, Sg: 'the interior.'
[49] S: 'the hosts.'
[50] Canticles vi, 3.

strengthen herself by means of the said bond and union of them, she entreated Him for this union in these words, saying: 'Strengthen me with flowers, compass me about with apples, for I am swooning with love.'[51] Meaning by the flowers, the virtues, and by the apples, the other gifts.

Annotation for the Stanza Following

I think it has been explained how by means of the interweaving[52] of these garlands and the planting of them in the soul this Bride-Soul endeavours to describe the Divine union of love that exists in this estate between her and God. The Spouse is the flowers, for, as He says,[53] He is the flower of the field[54] and the lily of the valleys. And the hair of the love of the soul is, as we have said, that which binds this flower of flowers and unites it with herself. Now, as the Apostle says, love is the bond of perfection,[55] which is union with God, and the soul is the sheaf[56] wherein these garlands are gathered together, since the soul is the subject of this glory, appearing not now to be that which it was aforetime, but the very flower of perfection with the perfection and beauty of all flowers; since this thread of love binds the two—that is to say, God and the soul[57]—with such firmness,[58] and so unites and transforms them and makes them one in love, that, although they differ in substance, yet in glory and in appearance the soul seems to be God and God the soul.

2. Such is this union. It is wondrous above all that can be

[51] Canticles ii, 5.

[52] Sg has *entretenimiento* ['arrangement'] for *entretejimiento* ['interweaving'].

[53] Canticles ii, 1.

[54] S modifies: 'the Bride desires in this last stanza to explain the Divine union of love which exists between God and her in this estate, since the Spouse, in [i.e., among] the flowers, is the flower of the field.'

[55] Colossians iii, 14. S adds: 'love must be maintained above all things.'

[56] Bg: 'exercise.'

[57] S: 'for since this thread of love binds God and the soul.'

[58] Sg: 'with such fury' [i.e., 'vehemence'].

expressed. Some conception of it may be formed from that which the Scripture says of Jonathan and David in the First Book of the Kings, where it says that the love which Jonathan had to David was so strait that it knit the soul of Jonathan with the soul of David.[59] If the love of one man for another man was so strong that it could knit one soul with another,[60] what will be the union[61] that is to be made between the soul and God its Spouse by the love which the soul has to God Himself, especially since the principal Lover here is God Himself,[62] Who with the omnipotence of His boundless love absorbs the soul in Himself, with more efficacy and force than that of a torrent of fire absorbing a drop of morning dew, which is wont to rise and dissolve[63] in the air? The hair, then, that performs such a work of union must needs, of a surety, be very strong and subtle, since with such great force it penetrates the parts that it binds; for the which cause, in the stanza following, the soul declares the properties of this her beauteous hair, saying:

[59] 1 Kings xviii, 1 [A.V., 1 Samuel xviii, 1].

[60] S reads [from the beginning of the paragraph]: 'Such is this union, wondrous above all that can be expressed. And of it some degree is described in that which the Scripture says in the First Book of the Kings, concerning the love which Jonathan had to David, which was so strait that it knit the soul of the one with the other. *Anima Jonatæ conglutinata est animæ David.* Then if the love of one man for another was so strong that it could knit their souls,' etc.

[61] [*Lit.*, 'the knitting.']

[62] Ej, G: 'that principal Lover is God Himself.' Sg: 'that Prince-Lover is God Himself.'

[63] [*Lit.*, 'to fly, dissolved in the air.'] Ej, G, Sg read: *resulta* ['issues,' 'results'] for *resuelta* ['dissolved'].

STANZA XXXI

By that hair alone   Which thou regardedst fluttering on my
  neck,
Beholding it upon my neck, thou wert captivated,   And wert
  wounded[1] by one of mine eyes.

Exposition

3. Three things are signified by the soul in this stanza.
First, she declares that that love[2] wherewith the virtues are
bound together is nothing less than a strong love, for in truth
it must be such in order that the virtues may be preserved.
Secondly, she says that God was greatly captivated by this her
hair of love, seeing that it was one only and was so strong.
Thirdly, she says that God was intimately enamoured of her,
seeing the purity and integrity of her faith. And she says
thus:

By that hair alone   Which thou regardedst fluttering on my
  neck,

4. The neck signifies that fortitude whereon, it is said, was
fluttering the hair of love, wherewith are interwoven the virtues, and this is love in fortitude. For it suffices not, in order
to keep the virtues together, that there be one hair only; it
must also be strong, so that no contrary vice may break it in
any part of[3] the garland of perfection. For the virtues are
bound together by this hair of the love of the soul in such a
way that, if it were to break[4] in any place, then, as we have
said, it would be lost in them all; for, where one of the virtues
is, there are they all, and likewise, where there is one lacking,
they are lacking all. And she says that this hair fluttered upon
her neck,[5] because, in the fortitude of the soul,[6] this love

1 [On this word, see p. 75, n. 5.]
2 Ej, Sg: 'that that hair.' G: 'that that hair-love.'
3 Bz: 'may anywhere enter.'
4 Av, Bz: 'to be lost.'
5 A: 'upon her hair.'
6 Ej, G, Sg add: 'that is, upon the neck of the soul.'

flies toward God with great fortitude and lightness, without
being hindered by aught soever. And, even as the breeze stirs
the hair and causes it to flutter upon the neck, even so does
the breeze of the Holy Spirit move and excite strong love
that it may make flights to God; for, without this Divine wind,
which moves the faculties to the practice of Divine love,
the virtues work not, neither have any effect,[7] although they
be in the soul. And, by saying that the Beloved regarded
this hair fluttering upon her neck, she signifies how great is
the love of God for strong love;[8] for to regard is to behold
with particular attention and esteem for that which one beholds, and strong love causes God to turn His eyes often to
behold it. She continues thus:

Beholding it upon my neck,

5. This the soul says, in order to convey the fact that not
alone did God prize and esteem this her love, when He saw
that it was alone,[9] but likewise that He loved it when He saw
that it was strong; because for God to look is for God to
love, even as for God to regard is, as we have said, for Him
to esteem that which He regards. And in this line she speaks
again of the neck, saying of the hair: 'Thou didst behold it
upon my neck,' because, as has been said, that is the cause of
His loving her so greatly, namely that He saw her in her fortitude, so that it is as if she had said: Thou didst love it when
Thou didst see that it was strong without weakness or fear,
and alone without any other love, fluttering with lightness
and fervour.

6. Until now God had not looked upon this hair[10] in such
a way as to be taken captive[11] by it, because He had not seen
it alone and detached[12] from the remaining hairs of other
loves and desires, affections and pleasures, and thus it[13] flut-

---

[7] [*Lit.*, 'make their effects.']
[8] Ej, G, Sg: 'for the strong soul.'
[9] Ej, G, Sg: 'when He saw that it was alone and strong.'
[10] Bz: 'this neck.'
[11] A, G, Bg, Ej, S read: *prenderse* ['be taken'] for *prendarse* ['be
taken captive'].
[12] Ej, G: 'strayed,' 'deviated.'
[13] S: 'wherewith it.'

tered not alone upon the neck of strength, but now that, through mortifications and trials and temptations and penance, it has succeeded in becoming so detached and so strong that it can be broken by no force[14] and by no occasion whatsoever, God looks upon it and takes and binds in it the flowers of these garlands, since it is now sufficiently strong to keep them bound together in the soul.

7. But what these temptations and trials are, and of what nature, and how far they can work[15] in the soul that it[16] may be able to attain to this strength of love, wherein God is united to the soul—of all this something is said in[17] the exposition of the four stanzas which begin: 'O living flame of love.' The soul, having passed through these experiences, has attained to such a degree of love that she has now merited Divine union. Wherefore she says next:

Thou wert captivated,

8. Oh, thing that art worthy of all acceptation[18] and joy, that God should be captivated by a hair! The cause of this so precious capture is that He has been pleased to stop to look at the fluttering of the hair,[19] as is said in the lines preceding; because, as we have said, for God to look is for Him to love. For if He, in His great mercy,[20] had not first beheld us and loved us, as Saint John says,[21] and humbled Himself, He would never have been captivated by the fluttering of the hair of our lowly love, since this love could not soar so high as to attain to the capture of this Divine bird of the heights. But

[14] Av, Bz: 'strength.'

[15] [Lit., 'reach.']

[16] G, Sg: 'reach to the height that it.'

[17] S: 'in the Dark Night and in.' [On the reference, see Vol. III, p. 4, of The Complete Works of St. John of the Cross, translated and edited by E. Allison Peers; The Newman Press; Westminster, Maryland.]

[18] Ej, G: 'of all attention.' S: 'of all esteem.'

[19] S adds: 'upon the neck.'

[20] A, S: 'in His grace and mercy.' G: 'in His grace of mercy.'

[21] 1 St. John iv, 10 [or 19].

since He humbled Himself to look upon us and to incite us[22] to fly in love and to make us to fly ever higher, and thus gave to our love the worth and strength necessary thereto,[23] He Himself was taken captive by the flight of this hair—that is, He Himself was glad and pleased, wherefore He was captivated; and this is the meaning of the phrase: 'Beholding it upon my neck, Thou wert captivated.' For it is a very credible thing that a bird of lowly flight should be able to capture a royal eagle flying high, if the eagle descends to its lowliness, desiring to be caught.

And wert wounded by one of mine eyes.

9. By the eye is here understood faith. She says by 'one' of them alone, and that He was 'wounded' by it, because if the faith and fidelity[24] of the soul toward God were not alone, but were mingled with respect or courtesy to some other, she would not succeed in wounding God by love. Wherefore it must be by but one eye alone that the Beloved is wounded, even as it is by one hair alone that He is taken captive. And the love wherewith the Spouse is taken captive by the Bride in this singleness and fidelity that He sees in her is so intimate that, if He was[25] taken captive by the hair of her love, by the eye of her faith His captivity is made closer with so fast a knot that there is inflicted upon Him a wound of love, through the great tenderness of the affection wherewith He loves her, and she enters into His love the more deeply.

10. This same figure of the hair and of the eye is used by the Spouse in the Songs, where He speaks with the Bride, saying: 'Thou hast wounded My heart, My sister; thou hast wounded My heart with one of thine eyes and with one hair of thy neck.'[26] Herein He twice declares that she has wounded His heart—namely, with the eye and with the hair. Wherefore the soul in the stanza describes the hair and the eye, de-

---

[22] Thus Ej, G, Sg [which P. Silverio follows]. The other authorities have: '. . . of the heights, to [i.e., that He might] look upon us and incite us.' S reads similarly with slight verbal differences.

[23] S adds: 'if He beheld not.'

[24] A: 'faith and felicity.'

[25] S: 'if He is.'

[26] Canticles iv, 9. [See p. 156, n. 13, above.]

noting therein the union which she has with God, according
to the understanding and according to the will; for faith, signified by the eye, is subdued in the understanding by faith
and in the will by love. In this union[27] the soul here glories
and gives thanks to her Spouse for this favour, which she has
received from His hand, esteeming it a great benefit that He
has been pleased to take pleasure in her love and to be captivated thereby. Here might one meditate upon the joy, gladness and delight which the soul will have with such a prisoner,
since she has for so long been His prisoner and for so long
has been enamoured of Him.

Annotation for the Stanza Following

Great is the power and the importunity of love, since it takes
captive and binds[28] God Himself.[29] Happy the soul that
loves, since it holds God a prisoner, subjected to all that it
wills; for He has this quality that, if He be taken by love, and
taken willingly, He will be made to do what is willed of Him;
but otherwise, one cannot speak to Him[30] or do aught with
Him, although one make the greatest efforts; for through love
He will be bound[31] with a hair. The soul, knowing this, and
also that, far in excess of her merits, He has granted her such
great favours as to raise her to such high love with such rich
endowments[32] of gifts and virtues, she attributes it all to
Him[33] in the following stanza, saying:

27 Ej, G, Sg modify: 'is subdued in the understanding, and love,
signified by the hair, in the will. Wherefore there is union in the
understanding by faith and in the will by love. In this union . . .'

28 A, Bg have *llaga* ['wounds'] for *liga* ['binds'].

29 Ej, G, Sg give this sentence to Stanza XXXI, and begin the
Annotation: 'Happy the soul . . .'

30 Av, Bz have: *hallarle* ['find Him'] for *hablarle* ['speak to
Him'].

31 So the MSS. Jaén reads: 'He is bound.'

32 [The Spanish word, *prendas,* is allied in derivation and meaning with the verb *prendar,* to take captive, used so frequently
above.]

33 Ej, G, Sg: 'with such just endowments of gifts and virtues, the
soul attributes it only [*solo lo* for *se lo*] to Him.'

STANZA XXXII

**When thou didst look on[1] me,   Thine eyes imprinted upon me
their grace;[2]
For this cause didst thou love me greatly,   Whereby mine eyes
deserved to adore that which they saw in thee.**

Exposition

2. It is the property of perfect love to be unwilling to accept or take aught for itself, and to attribute naught to itself, but all things to the Beloved. This is so even with our lower love—how much more, then, with love for God, which reason so urgently requires of us! Wherefore, since in the last two stanzas the Bride appears to have been attributing something to herself, as where she has said that she will make garlands together with the Spouse, and that they will be interwoven[3] with a hair of her head,[4] which is work of no small moment and esteem; and since afterwards she declares, exultingly, that the Spouse has been taken captive by this hair and wounded by her eye, wherein likewise she appears to be attributing to herself great deserving; now in the present stanza she desires to explain her meaning and to correct an erroneous conclusion which might be drawn from this, for she is apprehensive and fearful that some worth and merit will be attributed to her, and that for that reason there will be attributed to God less than that which is His due and than that which she desires. So she attributes it all to Him, and at the same time gives Him thanks for it, saying to Him that the reason for His being taken captive by the hair[5] of her love

---

[1] Cf. p. 237, n. 36, above.
[2] Sg: 'thy grace.' See p. 237, n. 37, above.
[3] S omits: 'and that they will be.'
[4] Av: 'with her neck.'
[5] A, B, Ej, G have 'taken' for 'taken captive.' Av: 'by the neck.'
[See also p. 157, n. 3.]

and wounded by the eye of her faith is that He has granted her the favour of looking upon her with love, and of thus making her graceful and pleasing in His sight; and that through this grace and worth which she has received of Him she has merited His love, and has now in herself become worthy to adore her Beloved pleasingly and to do works worthy of His grace and love. The stanza continues:

When thou didst look on me,

3. That is to say, with affection of love, for we have already said that for God to look signifies here for God to love.

Thine eyes imprinted upon me their grace;[6]

4. By the eyes of the Spouse is here understood His merciful Divinity, which, turning in mercy to the soul, imprints upon her and infuses in her His love and grace, beautifying her thereby and raising her up so as to make her the consort of His own Divinity. And, seeing the dignity and height wherein God has set her, the soul says:

For this cause didst thou love me greatly,

5. To love greatly[7] is more than to love simply: it is, as it were, to love doubly[8]—that is, for two motives or causes. And thus in this line the soul describes the two motives and causes for love which He has towards her; for the which not only[9] did He love her when He was taken captive by her hair, but He loved her greatly when He was wounded by her eye. And she says in this line that the reason for which He loved her so greatly and so intimately was that, when He looked upon her, He desired to grant her grace that He might be pleased with her, that she might give Him her love—that is, the hair—and that, by means of His charity, He might form faith[10] in her, which is her eye. And thus she says: 'For this cause didst Thou love me greatly.' Because for God to set His grace in

6 Sg: 'thy grace.'

7 See p. 158, n. 9, above.

8 Ej, G, Sg: 'to love delicately.'

9 Ej, G, Sg omit 'not only.' Sg omits the next few lines and reads: 'by her hair, that He might form in her, with His charity,' etc.

10 Bz, S read 'inform' for 'form.'

the soul is for Him to make her worthy and fit to love Him; and thus it is as if she had said: Since Thou hadst set Thy grace in me, giving me pledges worthy of Thy love, therefore didst Thou love me greatly—that is, for that reason didst Thou give me more grace.[11] This is that which is said by Saint John: That He gives grace for the grace that He has given,[12] which is to give more grace; for without His grace it is impossible to merit His grace.

6. For the understanding of this it is to be noted that, even as God loves naught apart from Himself, even so He loves naught in a lowlier way[13] than He loves Himself; for He loves all things with respect to Himself and thus love has the final reason; wherefore He loves not things for that which they are in themselves. Therefore for God to love the soul is for Him to set it, after a certain manner, in Himself, making it equal to Himself, and thus He loves the soul in Himself with the same love[14] wherewith He loves Himself. Wherefore, in each of its acts, inasmuch as each is performed in God, the soul merits the love of God, because, set as it is in this grace and in this lofty place, it merits God Himself in its every act. Wherefore the Bride next says:

Whereby mine eyes deserved[15] . . .

7. That is to say, in that favour and grace which the eyes of Thy mercy wrought in me, when Thou didst look on me, making me pleasing in Thine eyes and worthy to be seen of Thee, mine eyes deserved

. . . to adore that which they saw in thee.

8. This is as much as to say: The faculties of my soul, O my Spouse, which are the eyes wherewith Thou canst be seen

[11] Ej, G, Sg omit: 'that is . . . more grace.'
[12] St. John i, 16.
[13] So Jaén, A, B, Bz; also the Sanlúcar Codex (see p. 159, above). A corrector emended the Jaén MS. ('higher' for 'lowlier'). Ej, G, Sg have: 'more advantageous'; S: 'higher'; Av: 'loves naught more.'
[14] Ej, G, Sg read: 'making it equal to Himself with the same love.'
[15] See p. 159, n. 13, above.

of me, have deserved to rise and look upon Thee; the which aforetime, with the wretchedness of their base operation and natural possessions, had fallen and were very low. For that the soul should be able to look upon God is that it should do works[16] in the grace of God; and thus the faculties of the soul have had merit in adoration because they have adored in the grace of their God, wherein all operation is meritorious. Enlightened and raised up as they are, therefore, by His grace and favour, they have adored[17] that which they have already seen in Him, which by reason of their blindness and wretchedness they saw not aforetime. What, then, was it that they had already seen? They had seen greatness[18] of virtues, abundance of sweetness, immense goodness, love and mercy in God, numberless benefits which the soul had received of Him, both when[19] it was very near to God and when it was not so. All this the eyes of the soul have now deserved to adore meritoriously, because they are now full of grace and pleasing to the Spouse. Before this they deserved neither to adore nor to see, nor even to consider aught of this concerning God, for great is the grossness[20] and blindness of the soul that is without His grace.

9. There is much to be borne in mind here, and much at which to grieve, when we consider how far the soul unenlightened with the love of God[21] is from doing that which is of obligation for it. For it has an obligation to recognize these and innumerable other favours, both temporal[22] and spiritual, which it has received from Him, and which it receives at every moment, and to adore and serve God ceaselessly with all its faculties; yet not only does it not do this, but it is not even worthy to consider doing it and to have cognisance of it or to realize any such thing. As complete as this is the wretchedness of those who live (or, rather, who are dead) in sin.

[16] Ej, G, Sg: 'for it to be able to do works.'
[17] Sg: 'they have illumined.'
[18] S: 'It was greatness.'
[19] S: 'both in this estate when.'
[20] G: 'great is the lowness.'
[21] Ej, G, Sg: 'the soul unenlightened—that is, the soul that has not the love of God.'
[22] Ej, G, Sg: 'both bodily.'

Annotation for the Stanza Following

For the better understanding of what has been said, and of what follows, it must be known that the look of God works four blessings in the soul—namely, that it cleanses, beautifies, enriches and enlightens it, even as the sun, when it sends forth its rays, dries and warms and beautifies and makes resplendent. And after God has set these last three blessings[23] in the soul it becomes very pleasing to Him because of them, and thus He remembers no more the foulness and the sin that it had aforetime, even as He says through Ezechiel.[24] And thus, having taken away from it once and for all this sin and foulness, He never looks at them again, nor does He fail on their account to grant the soul more favours, since He judges not one thing twice.[25] Yet, although God forgets the evil and the sin after He has once pardoned them, it behoves the soul in no wise to consign its first sins to oblivion, for, as the Wise Man says, 'Concerning sin that is forgiven, be thou not without fear.'[26] And this for three reasons: first, that the soul may never more have occasion for presumption; second, that it may have matter for continual thanksgiving; third, that it may have greater confidence, and thus may receive more from God; for, if when it was in sin it received so much of God, how much greater favours shall it receive when it has set its love upon God and is free from sin![27]

2. The soul, then, being mindful here of all these mercies which it has received, and seeing itself placed with such dignity near to the Spouse, rejoices greatly with delight of thanksgiving and love, being greatly aided therein by the memory of that its first estate, so lowly[28] and so vile that it was unworthy and unprepared not only for God to look upon it, but even to

[23] Ej, G, Sg: 'these last four blessings.'
[24] Ezechiel xviii, 22.
[25] Nahum i, 9.
[26] Ecclesiasticus v, 5.
[27] Ej, G, Sg: 'when it is free from it [i.e., sin] and has set its love upon God!' Various other readings exist, but none adds to the sense or appreciably changes it.
[28] Ej, G, Sg: 'so bad.'

take His name upon its lips, according as He says through the prophet David.[29] Wherefore, seeing that there is no reason which comes from itself why God should behold it and exalt it, neither can there be such, but that the reason is of God, and consists in His fair grace and pure will,[30] the soul attributes its wretchedness[31] to itself, and to the Beloved all the blessings that it possesses, seeing that through them it now merits that which it merited not aforetime; and it takes courage and boldness to beg Him for the continuance of the Divine spiritual union, wherein favours may continue to be multiplied to it. All of which the soul expresses in the following stanza.

STANZA XXXIII

Despise me not,   For, if thou didst find me swarthy,
Now canst thou indeed look upon me,   Since thou didst look
upon me and leave in me grace and beauty.

Exposition

3. The Bride now takes courage; and, esteeming herself with respect to the pledges and the reward which she has of her Beloved (seeing that, since these things come from Him, though she of herself is of little worth and merits no esteem, she merits to be esteemed[1] because of them), makes bold to speak to her Beloved, begging Him not to despise her or hold her of no worth, since, if she once merited this by reason of the baseness of her fault and the wretchedness of her nature, now, since first He looked upon her and adorned her with His grace and clothed her with His beauty, He may well look

[29] Psalm xv, 4 [A.V., xvi, 4].
[30] Ej: 'and His mercy.' G, Sg: 'and merciful will.'
[31] Sg reads: *su misericordia* ['His (or "its") mercy'] for *su miseria* ['its wretchedness'].
[1] S adds: 'at least.'

upon her for the second time, and many times more, and
increase her grace and beauty, since there is reason and cause
sufficient for this in His having looked upon her when she
merited it not neither had the means of doing so.

Despise me not,

4. This soul says not this because she desires to be reputed
for aught, for the slights and insults are rather to be greatly
prized[2] by the soul that in truth loves God; and she sees that
of herself[3] she merits naught else, save through the grace
and the gifts that she has of God, even as she continues to
explain, saying:

For, if thou didst find me swarthy,

5. That is to say: For if ere Thou didst graciously look
upon me[4] Thou didst find in me the baseness and blackness
of faults and imperfections and wretchedness as to my condition by nature,

Now canst thou indeed look upon me,   Since thou didst look upon me

6. Since Thou didst look upon me, taking from me that
miserable swarthy colour of guilt wherewith I was not fit to be
seen, and wherein Thou gavest me grace the first time, now
canst Thou look upon me indeed; that is,[5] now can I indeed
be seen, and now do I deserve to be seen,[6] receiving more
grace from Thine eyes; since with Thine eyes not alone didst
Thou take from me my swarthiness when first Thou lookedst
upon me but likewise Thou didst make me worthier to be seen,
since with Thy look of love Thou didst

Leave in me grace and beauty.

[2] Bg: 'for the contempts and insults are held in no disesteem.'
[3] A omits: 'of herself.'
[4] Thus the MSS. Jaén omits 'upon me.'
[5] Ej begins this paragraph with the words 'that is.'
[6] B, Bg: 'deserve to serve Thee.' Ej, G, Sg: 'now canst Thou indeed and I deserve to be seen' [sic].

7. That which the soul has said in the two lines preceding is an exposition of that which Saint John says in the Gospel—namely, that God gives grace for grace[7]—for, when God sees that the soul is full of grace in His eyes, He is greatly moved to grant it more grace, inasmuch as He dwells within it, well pleased. This Moses knew, and he entreated God for more grace, desiring to constrain Him by the grace which he already had of Him, saying to God: 'Thou sayest that Thou knowest me by name and that I have found grace in Thy sight; if, then, I have found grace in Thy presence,[8] show me Thy face, that I may know Thee and may find grace in the sight of Thine eyes.'[9] And because the soul is magnified,[10] honoured and beautified by this grace in God's sight, as we have said, therefore it is loved by Him ineffably.[11] So that if, before it was in His grace, He loved it for His own sake, now that it is in His grace, He loves it not only for His own sake, but also for itself; and thus He is enamoured of its beauty, by its effects[12] and works, now that it is never without them,[13] and He continually communicates to it greater love and more graces, and, as He magnifies and honours it ever more, so does He ever become more captivated by it. For thus God declares in speaking with Jacob His friend in the Book of Isaias, saying: 'Since thou hast become honourable and glorious in Mine eyes, I have loved thee.'[14] Which is as much as to say: Since Mine eyes gave thee grace by looking upon thee, for which cause thou didst become glorious[15] and worthy of honour in My presence, thou hast merited more grace from My favours[16]—because for God to love more is for Him to grant more favours. This same thing the Bride declares to the other souls, in

7 St. John i, 16.

8 S: 'in the sight of Thy presence.'

9 Exodus xxxiii, 12–13.

10 Sg: 'gratified.'

11 Sg: 'and beautified ineffably.'

12 On 'effects,' see p. 161, n. 3, above.

13 [The reading in the text is that of S.] Jaén [which P. Silverio adopts] reads: 'now without them.'

14 Isaias xliii, 4. Av: 'I have honoured thee by loving thee.'

15 Sg: 'become gracious.'

16 Sg: 'from My mercies.'

the Divine Songs, saying:[17] 'I am swarthy but beautiful, daughters of Jerusalem; wherefore the King has loved me and brought me into the interior of his bed.'[18] Which is as if to say: Souls, ye that know not neither are aware of these favours, marvel not because the King of Heaven has wrought them in me so wondrously as to bring me even into the interior of His love, for though of myself I am swarthy, so often did He cast His eyes upon me, after He had first looked upon me, that He was not content till He had betrothed me to Himself, and brought me into the inner bed of His love.

8. Who can describe the extent of the exaltation of a soul by God when He is pleased to take delight in it? It cannot even be imagined;[19] but briefly, He acts like God, that He may show Who He is. This can only be understood to any extent by that property[20] of God according to which He keeps giving more to him who already has more; and that which He keeps giving is by multiplication, in proportion to that which the soul had before. This He explains in the Gospel, saying: 'Whosoever hath, to him more shall be given, even till he reach abundance; and whosoever hath not, from him shall be taken away even that which he hath.'[21] And thus the money which the servant had who was not in the grace of his lord was taken from him, and given to one that had more money than had all the rest together who were in the grace of their lord.[22] Wherefore the best and the principal blessings of His house—that is, of His Church, both mili-

[17] S gives the Latin text, and reads: 'And the Church adds in her name: *Ideo* . . .' [The latter part of the quotation is from an Office of the Blessed Virgin Mary, as well as being a paraphrase of Canticles i, 3 (A.V., i, 4) hence the different readings. The former part is from Canticles i, 4: A.V., i, 5.]

[18] Ej, G, Sg: 'into the interior cellar.'

[19] Ej, G, Sg: 'It cannot be expressed or even imagined.'

[20] [*Lit.,* 'by the property.'] Jaén reads *canción* ['stanza'] for *condición* ['erroneously,' says P. Silverio, who follows Bg here, as did P. Gerardo before him. But *canción* has also a popular meaning of 'mania,' 'insistent desire.']

[21] St. Matthew xiii, 12.

[22] [St. Matthew xxv, 14 ff.] S modifies: 'more money(s), so that he might have all of them together, (being) in the grace of his lord.'

tant and triumphant—God heaps upon him that is His greatest friend, ordaining it so in order the more to honour and glorify him; even as a great light absorbs into itself many small lights. This God also explained in the above-mentioned passage of Isaias, according to the spiritual sense, where He speaks with Jacob and says: 'I am the Lord thy God, the Holy One of Israel, thy Saviour; I have given Egypt for thy atonement, Ethiopia[23] and Saba for thee, and I will give men for thee and peoples for thy soul.'[24]

9. Well, therefore, now, my God, canst Thou look upon the soul, and greatly canst Thou prize her on whom Thou lookest, since with Thy look Thou dost leave in her the prize for which Thou prizest her and the pledges wherewith Thou art captivated;[25] wherefore not once alone, but many times, does she merit Thy looking upon her, since Thou hast looked upon her once; for, as is said by the Holy Spirit in the Book of Esther: 'Worthy of such honour is he whom the King is pleased to honour.'[26]

Annotation for the Following Stanza

The loving[27] gifts which the Spouse[28] bestows upon the soul in this estate are inestimable, and the praises and endearing words of Divine love, which with great frequency pass between the two, are ineffable. The soul is occupied in praising and thanking Him, and He in exalting,[29] praising and giving thanks to the soul, according as may be seen in the Songs, where He speaks with her and says: 'Behold, thou art fair, my

23 Some MSS. read: 'Egypt' for 'Ethiopia.'

24 Isaias xliii, 3–4.

25 See p. 436, n. 32, above.

26 Esther vi, 11.

27 [Lit., 'friendly,' but Spanish often uses 'friend,' 'friendly,' for 'love,' 'loving.' Ramon Lull's Book of the Lover and the Beloved is in Catalan Libre d'Amic e Amat (Libro del Amigo y del Amado). Cf. the quotation from Canticles i, 15, below, where the Spanish amiga mía ('my friend') is translated 'my love.']

28 Ej, G, Sg read 'God' for 'the Spouse.'

29 Av, Bz: 'exalting in His turn.' A, G, Sg: 'giving thanks' [using a different word from that used further on].

love; behold, thou art fair, and thine eyes are a dove's eyes.'[30] And many other gracious words and praises each one in the Songs continually addresses to the other. In the last stanza, the Bride has just depreciated herself, calling herself swarthy and vile, and has praised Him as being fair and gracious, since with His look He has given her grace and beauty. And He, being accustomed to exalt whom He humbles, casts His eyes upon her as she has begged Him to do, and, in the stanza next following, is occupied in praising her, calling her, not 'swarthy,' as she called herself, but 'white dove,'[31] and praising her for her good qualities, which are those of a dove and of a turtle-dove. And thus He says:

STANZA XXXIV

**The little white dove   Has returned to the ark with the bough,
And now the turtle-dove   Has found[1] the mate of her desire on
the green banks.**

Exposition

2. In this stanza it is the Spouse Who speaks, singing of the purity which the Bride now has in this estate, and of the riches and the prize which she has won, through having prepared herself and laboured to come to Him. Likewise He sings of the great happiness which she has experienced in finding her Spouse in this union, and He describes the fulfilment of her desires and the delight and refreshment which she possesses in Him, now that the labours of this life and of the time past are over. He says, then:

The little white dove

30 Canticles i, 14–15 [A.V., i, 15–16].
31 Ej, G, Sg: 'is occupied in calling her, not "swarthy," as she calls herself, but "dove."' Ej adds: 'or turtle-dove.'
1 Sg, here and at the end of § 4, reads: 'settled' for 'found' [destroying the sense of the stanza].

3. He calls the soul a little white dove by reason of the whiteness and cleanness which it has received of the grace that it has found in God. And He calls it 'dove,' because He calls it this in the Songs, to denote the simplicity and gentleness of its nature[2] and its loving contemplation. For the dove is not only simple and gentle, without gall, but it also has bright and loving eyes; for which reason, to indicate that quality of loving contemplation wherewith the soul regards God, the Spouse there said that it had a dove's eyes.[3] This dove, He says,

Has returned to the ark with the bough,

4. Here the Spouse makes a comparison between the soul and the dove from the ark of Noah, taking that coming and going of the dove to and from the ark as a figure of that which has come to pass[4] in the soul in this case. For, even as the dove came and went to and from the ark, because it found not where to rest its foot in the waters of the flood, until at last it returned to it with an olive branch in its beak, as a sign of the mercy of God in commanding the waters which had overwhelmed the earth to withdraw from it, even so the soul in such case, which left the ark of God's Omnipotence when He created it, has flown over the waters of the flood of sins and imperfections, found not where to rest its desire, and flown to and fro on the breezes of the yearnings of love to the ark of its Creator's bosom, yet has found no perfect entrance thereto[5] until God has caused all the waters of imperfections aforementioned to withdraw from the earth —that is, from the soul. Now it has returned with the olive branch (which is the victory that by means of clemency and mercy God has won over all things) to this happy and perfect recollection in the bosom of its Beloved, not only having won a victory over its opponents, but having also received the reward of its merits, for both these things are denoted by the olive branch. And thus does the little dove-soul not

---

[2] A: 'of its heart.'
[3] Canticles iv, 1.
[4] A, B: 'which has happened to.'
[5] [The original has 'perfect recollection therein.' Cf. the use of the phrase below.]

only now return to the Ark of its God, white and clean, even as it left that Ark when He created it, but it also brings something with it—namely, the branch, which is the reward and the peace that it has obtained through its victory over its own self.

And now the turtle-dove   Has found the mate of her desire on the green banks.

5. The Spouse also calls the soul here a turtle-dove, because in this matter of seeking its Spouse it has been like the turtle-dove when it found not the consort that it desired. For the understanding hereof it is to be known that it is said of the turtle-dove that when it finds not its consort it neither sits upon the green bough,[6] nor drinks of clear or cold water, nor settles beneath the shade, nor joins with other companions; but when it is united with him it then has fruition of all this. All these properties has the soul, and it must needs have them in order that it may reach this bond and union with the Spouse, the Son of God; for it must proceed with such love[7] and solicitude that it rest not the foot of its desire upon the green bough of any delight,[8] nor desire to drink the clear water of any honour and glory of the world, nor must it desire to taste the coolness of any temporal consolation or refreshment,[9] nor desire to stay beneath the shade of any favour or protection that is of creatures; desiring in no wise to rest in aught, or to find companionship in other affections, and sighing ever for solitude from all things until it find its Spouse in complete satisfaction.

6. And since the soul in such case, ere it reached this high estate, went about with great love[10] seeking its Beloved, and finding no satisfaction in aught save in Him, the same Spouse sings here of the end of the fatigues of the Bride and the fulfilment of her desires, saying that at last the turtle-dove has found the mate of her desire on the green banks. This is as

---

[6] Ej, G, Sg: 'green tree.'

[7] Sg: 'with such care.'

[8] Sg: 'upon any green tree of delight.'

[9] Ej, G, Sg: 'nor desire to taste it, or any temporal consolation or refreshment.'

[10] Ej, G, Sg add: 'and care.'

much as to say that the Bride-Soul now sits upon the green bough,[11] delighting in her Beloved; and that she now drinks the clear water of most high[12] contemplation and the wisdom of God, water which is cold, signifying the refreshment and delight that she has in God; and likewise settles beneath the shadow of His protection and favour,[13] which she had so greatly desired, wherein she is comforted, pastured and refreshed after a delectable and Divine manner, even as she declares joyously in the Songs, saying: 'I sat down under the shadow of Him that I had desired, and His fruit is sweet to my palate.'[14]

Annotation for the Stanza Following

Continuing, the Spouse describes the contentment that He derives from the blessing which the Bride has obtained by means of the solitude wherein aforetime she desired to live, which is stability of peace and blessing unchangeable. For, when the soul becomes confirmed in the tranquillity of her single and solitary love for the Spouse, as this soul has done of whom we here speak, she reposes so delectably and so lovingly in God, and God in her, that she has no need of other means or masters to lead her to God, since God is now her guide[15] and her light. For He fulfils in her that which He promised through Osee, saying: 'I will guide her[16] into solitude and will there speak to her heart.'[17] Here He declares that it is in solitude that He communicates and unites Himself to the soul; for to speak to her heart is to satisfy her heart, which is not satisfied with less than God. And thus the Spouse says:

[11] Ej, G, Sg: 'upon the tree.'

[12] Ej, G: 'most sublime.'

[13] G, Sg: 'and likewise [settles] beneath the shade of His favour and protection which she has in God.' Ej: 'and likewise sits beneath the shade of His protection, the which [shade] she . . .', etc.

[14] Canticles ii, 3.

[15] Jaén alone reads: 'her grace.' A has: 'her light, her guide and her law.' The other authorities all have: 'her guide.'

[16] S: 'I will bear her.'

[17] Osee ii, 14.

STANZA XXXV

**In solitude she lived   And in solitude now has built her nest,
And in solitude her dear one alone guides her,   Who likewise
in solitude was wounded by love.**

Exposition

2. In this stanza the Spouse does two things. The first is
to praise the solitude wherein aforetime the soul desired to
live, saying that it was a means whereby she might find and
enjoy[1] her Beloved, alone and far removed from all the pains
and fatigues which she experienced aforetime, for, as she desired to support herself in solitude, far from all pleasure and
consolation and support of the creatures, in order to reach the
companionship of her Beloved, and union with Him, she
merited to find possession of the peace of solitude in her Beloved, wherein she reposes, alone and far removed[2] from all
the said troubles. The second thing that the Spouse does is
to say[3] that, inasmuch as the soul has desired to be alone,[4]
for the sake of her dear one, and far from all created things,
He Himself, being enamoured of her because of this her soli-
tariness, has taken care of her, received her into His arms,
pastured her in Himself with all blessings and guided[5] her
spirit to the high places[6] of God. And He says, not only that
He is now her guide, but that He does these things alone,
without intermediaries—whether angels or men, or forms or
images—inasmuch as the soul, through this solitude, has now

[1] Ej, G, Sg omit: 'and enjoy.'
[2] Ej, G, Sg omit: 'removed,' but add: 'now.'
[3] [*Lit.*, 'the second is to say.']
[4] Jaén has: 'to give herself, alone.'
[5] Bg: 'and guarded.'
[6] [*Lit.*, 'high things.']

true liberty of spirit and is not bound[7] to any of these means. And the line says:

In solitude she lived

3. The little turtle-dove aforementioned, which is the soul, lived in solitude before it found the Beloved in this estate of union. For the soul that desires God is in no wise comforted by any company soever, but all things make and cause within it greater solitude until it find Him.

And in solitude now has built her nest,

4. The solitude wherein the soul lived aforetime was its desire to be without all the things and blessings[8] of the world, for the sake of its Spouse, even as we have said of the turtle-dove. It strove to become perfect, and to acquire perfect solitude, wherein the soul attains to union with the Word, and consequently to all refreshment and rest. It is this that is signified by the nest which is here spoken of—namely, rest and repose. And it is thus[9] as though He were to say: In that solitude wherein aforetime she lived, working therein with labour and anguish, because she was not perfect, she has now set her rest[10] and refreshment, since she has now acquired this solitude perfectly in God. Of this says David, speaking spiritually: 'The bird has indeed found herself a house, and the turtle-dove a nest wherein to rear[11] her young.'[12] That is, an abode in God where she may satisfy her desires and faculties.

And in solitude . . . guides her,

5. This signifies: In that solitude which the soul has with respect to all things and wherein she is alone with God, He guides and moves her and raises her to Divine things—that is to say, He raises her understanding to Divine intelligence,

---

[7] Sg: 'is not tied.'
[8] Ej, G, Sg: 'all the blessings.'
[9] S abbreviates: 'the nest which is spoken of. And it is thus.'
[10] Ej, G, Sg: 'her nest.'
[11] Bg: 'wherein to shelter.'
[12] Psalm lxxxiii, 4 [A.V., lxxxiv, 3].

since it is now alone and stripped of all other strange and contradictory intelligence; and He moves her will[13] freely to the love of God, for it is now alone and free from other affections; and He fills her memory with Divine knowledge, since it, too, is now alone and emptied of other imaginings and fancies. For, as soon as the soul disencumbers these faculties and voids them of all lower things and of all attachment to higher things, leaving them in solitude,[14] with naught else, God at once uses them for the invisible and Divine, and it is God Who guides the soul in this solitude, even as Saint Paul says concerning the perfect: *Qui spiritu Dei aguntur,*[15] etc. 'They are moved by the Spirit of God.' Which is the same as saying: In solitude there guides her

. . . her dear one alone

6. This signifies that not only does He guide her in her solitude, but that it is He Himself alone Who works in her, using no other intermediary. For it is the characteristic of this union of the soul with God in the Spiritual Marriage that God works in her and communicates Himself to her alone, not now by means of angels, as aforetime, neither by means of her natural ability. For the outward and inward senses, and all creatures, and even the soul herself, have very little to do with the receiving of these great and supernatural favours which God grants in this estate: they belong not to the ability[16] and natural working and diligence of the soul—He alone works them in her. And the reason for this is that He finds her alone, as has been said, and thus He will give her no other company, nor will He have her profit by any other, or trust[17] any other, save Himself only. And it is also fitting that, since the soul has now left all things and passed beyond all intermediaries, soaring above them all to God, God Himself should be her guide and the intermediary to Himself. Now that the soul has soared above everything, and is withdrawn

13 A, B, Bg: 'and her will is moved.'
14 Ej, G, Sg: 'leaving them all.'
15 Romans viii, 14.
16 S: 'because they are not contained in the ability.'
17 S: 'or have her trust.'

from everything, none of these things is now of any profit or service to her that she may soar higher, save the Word Himself, which is the Spouse. And He, because He is so greatly enamoured of her, desires to be Himself alone the One to work the favours aforementioned.[18] And so He next says:

Who likewise in solitude was wounded by love.

7. That is to say, by the love of the Bride. For, not only does the Spouse greatly love the solitude of the soul, but He is most deeply wounded with love for her, because she has desired to remain alone, and far from all things,[19] inasmuch as she has been wounded with love for Him. And thus He would not leave her alone; but rather, wounded by her through the solitude wherein for His sake she lives, and, seeing that she is content with naught else, He alone guides her to Himself, draws her to Himself and absorbs her in Himself; which He would not do in her had He not found her in spiritual solitude.

Annotation for the Stanza Following

A strange characteristic of those that are in love[20] is this, that they are far more desirous of enjoying each other's society when they are alone together and withdrawn from every creature[21] than of doing so in the company of any. For, although they be together, yet if there be any strange company present with them, even though they would not converse and speak together if they were away from them any more than they do in their presence, and though these others speak not neither converse at all, their very presence is sufficient[22] to prevent the lovers from having pleasure and enjoyment in each other. The reason for this is that, since love is the union of two only, these two desire to commune alone.

[18] Ej, G, Sg: 'to work these Divine favours.'

[19] Ej, G omit the clause: 'because . . . from all things.'

[20] Ej, G have: 'of the lovers'; the other authorities: 'of the beloved.'

[21] Sg: 'from every joy.'

[22] Ej, G, Sg abbreviate: '. . . would not converse and speak, their very presence is sufficient,' etc.

And now that the soul has been set upon this summit[23] of perfection and freedom of spirit in God, and the repugnances and contrarieties of its sensuality have been done away with, it has no longer aught to understand, or any other exercise wherein to employ itself, than the giving of itself up to the delights and joys of intimate love with the Spouse. It is written thus of holy Tobias in his book, where he says[24] that, after he had passed through the trials of his poverty and temptations, God illumined him, and that he spent all the rest of his days[25] in rejoicing.[26] And just so does this soul of which we are speaking spend them, since the blessings which it sees in itself give it such great joy and delight as Isaias attributes to the soul which, having exercised itself in works of perfection, has arrived at the point of perfection whereof we are speaking.

2. Here, then, speaking to the soul concerning this perfection, he says: 'Then shall thy light rise up in darkness, and thy darkness shall be as the noonday. And thy Lord God shall give thee rest for ever, and He shall fill thy soul with brightness, and shall deliver thy bones, and thou shalt be like a watered garden[27] and like a fountain of waters, whose waters shall not fail. In thee shall be builded up the solitary places of ages and thou shalt raise up the beginnings and foundations of one generation and another generation; and thou shalt be called a builder up of the hedges, turning aside thy paths and ways into quietness. If thou turn away thy work from leisure and from doing thy will on My holy day, and call the leisure delicate and holy,[28] glorious, of the Lord, and glorify Him, doing not thy own ways and fulfilling not thy will, then shalt thou delight thyself in the Lord, and I will lift thee up above the high places of the earth, and I will pasture thee upon the inheritance of Jacob.'[29] Thus far these

[23] Sg has *costumbre* ['custom'] for *cumbre* ['summit'].

[24] S omits: 'in his book, where he says.'

[25] S: 'and that he spent all the remainder of his life.'

[26] Tobias xiv, 4 [A.V., xiv, 2].

[27] Bg: 'and shall fill thy bones and veins like a watered garden.'

[28] Sg abbreviates: 'if thou turn away thy work from leisure delicate and holy.'

[29] Isaias lviii, 10–14. Ej, G, Sg abbreviate: 'and I will lift thee up upon the inheritance of Jacob.'

words are from Isaias, wherein the inheritance of Jacob is God Himself.[30] And therefore, as we have said, this soul has a care to do naught save to enjoy the delights of this pasture; only one thing remains for it to desire—namely, to enjoy Him perfectly in life eternal.[31] And thus, in the following stanza, and in the rest which follow, the soul is occupied in entreating the Beloved for this beatific pasture in the clear vision of God. And thus she says:

STANZA XXXVI

Let us rejoice, Beloved,   And let us go to see ourselves in thy beauty,
To the mountain and the hill where flows the pure water;   Let us enter farther into the thicket.

Exposition

3. Now that the perfect union of love is made between the soul and God, the soul desires to employ and exercise herself in the properties which pertain to love, and thus it is she who speaks in this stanza with the Spouse, praying Him for three things which are proper to love. First, she desires to receive the joy and sweetness of love, and for this she prays Him when she says:[1] 'Let us rejoice, Beloved.' The second desire is that she may become like to the Beloved, and for this she prays Him when she says: 'Let us go to see ourselves in Thy beauty.' And the third desire is to delve into the things and secrets of the same Beloved, and to know them,[2] and for this she prays Him when she says: 'Let us enter farther into the thicket.' There follows the line:

Let us rejoice, Beloved,

[30] S abbreviates: 'I will pasture thee upon the inheritance of Jacob, which is God Himself.'

[31] Ej, G, Sg: 'to enjoy Him in life eternal perpetually.'

[1] Av inadvertently omits the following passage: 'Let us rejoice . . . when she says.'

[2] Ej, G, Sg: 'and to desire to know them.'

4. That is to say, in the communication of the sweetness of love, not only in that which we already have in the habitual joining together and union of us both, but in that which overflows in the exercise of effective and actual love, whether interiorly[3] with the will in an act of affection, or exteriorly, in the performance of works belonging to the service of the Beloved. For, as we have said, love, where it has been firmly set, has this quality, that it desires ever to continue tasting its joys and sweetnesses, which are the exercise of loving interiorly and exteriorly, as we have said. All this the soul does that she may become more like to the Beloved, and thus she says next:

And let us go to see ourselves in thy beauty,

5. Which signifies:[4] Let us so act that, by means of this exercise of love aforementioned, we may attain to seeing ourselves in Thy beauty in life eternal: that is, that I may be so transformed in Thy beauty that, being alike in beauty, we may both see ourselves in Thy beauty, since I shall have Thy own beauty; so that, when one of us looks at the other, each may see in the other his beauty, the beauty of both being Thy beauty alone, and I being absorbed in Thy beauty;[5] and thus I shall see Thee in Thy beauty and Thou wilt see me in Thy beauty; and I shall see myself in Thee in Thy beauty; and Thou wilt see Thyself in me in Thy beauty; so that thus I may be like to Thee in Thy beauty and Thou mayest be like to me in Thy beauty, and my beauty may be Thy beauty, and Thy beauty my beauty; and thus I shall be Thou in Thy beauty and Thou wilt be I in Thy beauty,[6] because Thy beauty itself will be my beauty, and thus we shall each see the

---

[3] Ej, G, Sg alone have this word [which P. Silverio omits].

[4] There are many minor variants in this paragraph, due mainly to inadvertence, the playing upon words and phrases having confused the copyists. [The only changes that affect the translation are noted below.]

[5] S reads: 'absorbed therein.' Ej, G omit the following lines down to 'This is the adoption.'

[6] S: 'and my beauty may be Thine, and Thine, mine; and thus I shall be Thou in it, and Thou wilt be I in this same beauty of Thine.'

other in Thy beauty. This is the adoption[7] of the sons of God, who will truly say to God that which the Son Himself said through Saint John to the Eternal Father: 'All My things are Thine and Thy things are Mine.'[8] He by essence, being the Son by nature; and we by participation, being sons by adoption. And thus He spake, not only for Himself, Who is the Head, but for His whole mystical body, which is the Church, and which will share in the very beauty of the Spouse in the day of her triumph, which will be when she sees God face to face; for which cause the soul here entreats that she and the Spouse may go to see themselves in His beauty.

To the mountain and the hill

6. This means to the morning and essential knowledge of God, which is knowledge in[9] the Divine Word, Who, because of His height, is here understood by the mountain; as Isaias says, calling men to a knowledge of the Son of God, and saying: 'Come, let us go up to the mountain of the Lord.'[10] Again: 'The mountain of the house of the Lord shall be prepared.'[11] And to the hill[12]—that is, to the evening knowledge of God, which is the wisdom of God in His creatures and works and wondrous ordinances, which is here signified by the hill, since this wisdom is lower than that of the morning; but the soul prays for both morning and evening wisdom when she says: 'To the mountain and the hill.'[13]

7. When the soul, then, says: 'Let us go to the mountain to see ourselves in Thy beauty,' she means: Transform me in the beauty of Divine Wisdom, and make me like to It, which Wisdom, as we said, is the Word, the Son of God. And when she says: 'to the hill,' she is praying[14] God to inform her in the beauty of this other and lesser wisdom,[15] which is in His creatures and mysterious works, which also is beauty of the

---

[7] Ej, G: 'addition.'
[8] St. John xvii, 10.
[9] Ej, G: 'knowledge of.'
[10] Isaias ii, 3.
[11] Isaias ii, 2. A, B do not quote the Scriptural passage.
[12] Jaén alone omits: 'And to the hill.'
[13] Ej, G omit § 7 entirely.
[14] A, S: 'is telling.'
[15] Sg: 'and lesser knowledge of wisdom.'

Son of God wherein the soul desires to see herself enlightened.

8. The soul cannot see herself in the beauty of God save by being transformed in the Wisdom of God, wherein she sees herself to possess that which is above and that which is below. To this mountain and hill the Bride desired to come when she said: 'I will go to the mountain of myrrh and to the hill of frankincense'[16]—meaning by the mountain of myrrh the clear vision of God and by the hill of frankincense the knowledge of Him in the creatures, for the myrrh on the mountain is of a higher order than the frankincense on the hill.

Where flows the pure water;

9. This signifies: Where the knowledge and wisdom of God, which here she calls pure water, are given to the understanding, for they cleanse and strip it of accidents and phantasies, and clear it of the clouds of ignorance.[17] The soul has ever this desire to understand the Divine truths in a clear and pure[18] way; and the more she loves, the more deeply she desires to penetrate them; wherefore she makes her third request, saying:

Let us enter farther into the thicket.

10. Into the thicket of Thy[19] marvellous works and profound judgments, the multitude whereof is so great, and of such great variety, that it may be called a thicket. For therein is abundant wisdom, so full of mysteries that it can be called not only thick, but even curdled,[20] according as David says in these words: *Mons Dei, mons pinguis; Mons coagulatus.*[21] Which is to say: The mountain of God is a mountain thick and a mountain curdled. And this thicket of wisdom and knowledge of God is so profound and vast that, for all that the

16 Canticles iv, 6.
17 This is the reading of S. Jaén [which P. Silverio adopts] has: 'Where is given the knowledge and wisdom of God, which here she calls pure water, to the understanding, for [it is] clean and stripped of accidents and phantasies, and clear without clouds of ignorance.'
18 Ej, G: 'clear and distinct.' Sg: 'clear and distinct and pure.'
19 [P. Silverio reads 'my'—an apparent error. Cf. p. 204, § 6, above.]
20 Ej, G: 'that it may be called a thicket, but even curdled.'
21 Psalm lxvii, 16 [A.V., lxviii, 16].

soul may know thereof, she can ever enter farther still, so vast is it, and so incomprehensible are its riches, according as Saint Paul exclaims, saying: 'O the height of the riches of wisdom and knowledge of God! How incomprehensible are His judgments and incomprehensible[22] His ways!'[23]

11. But the soul desires to enter this thicket and incomprehensibility of judgments and ways, because she is dying with desire[24] to enter very far into the knowledge of them; for to have that knowledge is a priceless delight, exceeding all that can be felt. Wherefore David, speaking of their sweetness, said thus: The judgments of the Lord are true and have justice in themselves; they are more to be desired[25] and more coveted than gold[26] and than the precious stone of great worth; and they are sweet above honey and the honeycomb. So much so that thy servant loved and kept them.[27] Wherefore the soul greatly desires to be immersed in these judgments and to have a deeper knowledge of them; and to that end it would be a great consolation and joy to her to pass through all the afflictions and trials of the world, and through all else that[28] might be a means to her thereto, howsoever difficult and grievous it might be; and through the agonies and perils of death, that she might enter more deeply into her God.

12. Wherefore by the thicket which the soul here desires to enter may also very properly be understood the great number and multitude of trials and tribulations, whereinto this soul desires to enter, inasmuch as suffering is most delectable and most profitable to her; because suffering is a means to her of entering farther into the thicket of the delectable wisdom of God; for the purest suffering brings with it the most intimate and the purest knowledge,[29] and, in consequence, the purest and loftiest joy which comes from having penetrated into the

[22] B, Bg: 'and investigable [sic].'

[23] Romans xi, 33. Ej, G omit the Spanish text and only begin the Latin text.

[24] S: 'because she is moved by the desire.'

[25] [Lit., 'more desirable.'] S: 'more pleasant.'

[26] Ej, G here add: 'and silver.'

[27] Psalm xviii, 10–11 [A.V., xix, 9–11].

[28] Ej, G, Sg: 'and through all the torments that.'

[29] Sg: 'brings with it the purest and most intimate pleasure.'

deepest knowledge. So, not content with any manner of suffering, the soul says: 'Let us enter farther into the thicket.' That is to say, even to the perils of death, that I may see God. Wherefore Job, desiring this suffering in order to see God, said: 'Who will grant that my petition may be fulfilled and that God may give me that for which I hope, and that He that began me may destroy me and let loose His hand and cut me off, and that I may have this consolation, that He will afflict me with grief and will not pardon me?'[30]

13. Oh, that it might be perfectly understood how the soul cannot attain to the thicket and wisdom of the riches of God, which are of many kinds, save by entering into the thicket of many kinds of suffering, and by setting thereupon its consolation and desire! And how the soul that of a truth desires Divine wisdom first desires suffering, that it may enter therein —yea, into the thicket of the Cross! For this reason Saint Paul exhorted the Ephesians not to faint in tribulations, but to be very strong, and rooted in charity, that they might be able to comprehend with all the saints what is the breadth and the length and the height and the depth, and likewise to know the supereminent charity[31] of the knowledge of Christ, so as to be filled with all the fullness of God.[32] For the gate whereby one may enter into these riches of His wisdom is the Cross, which is a strait gate. And the desire to enter therein belongs to few,[33] but the desire for the joys to which it leads belongs to many.

Annotation for the Stanza Following

One of the principal reasons for which the soul desires to be set free and to see itself with Christ is that it may see Him there face to face, and its understanding may penetrate to the depths of His ways and the eternal mysteries of His Incarna-

---

[30] Job vi, 8–9. [On 'destroy,' see p. 206, n. 17, above.]

[31] Ej, G: 'the supervenient charity.'

[32] Ephesians iii, 18 [13–19].

[33] Ej, G, Sg: 'belongs to persons desirous of suffering, and [therefore] to few.'

tion, which is not the least part of its happiness; for, as Christ Himself says through Saint John, speaking with the Father: 'This is life eternal, that they may know Thee, one only, true God, and Thy Son Jesus Christ Whom Thou hast sent.'[34] Wherefore, even as the first thing that a person does, when he has arrived from afar, is to see and converse[35] with those[36] whom he greatly loves, so the first thing that the soul desires to do[37] when it attains to the vision of God is to know and enjoy the deep secrets and mysteries of the Incarnation and the ancient ways of God which depend thereon. Wherefore the soul, when it has ended saying that it desires to see itself in the beauty of God, says next the words of this stanza:

STANZA XXXVII

**And then we shall go forth   To the lofty caverns of the rock[1]
which are well hidden,
And there shall we enter   And taste the new wine of the
pomegranates.**

Exposition

2. One of the causes which move the soul most to desire to enter into this thicket of the wisdom of God and to have a deeper knowledge of the beauty of His Divine wisdom, is, as we have said, that it may pass on to a union of its understanding in God, according to the knowledge of the mysteries of the Incarnation, as of the loftiest and most delectable wisdom[2] of all His works. And thus the Bride in this stanza[3] says

[34] St. John xvii, 3.
[35] [*Lit.*, 'to converse with and see.'] Sg: 'to enter into and see.'
[36] [The form of the pronoun in Spanish is singular, but its meaning in the sixteenth century could be either singular or plural.]
[37] Av [for 'so . . .'] has: 'I mean that the first thing that [the soul] does and desires.'
[1] G: 'of the rocks.'
[2] Ej, G: 'most sovereign wisdom.'
[3] Ej, G, Sg: 'in the Songs.'

that, after having entered farther into the Divine wisdom
(that is, farther into the Spiritual Marriage which she is now
enjoying, which will be in glory, wherein the soul will see God
face to face and be united with this Divine wisdom, which is
the Son of God), the soul will know the sublime mysteries of
God and Man, which are sublimest in wisdom and are hidden
in God; and that they will enter into the knowledge thereof,
and the soul will be engulfed and absorbed in them, and that
she and the Spouse will have pleasure in the sweetness and
delight which is caused by the knowledge of them, and of the
virtues and attributes of God, which are known in God
through the said mysteries, such as justice, mercy, wisdom,
power, charity, etc.

**And then we shall go forth To the lofty caverns of the
rock . . .**

3. The rock of which she here speaks, according to Saint
Paul, is Christ.[4] The lofty caverns of this rock are the lofty
and high and deep[5] mysteries of the wisdom of God which are
in Christ, concerning the hypostatical union of human nature
with the Divine Word, and the correspondence to this which
is in the union of men in God, and in the agreement which
there is between the justice and mercy of God as to the salvation of the human race in the manifestation of His judgments.
These judgments are so high and so deep that she very properly calls them lofty caverns; lofty,[6] because of the height of
their lofty[7] mysteries, and caverns, because of the depth and
profundity of the wisdom of God in them. For, even as caverns are deep and have many recesses, even so each of the
mysteries that there are in Christ is most profound in wisdom,
and has many recesses, which are His secret judgments of
predestination and foreknowledge with respect to the sons of
men. Wherefore she says next:

. . . which are well hidden,

[4] 1 Corinthians x, 4.
[5] Ej, G, Sg: omit 'and deep.'
[6] So Ej, G, Sg, S. The other authorities omit 'lofty.'
[7] Ej, G, Sg, S omit 'lofty.'

4. So much so that, despite all the mysteries and wonders which have been discovered by holy doctors and understood by holy souls in this estate of life, there has remained much more to be said, and even to be understood, and thus there are great depths to be fathomed[8] in Christ. For He is like an abundant mine with many recesses containing treasures, of which, for all that men try to fathom them,[9] the end and bottom is never reached; rather in each recess men continue to find new veins of new riches[10] on all sides, as Saint Paul said of Christ Himself in these words: 'In Christ dwell hidden all treasures and wisdom,'[11] whereinto the soul cannot enter and whereto it cannot attain, unless first, as we have said, it pass through the strait place[12] of exterior and interior suffering into the Divine wisdom.[13] For even that degree of these mysteries of Christ to which a soul may attain in this life cannot be reached save through great suffering and until it has received from God many favours, both in the intellect and in the senses, and until many spiritual exercises have been first performed by it. For all these favours are inferior to the wisdom of the mysteries of Christ, for all are, as it were, preparations for coming thereto. Wherefore, when Moses prayed God to show him His glory, He answered him that he would be unable to see it in this life, but that He would show him 'all good'[14]—all, that is, that in this life is possible. And it came to pass that, after setting him in the cavern of the rock, which, as we have said, is Christ, He showed him His back— that is, He gave him a knowledge of the mysteries of the Humanity of Christ.

5. Into these caverns of Christ, then, the soul indeed desires earnestly to enter, that it may be wholly absorbed and trans-

---

[8] Ej, G: 'and thus there is far to go.' [This apparently extensive change is caused by the substitution of *andar* for *ahondar* in the original.]

[9] Ej, G: 'however far men go.' [A similar change to that described in the last note.]

[10] Ej, G: 'many veins of many riches.' Sg: 'many new veins of many riches.'

[11] Colossians ii, 3.

[12] S: 'the thicket.'

[13] S omits: 'into the Divine wisdom.'

[14] Exodus xxxiii, 19.

formed and inebriated in the love of the wisdom thereof, hiding itself in the breast of its Beloved. For to these clefts He invites it in the Songs, saying: 'Arise and make haste, My friend, My fair one, and come into the clefts of the rock and into the cavern of the enclosure.'[15] These clefts are the caverns which we are here describing, and to which the soul refers, saying:

And there shall we enter

6. There shall we enter—that is, into that knowledge and those Divine mysteries.[16] She says not: 'I shall enter alone,' which would seem more fitting, for the Spouse has no need to enter there again, but 'We shall enter'—that is, I and the Beloved; this in order to explain that it is not she who does this, but the Spouse with her; and over and above this, inasmuch as God and the soul are already united in this estate of the Spiritual Marriage whereof we are speaking, the soul does no work by itself without God. And to say: 'There shall we enter' is to say: There shall we be transformed—that is, I in Thee through the love of these delectable and Divine judgments aforementioned; for in the knowledge of the predestination of the just and the foreknowledge[17] of the wicked, wherein the Father prevented the just in the benedictions of His sweetness in His Son Jesus Christ, the soul is transformed after a most sublime and intimate manner[18] in the love of God according to this knowledge, giving thanks afresh to the Father and loving Him afresh with great sweetness and delight through His Son Jesus Christ; and this she does in union with Christ, together with Christ; and the sweetness of this praise is so delicate that it is altogether ineffable; but the soul speaks of it in the line which follows, saying:

And taste the new wine of the pomegranates.

[15] Canticles ii, 13–14.
[16] Ej, G: 'namely, into those Divine promises and that knowledge.'
[17] Ej, G: 'and the condemnation.'
[18] Ej, G, Sg: 'in His Son Jesus Christ, in Whom He condemned the wicked in perpetual anathema and malediction, the soul is transformed after a most intimate and sublime manner.'

7. The pomegranates here signify the mysteries of Christ, and the judgments of the wisdom of God, and the virtues and attributes of God which are known in God through the knowledge of these mysteries and judgments, which are innumerable. For, as the pomegranate has many small seeds, which have been born and are nourished in that one round orb,[19] so each of the attributes and mysteries[20] and judgments and virtues of God contains within itself a great multitude of wondrous ordinances and admirable effects of God, contained and nourished in the spherical orb[21] of virtue and mystery, etc., which belong to those effects. And we refer here to the spherical or circular shape of the pomegranate, because by each pomegranate we here understand some virtue and attribute of God, which attribute or virtue of God is God Himself, which is denoted by the spherical or circular figure, because it has no beginning or end. It was because there are such innumerable judgments and mysteries in the wisdom of God that the Bride said to the Spouse in the Songs: 'Thy belly is of ivory, set with sapphires';[22] by the which sapphires are denoted the said mysteries and judgments of the Divine Wisdom, which is here denoted by the belly, for sapphire is a precious stone of the colour of the heavens when they are clear and serene.

8. The new wine of these pomegranates, which the Bride says here that she and the Spouse will taste, is the fruition and delight of the love of God that in the knowledge and understanding of them overflows in the soul. For, even as from many pomegranate seeds there comes but one new wine when they are pressed, even so from all these wonders and grandeurs of God which are infused into the soul there overflows for her one fruition and one delight of love alone, which is the drink of the Holy Spirit; the which she offers at once to her God, the Word-Spouse, with great tenderness of love. For

[19] See p. 210, n. 11, above.
[20] S omits: 'and mysteries.'
[21] Thus A, Av, B, Bz, S. Jaén: 'in the seraphic orb.' Sg: 'in the same spherical God.' Ej, G: 'in the same spherical orb of God.' Bg: 'in the orb of virtue.' [See also p. 210, n. 11, above. The word *seno* can also be translated 'bosom.']
[22] Canticles v, 14.

this Divine drink she promised Him in the Songs, if He granted her these kinds of sublime knowledge,[23] saying: 'There Thou shalt teach me and I will give Thee to drink of spiced wine and the new wine of my pomegranates.'[24] She calls them (that is, the Divine knowledge) hers, although they are God's, since He has given them to her. The joy and fruition hereof in the wine of love she gives to her God as a drink, and this is signified by:[25] 'We will taste the new wine of the pomegranates.' For as He tastes it, He gives it to her to taste, and, as she tastes it, she gives it back to Him to taste, so that they both taste of it together.

Annotation for the Stanza Following

In these last two stanzas the Bride has been singing of the blessings which the Spouse is to give her in that eternal bliss —namely, that the Spouse is effectually to transform her into the beauty of His wisdom created and uncreated. And that He will transform her also into the beauty of the union of the Word with humanity, wherein she will then know Him, as well by His face as by His back. And now in the stanza following she says two things: first, she speaks of the manner wherein she is to enjoy that Divine 'new wine' of the sapphires or the pomegranates[26] whereof she has spoken; secondly, she sets before the Spouse the glory of her predestination which He will give her. Here it is well to note that, although these blessings of the soul are described one after the other, successively, they are all contained in the soul's one essential glory. She says, then, thus:

[23] [*Lit.*, 'if He set her in these sublime knowledge(s).'] S: 'if He should make her to enter' for 'if He set her.'
[24] Canticles viii, 2.
[25] S abbreviates: 'since He has given them to the soul, and she returns them as her own to God Himself, and this is signified by.'
[26] S omits: 'sapphires or the.'

STANZA XXXVIII

There wouldst thou show me[1]   **That which my soul desired,**[2]
And there at once, my life, wouldst thou give me[3]   **That which
thou gavest me the other day.**

Exposition

2. The end for which the soul desired to enter those caverns
was that she might reach the consummation of the love of
God which she had ever desired,[4] which is to come to love
God with the purity and perfection wherewith she is loved by
Him, in order to requite Him. And thus in this stanza she says
to the Spouse that He will show her that which she has so
greatly desired in all her acts and exercises, which is to show
her how to love Him with the perfection wherewith He loves
her.[5] And the second thing that she says He will give her
there is the essential glory to which He predestined her from
the day of His eternity. And thus she says:

There wouldst thou show me[6]   **That which my soul desired,**

3. This desire of the soul is the equality of love with God
for which, both naturally and supernaturally, she ever longs,
because the lover cannot be satisfied if he feels not that he
loves as much as he is loved. And as the soul sees that, notwithstanding the transformation in God which she is experiencing in this life, all the vastness of her love cannot succeed
in equalling the perfection of love wherewith she is loved by
God, she desires the clear transformation of glory, wherein

---

[1] Ej, G, Sg: 'wilt thou show me.'
[2] [See p. 212, n. 1, above.]
[3] Ej, G, Sg: 'wilt thou give me.'
[4] [*pretendido*. See p. 212, n. 1, above.]
[5] So S. The other authorities [followed by P. Silverio] have:
'wherewith He loves Himself.'
[6] Ej, G, Sg: 'wilt thou show me.'

she will succeed in equalling the said love. For, although in this high estate which the soul here enjoys[7] there is true union of the will, it cannot attain to the excellence[8] and strength of love which the soul will possess in that strong union of glory. For just as (in the words of Saint Paul) the soul will then know even as she is known of God,[9] so then she will also love God even as she is loved of Him. For even as her understanding will then be the understanding of God, and her will the will of God, even so will her love be the love of God. For, although the will of the soul is not destroyed there, it is so strongly united with the strength of the will of God wherewith it is loved of Him that it loves Him as strongly and perfectly as it is loved of Him, the two wills being united in one sole love of God; and thus the soul loves God with the will and strength of God Himself, united with the same strength of love wherewith she is loved of God, which strength is in the Holy Spirit, in Whom the soul is there transformed; and since He is given to the soul to strengthen this her love, He bestows upon her and supplies in her, by reason of this her transformation of glory, that in which she is wanting. Even in the perfect transformation of this estate of marriage to which the soul attains in this life, wherein she is altogether clothed[10] in grace, she still loves so greatly after some manner through the Holy Spirit, Who is given to her in this transformation.

4. Herein it is to be noted that the soul says not here that He will give her His love there, although He does in fact give it to her (for she means to say here only that God would love her), but that He will show her there how she is to love Him with the perfection to which she aspires. Inasmuch as He gives her His love there, He shows her how to love Him as she is loved by Him; for, besides teaching the soul to love purely, freely and disinterestedly, as He loves us, God makes her to love with the strength wherewith He loves her, transforming

[7] [*Lit.,* 'here has.']

[8] [*Lit.,* 'carats,' *quilates,* often used in Spanish metaphorically.]

[9] 1 Corinthians xiii, 12.

[10] Jaén, Av, Sg [followed by P. Silverio] have: 'altogether overflowing.' The other authorities read as in the text.

her in His love, as we have said, and thus giving her His own strength wherewith she can love Him, which is like placing an instrument in her hands, telling her how to use it, and continually using it together with her—which is to show the soul how to love and to give her the capacity for loving. Until she attains so far, the soul is not content, nor would she be content in the next life, if, as Saint Thomas says *in opusculo de Beatitudine*, she felt not that she loves God as greatly as she is loved by Him. And, as has been said, in this estate of the Spiritual Marriage whereof we are speaking, at this season, although there is not that perfection of glorious love, there is a certain vivid vision and image of that perfection which is altogether ineffable.[11]

And there at once, my life, wouldst thou give me[12]   That which thou gavest me the other day.

5. That which the soul here says that He would at once give her is essential glory, which consists in the vision of[13] the Being of God. Wherefore, before we proceed farther, it behoves us here to settle one question, which is: Why, since essential glory consists in seeing God and not in loving, does the soul say here that this love, and not essential glory, was her aspiration, and why does she speak of this love at the beginning of the stanza, and then, as if it were something that she esteemed less, make her petition concerning essential glory? There are two reasons:[14] first, that even as the end of all things is love, which is subject to the will, whose property is to give and not to receive, and the property of the understanding, which is the subject of essential glory,[15] is to receive and not to give, so the soul, being here inebriated with love, puts not in the first place the glory which God is to give her, but rather the giving of herself to God, in surrender of true

[11] Sg abbreviates: 'although there would not be that perfection of love which is altogether ineffable.'

[12] Ej: 'wilt thou give me.'

[13] [*Lit.*, 'in seeing.']

[14] Ej, G, Sg: 'two things.'

[15] Ej, G: 'the understanding, whose object is essential glory.' Sg: 'the understanding, for its object is essential glory.'

love, without any regard to her own advantage. The second reason is that in the first desire[16] the second is included also, and has been pre-supposed in the preceding stanzas; for it is impossible to attain to the perfect love of God without the perfect vision of God.[17] The difficulty in this question, however, is solved by the first reason, for through love the soul requites God that which she owes Him, and with the understanding she receives from God rather than gives.

6. Coming now to the exposition of these lines, let us see what day is that 'other' whereof the soul here speaks, and what is the 'that'[18] which God gave her on that day,[19] and which she begs Him to give her afterwards in glory. By that other day she understands the day of the eternity of God, which is 'other' than this day of time; in the which day of eternity God predestined the soul to glory, and therein determined the glory which He would give her, and gave it to her freely, without beginning, before He created her. And this 'that' is proper to this soul, in such wise that no happening or accident, high or low, will suffice to take it from her for ever; but she will come to possess without end 'that' to which God predestined her without beginning. And this is 'that' which He says He gave her on that other day, the which she desires now to possess openly[20] in glory. And what will be that which He will give her there? Eye has not seen it, neither has ear heard it, neither has it entered into the heart of man, as the Apostle says.[21] And again Isaias says: 'The eye hath not seen, Lord, besides Thee, that which Thou hast prepared,' etc.[22] Here, since it has no name, the soul calls it 'that.' It is, in fact, to see God, but what it is for the soul to see God has no other name than 'that.'

7. However, in order not to fail to say something of 'that,' let us say what Christ said of it to Saint John in the Apoca-

---

[16] Bg: 'the first question.'
[17] B, Bg: 'the perfect union of God.'
[18] G, Sg: 'and what is that "other" and what is "that."'
[19] Av, Bz: 'on that other day.'
[20] Ej, G, Sg omit the words 'now' and 'openly.'
[21] 1 Corinthians ii, 9.
[22] Isaias lxiv, 4.

lypse, using many terms and words and comparisons,[23] on seven occasions; since 'that' cannot comprehensively be described in one word or on one occasion; because even after all those occasions much still remains unsaid. Christ, then, says there: 'To him that overcometh I will give to eat of the tree of life, which is in the Paradise of My God.'[24] But since this 'that' is not fully expounded in that phrase, He then uses another, which is: 'Be thou faithful unto death and I will give thee the crown of life.'[25] And, since this phrase does not describe it, He uses another which is more obscure, yet which explains it better, saying: 'To him that overcometh will I give the hidden manna, and I will give him a white stone[26] and on the stone a new name written which no man knoweth, but he that receiveth it.'[27] And, since these terms suffice no better to express 'that,' the Son of God goes on to use others of great delight and power. 'To him that overcometh,' He says, 'and keepeth my works unto the end, I will give power over the nations, and he shall rule them with a rod of iron, and they shall be broken to pieces like a vessel of clay, as I also have received from My Father; and I will give him the morning star.'[28] And, not content with using these terms for the exposition of 'that,' He next says: 'He that overcometh after this manner shall be clothed in white raiment and I will not blot his name out of the book of life, and I will confess his name before My Father.'[29]

8. But, since all that has been said still falls short, He then uses many terms to explain 'that' thing, the which terms contain within themselves ineffable majesty and greatness. 'Him that overcometh,' He says, 'I will make a pillar in the temple of My God, and he shall go out no more, and I will write

[23] Sg omits: 'and comparisons.'
[24] Apocalypse ii, 7.
[25] Apocalypse ii, 10.
[26] [*cálculo*.] Ej, G, Sg add: 'and the *cálculo* is a precious stone as red [*lit.*, 'as enkindled'] as a coal.' Jaén also has this addition, as a marginal note.
[27] Apocalypse ii, 17. Ej, G, Sg, S have: 'receiveth it' [as in A.V.]. The other authorities have: 'writeth it.'
[28] Apocalypse ii, 26–8.
[29] Apocalypse iii, 5.

upon him[30] the name of My God and the name of the new
city of Jerusalem of My God, which cometh down out of
Heaven from My God, and also My new name.'[31] And next
He says the seventh thing to explain this 'that,' which is: 'To
him that overcometh[32] I will give to sit with Me in My throne,
as I also overcame and am sat down with My Father in His
throne. He that has ears to hear, let him hear,' etc.[33] To this
point these are the words of the Son of God whereby He
explains 'that'; which agree most perfectly with 'that' but yet
describe it not; for a thing of such immensity has this property,
that all excellent terms[34] that are of quality and greatness and
good agree with it, but none of these describes it—nay, nor
all of them together.

9. Let us now see if David says aught of this 'that.' In a
Psalm he says: 'How great is the multitude of Thy sweetness
which Thou hast hidden for them that fear Thee';[35] and elsewhere he speaks of 'that,' as of a torrent of pleasure, saying:
'Of the torrent of Thy pleasure Thou shalt give them to
drink.'[36] And, because David finds not even this name to be
sufficiently exact,[37] he calls it elsewhere a prevention of the
blessings of the sweetness of God.[38] So that a name which
exactly fits this 'that,' which the soul says is the bliss[39] to
which God predestined her, cannot be found. Let us, then,
keep the name of 'that,' which the soul gives it, and let us
expound the line after this manner: 'that which Thou gavest
me'—that is, that weight of glory whereunto Thou didst pre-
destine me, O my Spouse, in the day of Thine eternity, when
Thou wert pleased to determine to create me, Thou wilt give

[30] A: 'and I will write his name upon.'

[31] Apocalypse iii, 12.

[32] Here ends G. Ej adds the lines of Stanza XXXIII and ends
also.

[33] Apocalypse iii, 21–2. Sg has: 'in His nuptial-chamber
[*tálamo*]' for 'in His throne.'

[34] Sg: 'excellent roads.'

[35] Psalm xxx, 20 [A.V., xxxi, 19].

[36] Psalm xxxv, 9 [A.V., xxxvi, 8].

[37] Sg: 'sufficiently exact for the thing.'

[38] Psalm xx, 4 [A.V., xxi, 3]. [By 'prevention' understand 'fore-
taste.' Cf. A.V.]

[39] Bg: 'is the fidelity.'

me there, on the day of my betrothal and my marriage, and in my day of the joy[40] of my heart, when, setting me free from the flesh and making me to enter into the lofty caverns of Thy bridal chamber, transforming me gloriously into Thyself, Thou mayest drink with me the new wine of the sweet pomegranates.[41]

Annotation for the Stanza Following

But inasmuch as the soul in this estate of the Spiritual Marriage, whereof we are here treating, fails not to know something of 'that,' since, being transformed in God, it experiences something of it, it will not fail to say something of 'that' whereof it feels the pledges and the signs within itself already; for, as is said in the Book of Job,[42] Who can withhold the word which he has conceived within himself and not utter it?[43] And thus in the following stanza the soul is occupied in saying something of that fruition which it will then enjoy in the beatific vision,[44] describing, as far as is possible, what and of what nature will be that thing which will then come to pass.

STANZA XXXIX

The breathing of the air,   The song of the sweet philomel,
The grove and its beauty in the serene night,   With a flame
    that consumes and gives no pain.

2. In this stanza the soul describes and expounds that which she says the Spouse will give her in that beatific transformation, expounding it by means of five expressions. First, she

[40] Sg: 'of the glory.'
[41] Sg: 'Divine pomegranates.'
[42] So S. The other authorities read: 'in the prophet Job.'
[43] Job iv, 2.
[44] So Sg. Bg: 'in the most blessed sight.' B: 'in the beatified sight.' The other authorities read: 'in the beatific sight.'

says it is the aspiration[1] after her of the Holy Spirit of God, and her own aspiration after God. Secondly, jubilation before God in the fruition of God. Thirdly, the knowledge of the creatures and of the ordering of them. Fourthly, pure and clear contemplation of the Divine Essence. Fifthly, total transformation in the boundless love of God. The line, then, says:

The breathing of the air,

3. This breathing of the air is a property[2] which the soul says that God will give her there, in the communication of the Holy Spirit, Who, as one that breathes, raises the soul most sublimely with that His Divine breath, and informs and habilitates her, that she may breathe in God the same breath of love that the Father breathes in the Son and the Son in the Father, which is the same Holy Spirit that God breathes into the soul in the Father and the Son, in the said transformation, in order to unite her with Himself. For it would not be a true and total transformation if the soul were not transformed in the three Persons of the Most Holy Trinity, in a clearly revealed and manifest degree. And this said breathing[3] of the Holy Spirit in the soul, whereby God transforms her into Himself, is so sublime and delicate and profound a delight to her that it cannot be described by mortal tongue, nor can human understanding, as such, attain to any conception of it. For even that which passed in the soul with respect to this communication in this temporal transformation cannot be described, because the soul united and transformed in God breathes in God into God the same Divine breath[4] that God, when she is transformed in Him, breathes into her in Himself.

4. And in the transformation which the soul experiences in this life, this same breathing of God into the soul, and of the soul into God, is very frequent, and brings the most sub-

[1] [*aspiración.* Or 'breathing,' which word is used to translate the verbal noun *aspirar,* below.] Bg has: 'the explanation.' Sg: 'the aspiration of the air (of the Holy Spirit).' [The word *a,* rendered here 'after,' as befits the abstract 'aspiration,' is translated 'into,' at the end of the next paragraph, after the verb 'breathe.']

[2] See p. 215, n. 24, above.

[3] [*aspiración.* n. 1, above.]

[4] [*aspiración.*]

lime delight of love to the soul, albeit not in a degree revealed and manifest, as in the next life. For this, as I understand, was the meaning of Saint Paul when he said: 'Because you are sons of God, God sent the Spirit of His Son into your hearts, crying to the Father.'[5] This happens, after the manners described, to the blessed in the next life and to the perfect in this. And there is no need to consider it impossible that the soul should be capable of aught so high as to breathe in God as God breathes in her by a mode of participation. For, since God grants her the favour of uniting her in the Most Holy Trinity, wherein she becomes deiform and God by participation, how is it a thing incredible that she should also perform her work of understanding, knowledge and love—or, rather, should have it performed in the Trinity, together with It, like the Trinity Itself. This, however, comes to pass by a mode of communication and participation, which God effects in the soul herself; for this is to be transformed in the three Persons,[6] in power and wisdom and love; and herein the soul is like to God, for it was to the end that she might come to this that He created her in His image and likeness.

5. And how this comes to pass cannot be known, nor is it possible to express it, save by describing how the Son of God obtained for us this high estate and merited for us this sublime office, of being able to become sons of God, as says Saint John.[7] And thus He prayed to the Father, as says the same Saint John, saying: 'Father, I will that they whom Thou hast given Me may be also with Me where I am, that they may see the brightness which Thou gavest Me.'[8] That is to say, that they may work in Us by participation the same work which I do by nature, which is the breathing of the Holy Spirit. And He says further: 'I pray not, Father, only for these that are present, but for them also who through their teaching shall believe in Me, that they may all be one and the same thing; so that as Thou, Father, art in Me and I am in Thee, even

[5] Galatians iv, 6.
[6] Sg: 'in the three faculties.'
[7] [St. John i, 12.]
[8] St. John xvii, 24.

so may they be one and the same thing in Us;[9] and I have given them the brightness which Thou hast given Me, that they may be one and the same thing, as We are one and the same thing; I in Them, and Thou in Me, that they may be perfect in one; that the world may know that Thou hast sent Me, and hast loved them, as Thou hast loved Me';[10] namely, by communicating to them the same love as to the Son, though not naturally, as to the Son, but, as we have said, by unity and transformation of love. Neither is it to be understood here that the Son means to say to the Father that the saints are to be one thing in essence and nature, as are the Father and the Son; but rather that they may be so by union of love, as are the Father and the Son in unity of love.

6. Wherefore souls possess these same blessings by participation as He possesses by nature; for the which cause they are truly gods by participation, equals of God[11] and His companions. Wherefore Saint Peter said: 'Grace and peace be complete and perfect in you in the knowledge of God and of Christ Jesus our Lord, according as all things are given to us of His Divine virtue for life and godliness, through the knowledge of Him that has called us with His own glory and virtue; whereby He has given unto us most great and precious promises, that by these things we may be made companions of the Divine nature.'[12] Thus far are the words of Saint Peter, wherein it is clearly signified that the soul will have participation in God Himself, and that it will be performing in Him, in company with Him, the work of the Most Holy Trinity, after the manner whereof we have spoken, by reason of the substantial union between the soul and God. And, though this can be perfectly fulfilled only in the next life, nevertheless, in this life, when the estate of perfection is reached, as we say it is here reached by the soul, a clear trace and taste of it

9 Sg omits the sentence: 'So that . . . in Us.'

10 St. John xvii, 20–3.

11 S: 'like unto God.' [The Spanish is here identical with that of the first redaction, which, on account of the great importance of the passage, is quoted on p. 219, n. 13, above.]

12 2 St. Peter i, 2–4.

are attained, after the manner that we are describing, albeit, as we have said, this cannot be expressed.

7. O souls created for these grandeurs and called thereto! What do ye do? Wherein do ye occupy yourselves? Your desires[13] are meannesses, and your possessions miseries.[14] O wretched blindness of the eyes of your souls,[15] which are blind to so great a light and deaf to so clear a voice, seeing not that for so long as ye seek grandeurs and glories ye remain miserable and mean,[16] and have become ignorant and unworthy of so many blessings![17] There follows the second thing which the soul says in order to explain 'that' thing, namely:

The song of the sweet philomel,

8. That which is born in the soul from that breathing of the air is the sweet voice of the Beloved speaking to her, wherein the soul addresses to Him her own delectable jubilation; and both are here called the song of the philomel. For even as the song of the philomel, which is the nightingale,[18] is heard in the spring, when the cold, the rains and the changes of winter are all past, and makes melody to the ear and gives refreshment to the spirit, even so in this present communication and transformation of love which the soul now enjoys in this life, she is protected and freed from all temporal changes and disturbances, and detached and purged from the imperfections, penalties and mists,[19] both of sense and of spirit, and feels the new spring in liberty, enlargement and joy of spirit, wherein she hears the sweet voice of the Spouse, Who is her sweet philomel, by the which voice, re-

[13] [See p. 219, n. 15, above.]

[14] Sg: 'and your possessions, meannesses and miseries.'

[15] S: 'O wretched blindness of the sons of Adam!' Sg: 'O pitiableness and blindness of the eyes of your souls!' Bg: 'What do ye do? Where do ye stop and occupy your faculties, mean desires and wretched possessions?'

[16] B, Bg, Bz: 'and empty.'

[17] A: 'miserable and deprived of so many blessings!' [The difference between this reading and that of the first redaction (p. 219) in the Spanish is one of punctuation only.]

[18] [See p. 220, n. 16, above.]

[19] [See p. 135, n. 32, above.]

freshing and renewing the substance of her soul, so that it is
now well prepared for the journey to life eternal,[20] He calls
her sweetly and delectably, saying: 'Arise, make haste, My
friend,[21] My dove, My beautiful one, and come; for the winter is now past, the rain has now gone far away, the flowers
have now appeared in our land, the time of pruning[22] is
come, and the voice of the turtle-dove is heard in our land.'[23]

9. This voice of the Spouse, Who speaks to the Bride in the
inmost part of the soul, she perceives to be the end of her ills,
and the beginning of her blessings; and in the refreshment and
protection and delectable feeling which this causes her she
likewise lifts up her voice, as does the sweet philomel, in a new
song of jubilation to God, together with God, Who moves her
thereto. For this cause He gives her His voice,[24] that she may
sing to God with Him, for that is His aspiration[25] and desire,
that the soul may lift up her spiritual voice in jubilation to
God. This is also the desire of the same Spouse in the Songs,
where He says: 'Arise, make haste, My friend,[26] and come,
My dove, into the clefts of the rock, into the cavern of the
enclosure; show Me thy face, let thy voice sound in Mine
ears.'[27] By the ears of God are here meant the desires of God
that the soul may lift up to Him this voice of perfect jubilation; the which voice, that it may be perfect, the Spouse entreats the soul to send forth and cause to sound in the caverns
of the rock—that is, in the transformation of the mysteries of
Christ whereof we spoke above. For, because in this union the
soul rejoices and praises God together with God Himself, as
we said in speaking of their love, it is praise very perfect and
pleasing to God, for the soul, being in this perfection, performs works which are perfect. And thus this voice of jubilation is sweet to God and sweet to the soul. Wherefore the

[20] Sg: 'for the communication of life eternal.'
[21] [See p. 446, n. 27, above.]
[22] [*el tiempo del podar*. P. Silverio has *poder* ('be able') for
podar ('prune'), an evident error.]
[23] Canticles ii, 10–12.
[24] Sg: 'He gives His spiritual voice in jubilation.'
[25] [See p. 220, n. 22, above.]
[26] [See p. 446, n. 27, above.]
[27] Canticles ii, 13–14.

Spouse said: 'Thy voice is sweet.'[28] That is to say, not only for thee, but also for Me; for, being at one with Me, thou dost raise thy voice as a sweet philomel in unison with Me.

10. Of this kind is the song which is sung by[29] the soul in the transformation which it experiences in this life, the delectableness whereof is beyond all exaggeration. But, as it is not as perfect as the new canticle of the life of glory, the soul, having some experience of it through this which it here knows,[30] forms some conception,[31] through the sublimity of this song, of the excellence of that which it will have in glory, which exceeds it beyond all comparison. The Bride thinks upon it[32] and says that 'that' which He will give her will be the song of the sweet philomel. And she then says:

The grove and its beauty

11. This is the third thing which the soul says that the Spouse is to give her. By the grove, since it nurtures within itself many plants and animals, the soul here understands God, since He nurtures and gives being to all creatures, which have their life and root in Him; which is for God to show Himself and make Himself known to her as Creator. In the beauty of this grove, which the soul likewise entreats the Spouse to give her then, she prays for grace[33] and wisdom, and the beauty which not only each of the creatures, both terrestrial and celestial,[34] has from God, but which they make among themselves in the wise, ordered, gracious and loving mutual correspondence, both of the lower creatures among themselves, and of the higher likewise among themselves, and between the higher and the lower—a thing of which the knowledge

[28] Canticles ii, 14.

[29] [*Lit.*, 'which passes in.']

[30] [*Lit.*, 'feels.']

[31] [*rastreando: lit.*, tracking, following a track or clue (*rastro*). 'This song' is the 'track' by following which the soul gains some conception of the other.]

[32] [*hace memoria de él:* a phrase often used with this equivalence.]

[33] Sg: 'she understands grace.'

[34] Sg omits: 'both . . . celestial.'

gives the soul great beauty and delight. There follows the
fourth thing, which is:

In the serene night,

12. This night is contemplation, wherein the soul desires
to see these things. She calls it night, because contemplation
is dark, for which reason it is called by its other name, 'mystical theology,' which signifies secret or hidden wisdom of God,
wherein without noise of words and without the aid of any
bodily or spiritual sense, as if in silence and quiet, hidden by
darkness from all that is of the senses and of nature, God
teaches the soul after a most hidden and secret manner, without her knowing how; this is that which some spiritual men
call 'understanding yet understanding not.' This is not done
by the understanding which philosophers call active, the work
whereof is in the forms and fancies and apprehensions of the
bodily faculties; but it is done in the understanding inasmuch
as this is possible[35] and passive: without receiving such forms,
it passively receives substantial knowledge, stripped of all images, which is given to it without any work or active office
of its own.

13. And for this cause she calls this contemplation night,
wherein, in this life, by means of the transformation which it
already has, the soul after a most lofty manner knows this Divine grove and its beauty. But, lofty as this knowledge is, it is
nevertheless dark night by comparison with the beatific knowledge which the soul here entreats; wherefore, praying for
clear contemplation, she asks that this enjoyment of the grove
and its beauty, and of the other things which she has here entreated, may be in the serene night—that is, in clear and
beatific[36] contemplation—so that it may no longer be night in
the dark contemplation here below, but may turn into[37] the
contemplation of the clear and serene sight of God on high.
And thus to say 'in the serene night' is to say 'in clear and
serene contemplation of the sight of God.' Wherefore David,
referring to this night of contemplation, says: 'The night shall

---

[35] Sg has *pasible* [a synonym of *pasivo*, which follows].
[36] A: 'clear and serene and beatific.'
[37] Bg: 'and delights in.'

be my illumination[38] in my delights.'[39] Which is as though he
had said: When I am in my delights of the essential sight of
God, the night of contemplation will have dawned in the day
and light of my understanding. There follows the fifth thing:

With a flame that consumes and gives no pain.

14. By the flame she here understands the love of the Holy
Spirit. To consume[40] signifies here to complete and to perfect.
When the soul, then, says that all the things which she has
described in this stanza will be given to her by the Beloved
and that she will possess them with consummate and perfect
love, all of them being absorbed, and she with them, in perfect
love which causes no pain, she says this in order to describe
the complete perfection of this love. For, in order that it may
be perfect, it must have these two properties—namely, that it
may consume[41] and transform the soul in God, and that the
enkindling and the transformation of this flame in the soul
may not cause pain. This cannot be save in the beatific estate,
where this flame is already sweet love;[42] for in the transformation of the soul therein there is beatific satisfaction and
conformity on either side, and therefore there is no pain
caused by difference between the greater and the less, as there
was before the soul attained to the capacity of this perfect
love. For, now that the soul has attained thereto, its love of
God is so closely conformed to Him and so sweet that though
God, as Moses says, is a consuming fire,[43] He is not so now,
but a consummating[44] and a renewing fire. This new transformation is not like that which the soul experienced in this life;

[38] So A, Av, B, Bg, Bz. Sg: 'the serene night is my illumination.'
Jaén: 'the serene night my illumination.'

[39] Psalm cxxxviii, 11 [A.V., cxxxix, 11].

[40] [All the authorities have 'to consummate' (*consumar*), but 'to
consume' (*consumir*) is certainly meant, as it is used in the line
to be expounded and just quoted ('Con llama que *consume* . . .').]

[41] [Again, 'consummate' is used, this time with more reason. I
keep 'consume,' however, on account of the context.]

[42] S omits: 'this cannot be . . . sweet love.'

[43] Deuteronomy iv, 24.

[44] [There is a play on words here between 'consuming' (*con-
sumidor*) and 'consummating' (*consumador*).]

for, although the latter was most perfect, and effected the consummation of love, it was yet in some measure consuming and
detractive, like fire upon coals; and though these coals be
transformed and have become like to the fire, having none of
that smoke[45] which they gave out before they were transformed in it, yet, although they have become perfected by the
fire, it has nevertheless consumed them and reduced them
to ashes. This comes to pass in the soul that in this life is
transformed with perfection of love; for, although there is
conformity, still the soul suffers some degree of pain and detriment; first, because of the beatific transformation which the
spirit still lacks; and secondly, because of the detriment which
is suffered by weak and corruptible sense from its contact
with the fortitude and loftiness of love that is so great; for
anything that is excellent is detriment and grief to natural
weakness; for, even as it is written, *Corpus quod corrumpitur
aggravat animam.*[46] But in that beatific life it will feel no
detriment or pain, although its understanding will be exceeding deep and its love altogether boundless;[47] for God will
give it capacity for the one and fortitude for the other, and
will perfect its understanding with His wisdom and its will
with His love.[48]

15. And since in the preceding stanzas, as in that which we
are expounding, the Bride has prayed for boundless communications and knowledge of God, for which she needs the
strongest and the loftiest love, in order to love according to
the greatness and the loftiness of this knowledge, she here
prays that they may all be contained in this love, which is
consummate, perfective and strong.

[45] A, Sg: 'that brilliance [i.e., of flame] and smoke.' B, Bg:
'that brilliance and beauty.'
[46] Wisdom ix, 15. ['The corruptible body is a load upon the
soul.']
[47] Sg: 'will be exceeding deep, sweet and altogether boundless.'
[48] A omits the following paragraph. Sg heads it: 'Annotation
for the stanza following.'

STANZA XL

**For none saw it,   Neither did Aminadab appear,
And there was a rest from the siege,   And the cavalry came
down at the sight of the waters.**

Exposition and Annotation[1]

The Bride, then, now knows that the desire of her will is at
last detached from all things and is clinging to her God with
most intimate love; that the sensual part of the soul, with all
its powers, faculties and desires, is conformed with the spirit;[2]
and that its rebellions are quelled and are all over. She knows,
too, that the devil is now overcome and driven far away by
long and varied spiritual strife and exercise, and that her soul
is united and transformed[3] with abundance of celestial gifts
and riches; and that accordingly she herself is now ready and
strong and well prepared to go up, leaning upon her Beloved,[4]
through the wilderness of death, abounding in delights, to the
glorious seats and resting-places of her Spouse. Desiring, then,
that the Spouse will now bring this matter to a conclusion,
she endeavours to move Him thereto, by setting all these things
before Him in this last stanza, wherein she says five things.
The first thing is that her soul is detached and far away from
all things. The second, that the devil has now been conquered
and put to flight. The third, that the passions are now held
in bondage and the natural desires are mortified. The fourth
and fifth, that the lower and sensual part of the soul has
now been reformed and purified and has been brought into
conformity with the spiritual part, so as not only not to be
hindered from receiving spiritual blessings, but rather to be

---

[1] Sg omits: 'and annotation.'
[2] Sg: 'conformed with the desire.'
[3] A adds: 'in God.'
[4] Canticles viii, 5.

prepared for them, for, according to its capacity, it is already a partaker of those which it now has. And she says thus:

For none saw it,

2. This is as though she were to say: My soul is now stripped, detached, alone and far removed from all created things, both above and below, and has entered so far into interior recollection[5] with Thee, that none of the said things can come within sight of the intimate joy which I possess in Thee—that is, none of them by their sweetness can move my soul to desire them, nor by their wretchedness and misery to dislike and be troubled by them; for my soul is so far from them and in such deep joy with Thee that none of these things can come within sight of it. And not only so, but

Neither did Aminadab appear,

3. This Aminadab, in Divine Scripture, spiritually considered, signifies the devil, who is the adversary of the soul, and was ever giving her battle and disturbing her with the innumerable munitions of his artillery, that she might not enter into this fortress and secret place of interior recollection with the Spouse. When placed herein, the soul is so greatly favoured, so strong and so victorious with the virtues that she has there, and with the favour of the embrace[6] of God, that the devil not only dares not approach her, but flees very far from her in great terror and dares not even appear. And because of the exercise of the virtues, and by reason of the perfect estate wherein she now abides, the soul has so completely put him to flight and conquered him that he appears before her no longer. And so (says the soul) neither did Aminadab appear with any right to hinder me from receiving this blessing to which I aspire.

And there was a rest from the siege,

4. By this siege the soul here understands its passions and desires, which, when they are not conquered and mortified,

[5] Sg: 'interior knowledge.'
[6] So Jaén, A, Av, Bg, Bz, Sg. B, S: 'of the arm.'

besiege it round about, giving battle to it on every side, wherefore she calls these the siege. From this siege she says, too, that there is now a rest—that is, that the passions are ordered by reason and the desires mortified. Since this is so, then, the soul begs the Spouse not to fail to communicate to her the favours for which she has prayed Him, since the siege aforementioned can no longer be a hindrance. This she says because, until the soul has its four passions ordered and directed Godward, and the desires mortified and purged, it is not capable of seeing God.[7] And there follows:

And the cavalry came down at the sight of the waters.

5. By the waters are here understood the spiritual delights and blessings whereof in this estate the soul has fruition inwardly with God. By the cavalry are here understood the faculties of the sensual part, both interior and exterior, for these carry within them the phantasms[8] and figures of their objects. These, says the Bride here, come down in this estate at the sight of the spiritual waters,[9] for the lower and sensual part of the soul is now so purified and in some manner spiritualized in this estate of the Spiritual Marriage that she, together with her sensual faculties and natural forces, is recollected, and has participation and fruition, after her manner, of the spiritual grandeurs which God is communicating to the soul, in the inmost part of the spirit, even as David signified when he said: 'My heart and my flesh have rejoiced in the living God.'[10]

6. And it is to be noted that the Bride says not here that the cavalry came down to taste of the waters, but that it came down at the sight of them. For this sensual part with its faculties has not the capacity to taste essentially and properly of spiritual blessings, either in this life or even in the next; but through a certain overflowing of the spirit they receive in the

[7] A, Bg read: 'they are not in peace [*en paz*] to see God' for 'it is not capable [*capaz*] of seeing God.'

[8] S: 'the fantasies.'

[9] Bg: 'came down in this estate to the spiritual waters or at the sight of them.'

[10] Psalm lxxxiii, 3 [A.V., lxxxiv, 2].

senses refreshment and delight therefrom, whereby these senses and faculties[11] of the body are attracted into[12] that interior recollection wherein the soul is drinking of spiritual blessings, which is to come down at the sight of them rather than to drink of them[13] and taste of them as they are. And the soul says here that they came down, and says not that they went, nor uses any other word, in order to signify that, in this communication of the sensual part to the spiritual, when the said draught[14] of the spiritual waters is tasted, they come down from their natural operations, from which they cease, to interior recollection.

7. All these perfections and dispositions[15] the Bride sets before her Beloved, the Son of God, with the desire to be translated by Him out of the Spiritual Marriage to which God has been pleased to bring her in this Church Militant, to the glorious Marriage of the Church Triumphant; whereto may the sweetest Jesus be pleased to lead all such as call upon His name, the Spouse of faithful souls, to Whom, with the Father and the Holy Spirit, belong honour and glory, *in sæcula sæculorum*. Amen.[16]

[11] A, B omit: 'and faculties.'
[12] Sg: 'are drawn to.'
[13] A, Av, Bz: 'than to see them.'
[14] Sg: 'the said communication and draught.'
[15] Sg omits: 'and dispositions.'
[16] Sg adds: 'Laus Deo'; Av: 'Fr. Juan de la †'; A: 'End of the illumination, etc.'; Bg: 'Jesus, Mary, Joseph.'

APPENDIX

Passages from the Granada Codex showing extensive variations from the Sanlúcar Codex.

Beginneth the Exposition of the Stanzas between the Bride and the Spouse[1]

STANZA THE FIRST

Whither hast thou hidden thyself, And hast left me, O Beloved, to my sighing?
Thou didst flee like the hart,[2] having wounded me: I went out after thee, calling, and thou wert[3] gone.

Exposition

In this first stanza, the soul that is enamoured of the Word,[4] the Son of God, her Spouse, desiring to be united with Him through clear and essential vision, sets forth her love's anxiety, reproaching Him for His absence, the more so because, being wounded by her love, for the which she has abandoned all things, yea even herself, she has still to suffer the absence of her Beloved and is not yet loosed from her mortal flesh that she may be able to have fruition of Him in the glory of eternity. And thus she says:

Whither hast thou hidden thyself,

2. It is as though she said: O Word, my Spouse, show me the place where Thou art hidden. Wherein she begs Him to manifest His Divine Essence; for the place where the Son of

---

[1] [See p. 49, n. 1.] The notes which follow show such variants as are to be found in Codices similar to that of Granada, i.e., those not included in the Sanlúcar version.

[2] Bj, Bz: 'like a hart.' 8,654: 'For thou didst flee like a hart.'

[3] Bj, Lch: 'wert already.'

[4] Bj omits: 'the Word.'

God is hidden, as Saint John says, is 'the bosom of the Father,'[5] which is the Divine Essence, the which is removed and hidden from every mortal eye and from all understanding.[6] Which Isaias signified when he said: 'Verily Thou art a hidden God. Here it is to be noted that, however lofty are the communications with God of a soul that is in this life, and the revelations of His presence, and however high and exalted is its knowledge of Him, they are not God in His Essence, nor have they aught to do with Him. For in truth He is still hidden from the soul, and it ever beseems the soul, amid all these grandeurs, to consider Him as hidden, and to seek Him as One hidden, saying: 'Whither hast Thou hidden Thyself?' For neither[7] a sublime communication of Him nor a sensible revelation of His presence[8] is a clearer testimony of His presence, nor is aridity or the want of all these things[9] in the soul the less clear testimony thereof.[10] For which cause says the prophet Job: 'If He comes to me I shall not see Him; and if He departs, I shall not understand Him.' Wherein is to be understood that, if the soul should experience any great communication and feeling or knowledge of God, it must not for that reason persuade itself that it possesses God more completely or is more deeply in God; nor that that which it feels and understands is God in His Essence, however profound such experiences may be; and, if all these sensible communications fail, it must not for that reason think that God is failing it.[11] For in reality the one estate can give no assurance to a soul that it is in His grace, neither can the other, that it is outside it. So that the principal intent of the soul in the present line is not merely to beg for sensible and affective[12] devo-

[5] [The Scriptural references are not given in the notes to this Appendix; they can be found in the Sanlúcar version above.]

[6] Md adds: 'in this life.'

[7] The Granada MS., which lacks its first folio, begins with these words.

[8] Bj: 'His pre-eminence.'

[9] [*Lit.*, 'or the want' only.]

[10] Lch: '. . . of His presence, and a presence to be feared, nor are aridities and the want [of all these things] in the soul.'

[11] [See p. 50, n. 3, above.]

[12] Bz: 'and devotion.' Md: 'and devotion affectively.'

tion, wherein there is neither certainty nor evidence of the possession of the Spouse in this life, but to beg for the clear presence and vision of His Essence, wherein it desires to be certified and satisfied in glory.

3. This same thing was signified by the Bride in the Divine Songs when, desiring union with the Divinity of the Word her Spouse, she begged the Father for it, saying: 'Show me where thou feedest, and where thou liest in the midday.' For to enquire of Him where He fed was to beg that she might be shown the Essence of the Word, for the Father feeds upon naught else than His only Son. And to beg Him to show her where He lay was to beg that selfsame thing, since the Father lies not, neither is present, in aught save in His Son, in Whom He lies, communicating to Him all His Essence—'in the midday,' which is in Eternity, where He ever begets Him.[13] It is this pasture, then, where the Father feeds, and this flowery bed of the Word, whereon He lies hidden from every creature, that the Bride here entreats when she says: 'Whither hast Thou hidden Thyself?'

4. And it is to be observed, if one would learn how to find[14] this Spouse, that the Word, together with the Father and the Holy Spirit, is hidden essentially in the inmost centre of the soul. Wherefore the soul that would find Him must go forth from all things according to the will, and enter within itself in deepest recollection, which is to hold[15] all things as though they were not. Hence Saint Augustine, speaking with God in the *Soliloquies,* said: 'I found Thee not without, because I erred in seeking Thee without that wert within.' He is, then, hidden within the soul, and there the good contemplative must seek Him, saying: 'Whither hast Thou hidden Thyself?'

And hast left me, O Beloved, to my sighing?

5. The Bride calls Him 'Beloved,' in order the more to move and incline Him to her prayer, for, when God is loved, He hears the prayers of His lover with great readiness; and

[13] Bz: 'where He begets.' Lch: 'where He is begotten.'
[14] Bj has *hablar* ['to speak (to)'] for *hallar* ['to find'].
[15] Bj, 8,654, Lch, Md have 'esteeming' for 'which is to hold.' Bz has 'creatures' for 'things.'

then in truth He can be called Beloved when the soul is wholly with Him and has not its heart set on aught that is outside Him. Some call the Spouse 'Beloved' when He is not in truth their Beloved, because they have not their heart wholly with Him; and thus their petition before Him is of less effect.

6. And in the words which she then says: 'And hast left me to my sighing,' it is to be observed that the absence of the Beloved causes continual sighing in the lover, because apart from Him she loves naught, rests in naught and finds relief in naught; whence the man who indeed has love toward God will know it by this—namely, if he be content[16] with aught that is less than God. To this sighing Saint Paul referred clearly when he said: 'We[17] groan within ourselves, waiting for the adoption of the sons of God.' This, then, is the sighing which the soul ever makes, for sorrow at His absence, above all when, having enjoyed some kind of sweet and delectable communion with Him, she has remained dry and alone. And so there follows:

Thou[18] didst flee like the hart,

7. It is to be observed that in the Songs the Bride compares the Spouse to the hart and the mountain goat, saying: 'My Beloved is like to the goat, and to the young of the harts.' And this because of the swiftness wherewith He hides and reveals Himself, as the Beloved is wont to do in the visits which He makes to the soul, and in the withdrawals and absences which He makes them experience after such visits. In this way He makes them to grieve[19] the more bitterly for His absence, as the soul now declares when she says:

Having wounded me:

8. Which is as though she had said: Not sufficient of themselves were the sorrow and grief which I suffer ordinarily in Thy absence: Thou didst wound me yet more, by love, with

16 So Gr and 8,654. But Bj, Bz, Lch, Md read: 'with naught.'
17 Bj, Bz, 8,654, Md: 'We ourselves.'
18 8,654: 'For thou.'
19 Lch omits: 'after such . . . to grieve.'

Thine arrow; and, having increased my passion and desire for
the sight of Thee, didst flee with the swiftness of the hart and
allowedst not Thyself to be in the smallest degree comprehended.

9. For the further exposition of this line we must know
that, beside many other different ways wherein God visits the
soul, wounding it and upraising it in love, He is wont to bestow on it certain enkindling[20] touches of love, which like
fiery arrows strike and pierce the soul and leave it wholly cauterized with the fire of love. And these are properly called the
wounds of love,[21] whereof[22] the soul here speaks. So greatly
do these wounds enkindle the will in affection that the soul
finds itself burning in the fire and flame of love, so much so
that it appears to be consumed in that flame which causes it to
go forth from itself and be wholly renewed[23] and enter upon
another mode of being; like the phœnix, that is burned up
and re-born anew. Of this David speaks and says: 'My heart
was kindled and my reins were changed and I was brought to
nothing and I knew not.' The desires and affections, which
the Prophet here describes as reins, are all stirred, and in that
enkindlement of the heart are changed into Divine affections,
and the soul through love is reduced to naught, and knows
naught save love.[24] And at this season there takes place this
stirring of these reins, which is much like to a torture of yearning to see God—so much so that the rigour wherewith love
treats the soul seems to it intolerable; not because it is
wounded thereby (for aforetime it held such wounds of love
to be health), but because it is left thus grieving, and has not
been wounded further, even to the point of death, in the
which case it would see itself, and be united, together with
Him in life. Wherefore the soul magnifies or describes her
pain and says: 'Having wounded me.'

10. And thus there comes to pass this grief that is so great,

---

[20] 8,654 reads: *escondidos* ['hidden,' 'secret'] for *encendidos*
['enkindling'].

[21] Bj, Lch omit: 'And these . . . of love.'

[22] Md has 'of which wounds of love' for 'whereof.'

[23] Bz: 'and completely overflow.'

[24] Bj, Bz omit: 'and knows naught save love.'

inasmuch as when God inflicts that wound of love the will rises with sudden celerity to the possession of the Beloved, Whose touch it has felt. And with equal celerity it feels His absence and the sighing for it together. For these said visits that wound are not like others wherein God refreshes and satisfies the soul by filling it with gentle peace. But these visits He makes to wound the soul rather than to heal it, and to afflict rather than to satisfy, since they serve but to quicken the knowledge and increase the desire, and, consequently, the pain.[25] These are called wounds of love, and are most delectable to the soul, for the which cause it would fain be ever dying a thousand deaths from these lance-thrusts, for they cause it to issue forth from itself and enter into God. This the Bride expresses in the line following, saying:

I went out after thee, calling, and thou wert[26] gone.

11. There can be no medicine for the wounds of love save that which comes from him that dealt the wounds. For this cause the soul went out, calling, after Him that had wounded her, because of the violence of the burning[27] that was caused by the wound. And it must be known that this going out is understood in two ways: the one, a going forth from all things, which is done by abhorring and despising them; the other, a going forth from herself, by forgetting herself, which is done by the love of God; and this raises her after such wise that it makes her to go out from herself and from her judgment[28] and the ways that are natural to her, and to call for God. And to this the soul here refers when she says: 'I went out after Thee, calling'; for both these, and no less, are needful, for one that would go after God and enter within Him. And it is as though she said: By this Thy touch and wound of love, my Spouse, Thou hast not only drawn forth my soul from all things, but likewise Thou hast made it to go out from itself (for truly it seems that He is drawing her away from her very flesh) and hast raised it up to Thyself, so that

25 In Bj all the paragraph, as far as this point, is wanting.
26 Bj, Lch: 'wert already.'
27 [Lit., 'strength of the fire.']
28 [See p. 55, n. 18, above.]

it cries for Thee and looses itself from all things that it may cling to Thee. 'And Thou wert gone.'

12. As though she had said: At the time when I desired to possess Thy presence I found Thee not, and I was loosed, yet I bound not myself to Thee; I was buffeted woefully by[29] the gales of love and found support neither in myself nor in Thee. This going forth of the soul in order to go to the Beloved, as the soul here terms it, is called by the Bride in the Songs to 'rise,' where she says: 'I will rise and will seek Him Whom my soul loveth, going about the city, in the streets and the broad ways; I sought Him and I found Him not.'[30] To rise up is here understood, spiritually, as of an ascent from the low to the high, which is the same as to go out from oneself—that is, from one's own low way of life and love of self to the high love of God. But she says that she was wounded because she found Him not. Thus one that is enamoured lives ever in affliction, in absence, for he is already surrendered, and has expectation of being paid by the surrender of the Beloved, which is not granted him. He has lost himself already for His sake, yet has found no gain to compensate him for his loss, for he lacks the possession of the Beloved. Wherefore, if a man goes about afflicted for God, it is a sign that he has given himself to God and that God loves him.

13. This affliction and sorrow for the absence of God is wont to be so great in those that are approaching ever nearer to perfection, at the time of these Divine wounds, that, if[31] the Lord provided not for them, they would die. For, as they have kept the palate of the will and the spirit clean, healthy and well prepared for God, and as in that experience whereof we have spoken He gives them to taste something of the sweetness of love, for which they yearn above all things, therefore do they likewise suffer above all things. For there is shown to them in glimpses an immense good and it is not granted to them; wherefore their affliction and torment are unspeakable.

---

[29] [See p. 55, n. 20, above.]

[30] Canticles iii, 2.

[31] Lch abbreviates: 'is wont to be from these Divine wounds, so that, if . . .'

STANZA II

Shepherds, ye that go   Yonder, through the sheepcotes, to the hill,
If perchance ye see him that I most love,   Tell ye him that I languish, suffer and die.

Exposition

In this stanza the soul seeks to make use of intercessors and intermediaries with her Beloved, begging them to tell Him of her pain and affliction; for it is a characteristic of the lover, when she cannot commune with her Beloved because of His presence,[32] to do so by the best means that she may. And so at this point the soul would fain use her desires, affections and sighs as messengers, who are also able to make known the secrets of her heart. And thus she says:

Shepherds, ye that go

2. Calling the affections and desires shepherds, because they feed the soul on spiritual good things. For shepherd[33] signifies 'one who feeds,' and by their means God communicates Himself to her (which without them He does not). And she says: 'Ye that go.' That is to say, Ye that go forth from pure love; because they go not all to God, but those only that go forth from faithful love.

Yonder, through the sheepcotes, to the hill,

3. By the 'sheepcotes' she means the choirs of the angels, by whose ministry, from choir to choir, our sighs and prayers travel to God; Whom she here calls 'the hill,' because He is the greatest of all heights; and because in Him, as on the hill, are spied out[34] and seen all things, and the higher and lower

[32] Bz: 'His absence.'
[33] [See p. 57, n. 1, above.]
[34] [See p. 57, n. 2, above.]

sheepcotes; to Whom go our prayers, which the angels offer Him, as we have said; according as the angel said to Tobias, in these words: 'When thou didst pray with tears and didst bury the dead, I offered thy prayer unto God.' We can likewise understand by these shepherds of the soul the angels themselves, for not only do they bear messages to God but they also bring God's messages to our souls, feeding our souls, like good shepherds, with sweet inspirations and communications from God, which He also creates by means of them. And they protect us from the wolves, who are the evil spirits, and defend us from them like good shepherds

If perchance ye see . . .

4. This is as much as to say: If my good fortune and happiness are such that ye reach His presence so that He sees you and hears you. Here it is to be observed that, although it is true that God knows and understands all things, and sees and observes even the least of the thoughts[35] of the soul, yet He is said to see our necessities, or to hear them, when He relieves them or fulfils them; for not all necessities or all petitions reach such a point that God hears them in order to fulfil them, until in His eyes the number of them is sufficient and[36] there has arrived the proper time and season to grant them or relieve them. And then He is said to see them or to hear them, as may be seen in the Book of Exodus, where, after the four hundred years during which the children of Israel had been afflicted in the bondage of Egypt, God said to Moses: 'I have seen the affliction of My people and I am come down to deliver them'[37]—though He had ever seen them. Even so Saint Gabriel told Zacharias not to fear, because God had already heard his prayer by giving him the son for which he had been begging Him many years: yet He had ever heard him. And thus it is to be understood by every soul that, albeit God may not at once hearken to its necessity and prayer, yet it follows not that He will fail to hearken at an opportune time—He Who is a helper, as David says, in due time and in tribulation,

---

35 Bj, Lch: 'even the very thoughts.'
36 Lch omits: 'the number of them is sufficient and.'
37 Bj, Lch: 'to alleviate them.'

if the soul faint not and cease not from prayer. This, then, is signified here by the soul when she says, 'If perchance ye see . . .'; that is to say, 'If by good chance the time has arrived at which He sees well to grant them my petitions.'

. . . him that I most love,

5. That is to say: more than all things; which is, speaking spiritually, when naught that presents itself to the soul impedes her from doing and suffering, whatsoever it be, for His sake.

Tell ye him that I languish, suffer and die.

6. Three kinds of need the soul represents here, to wit: languor, suffering and death; for the soul that loves truly suffers ordinarily from the absence of God in three ways, according to the three faculties of the soul, which are understanding, will and memory. She says that she languishes in the understanding because she sees not God, Who is the health of the understanding. She says that she suffers as to the will, because she possesses not God, Who is the refreshment and delight of the will. She says that she dies as to the memory, because, remembering that she lacks all the blessings of the understanding, which are the sight of God, and all the delights of the will, which are the possession of Him, and that it is likewise very possible to be deprived of Him for ever, she suffers at this memory as it were death.

7. These three kinds of need Jeremias likewise represented to God in the Lamentations, saying: 'Remember my poverty, the wormwood and the gall.' The poverty refers to the understanding because to it belong the riches of the wisdom of God, wherein, as Saint Paul says, are hid all the treasures of God. The wormwood, which is a herb most bitter, refers to the will, for to this faculty belongs the sweetness of the possession of God: lacking which, the soul is left with its bitterness, even as the Angel said to Saint John in the Apocalypse, saying that his eating of the book would make his belly bitter, the belly being there taken to mean the will. The gall refers to the memory, which signifies the death of the soul, even as Moses writes in Deuteronomy, when he speaks of the damned, saying:

'Their wine will be the gall of dragons and the venom of asps, which is incurable.' This signifies there the lack of God, which is the death of the soul; and these three needs and afflictions are founded upon the three theological virtues—faith, charity and hope—which relate to the three faculties aforementioned: understanding, will and memory.[38]

8. And it is to be observed that in the line aforementioned the soul does no more than represent her need and affliction to the Beloved. For one that loves discreetly has no care to beg for that which he lacks and desires, but only shows forth his need, so that the Beloved may do that which seems good to Him. As when the Blessed Virgin spake to the beloved Son at the wedding in Cana of Galilee, not begging Him directly for wine, but saying: 'They have no wine.' Or as when the sisters of Lazarus sent to Him, not to say that He should heal their brother, but to tell Him to see how he whom He loved was sick. And this for three reasons. First, because the Lord knows that which is meet for us better than do we ourselves; second, because the Beloved has the greater compassion when He beholds the necessity of him that loves Him, and his resignation; third, because the soul is on surer ground with respect to self-love and love of possession if she represents her need than if she begs Him, as she thinks best, for that whereof she believes herself to have need. It is precisely this that the soul does now, when she represents her three necessities. And it is as though she were to say: Tell my Beloved this: Since I languish, and He alone is my health, may He give me my health; and since I suffer, and He alone is my joy, may He give me my joy; and since I die, and He alone is my life, may He give me my life.

[38] Md adds: 'although each one is not a proper subject for each of the three virtues.'

STANZA III

**Seeking my loves,   I will go o'er yonder mountains and banks;
I will neither pluck the flowers nor fear the wild beasts;   I will
pass by the mighty and cross the frontiers.**

Exposition

Not content with prayers and desires, and with making use of
intercessors in order that she may find the Beloved, as she did
in the preceding stanzas, the soul, over and above all this, sets
to work herself to seek Him. This she says in this stanza that
she must do: in the search for her Beloved, she must practise
virtues and mortifications in the contemplative and the active
life; and to this end she must accept no favours or good
things,[39] nor must all the powers and snares of the three enemies—world, devil and flesh—suffice to detain and hinder her.
So she says:

Seeking my loves,

2. That is to say, my Beloved.

I will go o'er yonder mountains and banks;

3. The virtues she calls 'mountains': first, by reason of their
loftiness; second, because of the difficulty and toil which are
experienced in climbing them, through the practice of the
contemplative life. And she describes as 'banks' the humilia-
tions and mortifications[40] and self-despising which she practises in the active life; for in order to acquire the virtues there
is need of both. This, then, is as much as to say: Seeking my
Beloved, I will ever put into practice the lofty virtues and
abase myself in mortifications and things lowly. This she says,

---

[39] Bj: 'or riches.'
[40] Bj, Bz, add: 'and subjections.'

because the way to seek God is ever to be doing good in God, and mortifying evil in oneself, after the manner following:

I will neither pluck the flowers . . .

4. Inasmuch as in order to seek God it is needful to have a heart that is detached and strong, free from all evil things and from good things that are not simply God,[41] she speaks, in this present line and in those which follow, of the liberty and the courage which she must have. And herein she says that she will not pluck the flowers that she may find on the way, whereby she means all the pleasures and satisfactions which may be offered her, which are of three kinds: temporal, sensual and spiritual. And because they all occupy the heart, and, if the soul pays heed to them or abides in them, are an impediment to the reaching of the true spiritual road, she says that she will not pluck these flowers or set her heart upon them. And it is as if she had said: I will not set my heart upon the riches and good things which the world may offer me, nor will I accept the satisfactions and delights of my flesh, neither will pay heed to the pleasures and consolations of my spirit, in such manner as to be kept from seeking my loves over the mountains and banks.[42] And this she says because she is doing that which David counsels upon this road, saying: 'If riches abound, set not your heart upon them'—that is, be not affectioned to them. This she understands of spiritual pleasures as also of other temporal blessings.[43] Here it is to be observed that not only do temporal blessings and corporeal delights and pleasures hinder and turn us aside from the road to God, but likewise spiritual delights and consolations, if we attach ourselves to them or seek after them, impede the road to the virtues. Wherefore it behoves him that will go forward not to turn aside for these flowers. And not only so, but it behoves him also to have the courage to say:

. . . nor fear the wild beasts;
I will pass by the mighty and cross the frontiers.

[41] Md adds: 'or lead not to God.'
[42] Bj, Bz: 'over the woods and banks.'
[43] Thus Gr, 8,654, Md. Bj, Bz: 'of sensual pleasures as of other temporal pleasures.'

5. In these lines the Bride speaks of the three enemies of the soul, which are world, devil and flesh, and these are they that war upon her and put difficulties in her way. By the 'wild beasts' she understands the world; by the 'mighty,' the devil; and by the 'frontiers,' the flesh.

6. She calls the world 'wild beasts,' because to the imagination of the soul that sets out upon the road to God the world seems to be represented after the manner of wild beasts, which threaten her fiercely, and principally in three ways. First, the favour of the world will leave her, and she will lose friends, credit and even property. Secondly, there is a wild beast no less terrifying—namely, that she must be able to bear the renunciation for ever of the satisfactions and delights of the world, and of all worldly comforts. Thirdly—and this is greater still—the tongues of men will rise up against her, and will mock her, and all will despise her. These things are wont to prejudice certain souls in such a way that it becomes supremely difficult for them, not only to persevere against these wild beasts, but even to set out upon the road at all.

7. But a few more generous souls meet other wild beasts, which are more interior and spiritual, in difficulties and temptations, tribulations and trials of many kinds, such as God sends to those whom He will prove as gold in the fire, even as in one place David says: That many are the afflictions of the just. But the soul that loves indeed, that prizes her Beloved above all things and trusts in the love of her Spouse and in His favour, will dare to say with courage: 'Nor will I fear the wild beasts.'

I will pass by the mighty and cross the frontiers.

8. Evil spirits, who are the second enemy of the soul, she calls 'the mighty,' because with a great display of strength they endeavour to seize the passes of this road, and likewise because their temptations and wiles are stronger and harder to overcome, and more difficult to penetrate, than those of the world and the flesh, and furthermore because they reinforce themselves with these other two enemies, the world and the flesh, in order to make vigorous warfare upon the soul. Wherefore David, in speaking of them, says of them: 'The

mighty sought after my soul.' Concerning their might, Job
says also: 'There is no power upon earth that can be compared
with that of the devil, who was made to fear no one.' That
is, no human power can be compared with his; and thus,
only the Divine power suffices to conquer him and only the
Divine light to penetrate his wiles. Wherefore the soul that
is to overcome his might will be unable to do so without
prayer, nor will it be able to penetrate his deceits without
humility and mortification. Hence Saint Paul, in counselling
the faithful, says these words: 'Brethren, put on the armour
of God, that you may be able to stand against the deceits of
the devil, for our wrestling is not against flesh and blood.' By
blood he means the world; and, by the armour of God, prayer
and the Cross of Christ, wherein is the humility and mortification whereof we have spoken.

9. She also says that she will cross the frontiers, whereby
she indicates the repugnance which of its nature the flesh has
to the spirit and the rebellions[44] which it makes against it; the
which flesh, as Saint Paul says, ever lusts against the spirit,
and sets itself, as it were, upon the frontier, and resists those
that travel on the spiritual road. And these frontiers the soul
must cross, by surmounting these difficulties and, by the force
and resolution of the spirit, overthrowing all the desires of
sense and the natural affections; for, so long as these remain
in the soul, the spirit is impeded by their weight so that it cannot pass on to true life and spiritual delight.[45] This Saint Paul
set clearly before us, when he said: 'If by the spirit you mortify the works of the flesh, you shall live.' This, then, is the
procedure which the soul says in this stanza that she must
needs follow in order to seek her Beloved—namely, constancy
and resolution not to stoop to pluck the flowers; courage not
to fear the wild beasts; and strength to pass by the mighty;
and she must determine only to go over the mountains and
banks after the manner already expounded.

[44] Bj, Lch have (by an error) 'revelations.'
[45] Md adds: 'from which we exclude not that of grace—rather
we assume it in one that is to journey to the perfection of the spiritual and mystical life.'

STANZA IV

**O woods and thickets   Planted by the hand[46] of the Beloved![47]
O meadow of verdure, enamelled with flowers,   Say if he has
passed by you.**

Exposition

After the soul has described the way wherein she will prepare
herself for setting out upon this road, namely, by courage not
to turn aside after delights and pleasures, and fortitude to conquer temptations and difficulties, wherein consists the practice
of self-knowledge, which is the first thing that the soul will
achieve in order to come to the knowledge of God, she now,
in this stanza, sets out upon her road, that of consideration
and knowledge of the creatures, to the knowledge of her Beloved, their Creator. For, after the practice of self-knowledge,
this consideration of the creatures is the first thing in order
upon this spiritual road to the knowledge of God; by means of
them the soul considers His greatness and excellence, according to that word of the Apostle where he says that the invisible
things of God are known by the soul, through the knowledge
of created things. The soul, then, in this stanza, speaks with
the creatures, asking them for news of her Beloved. And it is
to be observed that, as Saint Augustine says, the question that
the soul puts to the creatures is the meditation that she makes
by their means upon their Creator. And thus in this stanza is
contained a meditation on the elements and on the other
lower creatures, and a meditation upon the heavens and upon
the other creatures and material things that God has created
therein, and likewise a meditation upon the celestial spirits.
She says:

O woods and thickets

2. She describes as 'woods' the elements, which are earth,
water, fire, wind;[48] for, like the most pleasant woods, they are

---

46 Bj: 'by the hands.'
47 Lch, Md, 8,654: 'of my Beloved.'
48 Bj, Bz, Lch, 8,654, Md: 'water, air and fire.'

peopled thickly with creatures, by reason of their great number and the many differences which there are between them in each element. In the earth, innumerable varieties of animals; in the water, innumerable different species of fish; and likewise in the air, many diversities of birds; while the element of fire concurs with all in animating and preserving them; and thus each kind of animal lives in its element, and is located and planted therein as in its own wood, the region where it is born and nurtured. And in truth, God so commanded when He created them: He commanded the earth to produce animals; and the sea and the waters, fish; while He made the air the dwelling-place of birds. Wherefore, seeing that thus He commanded and that thus it was done, the soul then says:

Planted by the hand of the Beloved![49]

3. The consideration is this: that these wonders and varieties could be made only by the hand of her Beloved. Wherefore she says intentionally 'by the hand . . .'; for albeit God performs many other things by the hands of the angels, He never performs the act of creation save by His own hand. And thus the creatures greatly move the soul to love her Beloved, or she sees that they are things that have been made by His own hand. And she says furthermore:

O meadow of verdure,

4. This consideration is upon heaven, which she calls 'meadow of verdure,' because the things that are created therein never perish or wither with time; but, like fresh verdure, wherein the just take their pleasure and whereon they pasture, they are always unfading in their being; in the which consideration is likewise comprehended all the diversity of the stars and other celestial planets.

5. This name of verdure the Church gives likewise to heavenly things when, praying to God for the souls of the departed, and speaking to them, she says: May God set you among the delectable verdure.[50] And she says also that this meadow of verdure is likewise

---

[49] So Gr, 8,654. Lch, Md: 'of my Beloved.'
[50] G, V: 'celestial verdure.'

Enamelled with flowers,

6. By these flowers she understands the angels and the holy souls, wherewith that place is adorned and beautified like a graceful and costly enamel upon an excellent vase of gold.

Say if he has passed by you.

7. This question is the consideration spoken of above: Say what excellences He has created in you.

STANZA VIII

But, how, O life,[51] dost thou persevere,   Since thou livest not where thou livest,
And since the arrows make thee to die which thou receivest From the conceptions of the Beloved which thou formest within thee?

Exposition

As the soul sees herself to be dying of love, even as she has just said, and sees also that she is not dying wholly, in such a way as to be able to have the fruition of love freely, she makes complaint of the duration of her bodily life, by reason of which her spiritual life is delayed. And thus she addresses the life of her soul, laying stress upon this pain, saying: Life of my soul,[52] how canst thou persevere in this bodily life, since it is death to thee and privation of that wherein thou now livest in[53] love and desire? And especially since the wounds which thou receivest from the touches of the Beloved are sufficient to end thy life, as are also those of the vehement love caused in thee by that which thou feelest and understandest concerning Him—namely, the touches and wounds that slay with love?

But how, O life,[54] dost thou persevere,   Since thou livest not where thou livest,

51 Lch: 'O soul.'
52 [The word 'my' is omitted in the original.]
53 [The word 'in' is omitted in the original.]
54 Lch: 'O soul.'

2. For the understanding hereof it is to be known that the soul lives where it loves rather than in the body which it animates, because it has not its life in the body, but rather gives life to it, and has its life in that which is loved by it. But beside this life of love, whereby the soul lives in whatsoever it loves, the soul has its natural life in God, according to that which Saint Paul says to us: 'In Him we live and move and are.' And as the soul sees that she has her natural life in God, through the being that she has in Him, and likewise her spiritual life, through the love wherewith she loves Him, she complains because she is persevering so long in the life of the body, for this impedes her from truly living where she truly has her life, through essence and through love, as we have said. The insistence that the soul lays upon this is great, for she declares that she is suffering in two contrary ways, in these two short lines, for that which is said in them is as much as to say: 'My soul, how canst thou persevere thus, since thou livest without living truly where thou livest through love?'

Since the arrows make thee to die which thou receivest

3. As if she had said: And, apart from what I have said, since thou perseverest in the body, where thou hast not thy life, how dost thou still persevere, since the touches of love which thou receivest in thy heart, from that which thou feelest and understandest in thyself concerning the Beloved, alone suffice to slay thee? For this is what is meant by:

From the conceptions of the Beloved which thou formest within thee?

4. That is to say, of the beauty, greatness and wisdom and virtues that thou understandest of Him.

STANZA XIII

The sonorous rivers,

9. Rivers have three[55] properties: the first is that they assail and submerge all that they meet; the second, that they fill up

[55] Gr, by an oversight, omits: 'three.'

low and hollow places that are in their path; the third, that their sound is such as to drown and take the place of all sounds else. And because in this communication of the Beloved the soul feels in herself these three properties most delectably, she says that the Beloved is the sonorous rivers. With respect to the first, it must be known that the soul feels herself to be assailed by the torrent of the Spirit of God in this case, in such a manner, and taken possession of thereby with such force, that it seems to her that all the rivers of the world are coming upon her, assailing and overwhelming all her passions and actions which she had aforetime. Yet, though this is an experience of such violence, it is not for that reason an experience of torment; for these rivers are rivers of peace, even as the Spouse declares through Isaias, saying: 'See, I will come down upon her like a river of peace and like a torrent which overflows with glory as it advances.' And thus He fills it wholly with peace and glory. The second property which the soul says that she feels is that this Divine water fills up the low places of its humility[56] and also fills the empty places of its desires, even as Saint Luke says: 'He fills the hungry with good things.' The third property that the soul feels in the sonorous rivers of its Beloved is a spiritual voice and sound which is above all sounds and above all voices, the which voice drowns and exceeds every other sound. And in the exposition hereof we shall have to occupy ourselves a little.

10. This voice or sonorous sound[57] of these rivers which the soul here describes is a fulfilment so great that it fills the soul, and a power so powerful that it possesses the soul and appears to her not merely as the sound of rivers, but as most powerful thunderings. But it is a spiritual voice and is unaccompanied by those physical sounds, and by the pain of other sounds, but is accompanied by grandeur and strength and delight; but it is as an immense sound and voice which fills the soul with power. And thus, in order to make manifest this spiritual voice which, at the coming of the Holy Spirit, was inwardly produced in the spirits of the Apostles, that sound was heard from without as a vehement wind, whereby

[56] Lch adds: 'in order afterwards to raise it to greater glory.'
[57] [The word 'sound' does not appear in the original.]

was denoted the voice which the Apostles felt within themselves, which was, as we have said, a fulfilment of power and strength. And when once the Lord Jesus was praying to the Father in the peril and anguish which He suffered because of His enemies, even as is said in Saint John, there came to Him this inward voice from Heaven, strengthening Him according to His humanity, which the Jews heard from without, like a thunderclap, and thus some said that it was thunder, and others, that some angel had spoken to Him; the fact being that by that voice from without was denoted the strength and power which was given to Jesus, according to His humanity, from within. Whence it is to be known that the spiritual voice is the effect which the voice makes. It was this that David meant when he said: *Ecce dabit voci suæ vocem virtutis.* That is to say: See that He will give to His voice a voice of virtue. By this it must be understood that God is an infinite voice, and that the voice which He utters in the soul is the effect that He makes in it.

11. And this voice Saint John heard in the Apocalypse and he says that the voice that he heard from Heaven was *tanquam vocem aquarum multarum, et tanquam vocem tonitrui magni.* Which is to say: That the voice which he heard was as a voice of many waters and as the voice of a great thunder. And that it may not be inferred that this voice, because it was so great, was harsh and disagreeable, he adds at once that this same voice was so soft that *erat sicut citharedorum citharizantium in citharis suis.* Which signifies: It was as of many harpers who harped upon their harps. And Ezechiel says that this sound as of many waters was *quasi sonum sublimis Dei,* which is to say: as a sound of the Most High God. That is, that He made His communication therein after a manner most high and likewise most gentle. This voice is infinite, for, as we said, it is God Himself Who communicates Himself, speaking in the soul: but He limits Himself by the capacity of each soul, uttering a voice of virtue such as befits its limitations; and He produces in the soul great delight and grandeur. For this cause the Bride said in the Songs: *Sonet vox tua in auribus meis, vox tua dulcis.* This signifies: Let Thy voice sound in my ears, for Thy voice is sweet. The line continues:

STANZA XX

Exposition

In this stanza the soul makes answer to a tacit reproach[58] which might be addressed to her by those of the world, and which they are wont to direct to such as give themselves truly to God; they call them extravagant in their aloofness and queerness and in their general behaviour, and likewise consider them to be useless and lost with respect to all things that the world prizes and esteems. This reproach the soul meets in an excellent way, and very gladly faces both this and all else that the world can impute to it, taking little heed thereof when it has attained to living love; rather it glories and boasts of having done those things for the Beloved. And thus the Bride herself confesses them in this stanza, saying to those of the world that if they see her not in the places which formerly knew her, and following her former pastimes, they are to say that she has become lost to them and is withdrawn from them, and that she considers this so great a gain that she has herself desired thus to be lost in going after her Beloved, through works of virtue, and seeking Him, enkindled as she is with love for Him. And, that they may see how great a gain to her is this loss, and may not judge it to be delusion, she says that this loss was her gain and that she became lost of set purpose.

STANZA XXIV

Despise me not,   For, if thou didst find me swarthy,
Now canst thou indeed look upon me,[59]   Since thou didst look
    upon me and leave in me grace and beauty.

Exposition

The Bride now takes courage; and, esteeming herself with respect to the pledges and the reward which she has of her

---

[58] Bj: 'to a tacit objection or reproach.' Bz: 'to a tacit obligation or reproach.'

[59] Bz: 'Now wilt thou indeed be able to look upon me.'

Beloved (seeing that, since these things come from Him, though she of herself is of little worth and merits no esteem, she merits to be esteemed because of them), makes bold to speak to her Beloved, begging Him not to despise her or hold her of no worth, since if she once merited this by reason of the baseness of her fault and the wretchedness of her nature, now, since first He looked upon her and adorned her with His grace and clothed her with His beauty, He may well look upon her for the second time, and many times more, and increase her grace and beauty, since there is reason and cause sufficient for this in His having looked upon her when she merited it not neither had the means of doing so.

Despise me not,

2. As though she had said: Since this is so, do Thou not hold me as of little worth.

For, if thou didst find me swarthy,

3. For if, ere Thou lookedst upon me, Thou didst find in me baseness of faults and imperfections and wretchedness as to my condition[60] by nature,

Now canst thou indeed look upon me,   Since thou didst look upon me

4. Since Thou didst look upon me,[61] and take from me that miserable swarthy colour wherewith I was not fit to be seen, now canst Thou look upon me indeed, again and again; since not alone didst Thou take from me my swarthiness when first Thou lookedst upon me, but likewise Thou didst make me worthier to be seen, for Thou didst

Leave in me grace and beauty.

5. Greatly pleasing to God is the soul that has His grace,[62] since He abides, well pleased, within her, and she is exalted in Him; wherefore He loves her with an ineffable love, and communicates to her ever more love and gifts in all her seasons[63]

[60] Lch: 'my consideration.'
[61] Md omits: 'Since Thou didst look upon me.'
[62] Md: 'the soul to whom He has given His grace.'
[63] Bj, Bz: 'actions' for 'seasons.'

and works; for the soul attains much that has reached a lofty estate of love and is honoured in God. And thus God declares in speaking with Jacob His friend in the Book of Isaias,[64] saying: *Ex quo honorabilis factus es in oculis meis, et gloriosus, ego dilexi te.* Which signifies: Since thou hast become honourable and glorious in Mine eyes, I loved thee; that is, thou hast merited more love from Me, and therein more grace from My favours, through the honour and beauty of glory which thou hadst of Me.

This the Bride also declares in the Songs, saying to the daughters of Jerusalem: *Nigra sunt sed formosa filiæ Jerusalem, ideo dilexit me rex et introduxit me in cubiculum suum.* Which is to say: I am swarthy, daughters of Jerusalem, but beautiful; wherefore the King has loved me and brought me into the interior of his bed. That is to say: Though of myself I am swarthy, I am beautiful through Him, and therefore He communicated more love to me and brought me farther within, granting me greater favours.

6. Well, my God, canst Thou now look upon me, since Thou didst look upon me, and with Thy first look didst leave in me grace and beauty of honour and glory and riches.

STANZA XXV

Catch us the foxes, For our vineyard is now in flower,[65] While we make a bunch[66] of roses, And let none appear upon the hill.[67]

Exposition

The Bride, seeing that the virtues of her soul have now reached the point of perfection, so that she is now enjoying their delight and sweetness[68] and fragrance,[69] even as one

[64] [*Lit.*, 'through Isaias.']
[65] Bz: 'is now flowering.'
[66] [See p. 162, n. 2, above.]
[67] Lch: 'upon the countryside.'
[68] Lch: 'delight and wisdom.'
[69] Bj, Bz: 'sweetness and glory.'

enjoys the beauty and fragrance of plants when they are flowering, longs to continue this sweetness and desires that there may be naught to intercept and hinder[70] her from so doing. In this stanza, therefore, she begs that all those things may be caught and kept from her that may tear down and crumple[71] the flower of her virtues—as, for example, all the disturbances, temptations, causes of unrest, desires, imaginations and other motions, which are wont to keep from the soul inward sweetness and quiet and peace, at the time when the soul is wont to be most contentedly enjoying all the virtues together, in her Beloved. For the soul is wont at times in her spirit to see all the virtues which God has given to her (when He gives her that light), and then with wondrous delight and fragrance of love she gathers them all together and offers them to the Beloved as it were a bunch of flowers. In accepting them—and accept them indeed He does—the Beloved at the same time accepts a great service; for together with the virtues the soul offers herself, which is the greatest service that she can render Him; and this delight that the soul receives from this kind of gift which she makes to the Beloved is one of the greatest delights that she is wont to receive in her intercourse with God. Thus the Bride desires that naught may hinder her from this inward delight, which is the flowering vineyard, and desires that not only may these things aforementioned be taken from her, but that likewise she may be withdrawn far from all things,[72] so that in all her exterior and interior desires and faculties there may be no form or image or other such thing to appear and present itself before the soul and the Beloved, who, withdrawn from all else and united with each other, are making this nosegay and having joy therein.

Catch us the foxes,   For our vineyard is now in flower,[73]

2. The vineyard is the nursery of all the virtues, which is in the soul and which gives to the soul a wine of sweet savour. This vineyard of the soul is flowering when in the union of the

70 Lch: 'hinder and withdraw.'
71 Bz: 'tear down and smother.'
72 Lch omits: 'but that . . . all things.'
73 Bz: 'is now flowering.' Bj: 'is now full-flowering.'

will with the Beloved the soul is delighting itself and rejoicing in all these virtues together; and at this season there are wont to resort to the imaginative memory many and various forms and imaginations, and in the sensual part of the soul are many and various motions and desires which make the soul uneasy, and, by their great subtlety and agility, cause it to lose the pleasure and sweetness wherein at that time it is rejoicing, and trouble it greatly. And at this time there are wont to be many disturbances and horrors and fears,[74] which evil spirits are wont to set in the soul, and all these things she here calls foxes. For, even as the agile little foxes, with their subtle bounds, are in the habit of tearing down and maltreating the blossom of the vineyards, even so do these imaginations and motions, with their nimbleness,[75] keep from the soul, and tear down, the flower of sweetness, which, as we have said, the soul is enjoying; and also because, just as the foxes are malicious and shrewd in doing harm, even so do these imaginations and the evil spirits with them contrive to injure and tear down the flower of the soul's sweetness, so that it may give no fruit.

3. This same request is made by the Bride in the Songs, where she says: *Capite nobis vulpes parvulas, quæ demoliuntur vineas: nam vinea nostra floruit.* Which is to say: Drive us away the little foxes that spoil the vineyards, for our vineyard is flowering. And for that reason the soul desires them to be driven away, and likewise so that there may be room to do that which follows, namely:

While we make a bunch of roses,

4. At this season wherein the soul is taking her delight, upon the breast of her Beloved, in the flower of this vineyard, it comes to pass that the virtues stand out clearly to view, as we have said, and are at their best, showing to the soul and bestowing upon her their fragrance and sweetness, in the soul herself and in God, so that they seem to the soul to be a vineyard full-flowering, of the virtues and of the Beloved, and then she gathers them all together, and in each one of them and in

[74] Lch, 8,654 omit: 'and fears.'
[75] Lch, 8,654, Bz: 'nimbleness and lightness.' Md: 'lightness and nimbleness.'

all of them together makes most delectable acts of love. And so she offers these to the Beloved all together with great tenderness of love and sweetness; wherein the Beloved aids her; wherefore she says: 'We make a nosegay'—that is to say, He and I.

5. And thus this gathering together of virtues is like a cone or nosegay of roses,[76] because, even as a pine-cone[77] is strong[78] and contains within itself many pieces, strong and strongly bound together, which are the pine-kernels, even so this cone or nosegay which the soul makes for her Beloved is one single perfection of the soul, which firmly and in an ordered manner embraces within itself many perfections of virtues which are very strong, and gifts which are very precious, for all the perfections of virtues[79] are combined and ordered into one firm perfection of the soul. Inasmuch as this perfection is being formed and offered to the Beloved in the spirit, it is fitting that the foxes be driven away. And not only so, but likewise

And let none appear upon the hill.[80]

6. This Divine interior exercise also requires withdrawal and detachment from all things that might present themselves to the soul, whether from the lower part, which is that of the senses, or from the higher part, which is that of the reason, which are the parts wherein are comprised the entire harmony of the faculties and senses of the whole man, which she here calls a hill. She begs that none may appear thereon, that is to say, that no forms or figures or objects or other natural operations may appear in the faculties and senses,[81] because in this case, if the inward and outward senses work, they cause disturbance; so also let no other of her operations and exercises appear in the spiritual faculties, for when the soul reaches the delight[82] of union of love, the spiritual faculties no longer

[76] [See p. 162, n. 2, above.]
[77] [piña.]
[78] [Lit., 'a strong piece.' Cf. the following clause.]
[79] Lch: 'of virtues and gifts.'
[80] Lch: 'upon the countryside.'
[81] For sentidos ['senses'], Bj, Bz, Lch, 8,654, Md read: sentidos sensitivos ['senses of sense'].
[82] Md reads: al saber ['the knowledge'] for al sabor ['the delight'].

work, neither is it fitting that they should work, since the work of union is now done through love,[83] even as, when the end is reached, the means cease. Let none, then, appear upon the hill; let the will alone be present before the Beloved after the manner aforementioned.

STANZA XXXVIII

The breathing of the air,

2. This property[84] for which the soul prays so that she may love perfectly she here calls the breathing of the air, because it is a most delicate touch and feeling[85] which the soul feels at this time in the communication of the Holy Spirit; Who, sublimely breathing with that His Divine breath, raises the soul and informs her that she may breathe into God the same breath of love that the Father breathes[86] into the Son and the Son into the Father, which is the same[87] Holy Spirit that they breathe into her[88] in the said transformation. For it would not be a true transformation if the soul were not united and transformed also in the Holy Spirit, albeit not in a degree revealed and manifest,[89] by reason of the lowliness of this life. This is for the soul of such great glory and delight that it cannot be described by mortal tongue, neither does human understanding attain to any conception of it.[90]

3. But the soul that is united and transformed in God breathes in God into God the same Divine breath that God, being in her, breathes into her in Himself, which, as I understand, was the meaning of Saint Paul when he said: *Quoniam autem estis filii Dei, misit Deus Spiritum Filii sui in corda*

[83] Md: 'is now done through loving that which is understood.'

[84] [See p. 217, n. 5, above.]

[85] Lch: 'touch and understanding.'

[86] Md: 'that she may breathe into God a most sublime breath of love, like to that which the Father breathes.'

[87] Md omits 'same.'

[88] Md: 'that they give her.'

[89] Bz: 'which is the same Holy Spirit, although not in a manifest degree.'

[90] Md: 'neither does human understanding attain to it.'

clamantem: Abba, Pater. Which in the perfect is according to the manner described. And there is no need to wonder that the soul should be capable of aught so high; for, since God grants her the favour of attaining to being deiform and united in the Most Holy Trinity, how is it a thing incredible that she should perform her work of understanding, knowledge and love in the Trinity, together with It, like It, by a mode of participation, which God effects in her?

4. And how this comes to pass cannot be known, nor is it possible to express it, save by describing how the Son of God obtained for us and granted us to merit this high estate and office, as He said to the Father, in Saint John: *Volo ut quos dedisti mihi, ut ubi sum ego, et illi sint mecum.* Which signifies: Father, I will that they whom Thou hast given Me may be also with Me, where I am. That is to say, doing the same work as I, by participation. And He says also: 'I pray not only for these that are present, but for them also who through their teaching shall believe in Me, that they may all be one and the same thing; so that as Thou, Father, art in Me, and I am in Thee, even so they may be one and the same thing in Us; and I have given them the brightness which Thou hast given Me, that they may be one and the same thing, as We are one and the same thing: I in them, and Thou in Me, that they may be perfect in one; that the world may know that Thou hast sent Me, and hast loved them, as Thou hast loved Me'; namely, by communicating to them the same love as to the Son, though not naturally, as to the Son, but, as we have said, by unity and transformation of love. Neither is it to be understood here that the Son means to say to the Father[91] that the saints are to be one thing in essence and nature, as are the Father and the Son; but rather that they may be so by union of love, as are the Father and the Son in unity of love. Wherefore the souls possess these same blessings by participation as He possesses by nature; for the which cause they are truly gods by participation, equals of God and His companions. Wherefore Saint Peter said: 'Grace and peace be complete and perfect in you in the knowledge of God and of Christ Jesus our Lord, according as all things are given to us of His Divine virtue for

[91] Gr omits: 'to the Father.'

life and godliness, through the knowledge of Him that has called us with His own glory and virtue; whereby He has promised and given unto us most great and precious promises, that by these things we may be made companions of the Divine nature'; which is, after the manner that we have said, for the soul to have participation in work with the Trinity, in the union aforementioned. And though this can be perfectly fulfilled only in the next life, nevertheless, in this life, when the estate of perfection is reached, a clear trace and taste of it are attained, after the manner that we are describing, albeit this cannot be expressed.

5. O souls created for these grandeurs and called thereto! What do ye do? Wherein do ye occupy yourselves?[92] O wretched blindness[93] of the sons of Adam, being blind to so great a light and deaf to so clear a voice, since for so long as they seek grandeurs and glory they remain miserable and mean, unworthy of so many blessings! There follows the second thing.

In the serene night,

9. This night, wherein the soul desires to see these things, is contemplation; for contemplation is dark, and for that reason is called by its other name, 'mystical theology,' which signifies secret and hidden wisdom of God, wherein, without noise of words and without accessory and argument,[94] as in the silence and quiet of the night, hidden by darkness from all that is felt, God teaches the soul after a most hidden[95] and secret manner, without her knowing how; this is that which is called 'understanding yet understanding not.' For this is not done by the active understanding, as the philosophers call it, which works in forms and fancies of things; but it is done in the understanding inasmuch as it is possible[96] and passive, when, without receiving such forms and fancies, it passively receives substantial knowledge, which is given to it without any active office or work of its own.

[92] Gr omits: 'O souls . . . occupy yourselves?'
[93] Gr: 'O wretched war.'
[94] Md: 'and without turmoil and argument.'
[95] Bz: 'a most high.'
[96] Cf. p. 222, n. 24, above.

10. And for this cause she here calls this contemplation serene night; for even as the night is called serene because it is free from clouds and vapours in the air, which disturb serenity, so this night of contemplation is, to the sight of the understanding, empty of and withdrawn from every cloud of forms and fancies and particular[97] knowledge which may enter by the senses; it is clean likewise of all kinds of vapour from the affections and desires;[98] and thus it is night to the natural understanding and sense, even as the philosopher teaches, saying that, even as the eye of the bat is darkened in the sunlight,[99] even so is our understanding with the greatest natural light.

With a flame that consumes and gives no pain.

11. This flame is the love, now perfect, of God in the soul; which love has now consumed and transformed the soul in itself.[100] For, in order to be perfect, it must have these two properties, namely: that it may consume and transform the soul in God and that the enkindling and transformation of this flame in the soul may give no pain; and thus it is sweet love; inasmuch as there is conformity and fulfilment on either side, and therefore there is no pain caused by difference between the greater and the less, as there was before, when the soul was not capable of perfect love. For it is now like burning coal which, with great conformity, is now made identical with[101] the fire, and is transformed therein, without that smoking and flaming[102] that it gave forth aforetime, and without the darkness and accidents proper to it which it had before the fire had entered into it completely. These things the soul has to trouble it until it arrive at a degree of perfect love wherein love fully and completely and gently possesses it, and does so without the pain of the smoke of the natural

[97] Bj, Bz, Lch, 8,654, Md omit: 'particular.'
[98] Lch omits: 'from the affections.' Bz omits: 'from the affections and desires.'
[99] See p. 222, n. 26, above.
[100] Bj, Bz, Lch, 8,654, Md omit all that follows down to: 'and thus it is sweet love.'
[101] Md: 'is now very much like.'
[102] Md: 'and crackling.'

accidents and passions, but transformed into a gentle flame, which consumes it and changes it into the motions and actions of God, in the which flame the Bride says that He will show her and grant her all the things whereof she has spoken in this stanza, for she possesses and esteems and enjoys them all in perfect and sweet love of God.

STANZA XXXIX

Neither did Aminadab appear,

3. This Aminadab, in Divine Scripture, signifies the devil, who is the adversary of the soul, and who was ever giving her battle and disturbing her with the innumerable munitions of his temptations, that she might not enter into this fortress and secret place of recollection in union with the Beloved. The soul placed herein is so greatly favoured and victorious and strong in virtues that the devil dares not appear[103] before her. Wherefore, since she is in the favour of such an embrace, and the devil is so completely put to flight, and because, too, when a soul has gained a perfect victory over the devil, as the soul has done that has reached this estate, he no longer appears before her, she thus very truly says that neither did Aminadab appear.

And there was a rest from the siege,

4. By the siege she here understands the passions and desires of the soul, which besiege and give battle to it round about[104] when they are not conquered; from the which she says, too, that there is now a rest, because in this estate the passions are in such wise set at rest, and the desires mortified, that they can neither disturb the soul[105] nor make war upon it.

And the cavalry came down at the sight[106] of the waters.

[103] Bz, Lch: 'dares not stop.'
[104] Bz omits: 'round about.'
[105] Md: 'may hardly disturb the soul.'
[106] Bz: 'at the siege.'

5. By the waters she here understands the spiritual blessings which in this estate are given to the soul. By the cavalry are understood the faculties of the sensual part, both interior and exterior, which, says the Bride, come down in this estate at the sight of these spiritual waters. For the sensual part of the soul is so purified and spiritualized in this estate that the soul with its sensual faculties and natural forces is recollected and has participation and fruition, after its manner, of the spiritual grandeurs which God is communicating to the spirit, even as David indicated when he said: *Cor meum et caro mea exultaverunt in Deum vivum.* Which is to say: My spirit and flesh together have rejoiced and delighted in the living God.

6. And it is to be noted that the Bride says not here that the cavalry came down here to taste of the waters, but that it came down at the sight of them. For this sensual part with its faculties cannot essentially and properly taste of spiritual blessings because they have not a proportionate capacity[107] for this, either in this life or in the next; but through a certain spiritual overflowing they receive them with refreshment[108] and delight, whereby these faculties are attracted into that recollection wherein the soul is drinking of[109] spiritual blessings. This is to come down[110] at the sight of them rather than to the essential taste of them; and thus they taste of the overflowing which is communicated from the soul to them. She says that they came down, and uses no other word, in order to signify that these faculties descend and come down from their operations to the soul's recollection; wherein may the Lord Jesus,[111] the sweetest Spouse, be pleased to set all such as invoke His Name. Amen.

[107] Bz: 'they have no proportion or capacity.'
[108] Bj, Md, 8,654: 'they receive refreshment.'
[109] Bz: 'is enjoying.'
[110] Lch: 'These come down.'
[111] Lch: 'may the holy Jesus.'